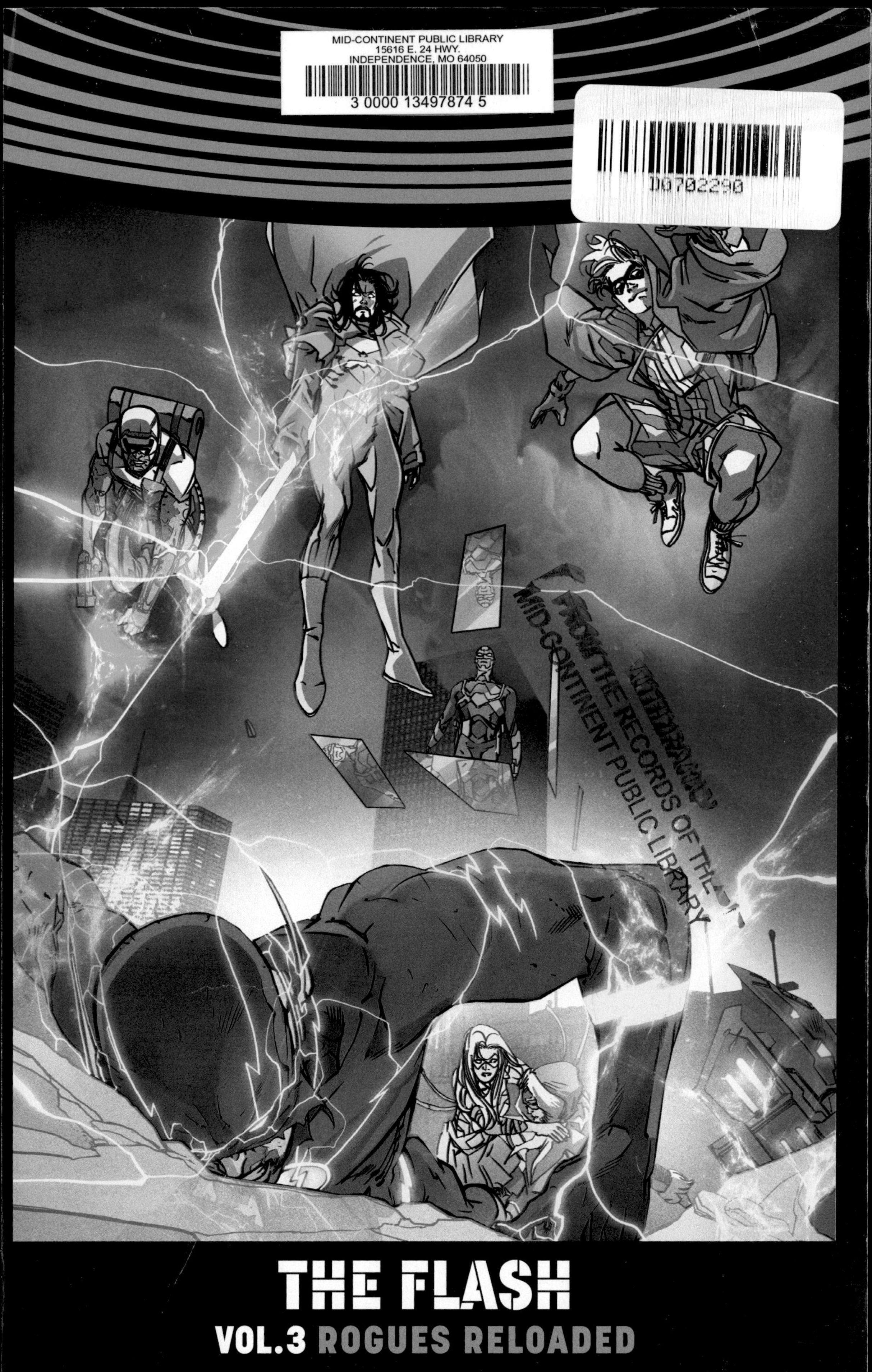

THE FLASH

VOL.3 ROGUES RELOADED

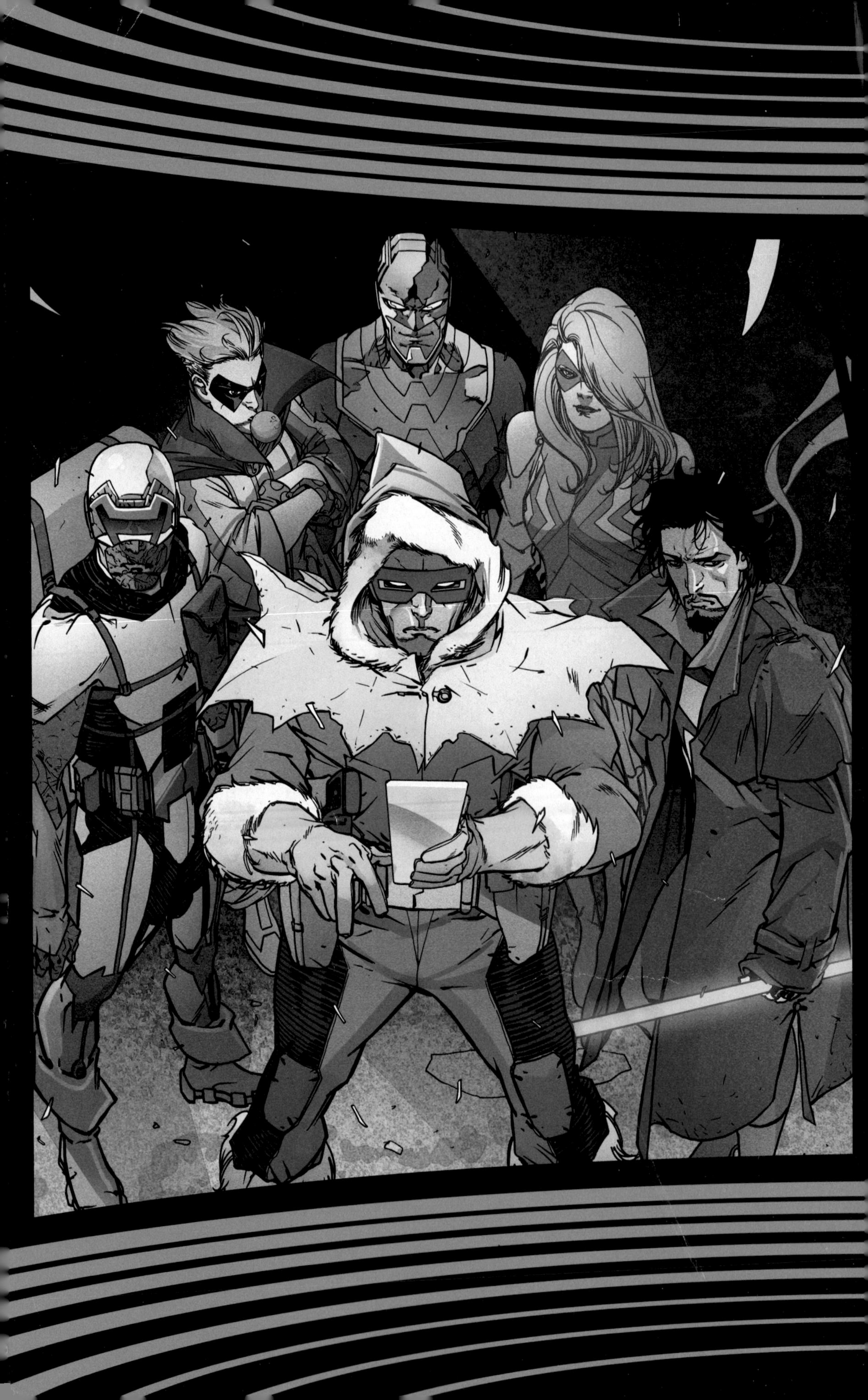

THE FLASH
VOL.3 ROGUES RELOADED

JOSHUA WILLIAMSON
writer

CARMINE DI GIANDOMENICO * **DAVIDE GIANFELICE**
NEIL GOOGE * **JESUS MERINO** * **ANDY OWENS**
artists

IVAN PLASCENCIA * **CHRIS SOTOMAYOR**
colorists

STEVE WANDS
letterer

CARMINE DI GIANDOMENICO
series and collection cover artists

BRIAN CUNNINGHAM Editor - Original Series ⁎ **AMEDEO TURTURRO DIEGO LOPEZ** Assistant Editors - Original Series
JEB WOODARD Group Editor - Collected Editions ⁎ **PAUL SANTOS** Editor - Collected Edition
STEVE COOK Design Director - Books ⁎ **MONIQUE GRUSPE** Publication Design

BOB HARRAS Senior VP - Editor-in-Chief, DC Comics

DIANE NELSON President ⁎ **DAN DiDIO** Publisher ⁎ **JIM LEE** Publisher ⁎ **GEOFF JOHNS** President & Chief Creative Officer
AMIT DESAI Executive VP - Business & Marketing Strategy, Direct to Consumer & Global Franchise Management ⁎ **SAM ADES** Senior VP - Direct to Consumer
BOBBIE CHASE VP - Talent Development ⁎ **MARK CHIARELLO** Senior VP - Art, Design & Collected Editions
JOHN CUNNINGHAM Senior VP - Sales & Trade Marketing ⁎ **ANNE DePIES** Senior VP - Business Strategy, Finance & Administration
DON FALLETTI VP - Manufacturing Operations ⁎ **LAWRENCE GANEM** VP - Editorial Administration & Talent Relations
ALISON GILL Senior VP - Manufacturing & Operations ⁎ **HANK KANALZ** Senior VP - Editorial Strategy & Administration
JAY KOGAN VP - Legal Affairs ⁎ **THOMAS LOFTUS** VP - Business Affairs
JACK MAHAN VP - Business Affairs ⁎ **NICK J. NAPOLITANO** VP - Manufacturing Administration
EDDIE SCANNELL VP - Consumer Marketing ⁎ **COURTNEY SIMMONS** Senior VP - Publicity & Communications
JIM (SKI) SOKOLOWSKI VP - Comic Book Specialty Sales & Trade Marketing ⁎ **NANCY SPEARS** VP - Mass, Book, Digital Sales & Trade Marketing

THE FLASH VOL. 3: ROGUES RELOADED

DC Comics, 2900 West Alameda Ave., Burbank, CA 91505.
Printed by LSC Communications, Owensville, MO, USA. 6/23/17. First Printing.
ISBN: 978-1-4012-7157-2

Library of Congress Cataloging-in-Publication Data is available.

PEFC Certified

Printed on paper from
sustainably managed
forests, controlled
sources

PEFC/29-31-337   www.pefc.org

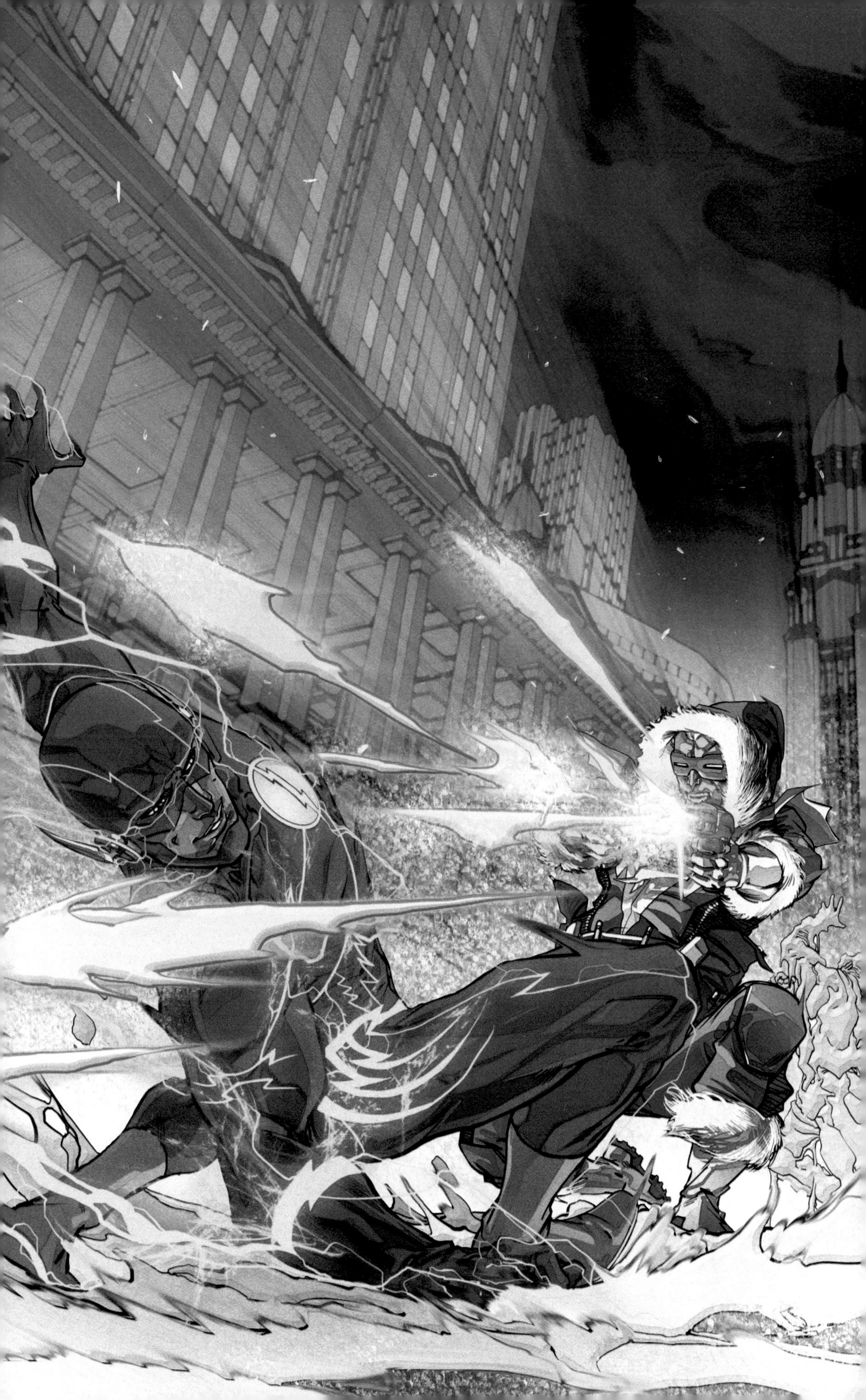

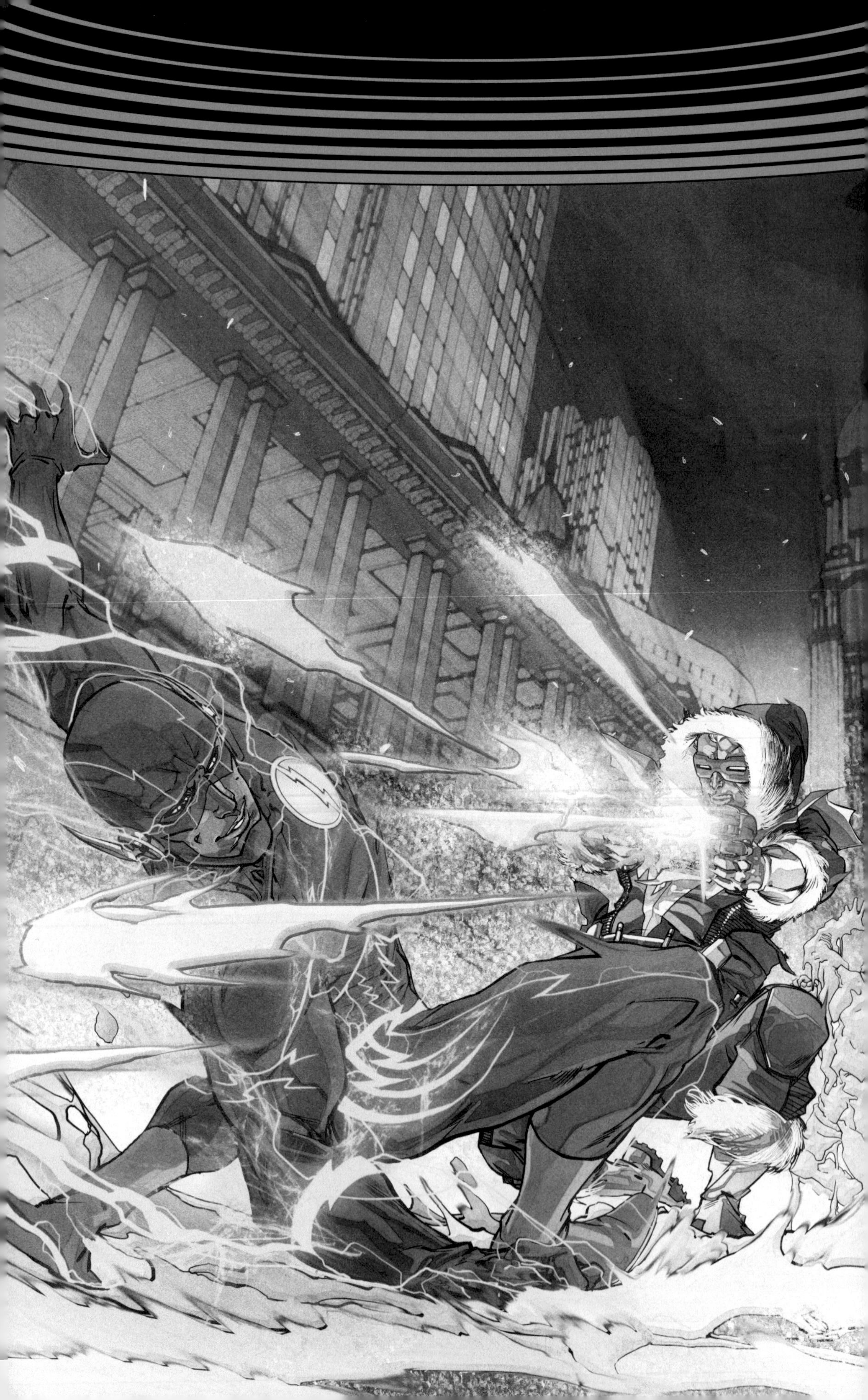

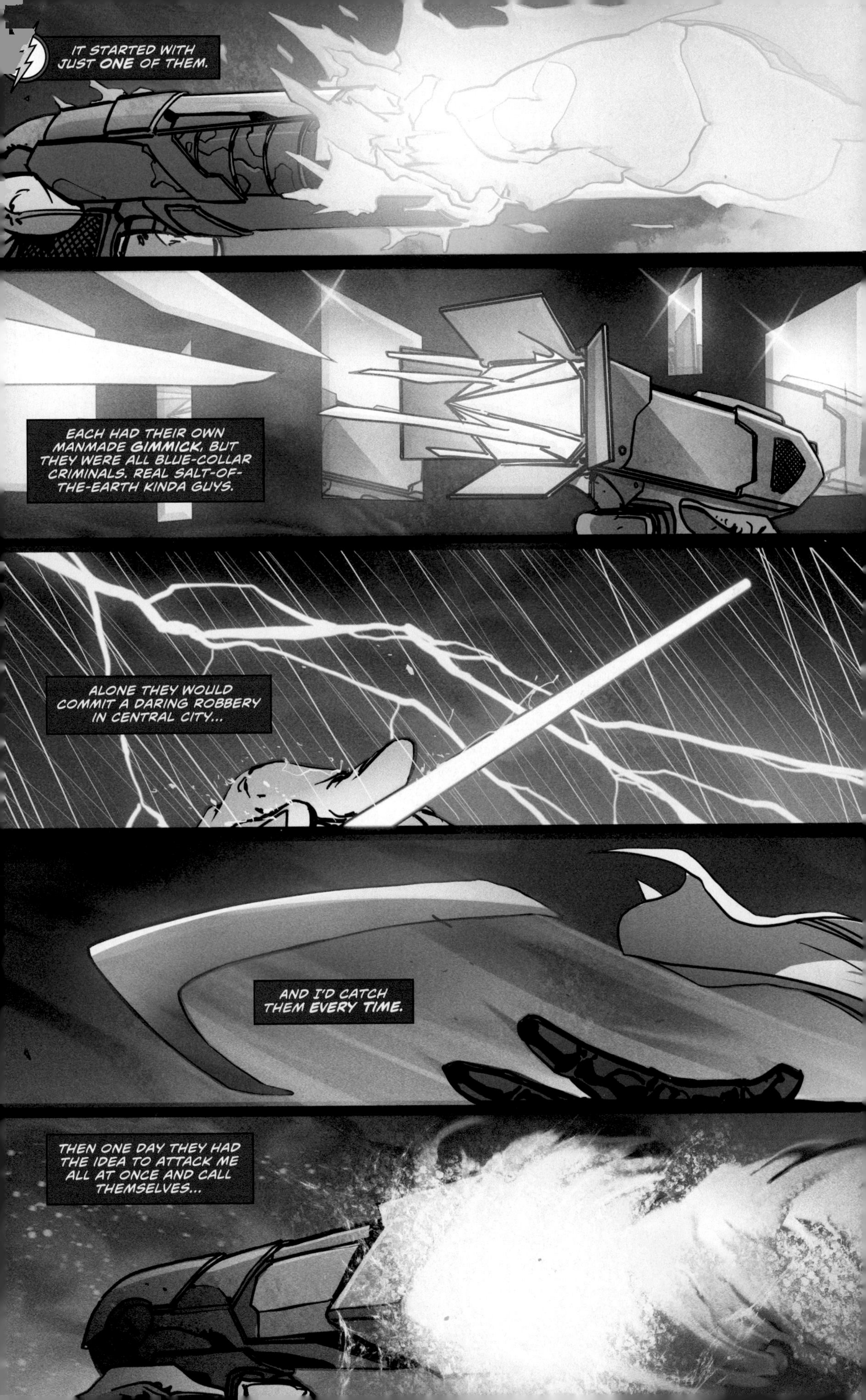
IT STARTED WITH JUST ONE OF THEM.
EACH HAD THEIR OWN MANMADE GIMMICK, BUT THEY WERE ALL BLUE-COLLAR CRIMINALS. REAL SALT-OF-THE-EARTH KINDA GUYS.
ALONE THEY WOULD COMMIT A DARING ROBBERY IN CENTRAL CITY...
AND I'D CATCH THEM EVERY TIME.
THEN ONE DAY THEY HAD THE IDEA TO ATTACK ME ALL AT ONCE AND CALL THEMSELVES...

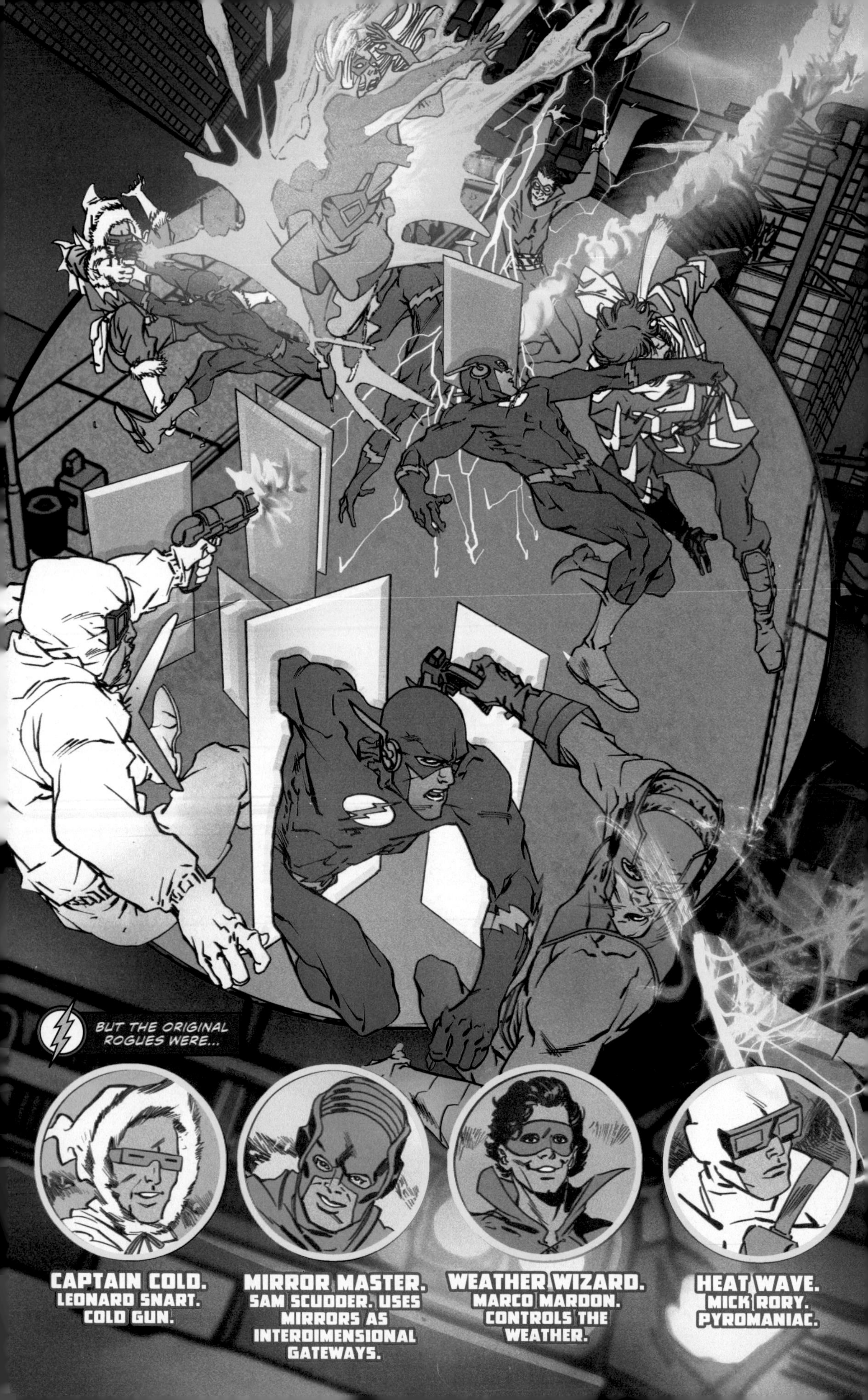
BUT THE ORIGINAL ROGUES WERE...
CAPTAIN COLD. LEONARD SNART. COLD GUN.
MIRROR MASTER. SAM SCUDDER. USES MIRRORS AS INTERDIMENSIONAL GATEWAYS.
WEATHER WIZARD. MARCO MARDON. CONTROLS THE WEATHER.
HEAT WAVE. MICK RORY. PYROMANIAC.

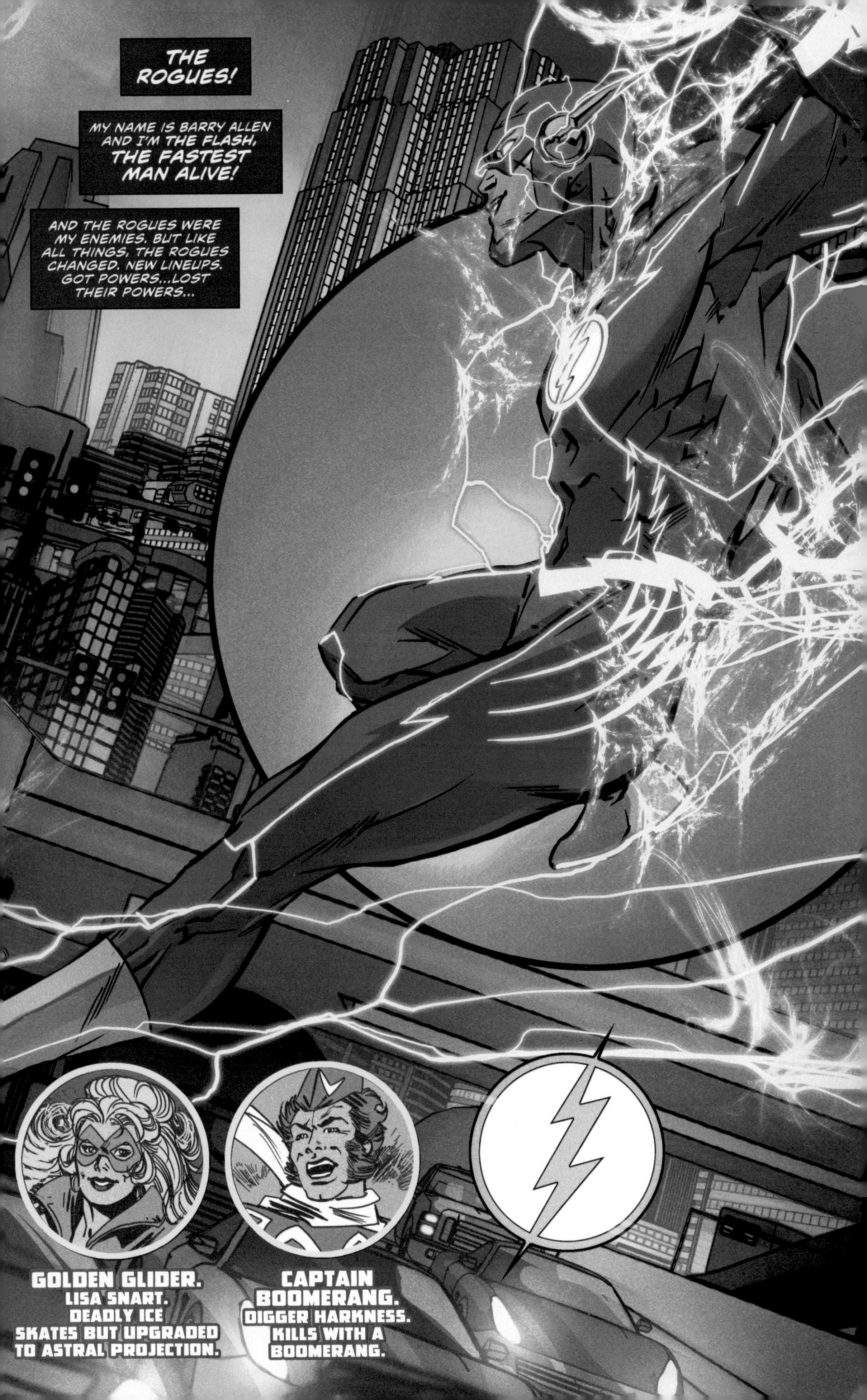
THE ROGUES!
MY NAME IS BARRY ALLEN AND I'M THE FLASH, THE FASTEST MAN ALIVE!
AND THE ROGUES WERE MY ENEMIES. BUT LIKE ALL THINGS, THE ROGUES CHANGED. NEW LINEUPS. GOT POWERS...LOST THEIR POWERS...
GOLDEN GLIDER. LISA SNART. DEADLY ICE SKATES BUT UPGRADED TO ASTRAL PROJECTION.
CAPTAIN BOOMERANG. DIGGER HARKNESS. KILLS WITH A BOOMERANG.

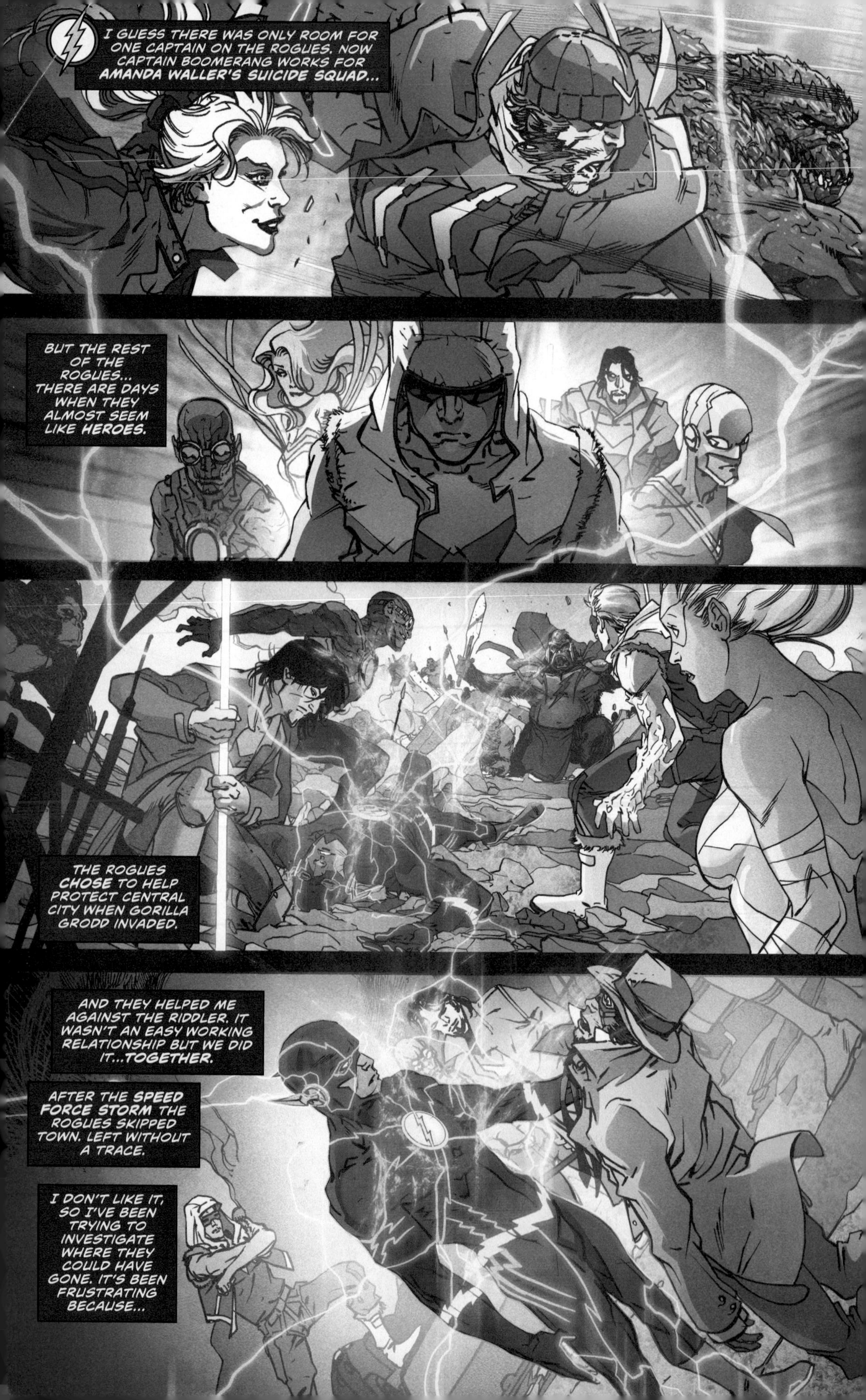
I GUESS THERE WAS ONLY ROOM FOR ONE CAPTAIN ON THE ROGUES. NOW CAPTAIN BOOMERANG WORKS FOR AMANDA WALLER'S SUICIDE SQUAD...
BUT THE REST OF THE ROGUES... THERE ARE DAYS WHEN THEY ALMOST SEEM LIKE HEROES.
THE ROGUES CHOSE TO HELP PROTECT CENTRAL CITY WHEN GORILLA GRODD INVADED.
AND THEY HELPED ME AGAINST THE RIDDLER. IT WASN'T AN EASY WORKING RELATIONSHIP BUT WE DID IT...TOGETHER.
AFTER THE SPEED FORCE STORM THE ROGUES SKIPPED TOWN. LEFT WITHOUT A TRACE.
I DON'T LIKE IT, SO I'VE BEEN TRYING TO INVESTIGATE WHERE THEY COULD HAVE GONE. IT'S BEEN FRUSTRATING BECAUSE...

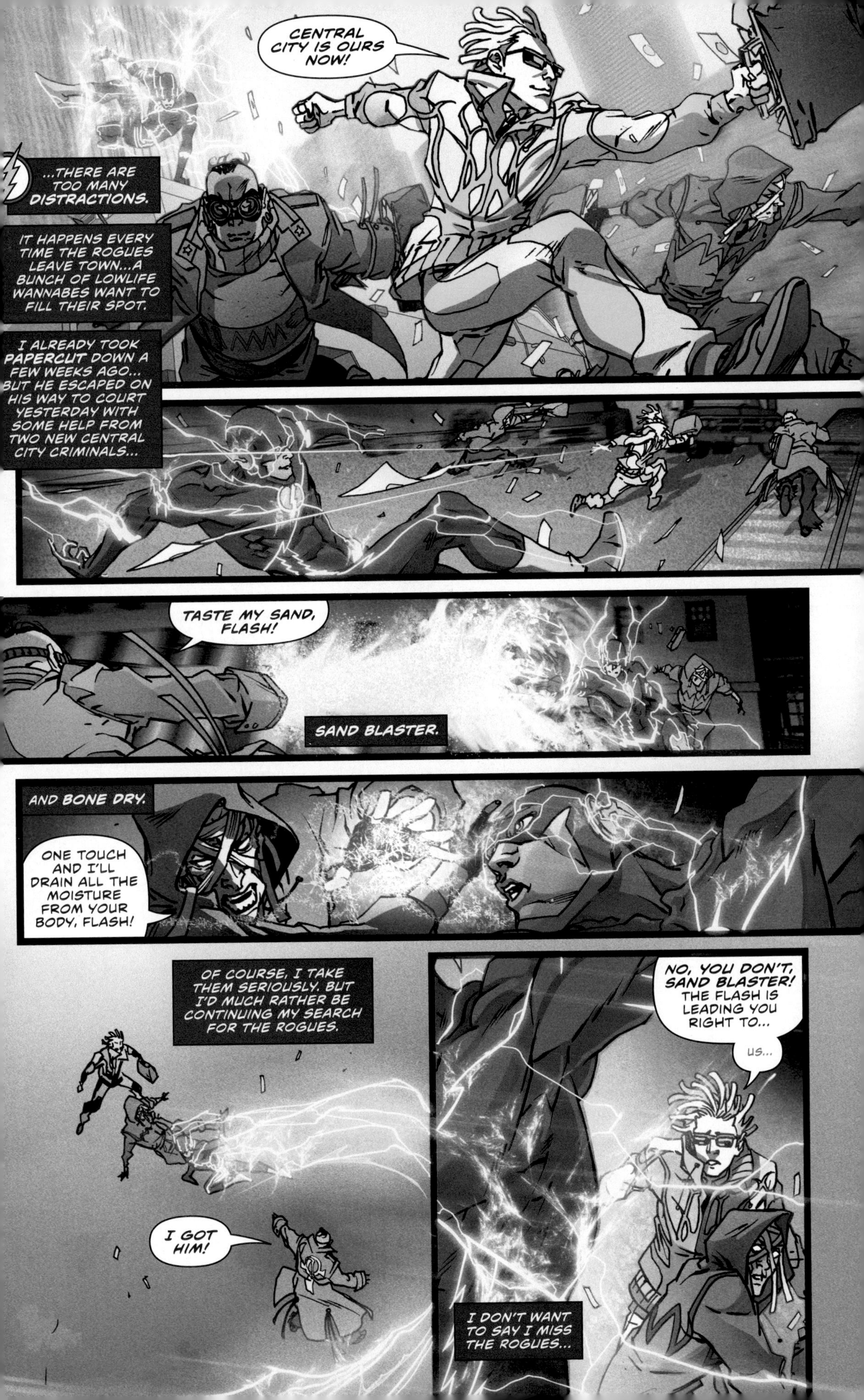
CENTRAL CITY IS OURS NOW!
...THERE ARE TOO MANY DISTRACTIONS.
IT HAPPENS EVERY TIME THE ROGUES LEAVE TOWN...A BUNCH OF LOWLIFE WANNABES WANT TO FILL THEIR SPOT.
I ALREADY TOOK PAPERCUT DOWN A FEW WEEKS AGO... BUT HE ESCAPED ON HIS WAY TO COURT YESTERDAY WITH SOME HELP FROM TWO NEW CENTRAL CITY CRIMINALS...
TASTE MY SAND, FLASH!
SAND BLASTER.
AND BONE DRY.
ONE TOUCH AND I'LL DRAIN ALL THE MOISTURE FROM YOUR BODY, FLASH!
OF COURSE, I TAKE THEM SERIOUSLY. BUT I'D MUCH RATHER BE CONTINUING MY SEARCH FOR THE ROGUES.
I GOT HIM!
NO, YOU DON'T, SAND BLASTER! THE FLASH IS LEADING YOU RIGHT TO...
US...
I DON'T WANT TO SAY I MISS THE ROGUES...

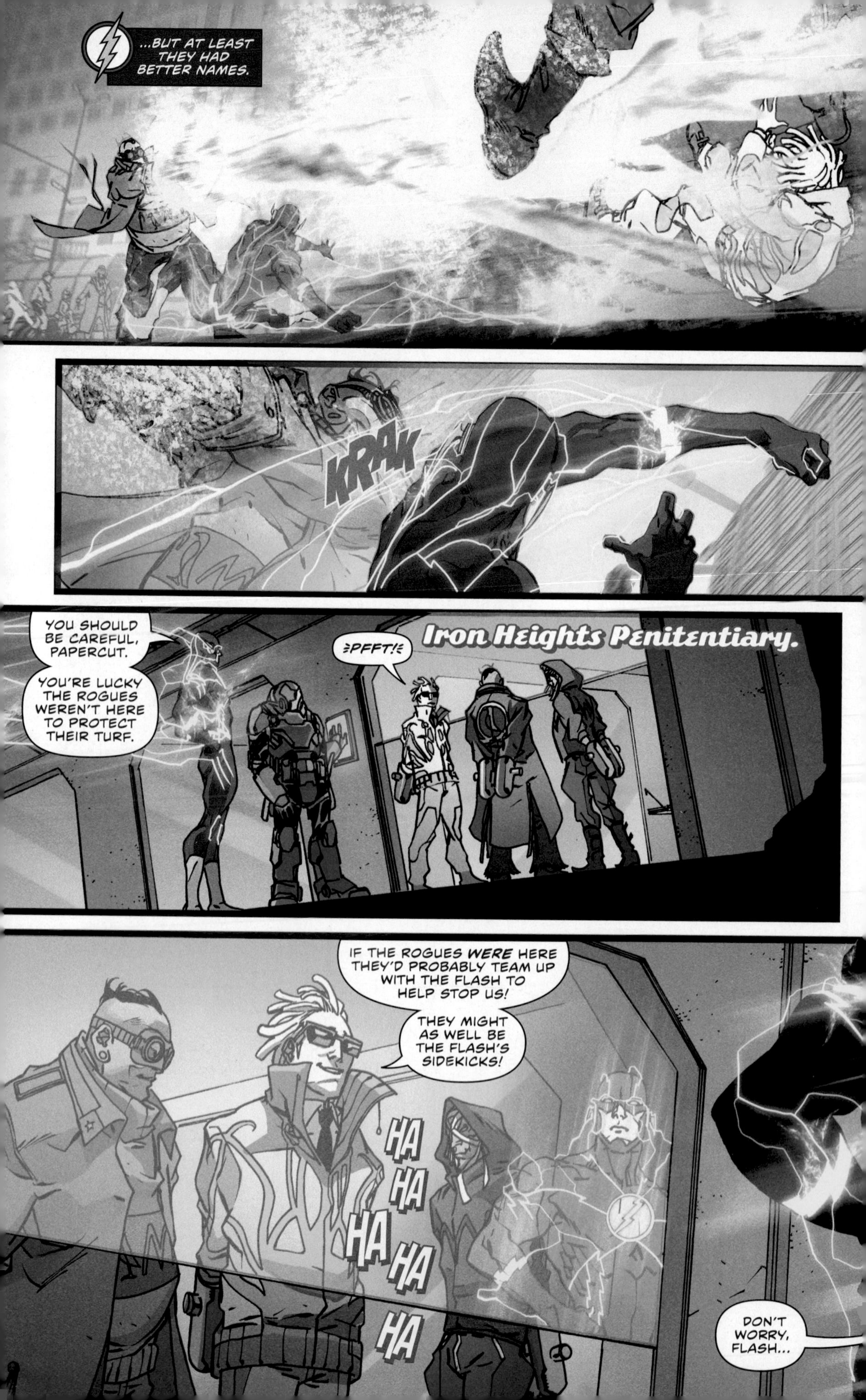
...BUT AT LEAST THEY HAD BETTER NAMES.
KRAK
YOU SHOULD BE CAREFUL, PAPERCUT.
YOU'RE LUCKY THE ROGUES WEREN'T HERE TO PROTECT THEIR TURF.
PFFT!
Iron Heights Penitentiary.
IF THE ROGUES WERE HERE THEY'D PROBABLY TEAM UP WITH THE FLASH TO HELP STOP US!
THEY MIGHT AS WELL BE THE FLASH'S SIDEKICKS!
HA HA HA HA HA
DON'T WORRY, FLASH...

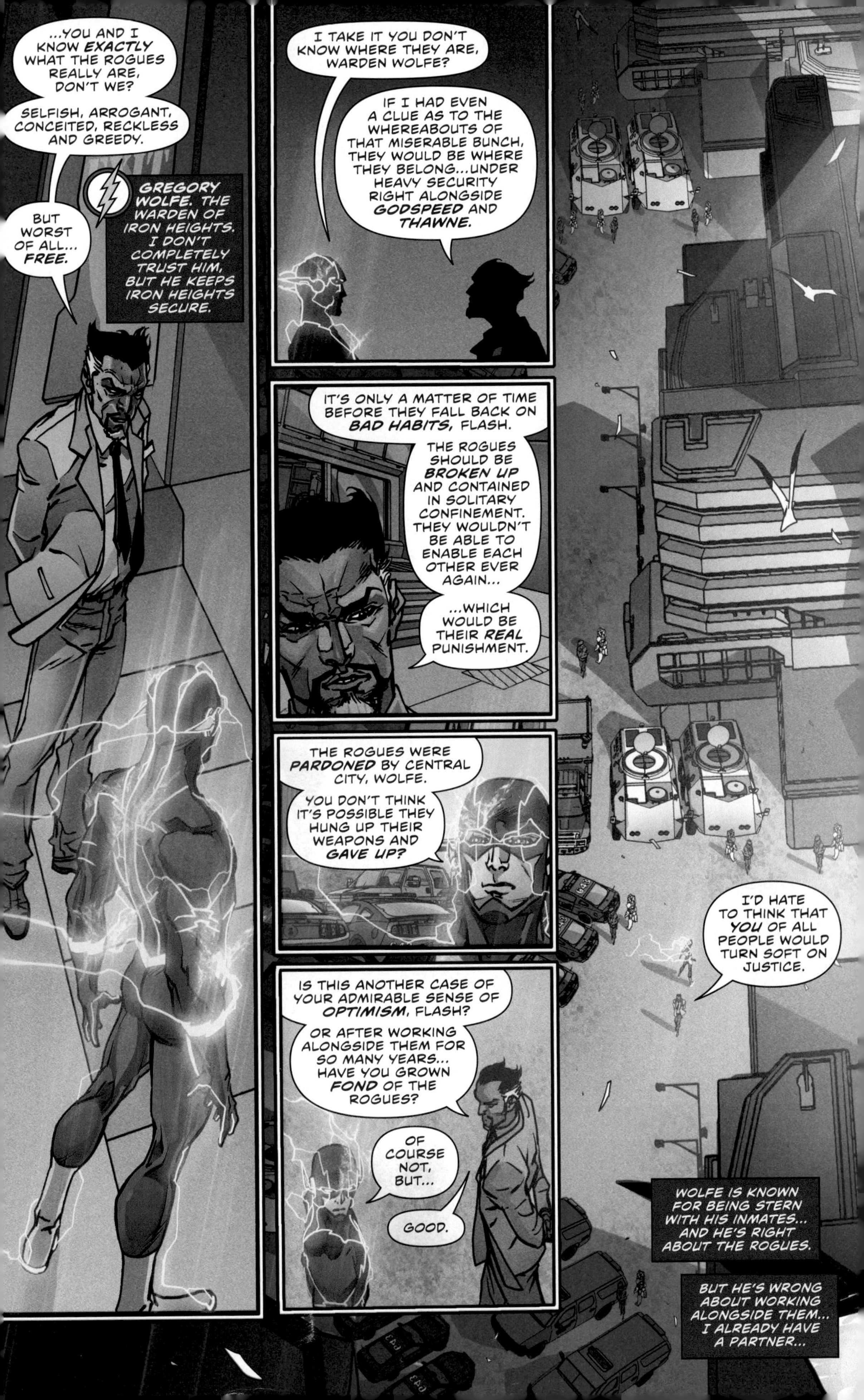

...YOU AND I KNOW EXACTLY WHAT THE ROGUES REALLY ARE, DON'T WE?
SELFISH, ARROGANT, CONCEITED, RECKLESS AND GREEDY.
BUT WORST OF ALL... FREE.
GREGORY WOLFE. THE WARDEN OF IRON HEIGHTS. I DON'T COMPLETELY TRUST HIM, BUT HE KEEPS IRON HEIGHTS SECURE.
I TAKE IT YOU DON'T KNOW WHERE THEY ARE, WARDEN WOLFE?
IF I HAD EVEN A CLUE AS TO THE WHEREABOUTS OF THAT MISERABLE BUNCH, THEY WOULD BE WHERE THEY BELONG...UNDER HEAVY SECURITY RIGHT ALONGSIDE GODSPEED AND THAWNE.
IT'S ONLY A MATTER OF TIME BEFORE THEY FALL BACK ON BAD HABITS, FLASH.
THE ROGUES SHOULD BE BROKEN UP AND CONTAINED IN SOLITARY CONFINEMENT. THEY WOULDN'T BE ABLE TO ENABLE EACH OTHER EVER AGAIN...
...WHICH WOULD BE THEIR REAL PUNISHMENT.
THE ROGUES WERE PARDONED BY CENTRAL CITY, WOLFE.
YOU DON'T THINK IT'S POSSIBLE THEY HUNG UP THEIR WEAPONS AND GAVE UP?
IS THIS ANOTHER CASE OF YOUR ADMIRABLE SENSE OF OPTIMISM, FLASH?
OR AFTER WORKING ALONGSIDE THEM FOR SO MANY YEARS... HAVE YOU GROWN FOND OF THE ROGUES?
OF COURSE NOT, BUT...
GOOD.
I'D HATE TO THINK THAT YOU OF ALL PEOPLE WOULD TURN SOFT ON JUSTICE.
WOLFE IS KNOWN FOR BEING STERN WITH HIS INMATES... AND HE'S RIGHT ABOUT THE ROGUES.
BUT HE'S WRONG ABOUT WORKING ALONGSIDE THEM... I ALREADY HAVE A PARTNER...

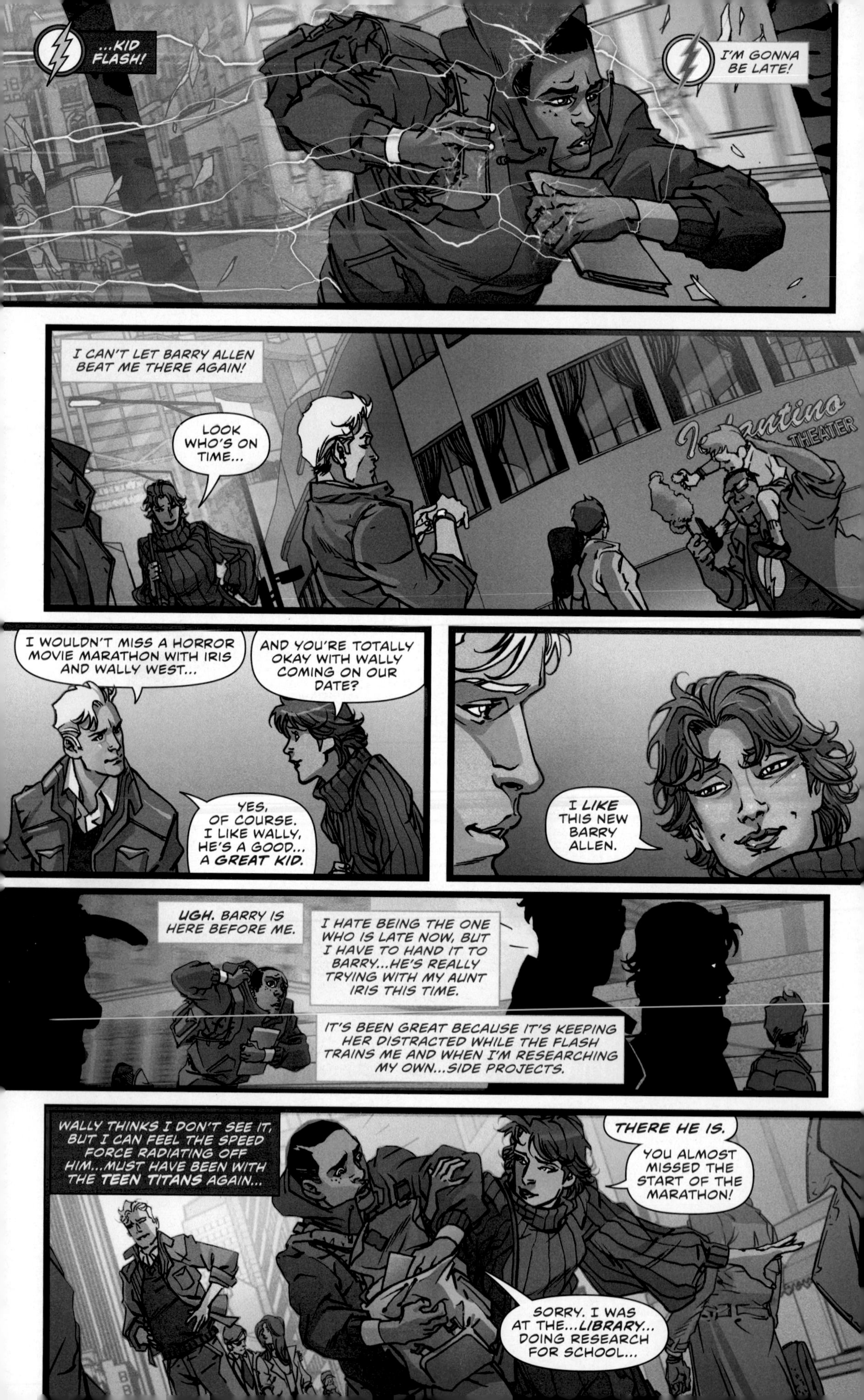
...KID FLASH!
I'M GONNA BE LATE!
I CAN'T LET BARRY ALLEN BEAT ME THERE AGAIN!
LOOK WHO'S ON TIME...
THEATER
I WOULDN'T MISS A HORROR MOVIE MARATHON WITH IRIS AND WALLY WEST...
AND YOU'RE TOTALLY OKAY WITH WALLY COMING ON OUR DATE?
YES, OF COURSE. I LIKE WALLY, HE'S A GOOD... A GREAT KID.
I LIKE THIS NEW BARRY ALLEN.
UGH. BARRY IS HERE BEFORE ME.
I HATE BEING THE ONE WHO IS LATE NOW, BUT I HAVE TO HAND IT TO BARRY...HE'S REALLY TRYING WITH MY AUNT IRIS THIS TIME.
IT'S BEEN GREAT BECAUSE IT'S KEEPING HER DISTRACTED WHILE THE FLASH TRAINS ME AND WHEN I'M RESEARCHING MY OWN...SIDE PROJECTS.
WALLY THINKS I DON'T SEE IT, BUT I CAN FEEL THE SPEED FORCE RADIATING OFF HIM...MUST HAVE BEEN WITH THE TEEN TITANS AGAIN...
THERE HE IS.
YOU ALMOST MISSED THE START OF THE MARATHON!
SORRY. I WAS AT THE...LIBRARY... DOING RESEARCH FOR SCHOOL...

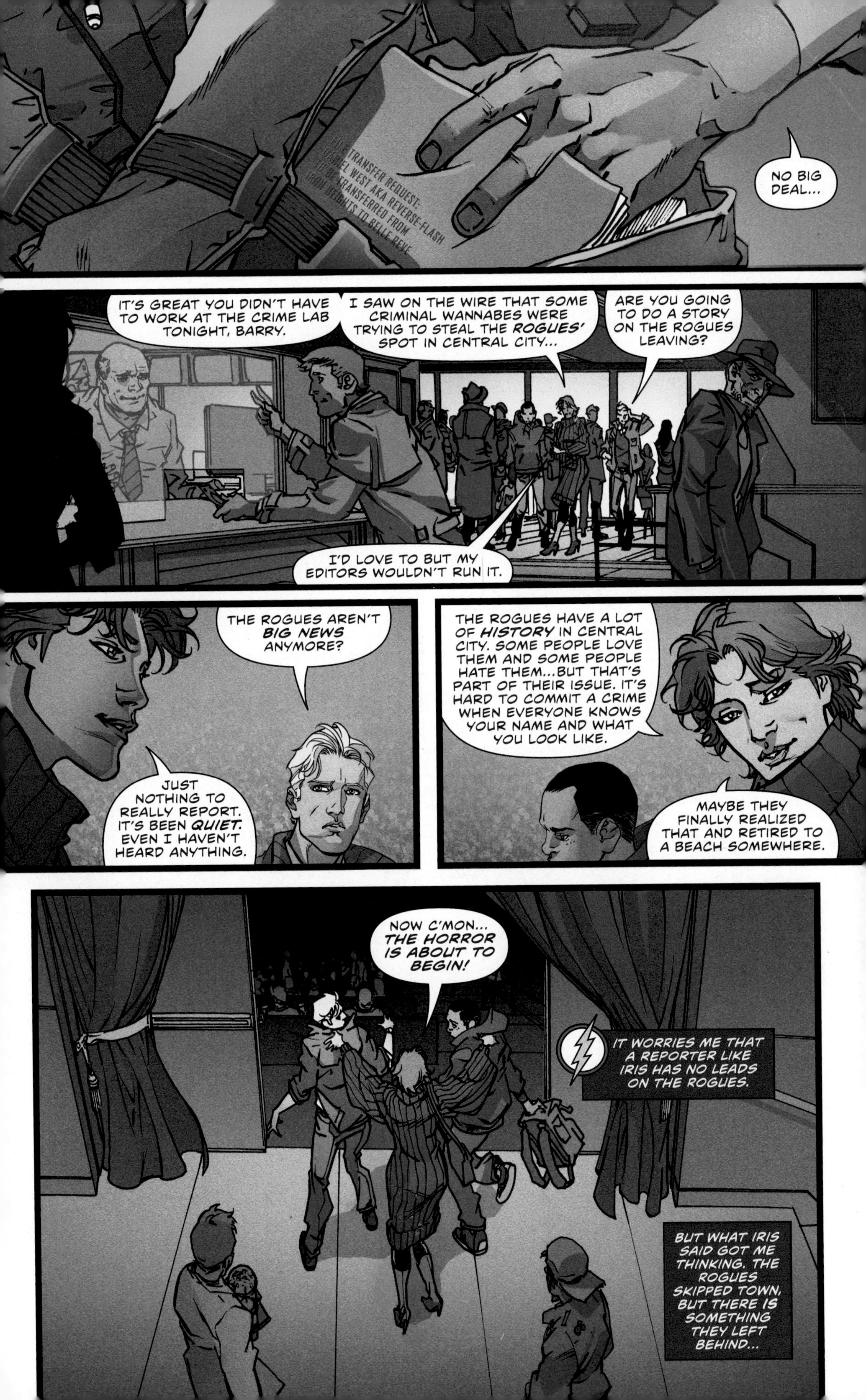
FILE TRANSFER REQUEST:
DANIEL WEST AKA REVERSE-FLASH
TO BE TRANSFERRED FROM
IRON HEIGHTS TO BELLE REVE
NO BIG DEAL...
IT'S GREAT YOU DIDN'T HAVE TO WORK AT THE CRIME LAB TONIGHT, BARRY.
I SAW ON THE WIRE THAT SOME CRIMINAL WANNABES WERE TRYING TO STEAL THE ROGUES' SPOT IN CENTRAL CITY...
ARE YOU GOING TO DO A STORY ON THE ROGUES LEAVING?
I'D LOVE TO BUT MY EDITORS WOULDN'T RUN IT.
THE ROGUES AREN'T BIG NEWS ANYMORE?
JUST NOTHING TO REALLY REPORT. IT'S BEEN QUIET. EVEN I HAVEN'T HEARD ANYTHING.
THE ROGUES HAVE A LOT OF HISTORY IN CENTRAL CITY. SOME PEOPLE LOVE THEM AND SOME PEOPLE HATE THEM...BUT THAT'S PART OF THEIR ISSUE. IT'S HARD TO COMMIT A CRIME WHEN EVERYONE KNOWS YOUR NAME AND WHAT YOU LOOK LIKE.
MAYBE THEY FINALLY REALIZED THAT AND RETIRED TO A BEACH SOMEWHERE.
NOW C'MON... THE HORROR IS ABOUT TO BEGIN!
IT WORRIES ME THAT A REPORTER LIKE IRIS HAS NO LEADS ON THE ROGUES.
BUT WHAT IRIS SAID GOT ME THINKING. THE ROGUES SKIPPED TOWN, BUT THERE IS SOMETHING THEY LEFT BEHIND...

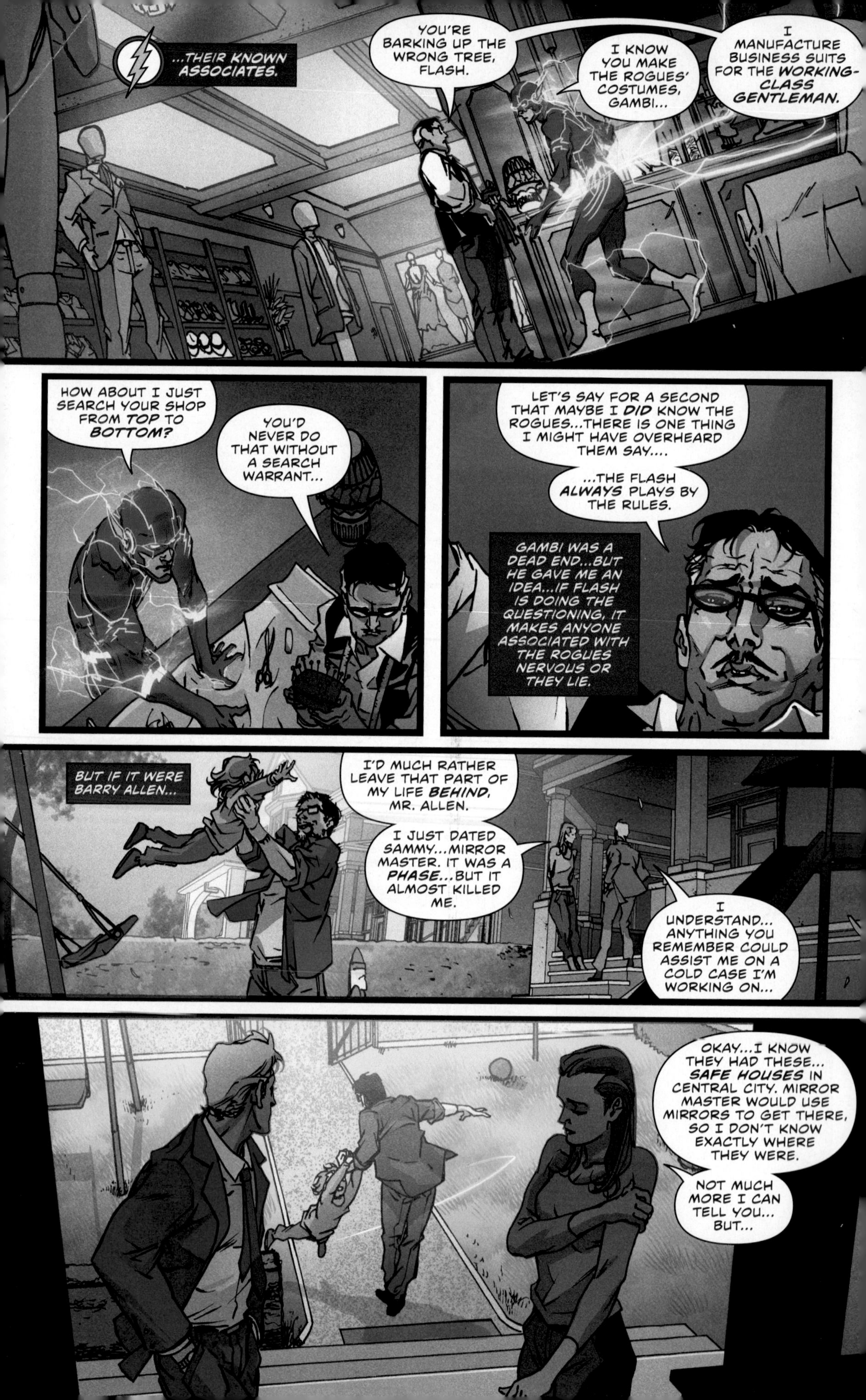
...THEIR KNOWN ASSOCIATES.
YOU'RE BARKING UP THE WRONG TREE, FLASH.
I KNOW YOU MAKE THE ROGUES' COSTUMES, GAMBI...
I MANUFACTURE BUSINESS SUITS FOR THE WORKING-CLASS GENTLEMAN.
HOW ABOUT I JUST SEARCH YOUR SHOP FROM TOP TO BOTTOM?
YOU'D NEVER DO THAT WITHOUT A SEARCH WARRANT...
LET'S SAY FOR A SECOND THAT MAYBE I DID KNOW THE ROGUES...THERE IS ONE THING I MIGHT HAVE OVERHEARD THEM SAY....
...THE FLASH ALWAYS PLAYS BY THE RULES.
GAMBI WAS A DEAD END...BUT HE GAVE ME AN IDEA...IF FLASH IS DOING THE QUESTIONING, IT MAKES ANYONE ASSOCIATED WITH THE ROGUES NERVOUS OR THEY LIE.
BUT IF IT WERE BARRY ALLEN...
I'D MUCH RATHER LEAVE THAT PART OF MY LIFE BEHIND, MR. ALLEN.
I JUST DATED SAMMY...MIRROR MASTER. IT WAS A PHASE...BUT IT ALMOST KILLED ME.
I UNDERSTAND... ANYTHING YOU REMEMBER COULD ASSIST ME ON A COLD CASE I'M WORKING ON...
OKAY...I KNOW THEY HAD THESE... SAFE HOUSES IN CENTRAL CITY. MIRROR MASTER WOULD USE MIRRORS TO GET THERE, SO I DON'T KNOW EXACTLY WHERE THEY WERE.
NOT MUCH MORE I CAN TELL YOU... BUT...

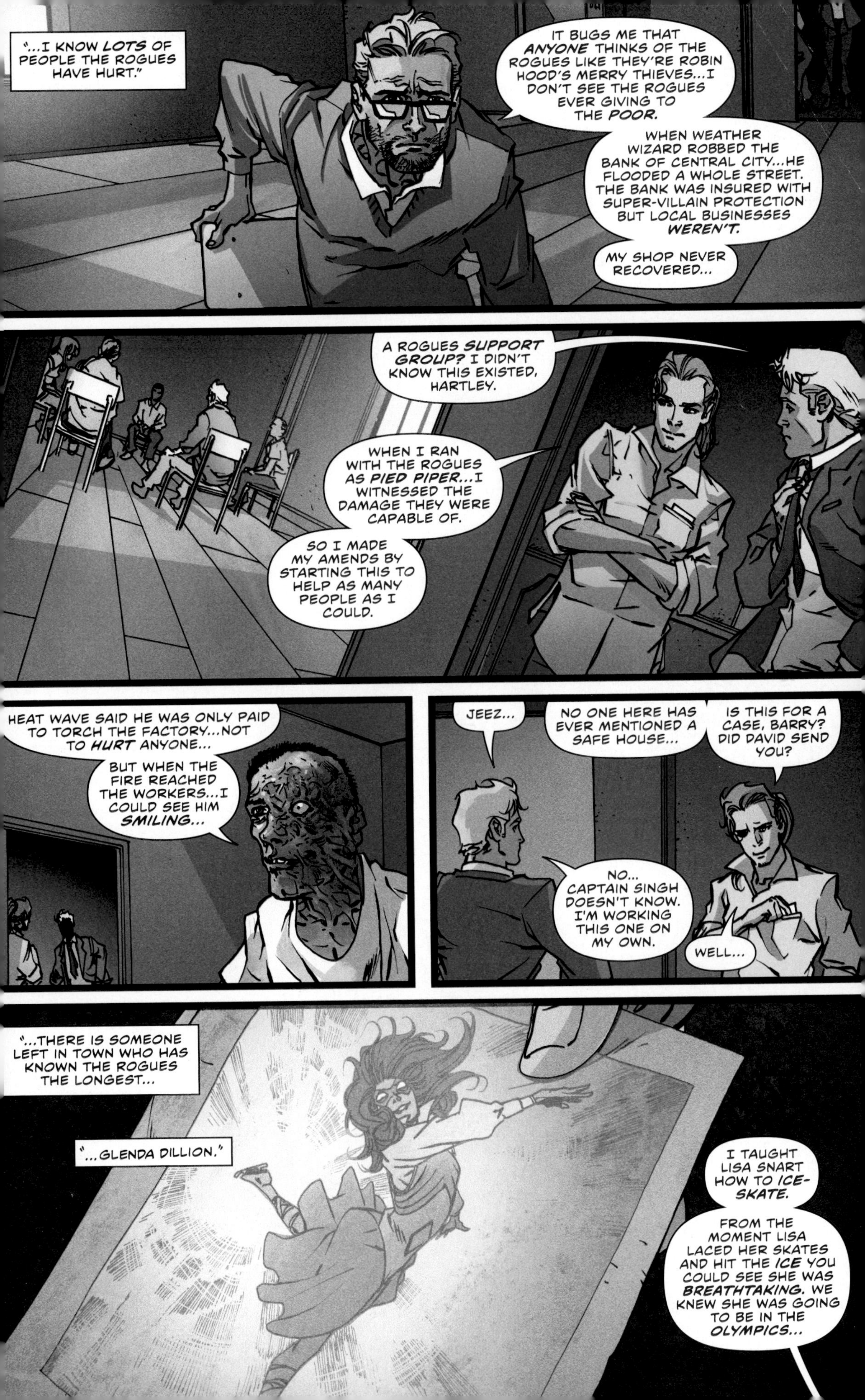
"...I KNOW LOTS OF PEOPLE THE ROGUES HAVE HURT."
IT BUGS ME THAT ANYONE THINKS OF THE ROGUES LIKE THEY'RE ROBIN HOOD'S MERRY THIEVES...I DON'T SEE THE ROGUES EVER GIVING TO THE POOR.
WHEN WEATHER WIZARD ROBBED THE BANK OF CENTRAL CITY...HE FLOODED A WHOLE STREET. THE BANK WAS INSURED WITH SUPER-VILLAIN PROTECTION BUT LOCAL BUSINESSES WEREN'T.
MY SHOP NEVER RECOVERED...
A ROGUES SUPPORT GROUP? I DIDN'T KNOW THIS EXISTED, HARTLEY.
WHEN I RAN WITH THE ROGUES AS PIED PIPER...I WITNESSED THE DAMAGE THEY WERE CAPABLE OF.
SO I MADE MY AMENDS BY STARTING THIS TO HELP AS MANY PEOPLE AS I COULD.
HEAT WAVE SAID HE WAS ONLY PAID TO TORCH THE FACTORY...NOT TO HURT ANYONE...
BUT WHEN THE FIRE REACHED THE WORKERS...I COULD SEE HIM SMILING...
JEEZ...
NO ONE HERE HAS EVER MENTIONED A SAFE HOUSE...
IS THIS FOR A CASE, BARRY? DID DAVID SEND YOU?
NO... CAPTAIN SINGH DOESN'T KNOW. I'M WORKING THIS ONE ON MY OWN.
WELL...
"...THERE IS SOMEONE LEFT IN TOWN WHO HAS KNOWN THE ROGUES THE LONGEST...
"...GLENDA DILLION."
I TAUGHT LISA SNART HOW TO ICE-SKATE.
FROM THE MOMENT LISA LACED HER SKATES AND HIT THE ICE YOU COULD SEE SHE WAS BREATHTAKING. WE KNEW SHE WAS GOING TO BE IN THE OLYMPICS...

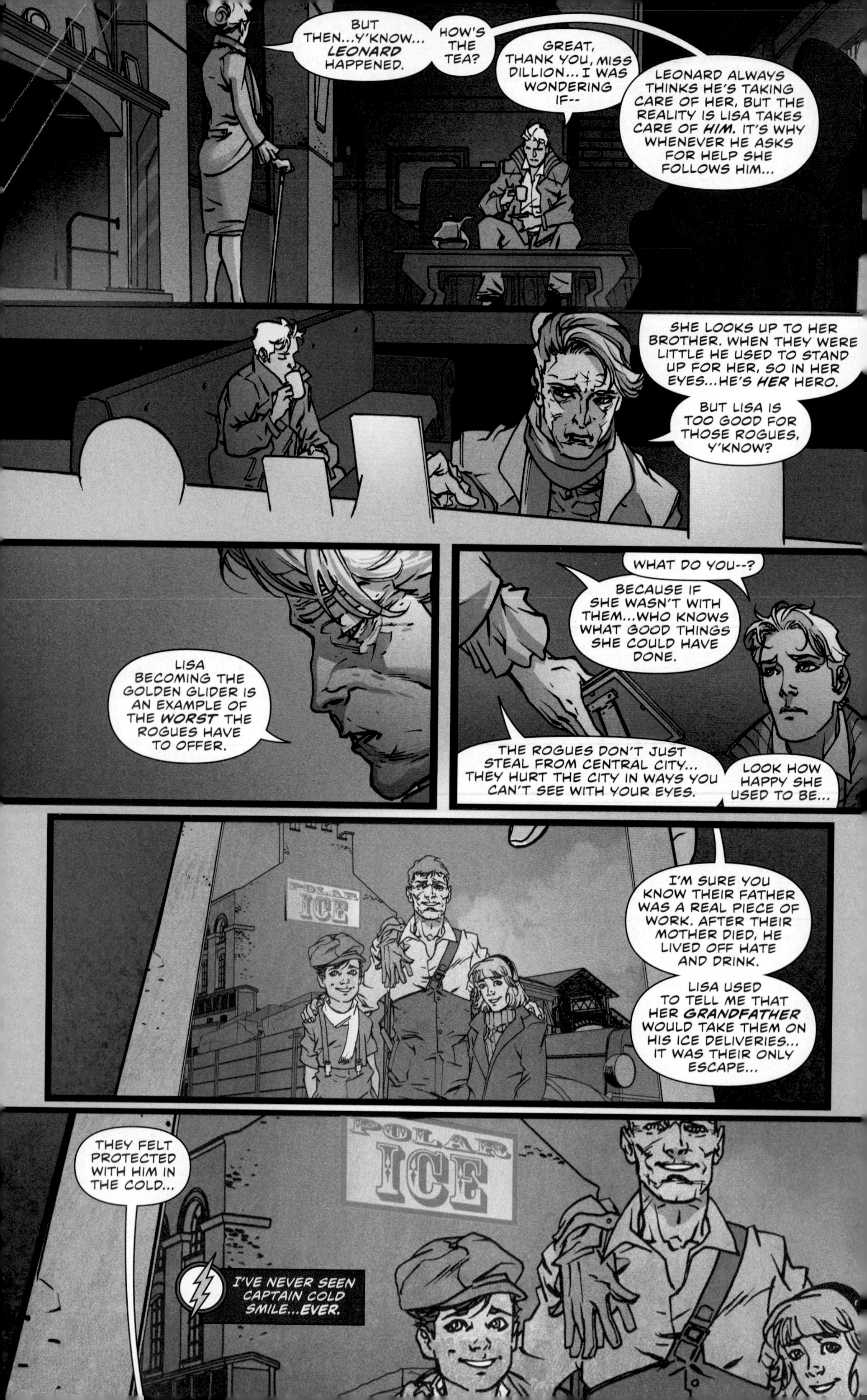

BUT THEN...Y'KNOW... LEONARD HAPPENED.
HOW'S THE TEA?
GREAT, THANK YOU, MISS DILLION... I WAS WONDERING IF--
LEONARD ALWAYS THINKS HE'S TAKING CARE OF HER, BUT THE REALITY IS LISA TAKES CARE OF HIM. IT'S WHY WHENEVER HE ASKS FOR HELP SHE FOLLOWS HIM...
SHE LOOKS UP TO HER BROTHER. WHEN THEY WERE LITTLE HE USED TO STAND UP FOR HER, SO IN HER EYES...HE'S HER HERO.
BUT LISA IS TOO GOOD FOR THOSE ROGUES, Y'KNOW?
LISA BECOMING THE GOLDEN GLIDER IS AN EXAMPLE OF THE WORST THE ROGUES HAVE TO OFFER.
WHAT DO YOU--?
BECAUSE IF SHE WASN'T WITH THEM...WHO KNOWS WHAT GOOD THINGS SHE COULD HAVE DONE.
THE ROGUES DON'T JUST STEAL FROM CENTRAL CITY... THEY HURT THE CITY IN WAYS YOU CAN'T SEE WITH YOUR EYES.
LOOK HOW HAPPY SHE USED TO BE...
POLAR ICE
I'M SURE YOU KNOW THEIR FATHER WAS A REAL PIECE OF WORK. AFTER THEIR MOTHER DIED, HE LIVED OFF HATE AND DRINK.
LISA USED TO TELL ME THAT HER GRANDFATHER WOULD TAKE THEM ON HIS ICE DELIVERIES... IT WAS THEIR ONLY ESCAPE...
THEY FELT PROTECTED WITH HIM IN THE COLD...
POLAR ICE
I'VE NEVER SEEN CAPTAIN COLD SMILE...EVER.

POLAR ICE... THE ONLY PLACE LEONARD EVER FELT SAFE.

NO ONE HAS BEEN HERE IN YEARS.

BUT THAT'S EXACTLY WHAT THE ROGUES WOULD WANT PEOPLE TO THINK.

VVRR RRRRR

BINGO.

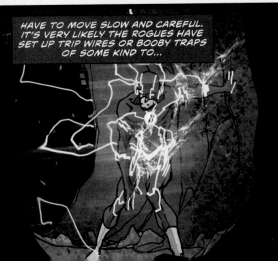

HAVE TO MOVE SLOW AND CAREFUL. IT'S VERY LIKELY THE ROGUES HAVE SET UP TRIP WIRES OR BOOBY TRAPS OF SOME KIND TO...

AH... DANG...

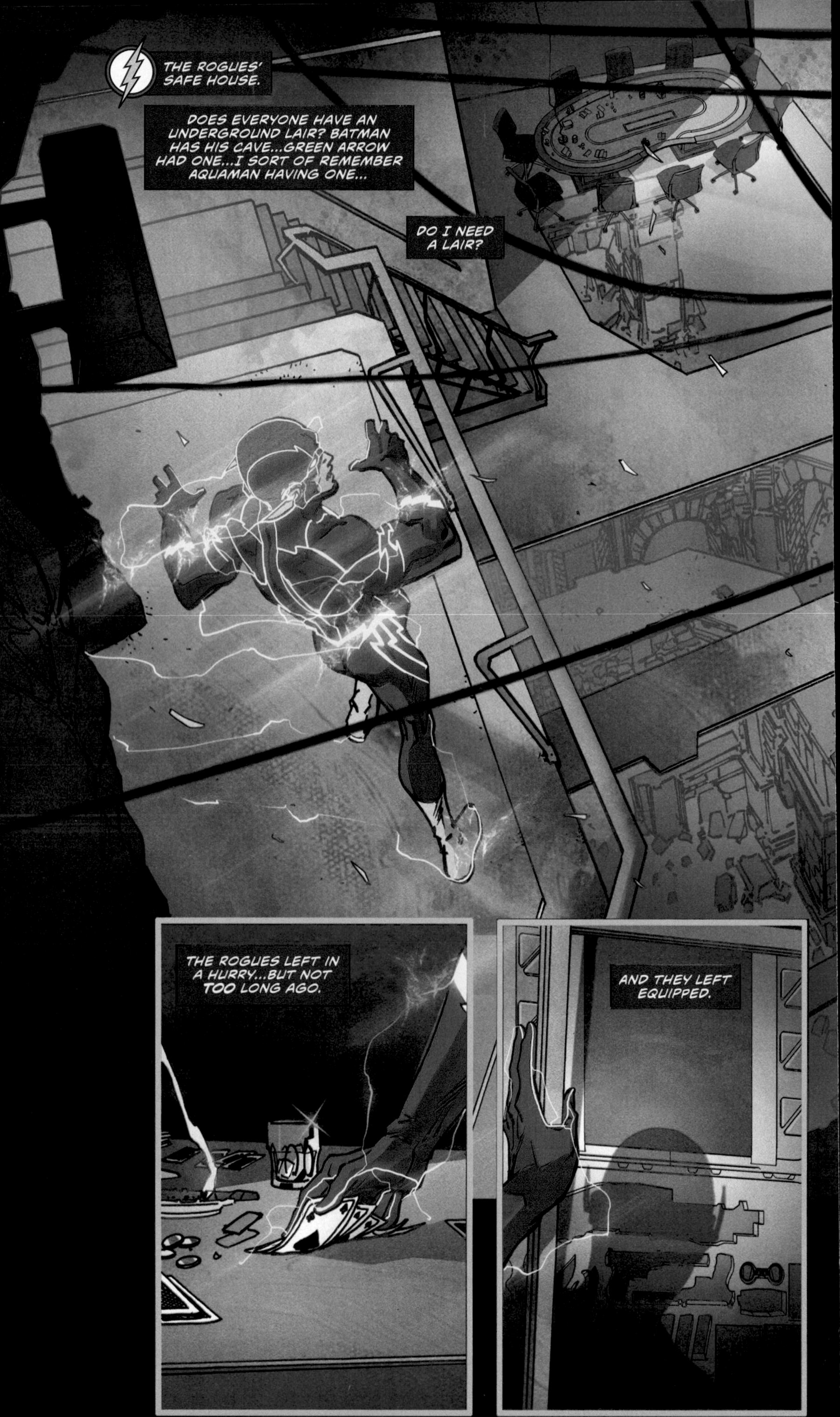
THE ROGUES' SAFE HOUSE.
DOES EVERYONE HAVE AN UNDERGROUND LAIR? BATMAN HAS HIS CAVE...GREEN ARROW HAD ONE...I SORT OF REMEMBER AQUAMAN HAVING ONE...
DO I NEED A LAIR?
THE ROGUES LEFT IN A HURRY...BUT NOT TOO LONG AGO.
AND THEY LEFT EQUIPPED.

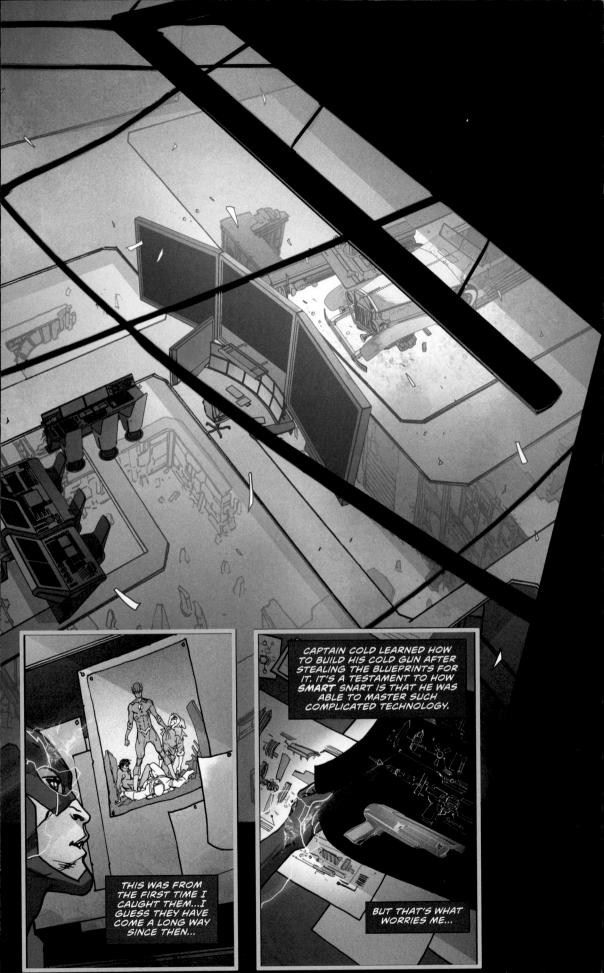

CAPTAIN COLD LEARNED HOW TO BUILD HIS COLD GUN AFTER STEALING THE BLUEPRINTS FOR IT. IT'S A TESTAMENT TO HOW **SMART** SNART IS THAT HE WAS ABLE TO MASTER SUCH COMPLICATED TECHNOLOGY.

THIS WAS FROM THE FIRST TIME I CAUGHT THEM...I GUESS THEY HAVE COME A LONG WAY SINCE THEN...

BUT THAT'S WHAT WORRIES ME...

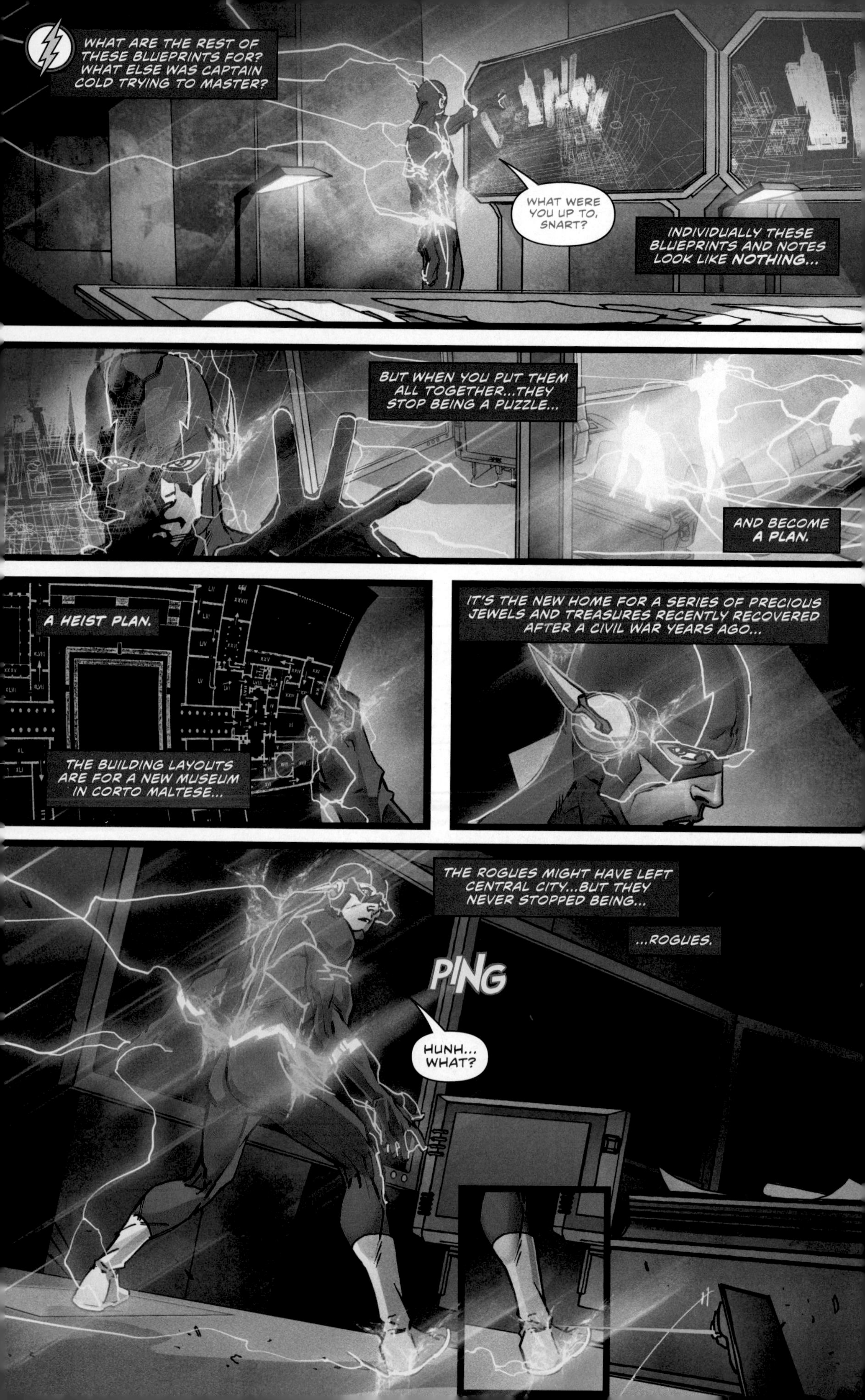
WHAT ARE THE REST OF THESE BLUEPRINTS FOR? WHAT ELSE WAS CAPTAIN COLD TRYING TO MASTER?
WHAT WERE YOU UP TO, SNART?
INDIVIDUALLY THESE BLUEPRINTS AND NOTES LOOK LIKE NOTHING...
BUT WHEN YOU PUT THEM ALL TOGETHER...THEY STOP BEING A PUZZLE...
AND BECOME A PLAN.
A HEIST PLAN.
THE BUILDING LAYOUTS ARE FOR A NEW MUSEUM IN CORTO MALTESE...
IT'S THE NEW HOME FOR A SERIES OF PRECIOUS JEWELS AND TREASURES RECENTLY RECOVERED AFTER A CIVIL WAR YEARS AGO...
THE ROGUES MIGHT HAVE LEFT CENTRAL CITY...BUT THEY NEVER STOPPED BEING...
...ROGUES.
PING
HUNH... WHAT?

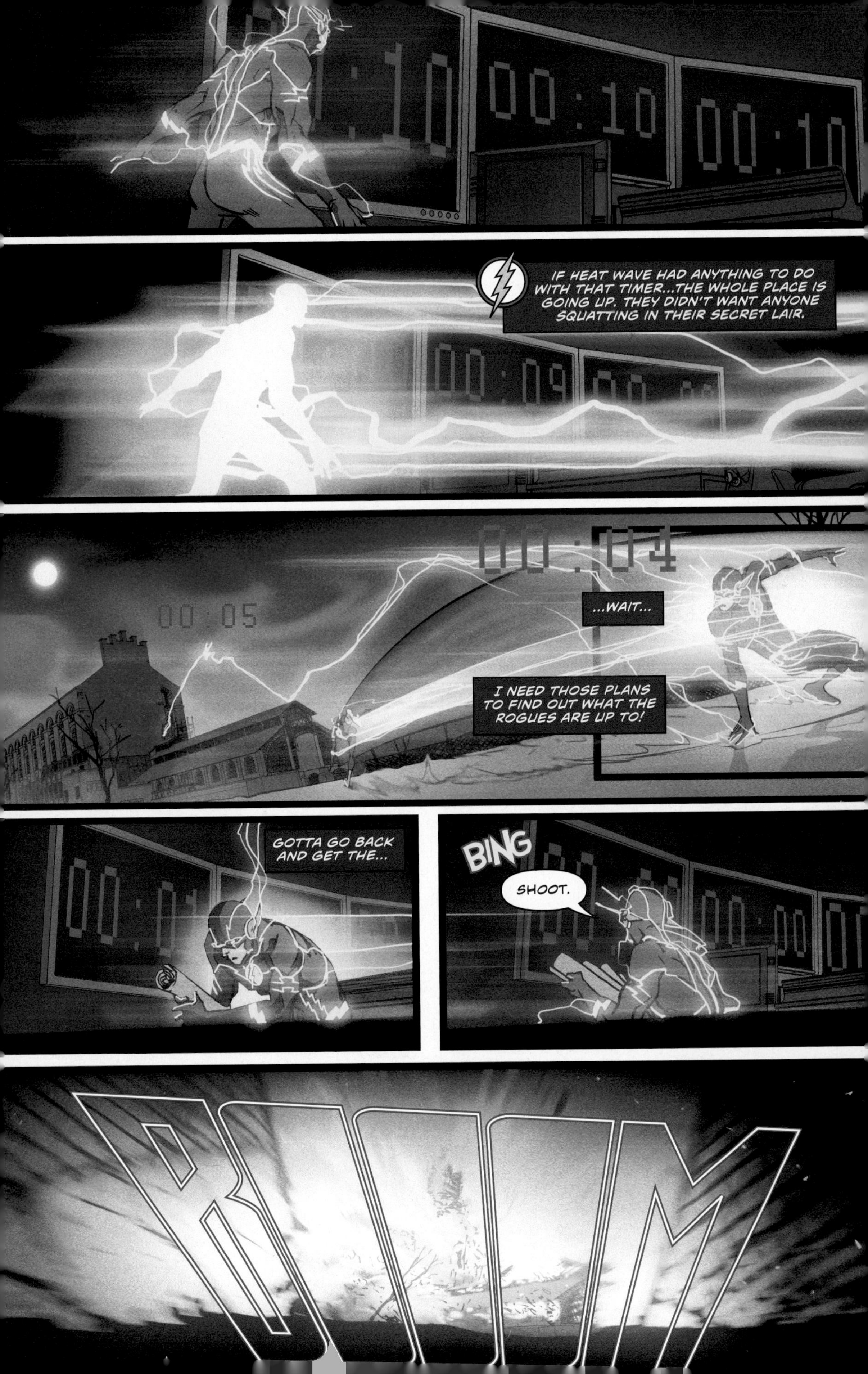
IF HEAT WAVE HAD ANYTHING TO DO WITH THAT TIMER...THE WHOLE PLACE IS GOING UP. THEY DIDN'T WANT ANYONE SQUATTING IN THEIR SECRET LAIR.
00:05
00:04
...WAIT...
I NEED THOSE PLANS TO FIND OUT WHAT THE ROGUES ARE UP TO!
GOTTA GO BACK AND GET THE...
BING
SHOOT.
BOOOM

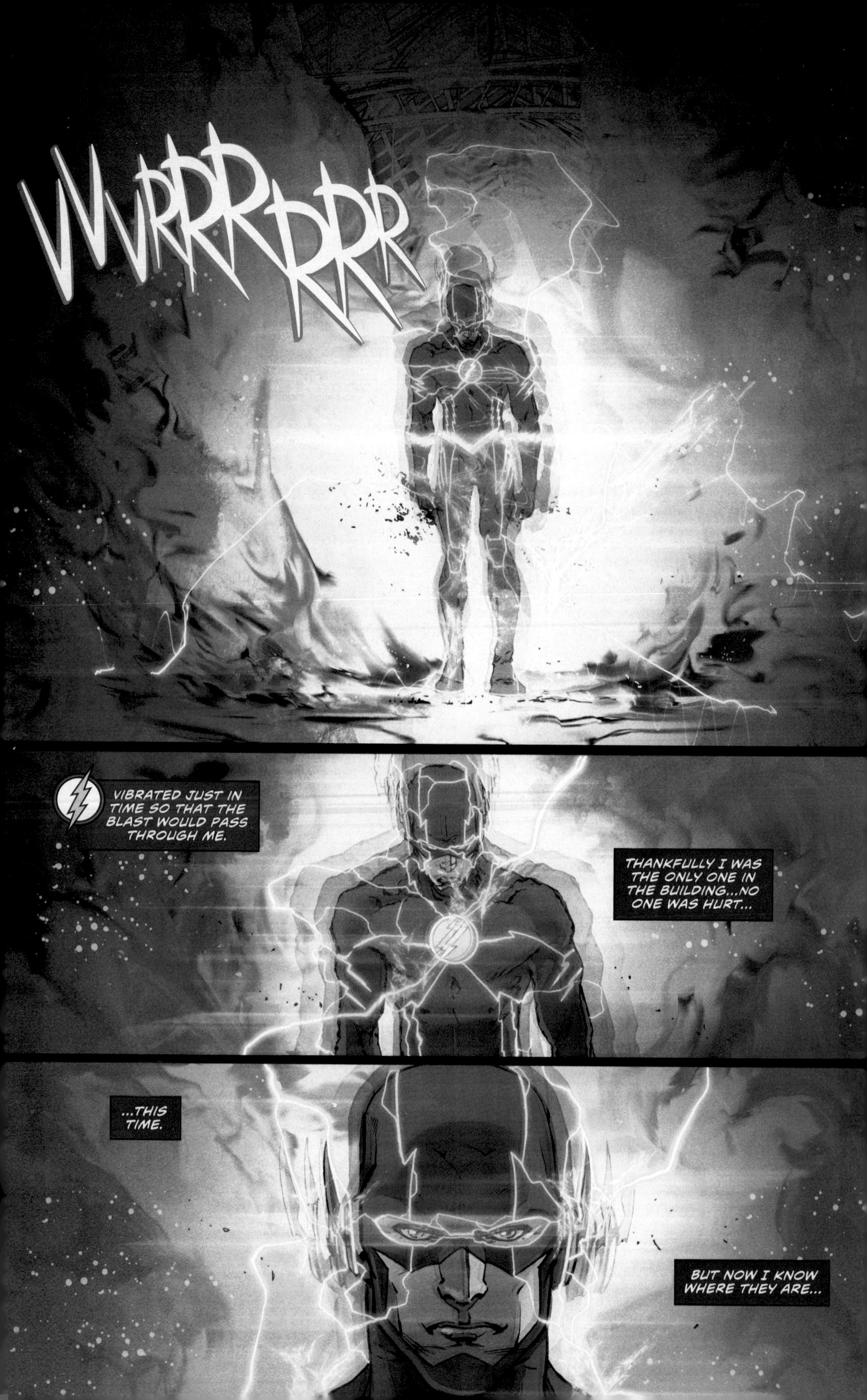
VVVRRRRRRR
VIBRATED JUST IN TIME SO THAT THE BLAST WOULD PASS THROUGH ME.
THANKFULLY I WAS THE ONLY ONE IN THE BUILDING...NO ONE WAS HURT...
...THIS TIME.
BUT NOW I KNOW WHERE THEY ARE...

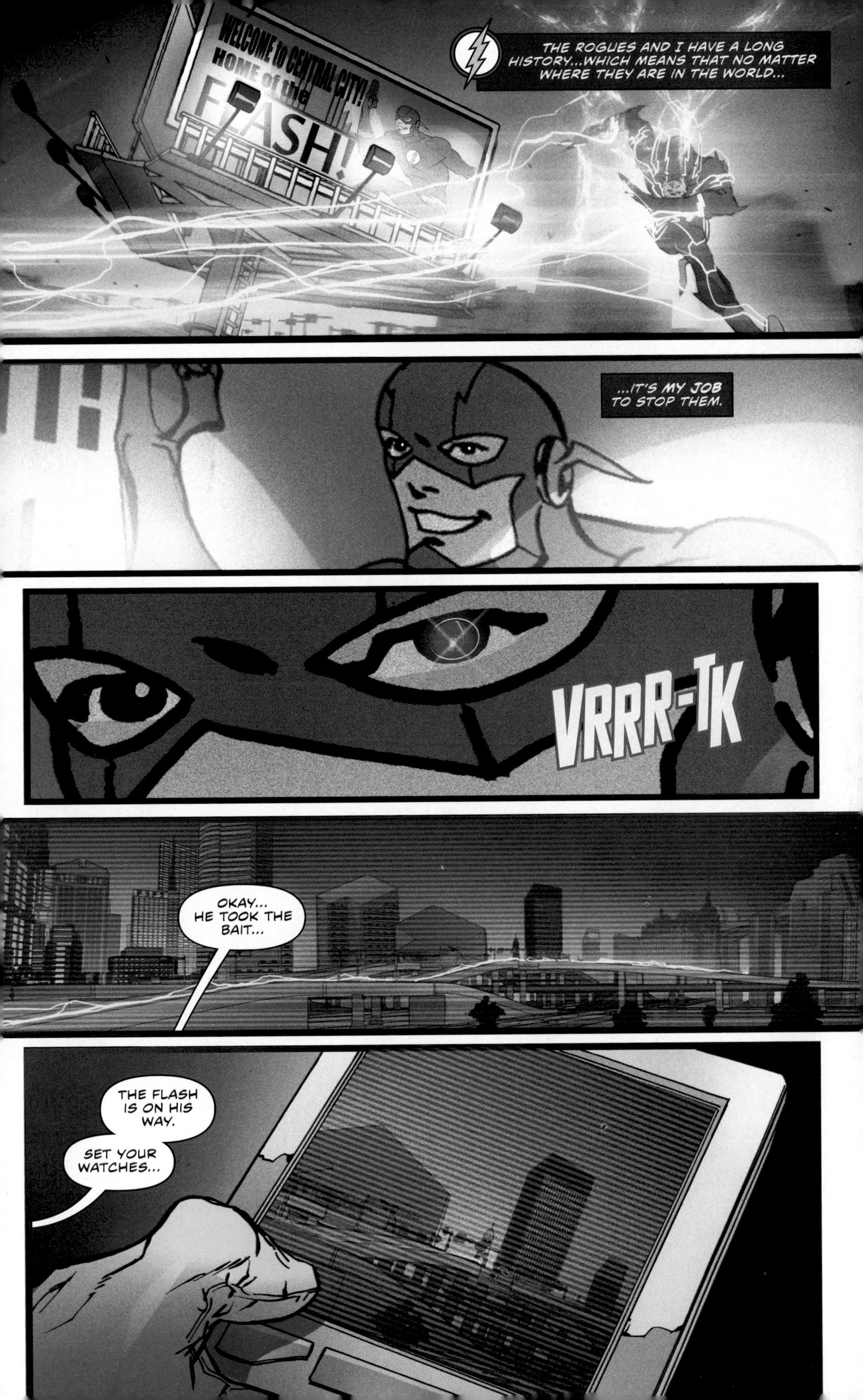
WELCOME to CENTRAL CITY! HOME of the FLASH!
THE ROGUES AND I HAVE A LONG HISTORY...WHICH MEANS THAT NO MATTER WHERE THEY ARE IN THE WORLD...
...IT'S MY JOB TO STOP THEM.
VRRR-TK
OKAY... HE TOOK THE BAIT...
THE FLASH IS ON HIS WAY.
SET YOUR WATCHES...

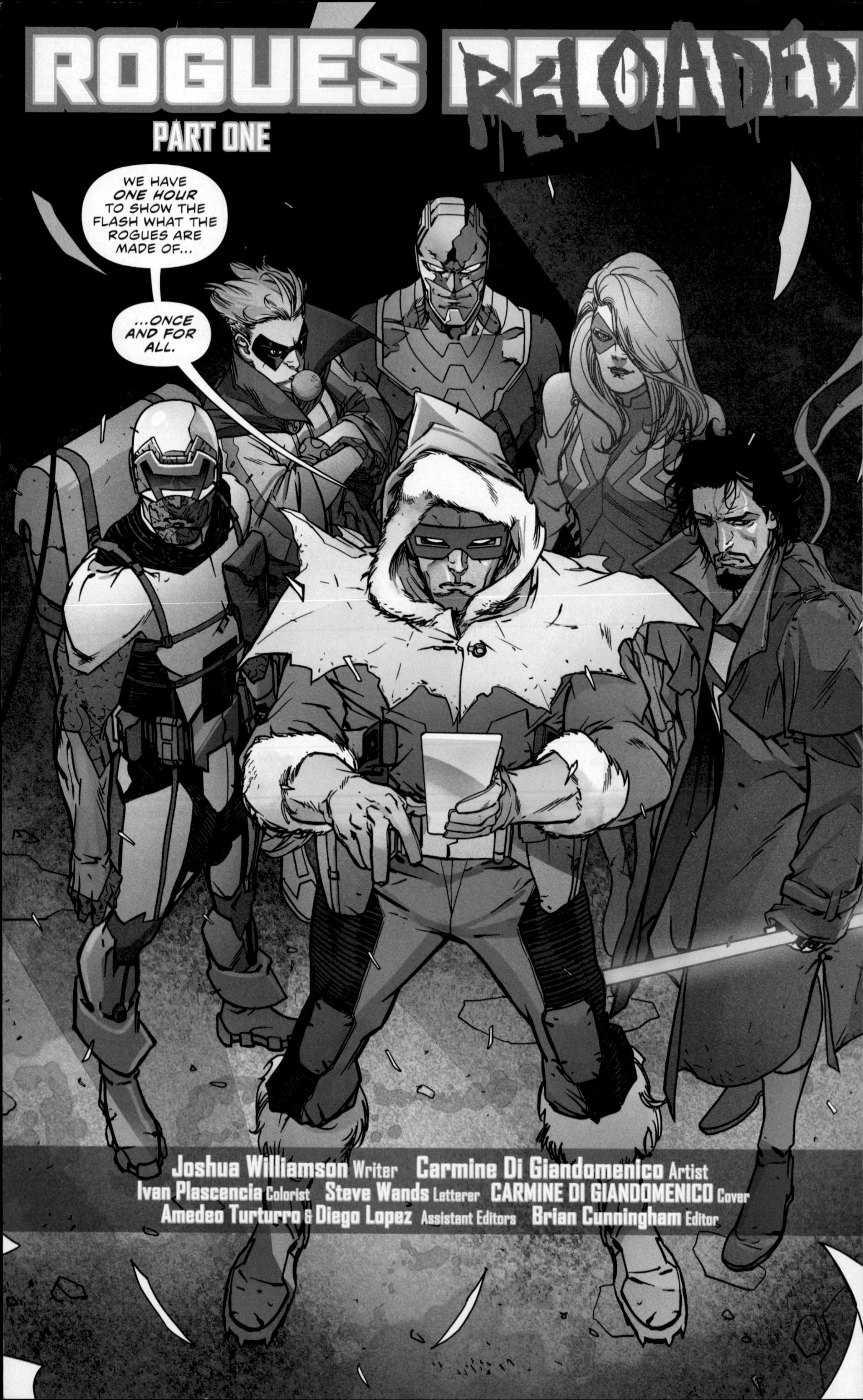
ROGUES RELOADED
PART ONE
WE HAVE ONE HOUR TO SHOW THE FLASH WHAT THE ROGUES ARE MADE OF...
...ONCE AND FOR ALL.
Joshua Williamson Writer Carmine Di Giandomenico Artist
Ivan Plascencia Colorist Steve Wands Letterer CARMINE DI GIANDOMENICO Cover
Amedeo Turturro & Diego Lopez Assistant Editors Brian Cunningham Editor

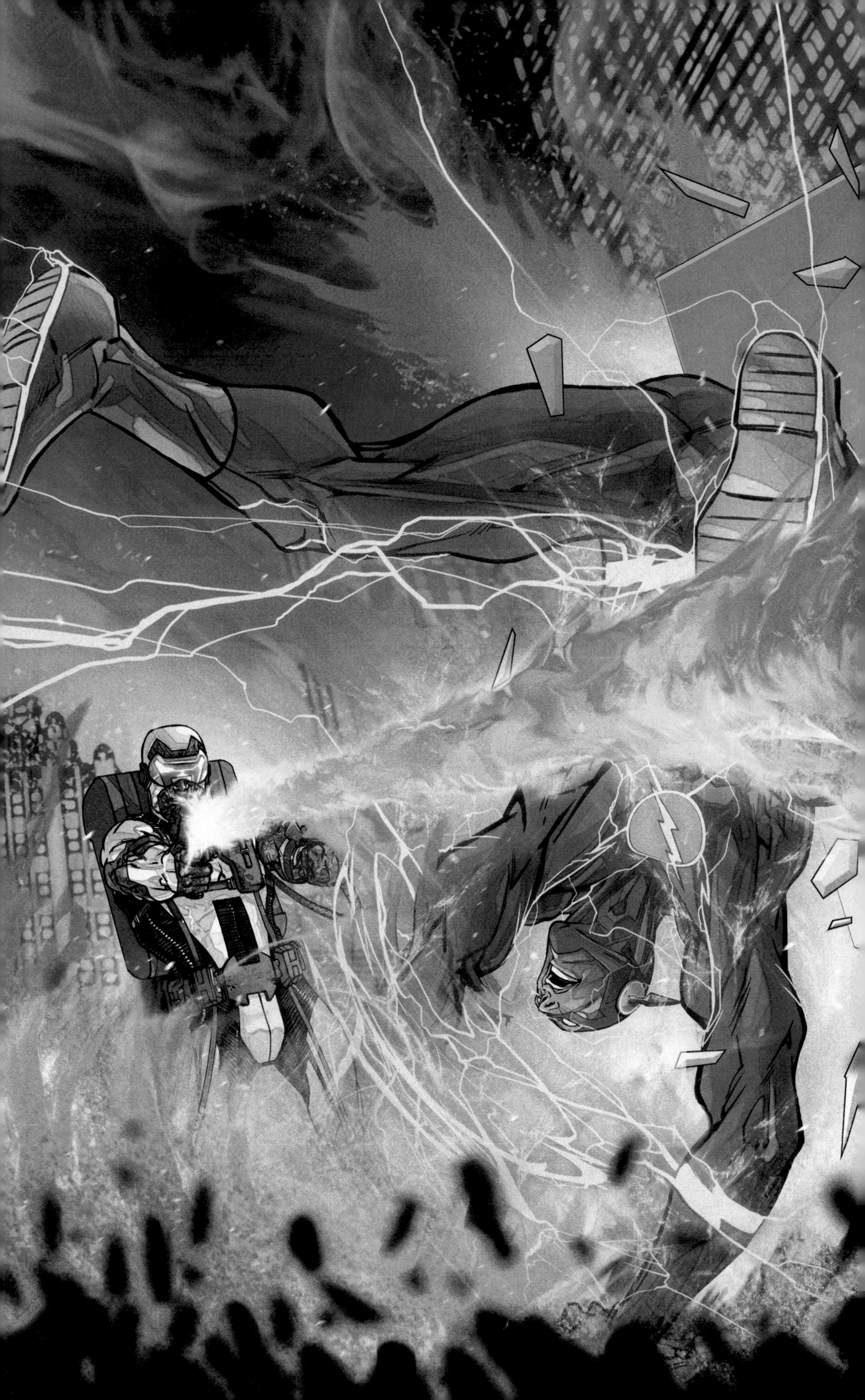

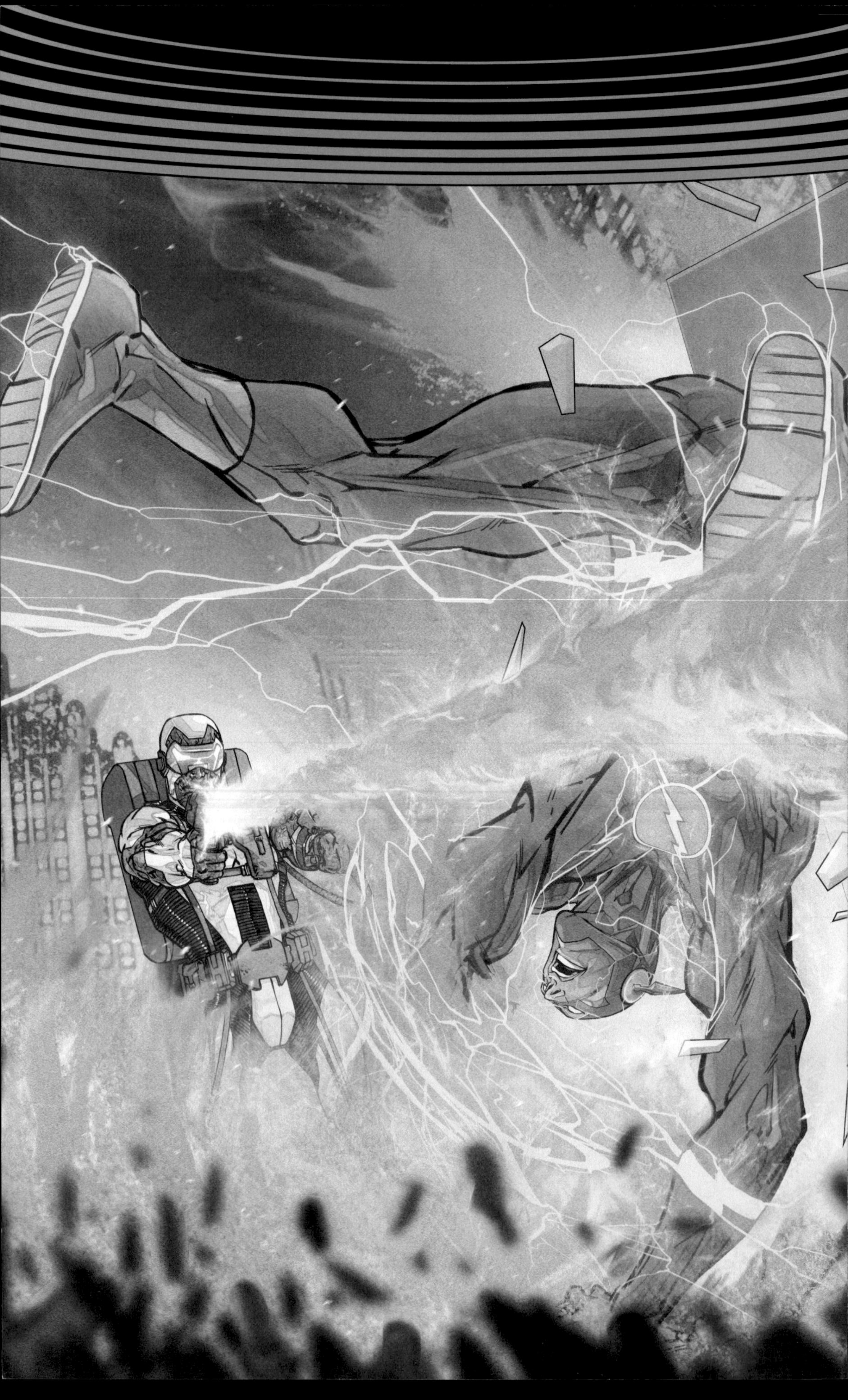

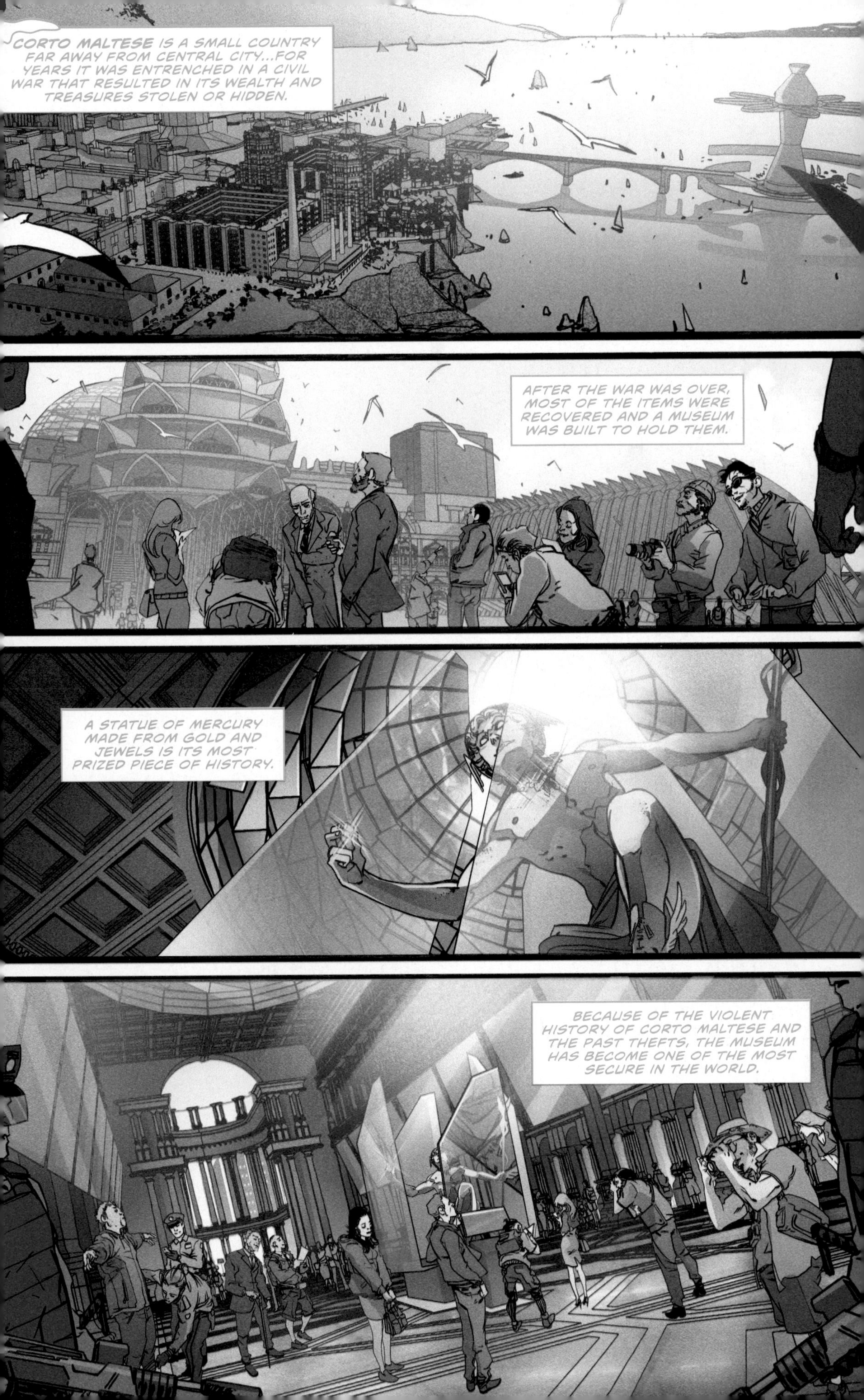
CORTO MALTESE IS A SMALL COUNTRY FAR AWAY FROM CENTRAL CITY...FOR YEARS IT WAS ENTRENCHED IN A CIVIL WAR THAT RESULTED IN ITS WEALTH AND TREASURES STOLEN OR HIDDEN.
AFTER THE WAR WAS OVER, MOST OF THE ITEMS WERE RECOVERED AND A MUSEUM WAS BUILT TO HOLD THEM.
A STATUE OF MERCURY MADE FROM GOLD AND JEWELS IS ITS MOST PRIZED PIECE OF HISTORY.
BECAUSE OF THE VIOLENT HISTORY OF CORTO MALTESE AND THE PAST THEFTS, THE MUSEUM HAS BECOME ONE OF THE MOST SECURE IN THE WORLD.

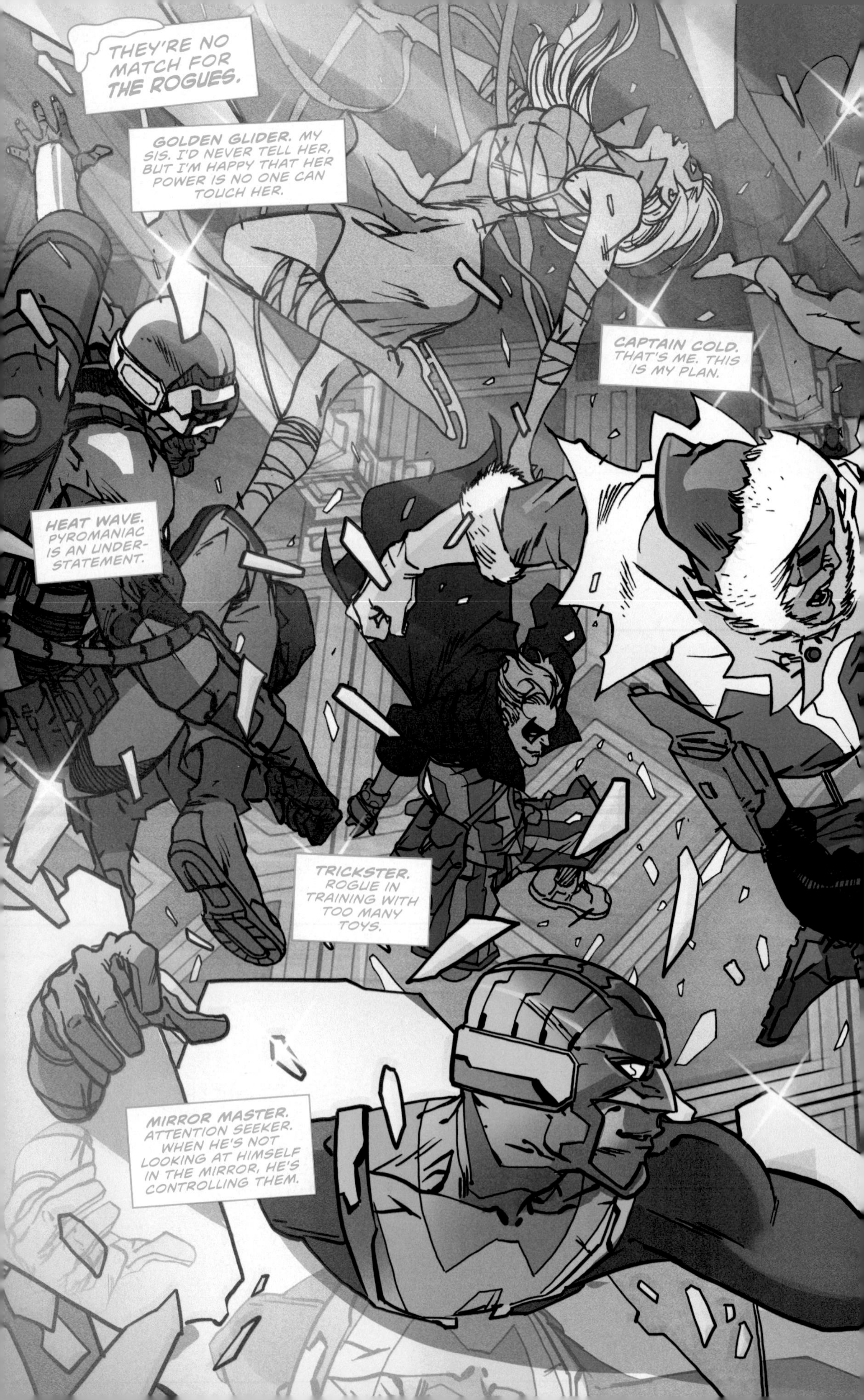
THEY'RE NO MATCH FOR THE ROGUES.
GOLDEN GLIDER. MY SIS. I'D NEVER TELL HER, BUT I'M HAPPY THAT HER POWER IS NO ONE CAN TOUCH HER.
CAPTAIN COLD. THAT'S ME. THIS IS MY PLAN.
HEAT WAVE. PYROMANIAC IS AN UNDER-STATEMENT.
TRICKSTER. ROGUE IN TRAINING WITH TOO MANY TOYS.
MIRROR MASTER. ATTENTION SEEKER. WHEN HE'S NOT LOOKING AT HIMSELF IN THE MIRROR, HE'S CONTROLLING THEM.

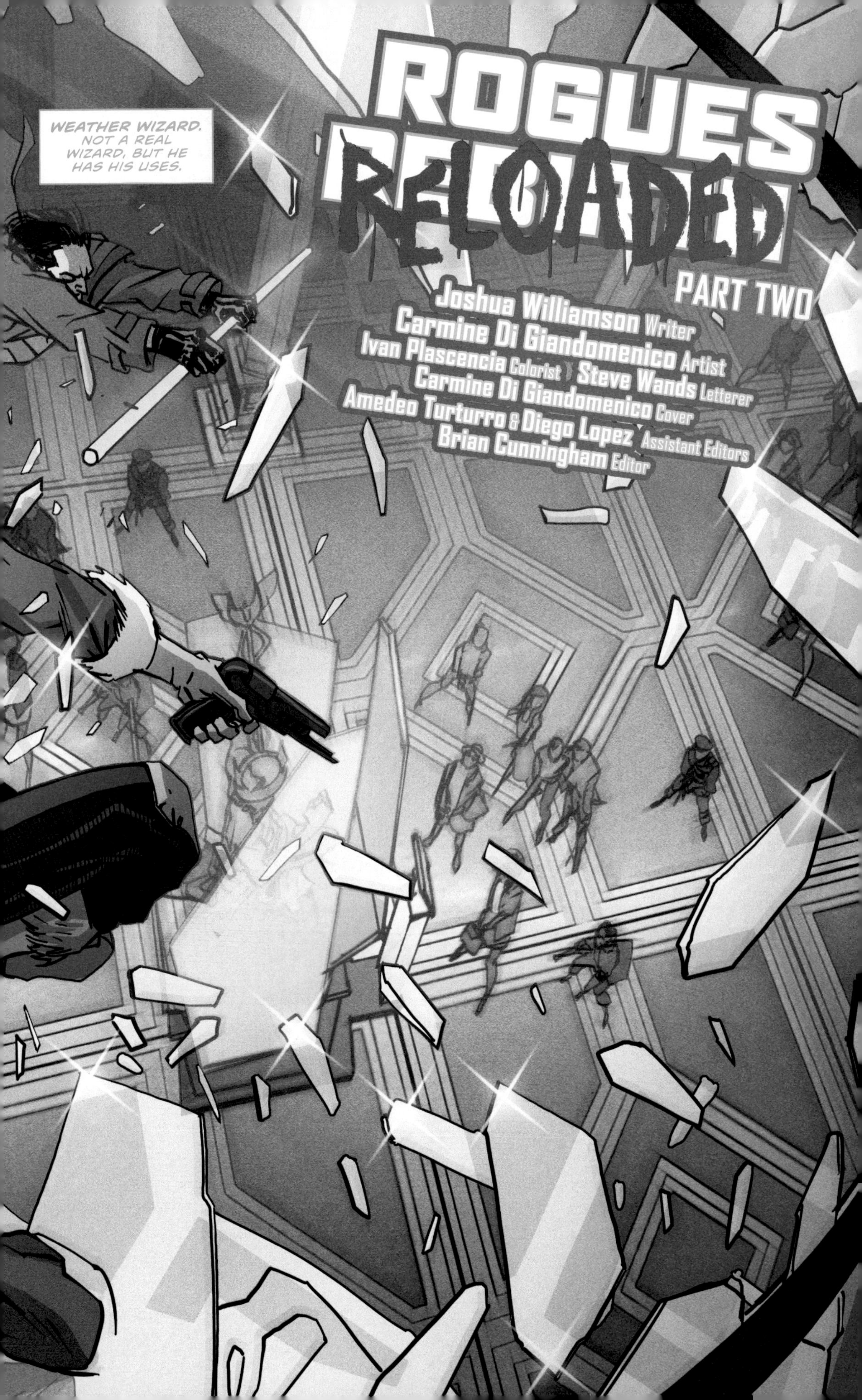
WEATHER WIZARD. NOT A REAL WIZARD, BUT HE HAS HIS USES.
ROGUES RELOADED
PART TWO
Joshua Williamson Writer
Carmine Di Giandomenico Artist
Ivan Plascencia Colorist Steve Wands Letterer
Carmine Di Giandomenico Cover
Amedeo Turturro & Diego Lopez Assistant Editors
Brian Cunningham Editor

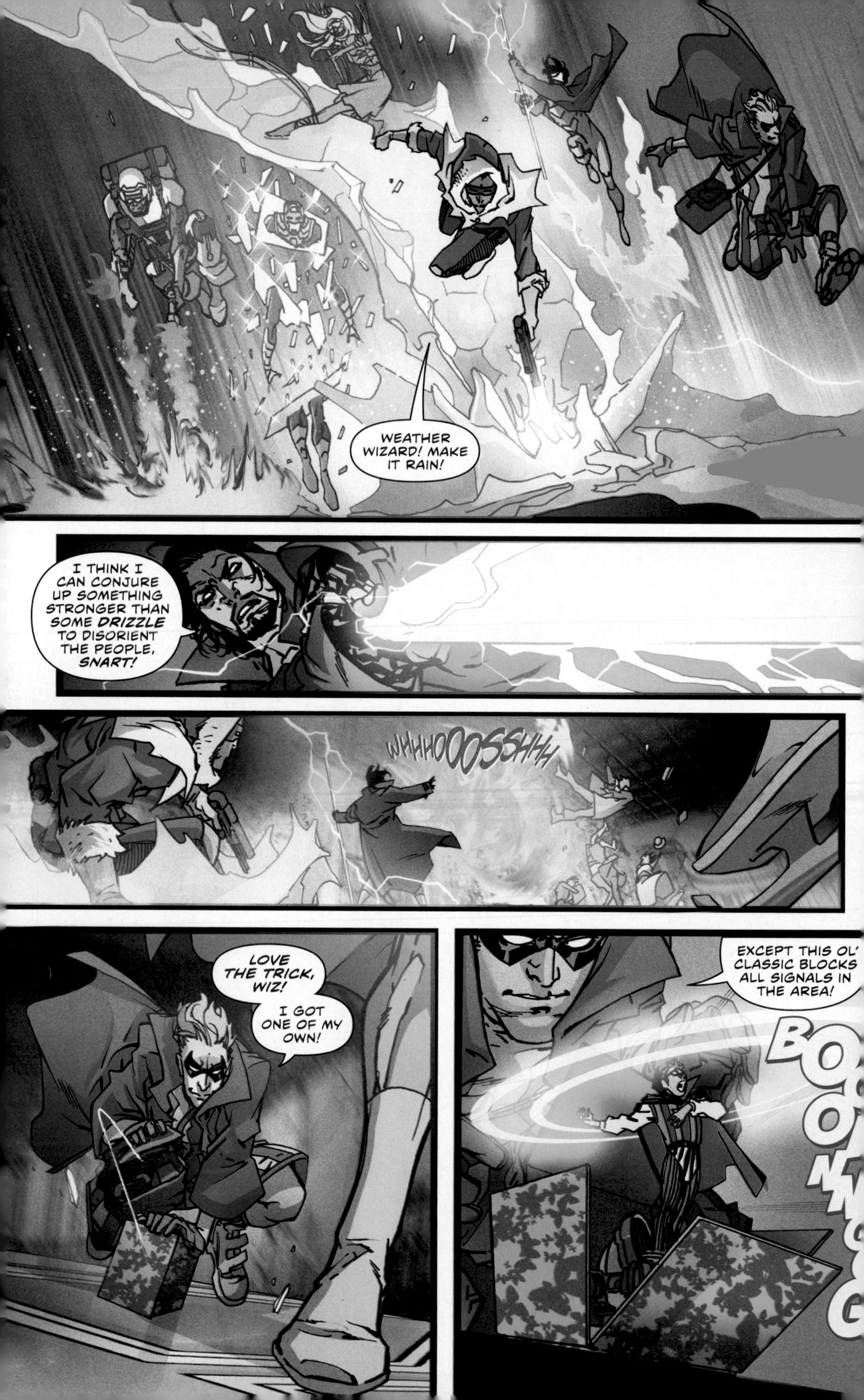
WEATHER WIZARD! MAKE IT RAIN!
I THINK I CAN CONJURE UP SOMETHING STRONGER THAN SOME *DRIZZLE* TO DISORIENT THE PEOPLE, *SNART!*
WHHHOOOSSHHH
LOVE THE TRICK, WIZ!
I GOT ONE OF MY OWN!
EXCEPT THIS OL' CLASSIC BLOCKS ALL SIGNALS IN THE AREA!

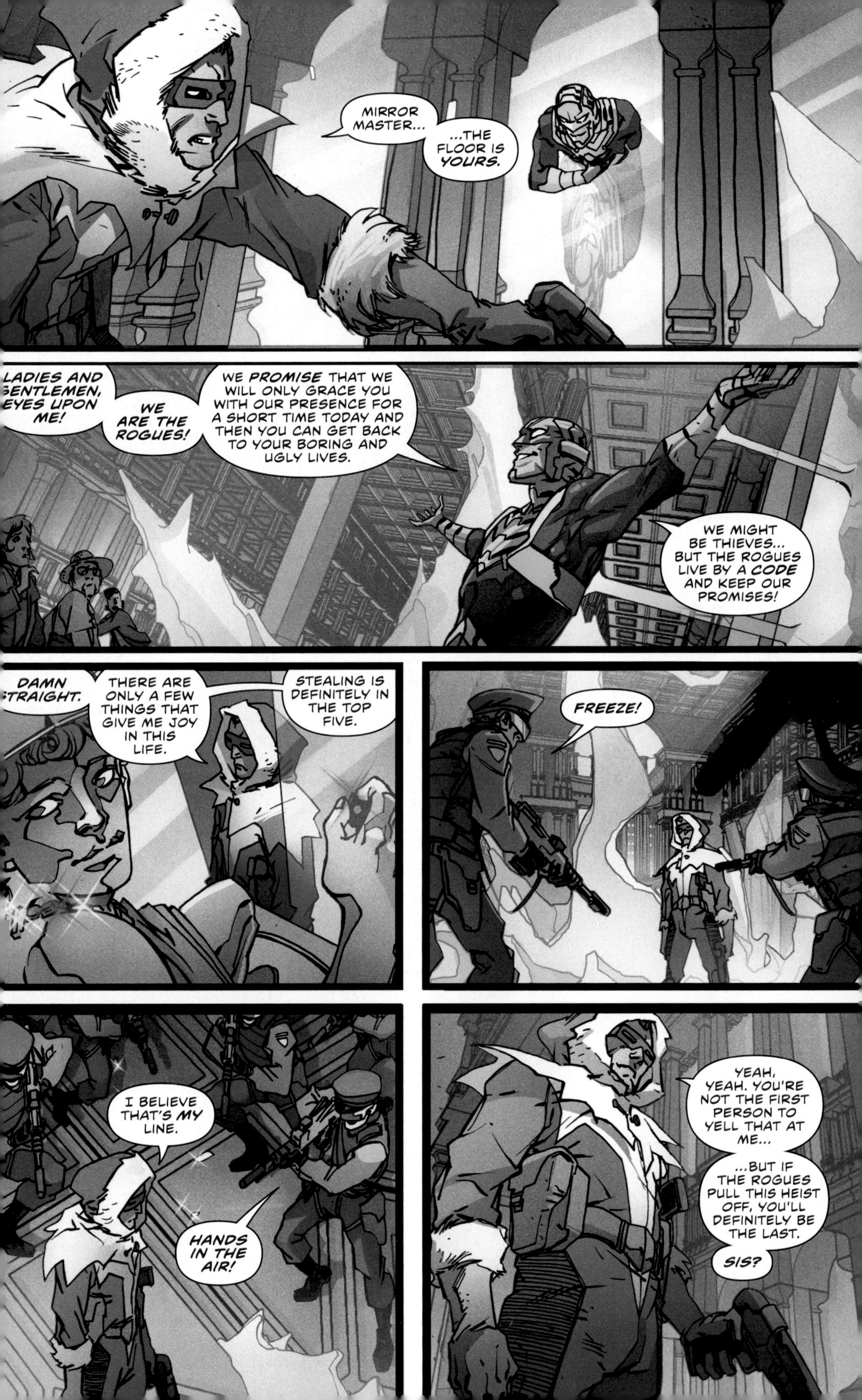
MIRROR MASTER...
...THE FLOOR IS YOURS.
LADIES AND GENTLEMEN, EYES UPON ME!
WE ARE THE ROGUES!
WE PROMISE THAT WE WILL ONLY GRACE YOU WITH OUR PRESENCE FOR A SHORT TIME TODAY AND THEN YOU CAN GET BACK TO YOUR BORING AND UGLY LIVES.
WE MIGHT BE THIEVES... BUT THE ROGUES LIVE BY A CODE AND KEEP OUR PROMISES!
DAMN STRAIGHT.
THERE ARE ONLY A FEW THINGS THAT GIVE ME JOY IN THIS LIFE.
STEALING IS DEFINITELY IN THE TOP FIVE.
FREEZE!
I BELIEVE THAT'S MY LINE.
HANDS IN THE AIR!
YEAH, YEAH. YOU'RE NOT THE FIRST PERSON TO YELL THAT AT ME...
...BUT IF THE ROGUES PULL THIS HEIST OFF, YOU'LL DEFINITELY BE THE LAST.
SIS?

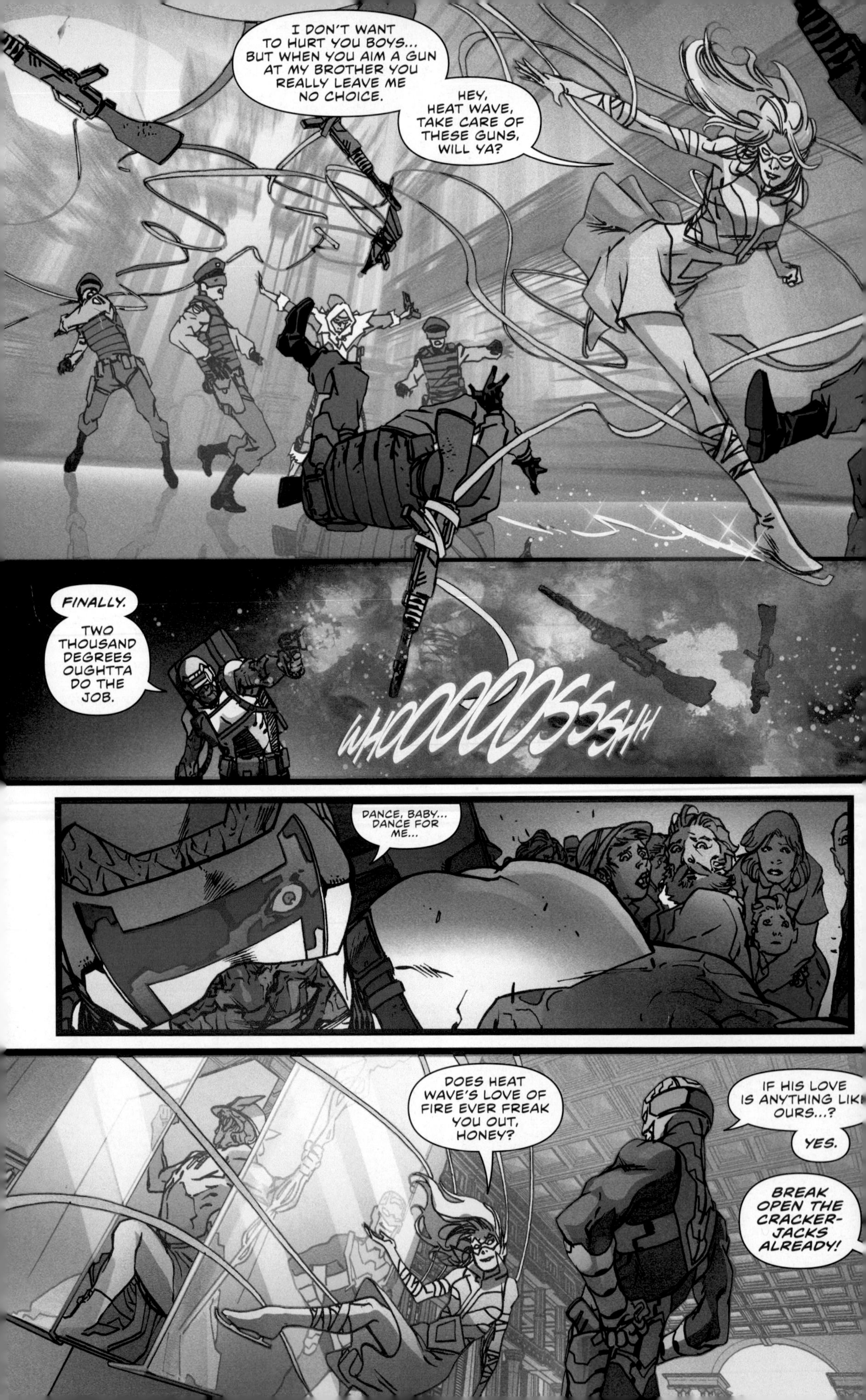
I DON'T WANT TO HURT YOU BOYS... BUT WHEN YOU AIM A GUN AT MY BROTHER YOU REALLY LEAVE ME NO CHOICE.
HEY, HEAT WAVE, TAKE CARE OF THESE GUNS, WILL YA?
FINALLY.
TWO THOUSAND DEGREES OUGHTTA DO THE JOB.
WHOOOOOOSSSHH
DANCE, BABY... DANCE FOR ME...
DOES HEAT WAVE'S LOVE OF FIRE EVER FREAK YOU OUT, HONEY?
IF HIS LOVE IS ANYTHING LIK OURS...?
YES.
BREAK OPEN THE CRACKER-JACKS ALREADY!

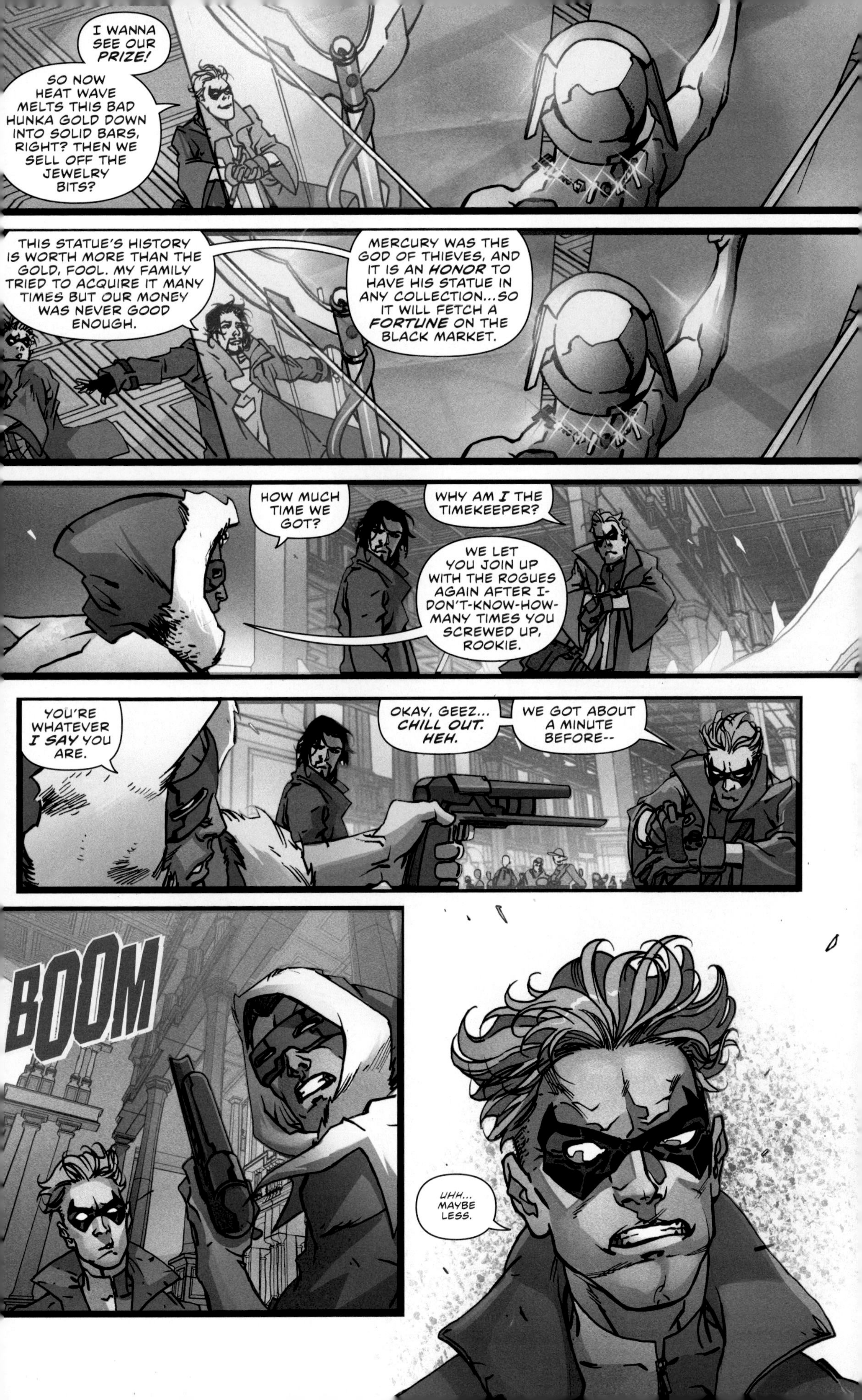
I WANNA SEE OUR PRIZE!
SO NOW HEAT WAVE MELTS THIS BAD HUNKA GOLD DOWN INTO SOLID BARS, RIGHT? THEN WE SELL OFF THE JEWELRY BITS?
THIS STATUE'S HISTORY IS WORTH MORE THAN THE GOLD, FOOL. MY FAMILY TRIED TO ACQUIRE IT MANY TIMES BUT OUR MONEY WAS NEVER GOOD ENOUGH.
MERCURY WAS THE GOD OF THIEVES, AND IT IS AN HONOR TO HAVE HIS STATUE IN ANY COLLECTION...SO IT WILL FETCH A FORTUNE ON THE BLACK MARKET.
HOW MUCH TIME WE GOT?
WHY AM I THE TIMEKEEPER?
WE LET YOU JOIN UP WITH THE ROGUES AGAIN AFTER I-DON'T-KNOW-HOW-MANY TIMES YOU SCREWED UP, ROOKIE.
YOU'RE WHATEVER I SAY YOU ARE.
OKAY, GEEZ... CHILL OUT. HEH.
WE GOT ABOUT A MINUTE BEFORE--
BOOM
UHH... MAYBE LESS.

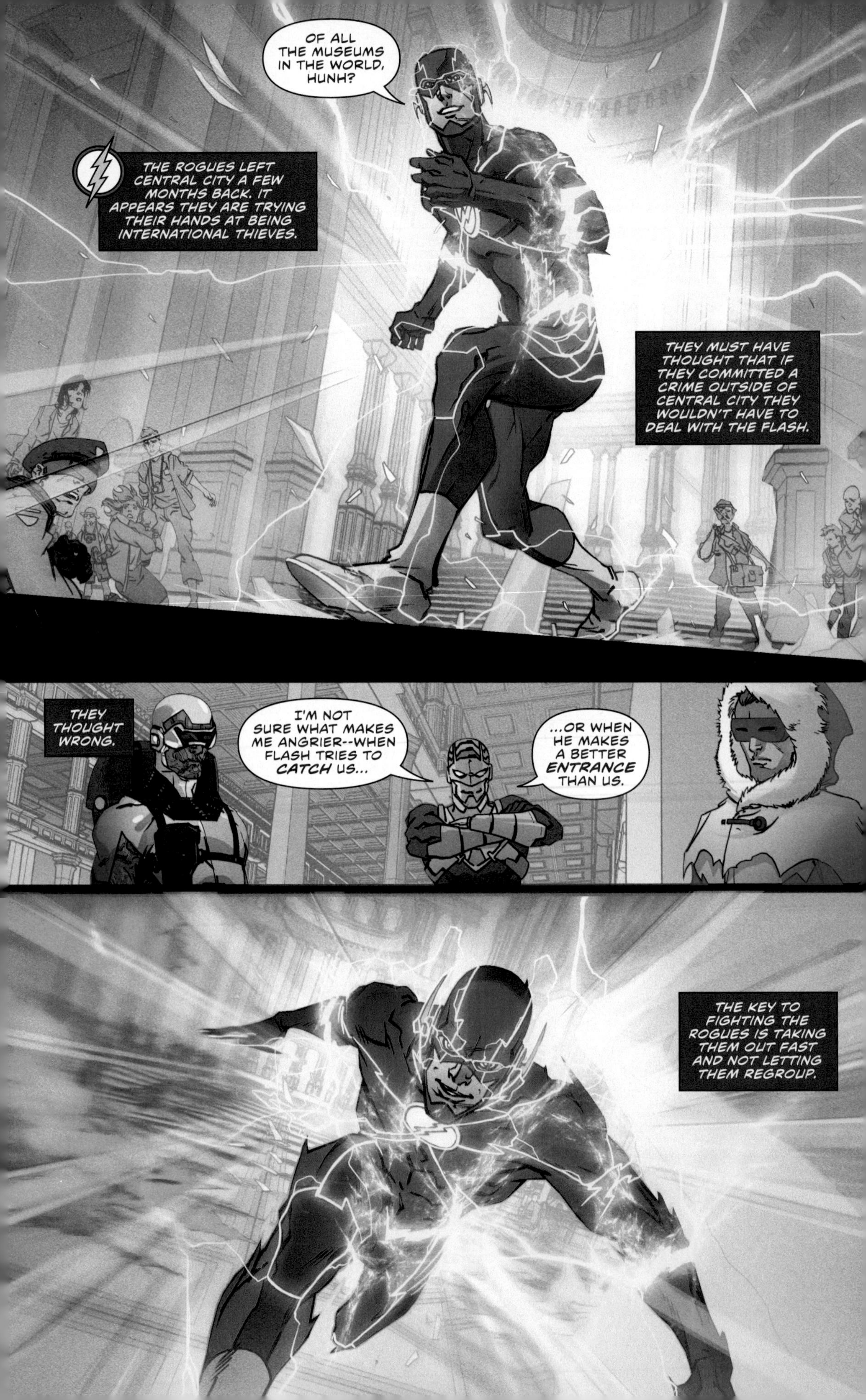
OF ALL THE MUSEUMS IN THE WORLD, HUNH?
THE ROGUES LEFT CENTRAL CITY A FEW MONTHS BACK. IT APPEARS THEY ARE TRYING THEIR HANDS AT BEING INTERNATIONAL THIEVES.
THEY MUST HAVE THOUGHT THAT IF THEY COMMITTED A CRIME OUTSIDE OF CENTRAL CITY THEY WOULDN'T HAVE TO DEAL WITH THE FLASH.
THEY THOUGHT WRONG.
I'M NOT SURE WHAT MAKES ME ANGRIER--WHEN FLASH TRIES TO CATCH US...
...OR WHEN HE MAKES A BETTER ENTRANCE THAN US.
THE KEY TO FIGHTING THE ROGUES IS TAKING THEM OUT FAST AND NOT LETTING THEM REGROUP.

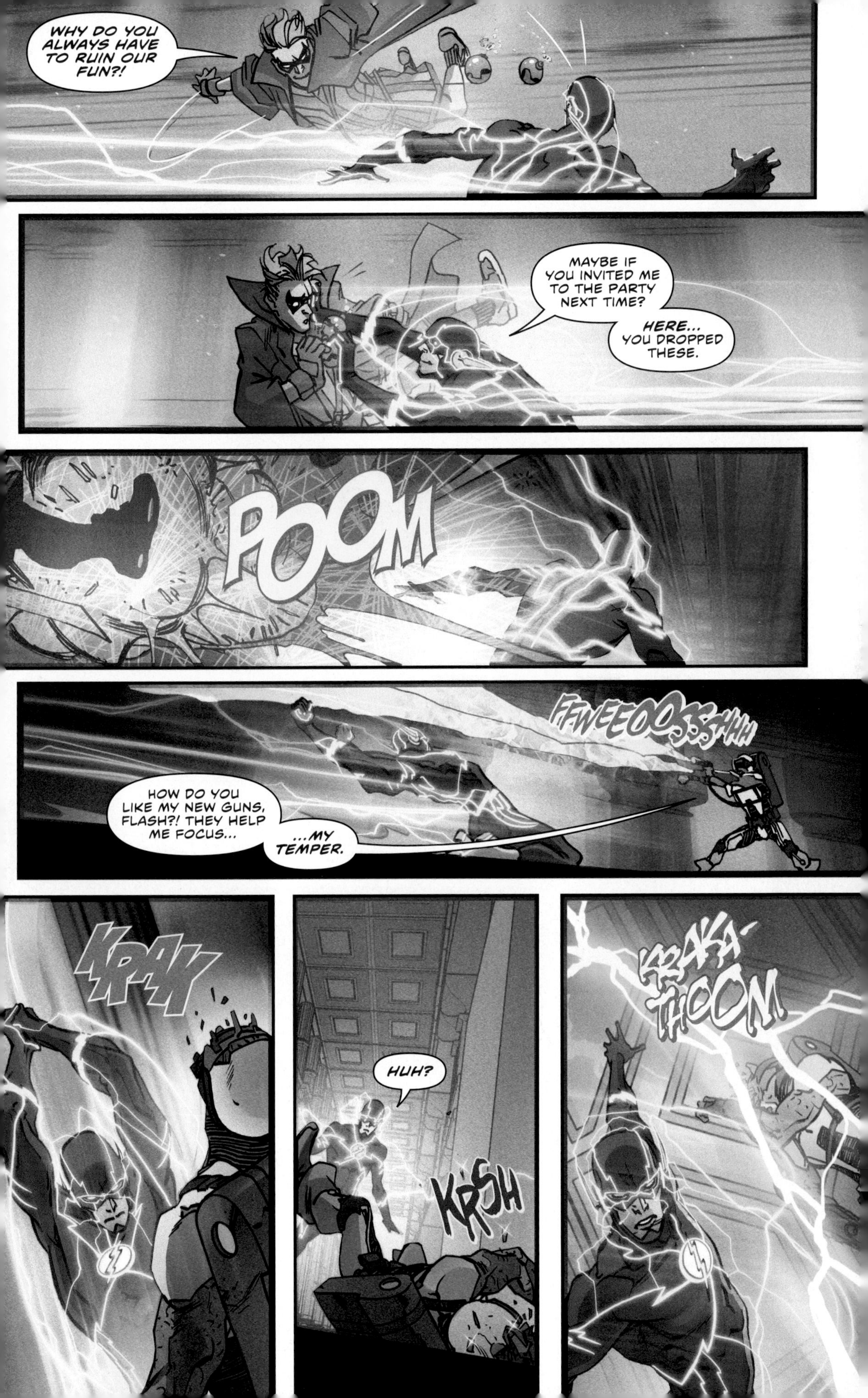
WHY DO YOU ALWAYS HAVE TO RUIN OUR FUN?!
MAYBE IF YOU INVITED ME TO THE PARTY NEXT TIME?
HERE... YOU DROPPED THESE.
POOM
FFWEEOOSSSHHH
HOW DO YOU LIKE MY NEW GUNS, FLASH?! THEY HELP ME FOCUS...
...MY TEMPER.
KRAK
HUH?
KRSH
KRAKA-THOOM

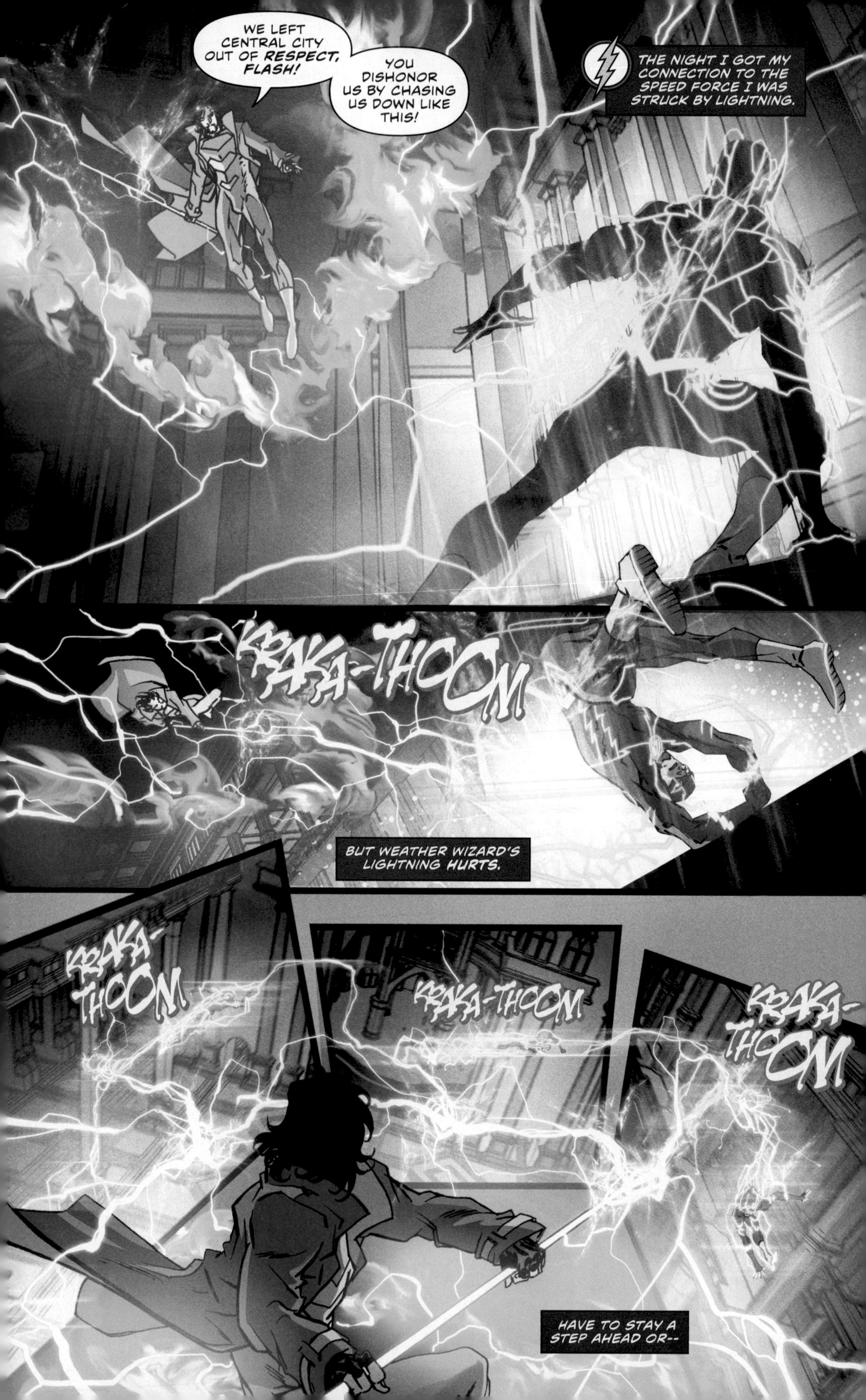
WE LEFT CENTRAL CITY OUT OF RESPECT, FLASH!
YOU DISHONOR US BY CHASING US DOWN LIKE THIS!
THE NIGHT I GOT MY CONNECTION TO THE SPEED FORCE I WAS STRUCK BY LIGHTNING.
KRAKA-THOOM
BUT WEATHER WIZARD'S LIGHTNING HURTS.
KRAKA-THOOM
KRAKA-THOOM
KRAKA-THOOM
HAVE TO STAY A STEP AHEAD OR--

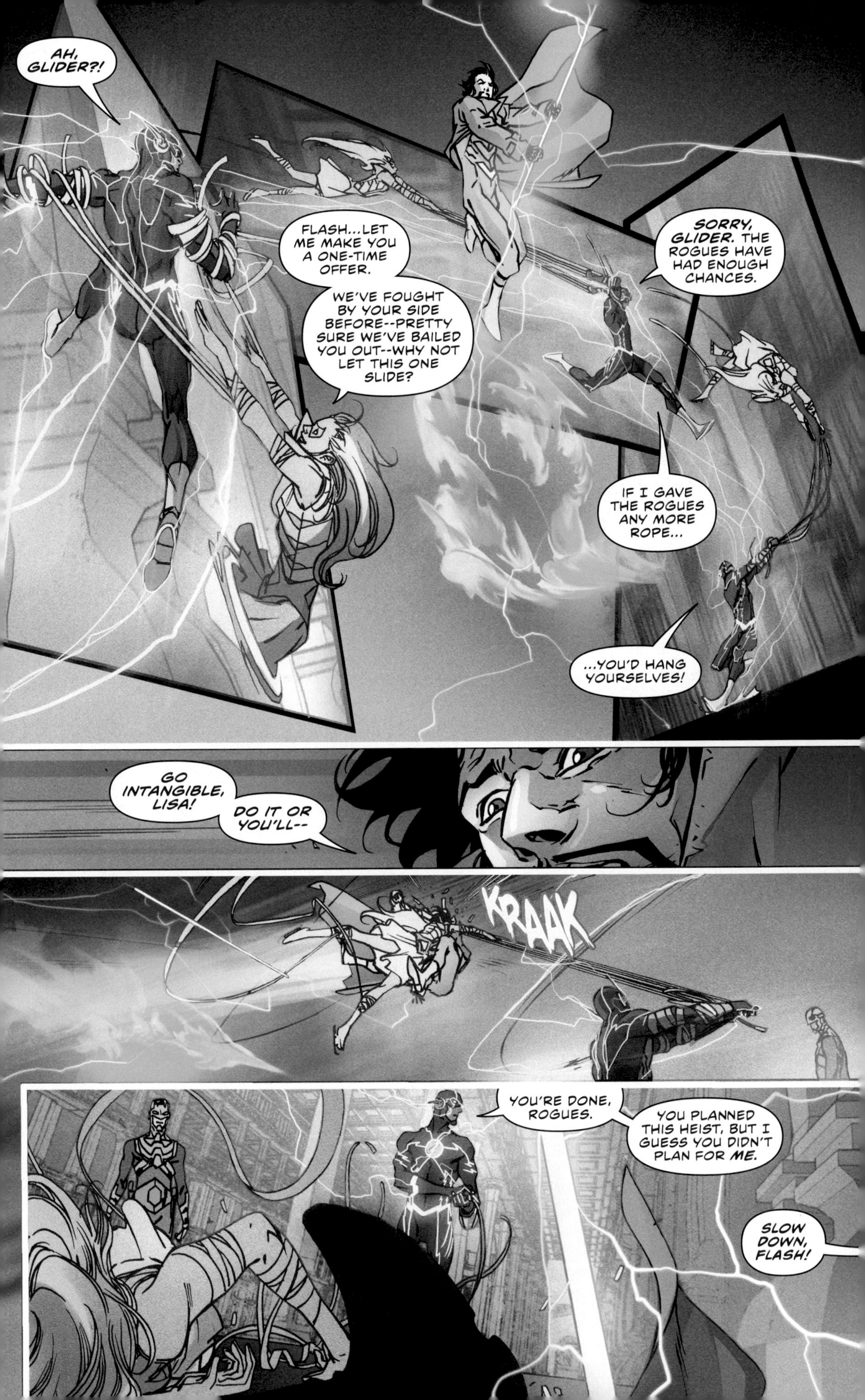
AH, GLIDER?!
FLASH...LET ME MAKE YOU A ONE-TIME OFFER.
WE'VE FOUGHT BY YOUR SIDE BEFORE--PRETTY SURE WE'VE BAILED YOU OUT--WHY NOT LET THIS ONE SLIDE?
SORRY, GLIDER. THE ROGUES HAVE HAD ENOUGH CHANCES.
IF I GAVE THE ROGUES ANY MORE ROPE...
...YOU'D HANG YOURSELVES!
GO INTANGIBLE, LISA!
DO IT OR YOU'LL--
KRAAK
YOU'RE DONE, ROGUES.
YOU PLANNED THIS HEIST, BUT I GUESS YOU DIDN'T PLAN FOR ME.
SLOW DOWN, FLASH!

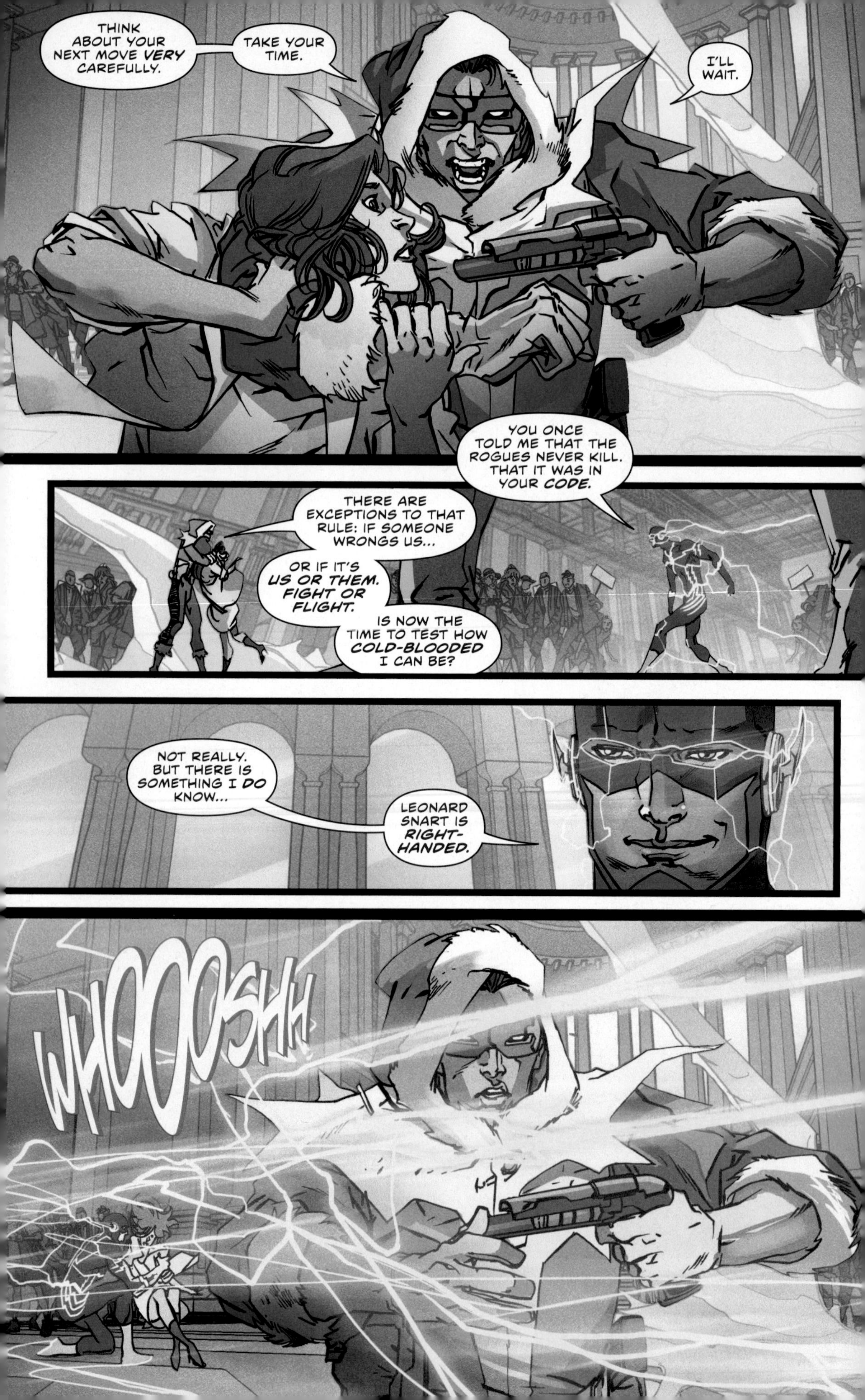
THINK ABOUT YOUR NEXT MOVE VERY CAREFULLY.
TAKE YOUR TIME.
I'LL WAIT.
YOU ONCE TOLD ME THAT THE ROGUES NEVER KILL. THAT IT WAS IN YOUR CODE.
THERE ARE EXCEPTIONS TO THAT RULE: IF SOMEONE WRONGS US...
OR IF IT'S US OR THEM. FIGHT OR FLIGHT.
IS NOW THE TIME TO TEST HOW COLD-BLOODED I CAN BE?
NOT REALLY. BUT THERE IS SOMETHING I DO KNOW...
LEONARD SNART IS RIGHT-HANDED.
WHOOOSHH

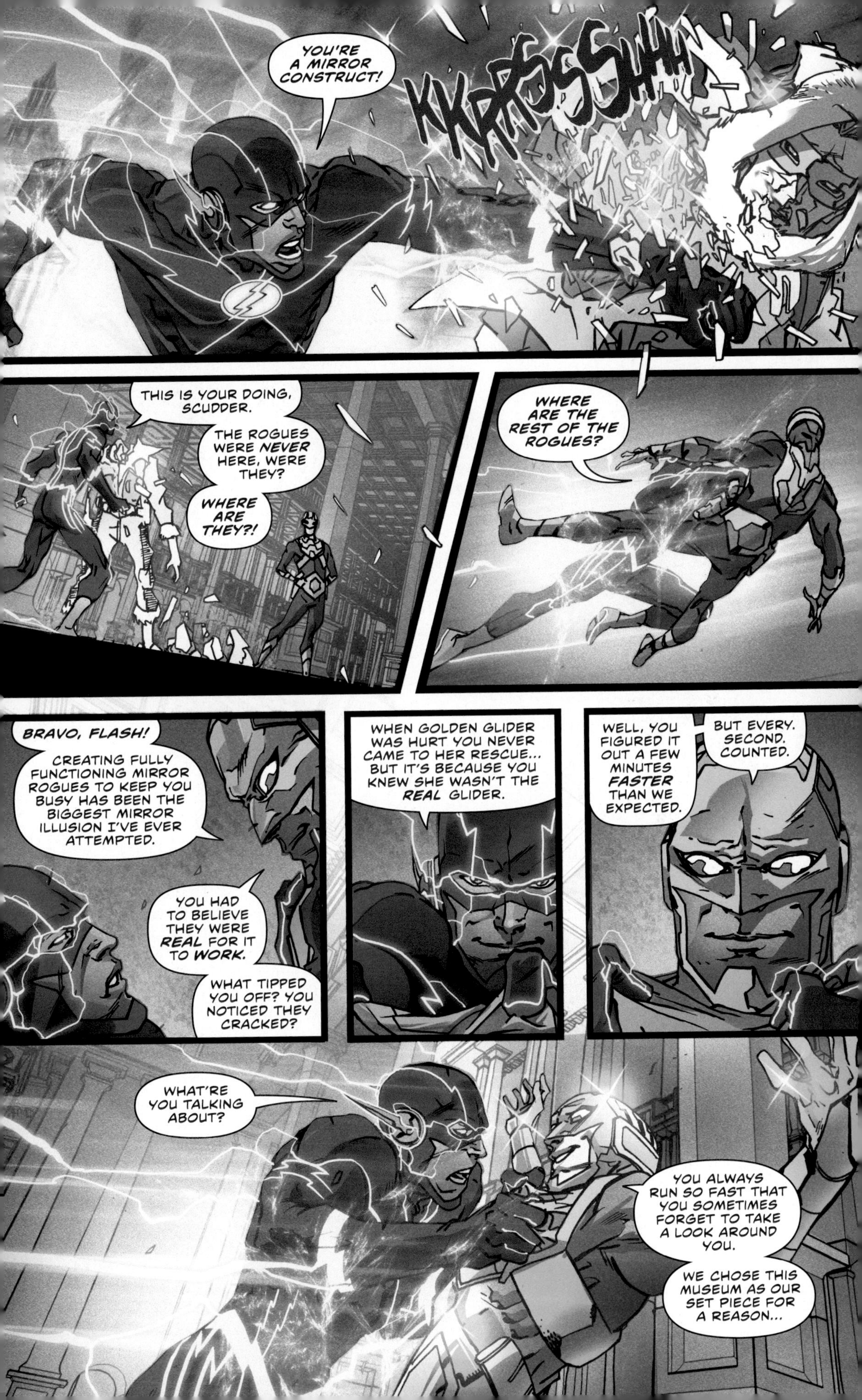

YOU'RE A MIRROR CONSTRUCT!
KKRRSSSHHH
THIS IS YOUR DOING, SCUDDER.
THE ROGUES WERE NEVER HERE, WERE THEY?
WHERE ARE THEY?!
WHERE ARE THE REST OF THE ROGUES?
BRAVO, FLASH!
CREATING FULLY FUNCTIONING MIRROR ROGUES TO KEEP YOU BUSY HAS BEEN THE BIGGEST MIRROR ILLUSION I'VE EVER ATTEMPTED.
YOU HAD TO BELIEVE THEY WERE REAL FOR IT TO WORK.
WHAT TIPPED YOU OFF? YOU NOTICED THEY CRACKED?
WHEN GOLDEN GLIDER WAS HURT YOU NEVER CAME TO HER RESCUE... BUT IT'S BECAUSE YOU KNEW SHE WASN'T THE REAL GLIDER.
WELL, YOU FIGURED IT OUT A FEW MINUTES FASTER THAN WE EXPECTED.
BUT EVERY. SECOND. COUNTED.
WHAT'RE YOU TALKING ABOUT?
YOU ALWAYS RUN SO FAST THAT YOU SOMETIMES FORGET TO TAKE A LOOK AROUND YOU.
WE CHOSE THIS MUSEUM AS OUR SET PIECE FOR A REASON...

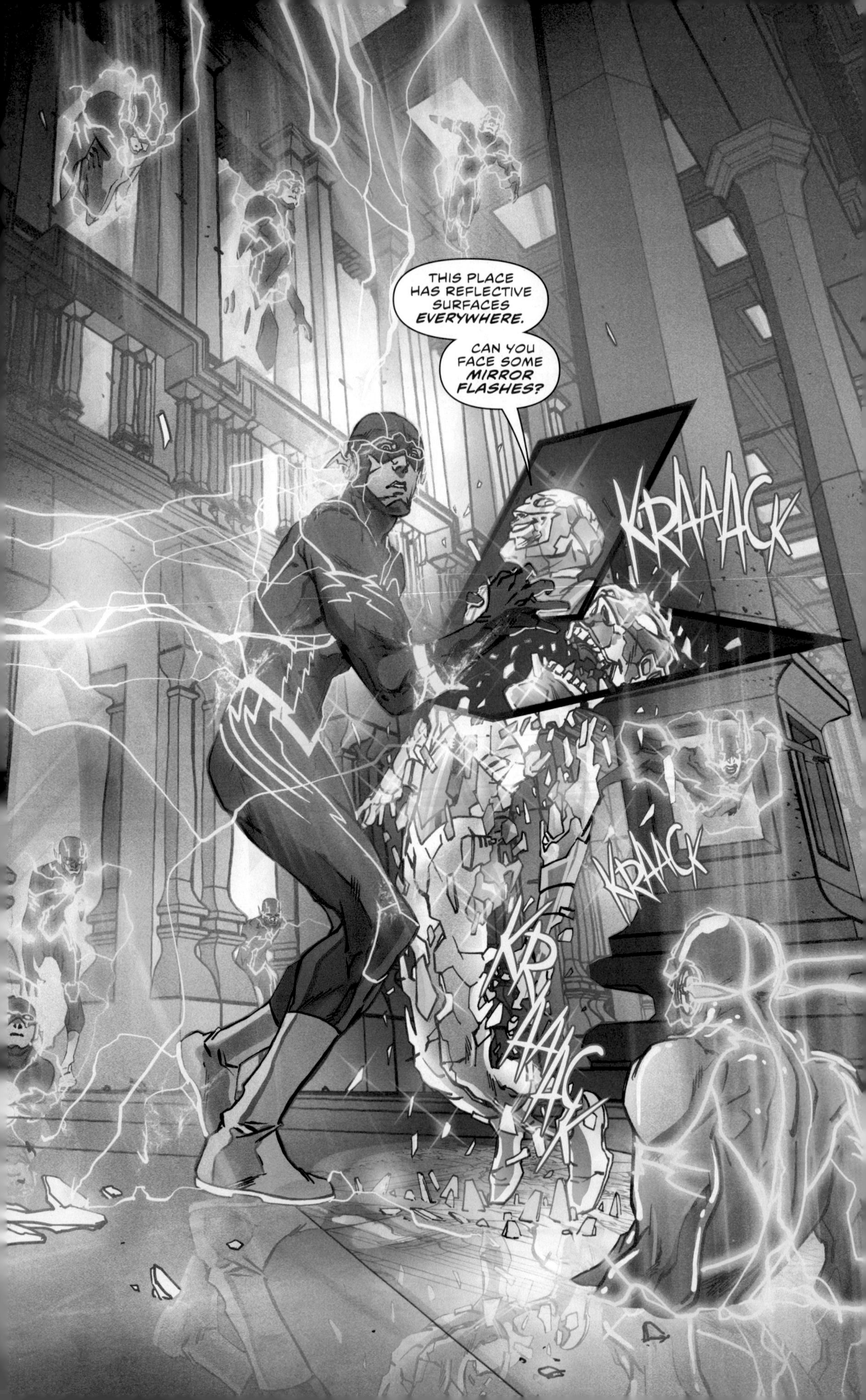

THIS PLACE HAS REFLECTIVE SURFACES *EVERYWHERE.*
CAN YOU FACE SOME *MIRROR FLASHES?*
KRAAACK
KRAACK
KRAAAACK

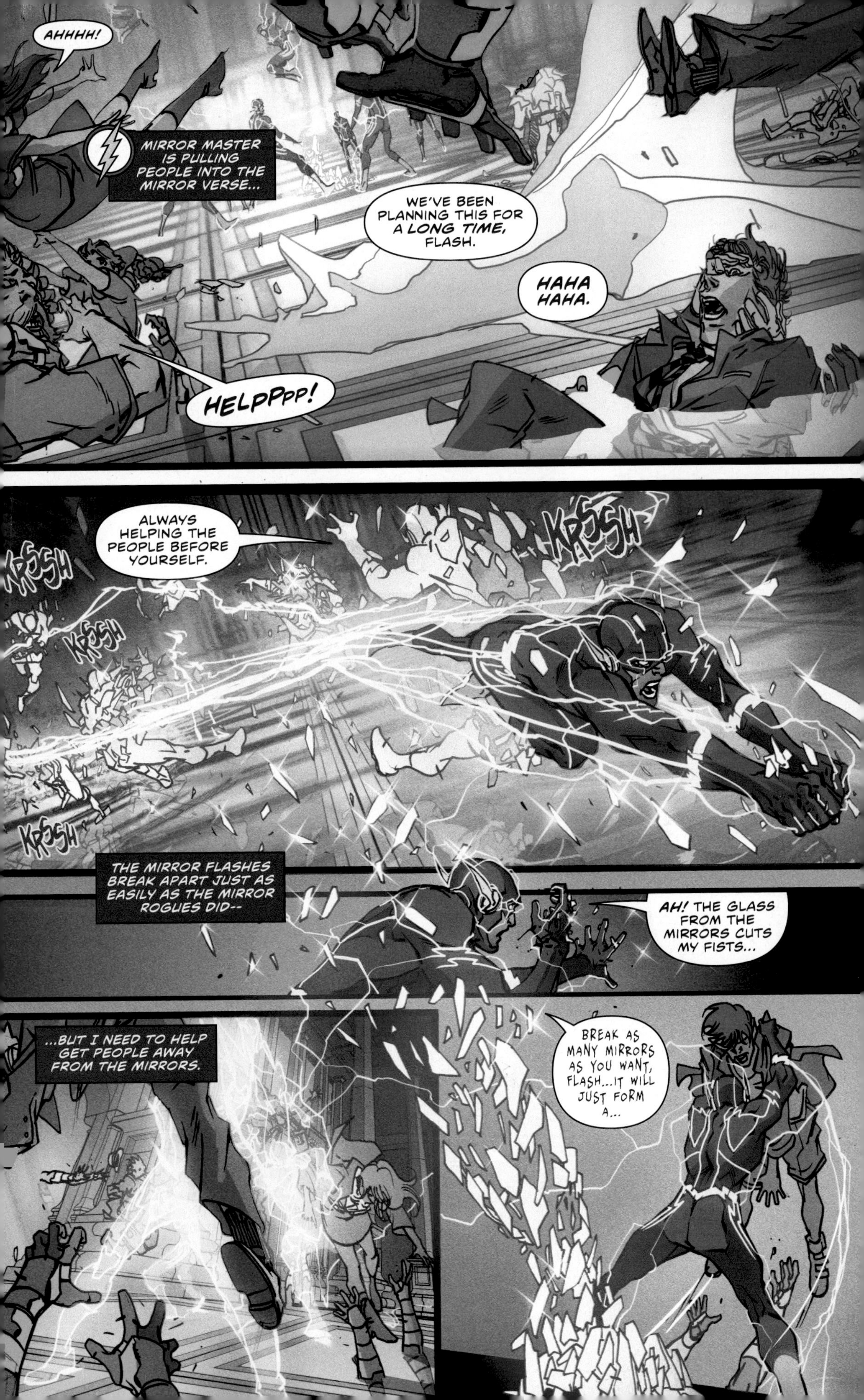
AHHHH!
MIRROR MASTER IS PULLING PEOPLE INTO THE MIRROR VERSE...
WE'VE BEEN PLANNING THIS FOR A LONG TIME, FLASH.
HAHA HAHA.
HELPPPP!
ALWAYS HELPING THE PEOPLE BEFORE YOURSELF.
KRSSH
KRSSH
KRSSH
KRSSH
THE MIRROR FLASHES BREAK APART JUST AS EASILY AS THE MIRROR ROGUES DID--
AH! THE GLASS FROM THE MIRRORS CUTS MY FISTS...
...BUT I NEED TO HELP GET PEOPLE AWAY FROM THE MIRRORS.
BREAK AS MANY MIRRORS AS YOU WANT, FLASH...IT WILL JUST FORM A...

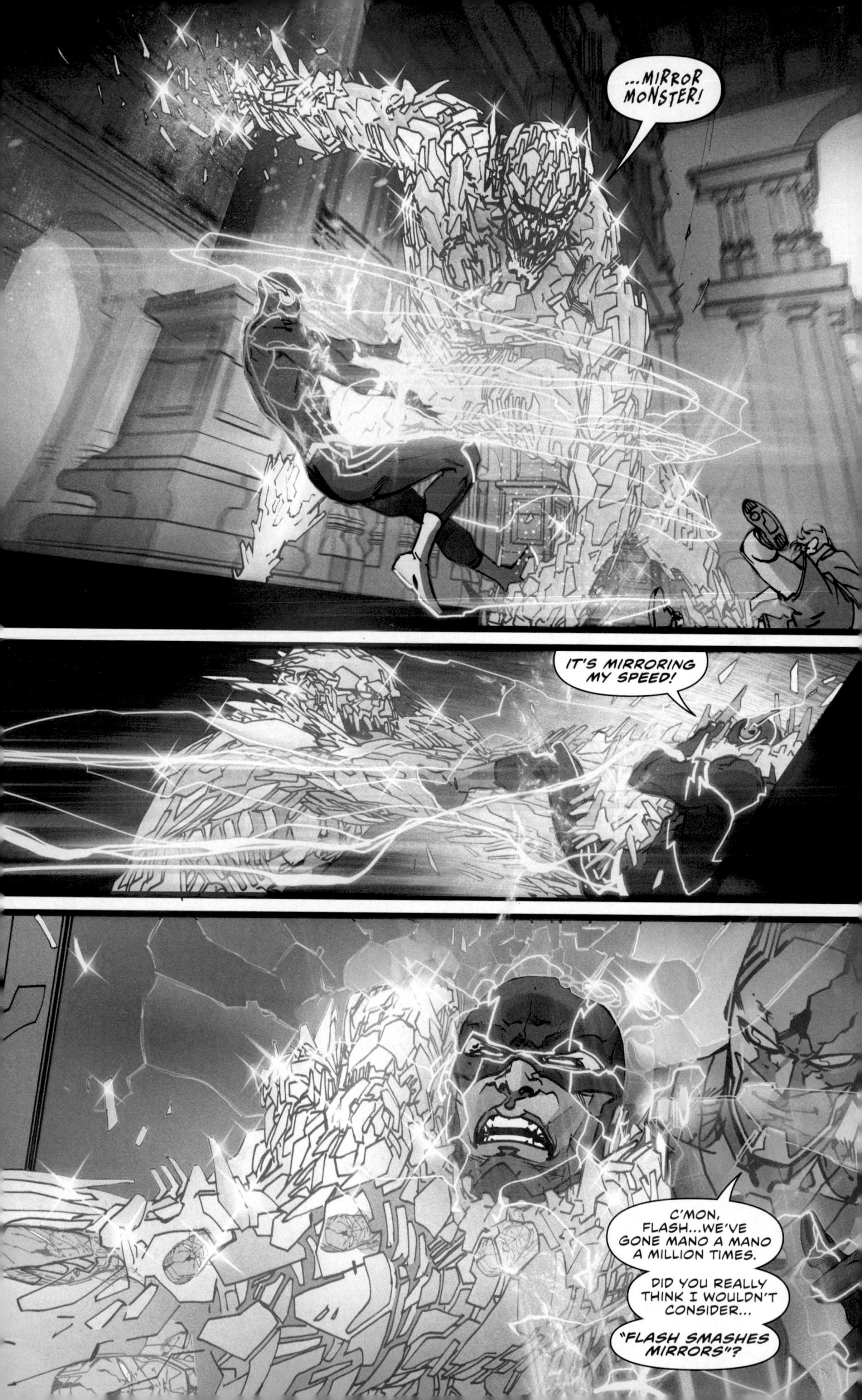
...MIRROR MONSTER!
IT'S MIRRORING MY SPEED!
C'MON, FLASH...WE'VE GONE MANO A MANO A MILLION TIMES.
DID YOU REALLY THINK I WOULDN'T CONSIDER...
"FLASH SMASHES MIRRORS"?

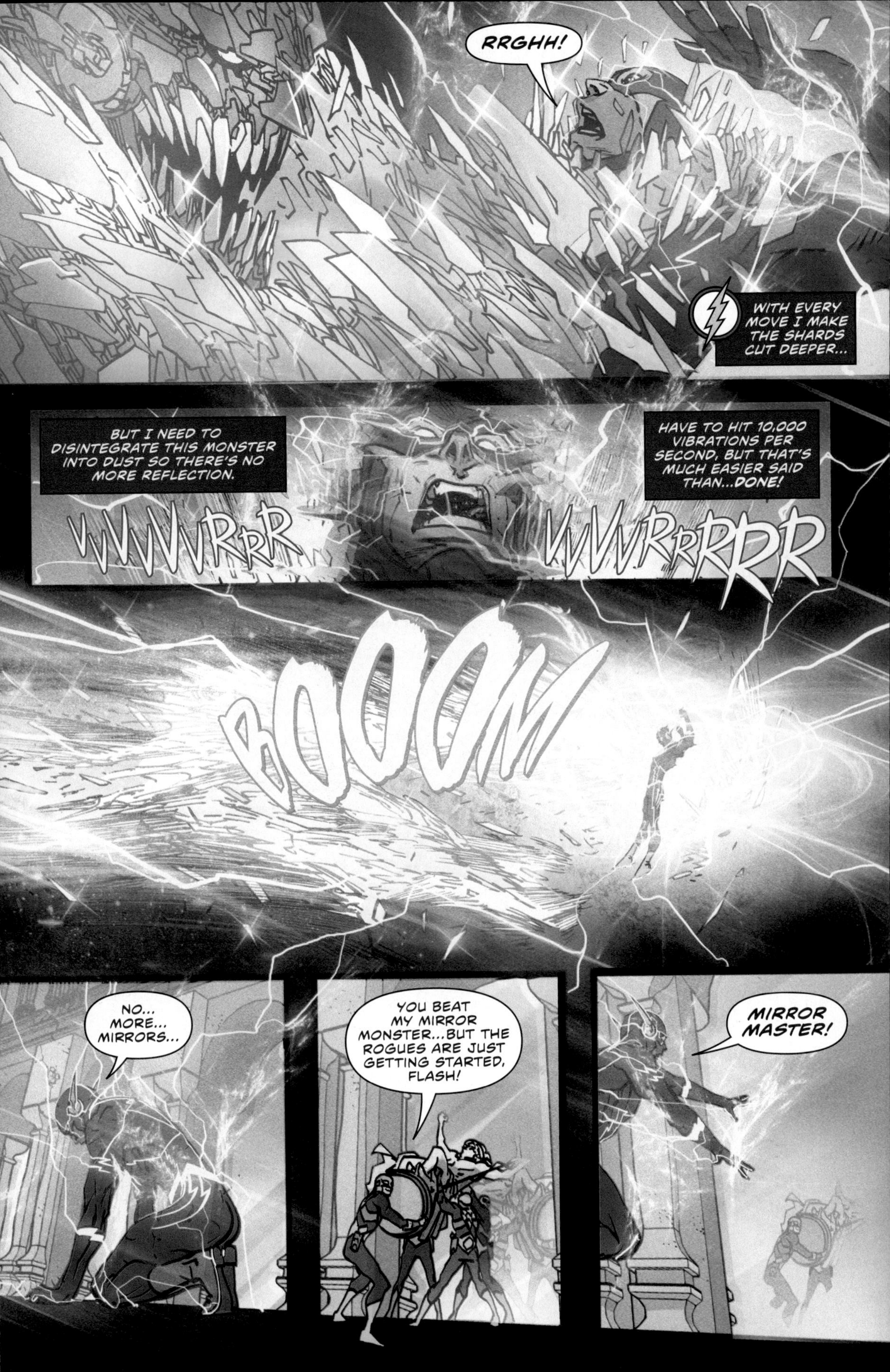
RRGHH!
WITH EVERY MOVE I MAKE THE SHARDS CUT DEEPER...
BUT I NEED TO DISINTEGRATE THIS MONSTER INTO DUST SO THERE'S NO MORE REFLECTION.
HAVE TO HIT 10,000 VIBRATIONS PER SECOND, BUT THAT'S MUCH EASIER SAID THAN...DONE!
VVVVVVRRR
VVVVRRRRR
BOOOM
NO... MORE... MIRRORS...
YOU BEAT MY MIRROR MONSTER...BUT THE ROGUES ARE JUST GETTING STARTED, FLASH!
MIRROR MASTER!

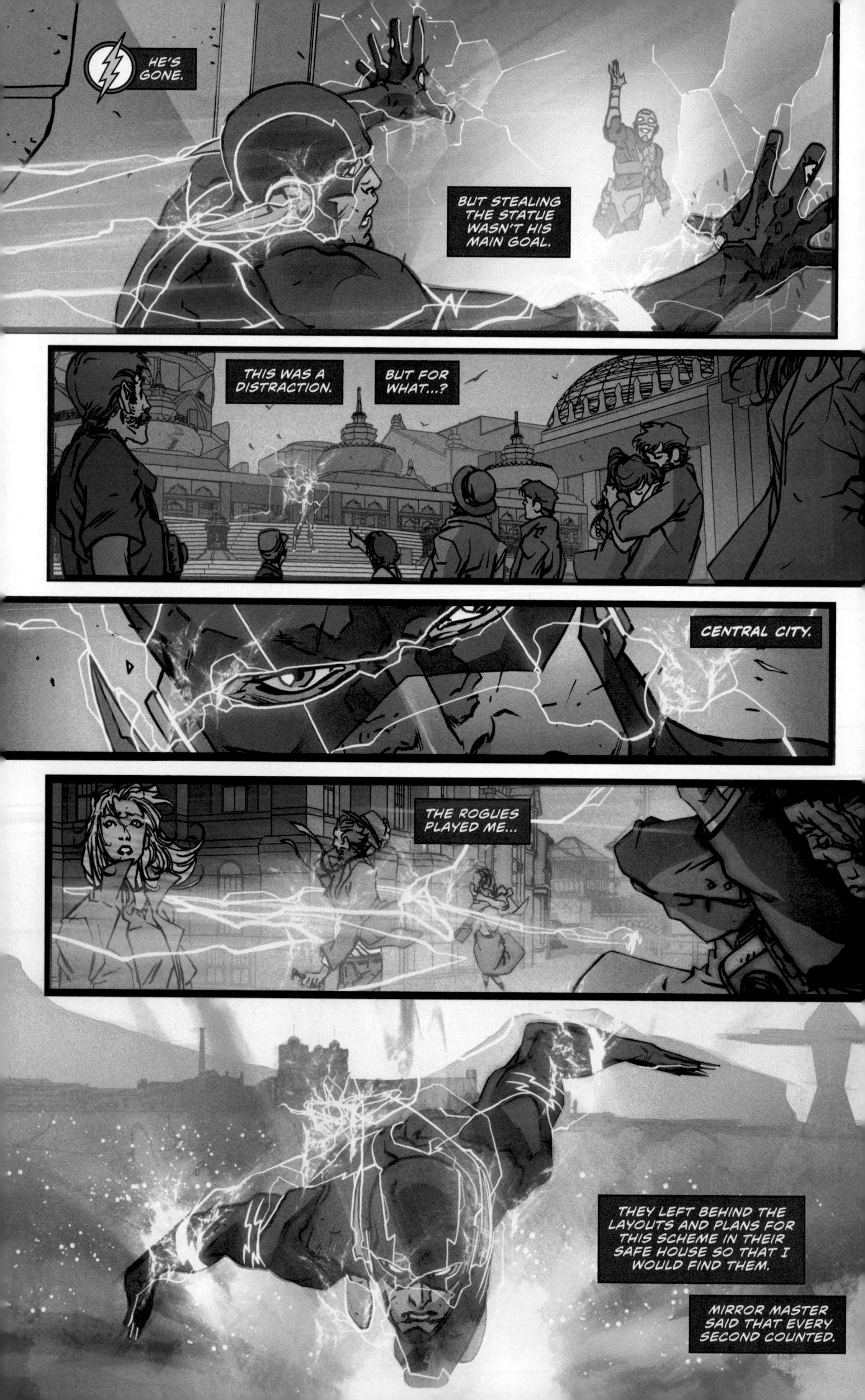
HE'S GONE.
BUT STEALING THE STATUE WASN'T HIS MAIN GOAL.
THIS WAS A DISTRACTION.
BUT FOR WHAT...?
CENTRAL CITY.
THE ROGUES PLAYED ME...
THEY LEFT BEHIND THE LAYOUTS AND PLANS FOR THIS SCHEME IN THEIR SAFE HOUSE SO THAT I WOULD FIND THEM.
MIRROR MASTER SAID THAT EVERY SECOND COUNTED.

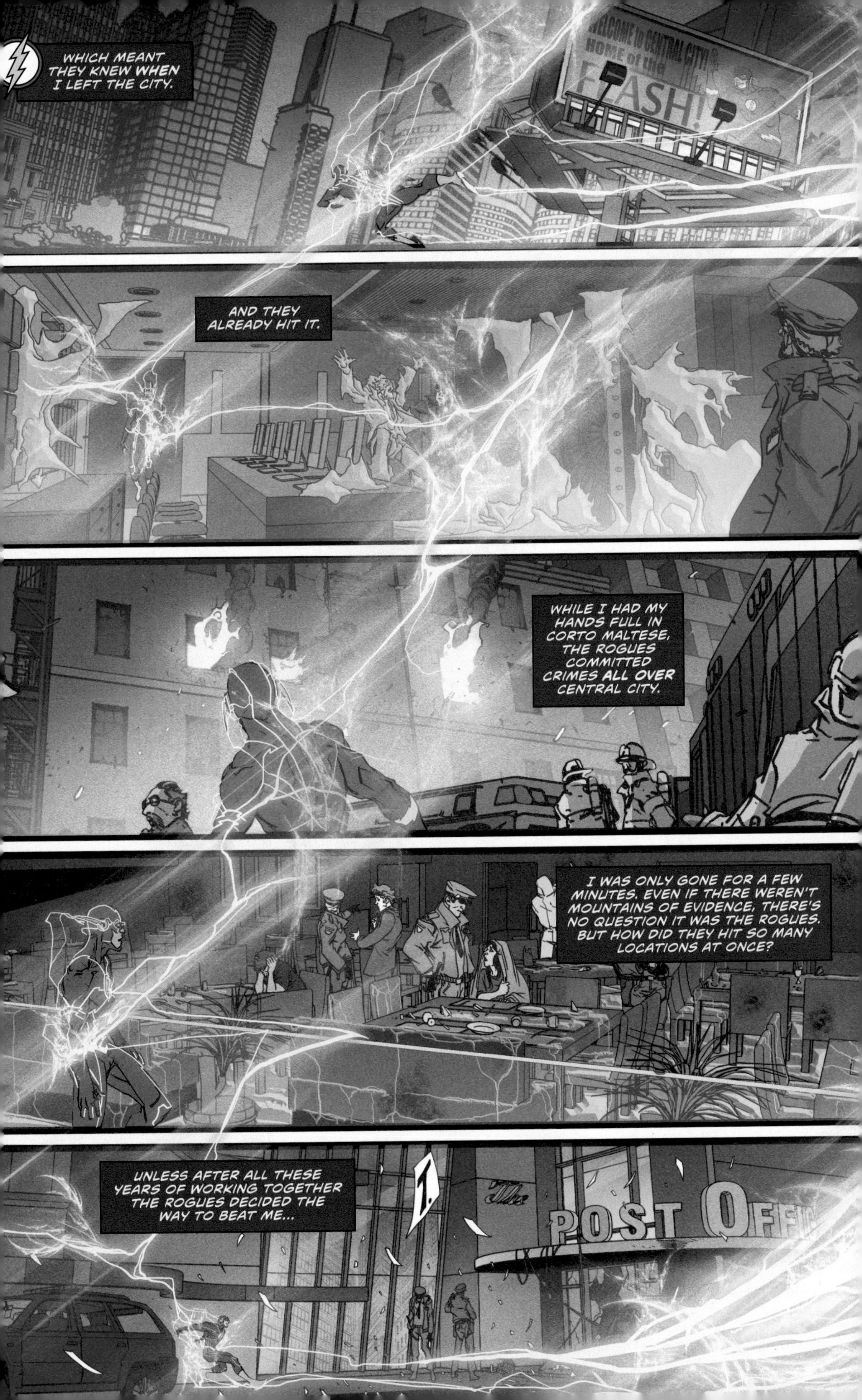
WHICH MEANT THEY KNEW WHEN I LEFT THE CITY.
WELCOME to CENTRAL CITY! HOME of the FLASH!
AND THEY ALREADY HIT IT.
WHILE I HAD MY HANDS FULL IN CORTO MALTESE, THE ROGUES COMMITTED CRIMES ALL OVER CENTRAL CITY.
I WAS ONLY GONE FOR A FEW MINUTES. EVEN IF THERE WEREN'T MOUNTAINS OF EVIDENCE, THERE'S NO QUESTION IT WAS THE ROGUES. BUT HOW DID THEY HIT SO MANY LOCATIONS AT ONCE?
UNLESS AFTER ALL THESE YEARS OF WORKING TOGETHER THE ROGUES DECIDED THE WAY TO BEAT ME...
The POST OFFIC

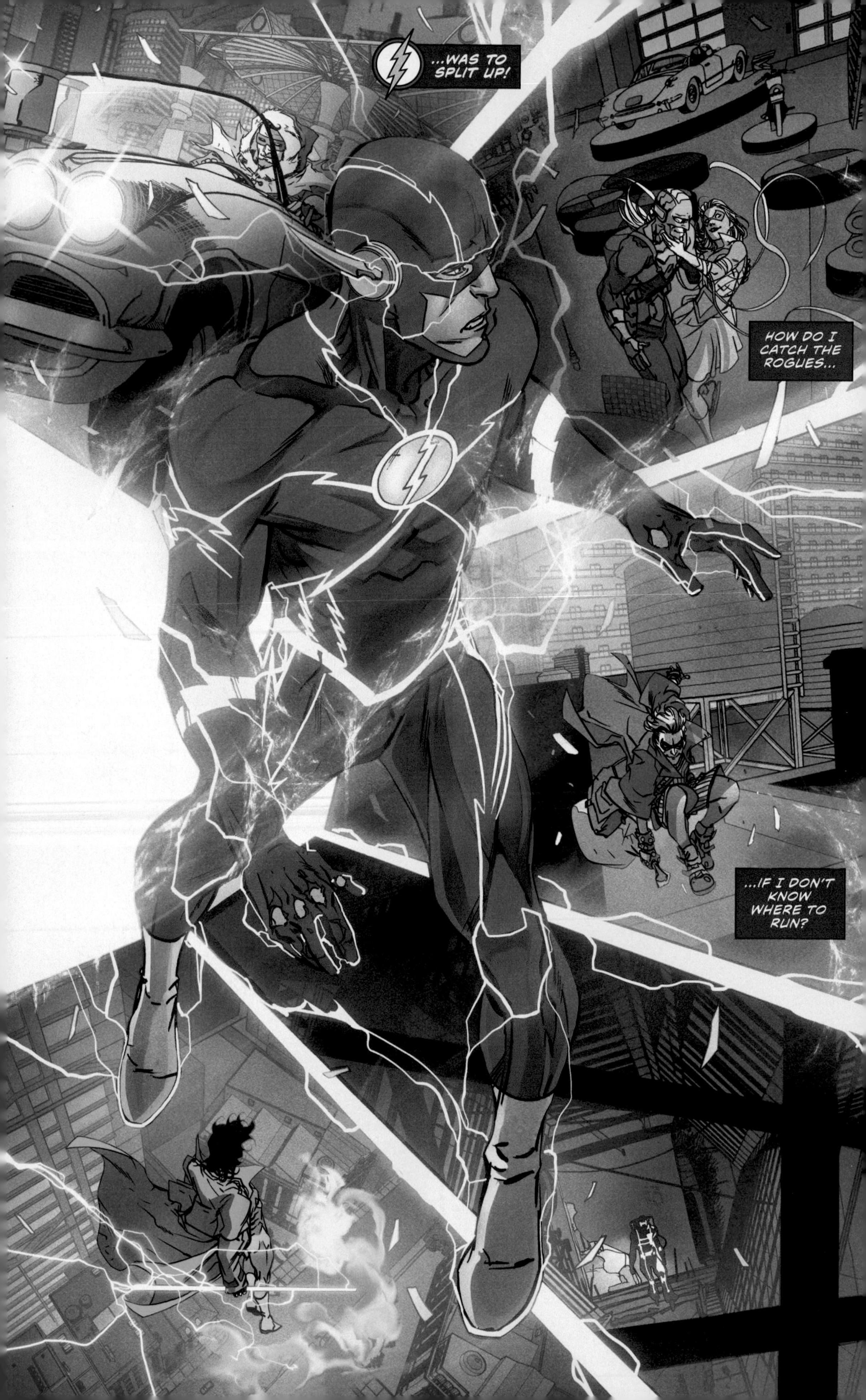
...WAS TO SPLIT UP!
HOW DO I CATCH THE ROGUES...
...IF I DON'T KNOW WHERE TO RUN?

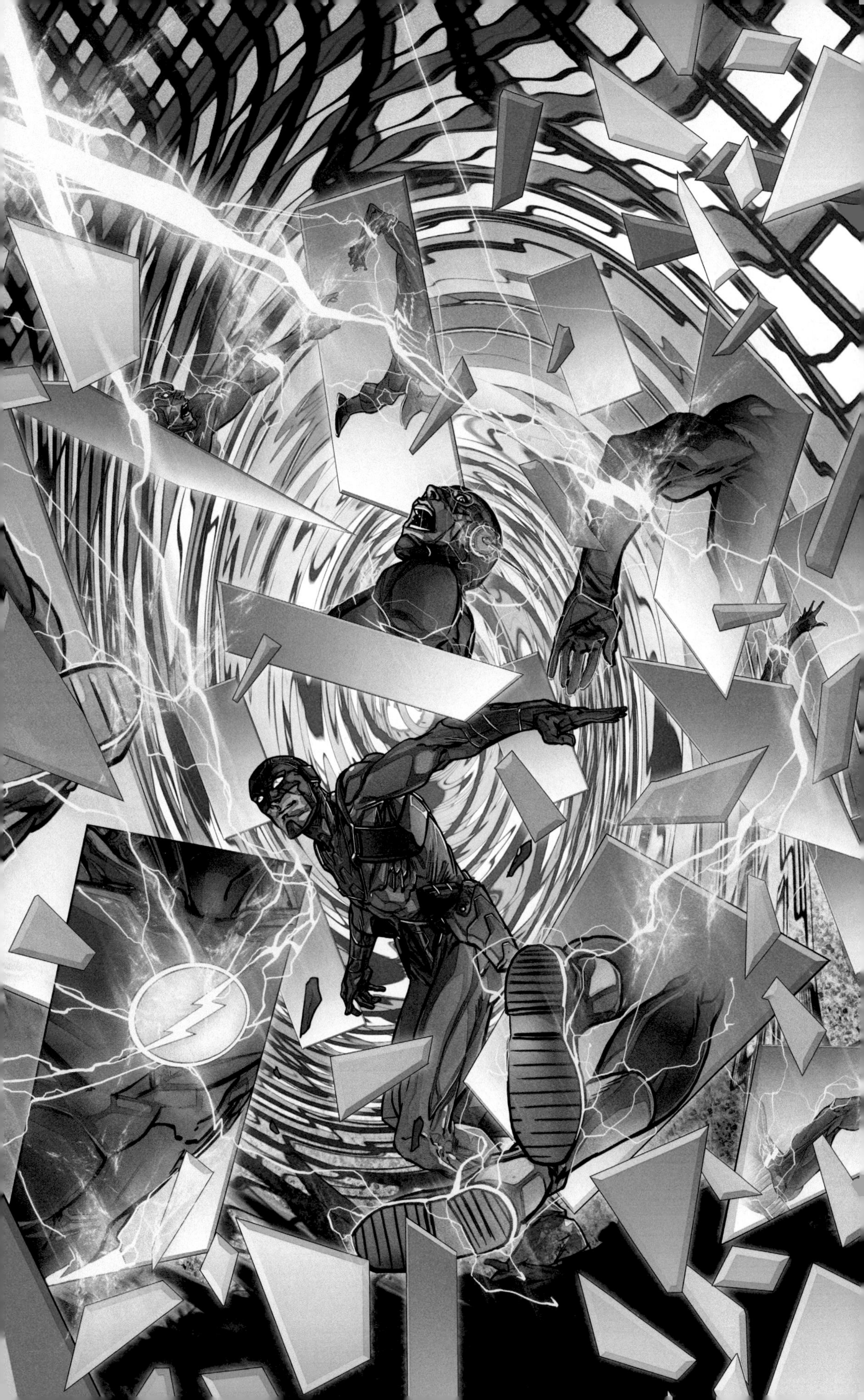

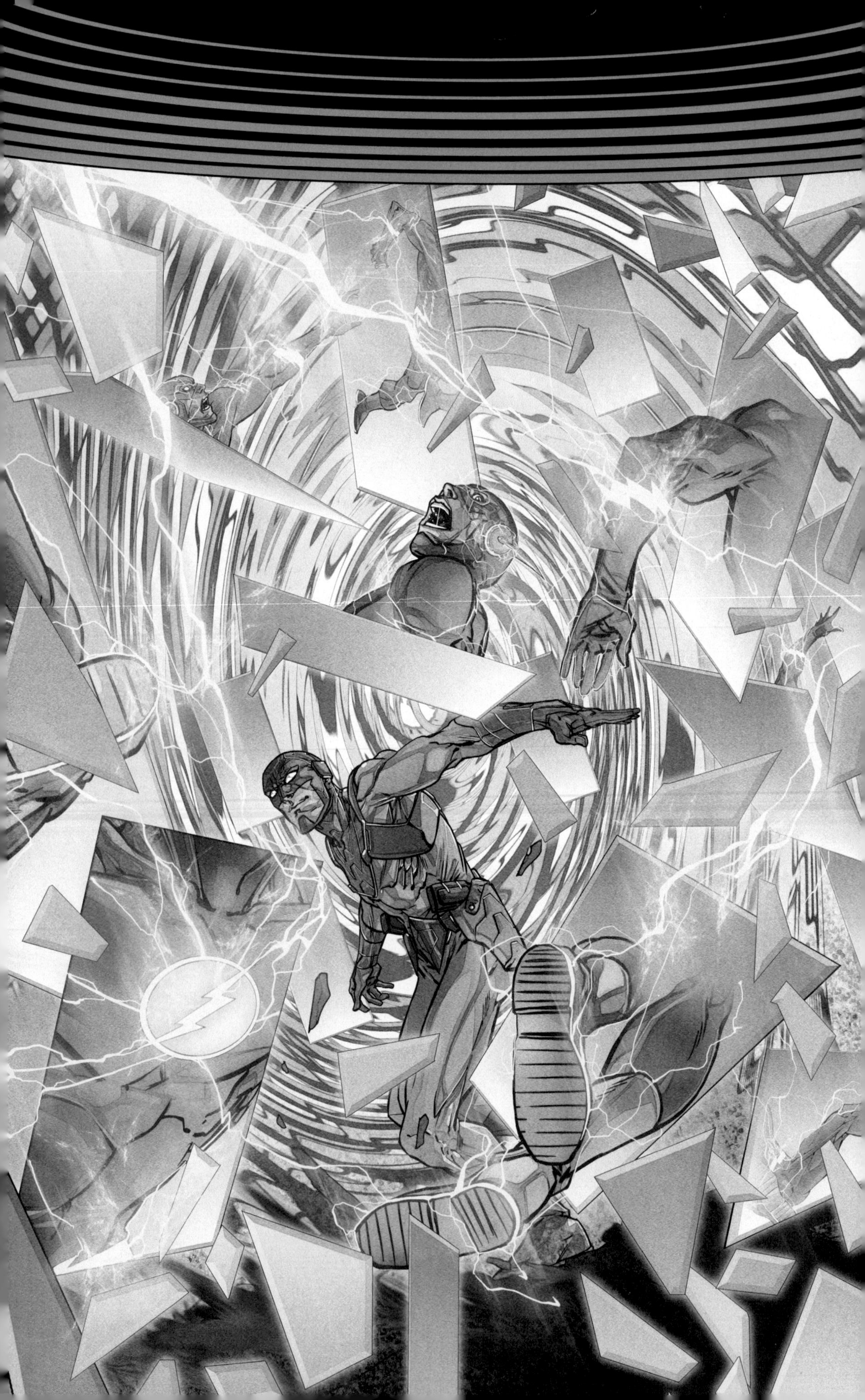

MY HOME CITY BURNS AND IT'S ALL MY FAULT. SORT OF.

THE REAL GUILTY PARTY IS MICK RORY. **HEAT WAVE.** HE'S A PYROMANIAC. HIS FILE AT CCPD SAYS HE BECAME OBSESSED WHEN HIS HOME CAUGHT FIRE AND HIS FAMILY WAS BURNED ALIVE.

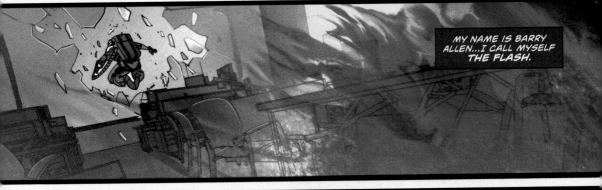

MY NAME IS BARRY ALLEN...I CALL MYSELF THE FLASH.

EVEN THOUGH I'M THE FASTEST MAN ALIVE, I HAVE A BAD HABIT OF ARRIVING A BIT LATE.

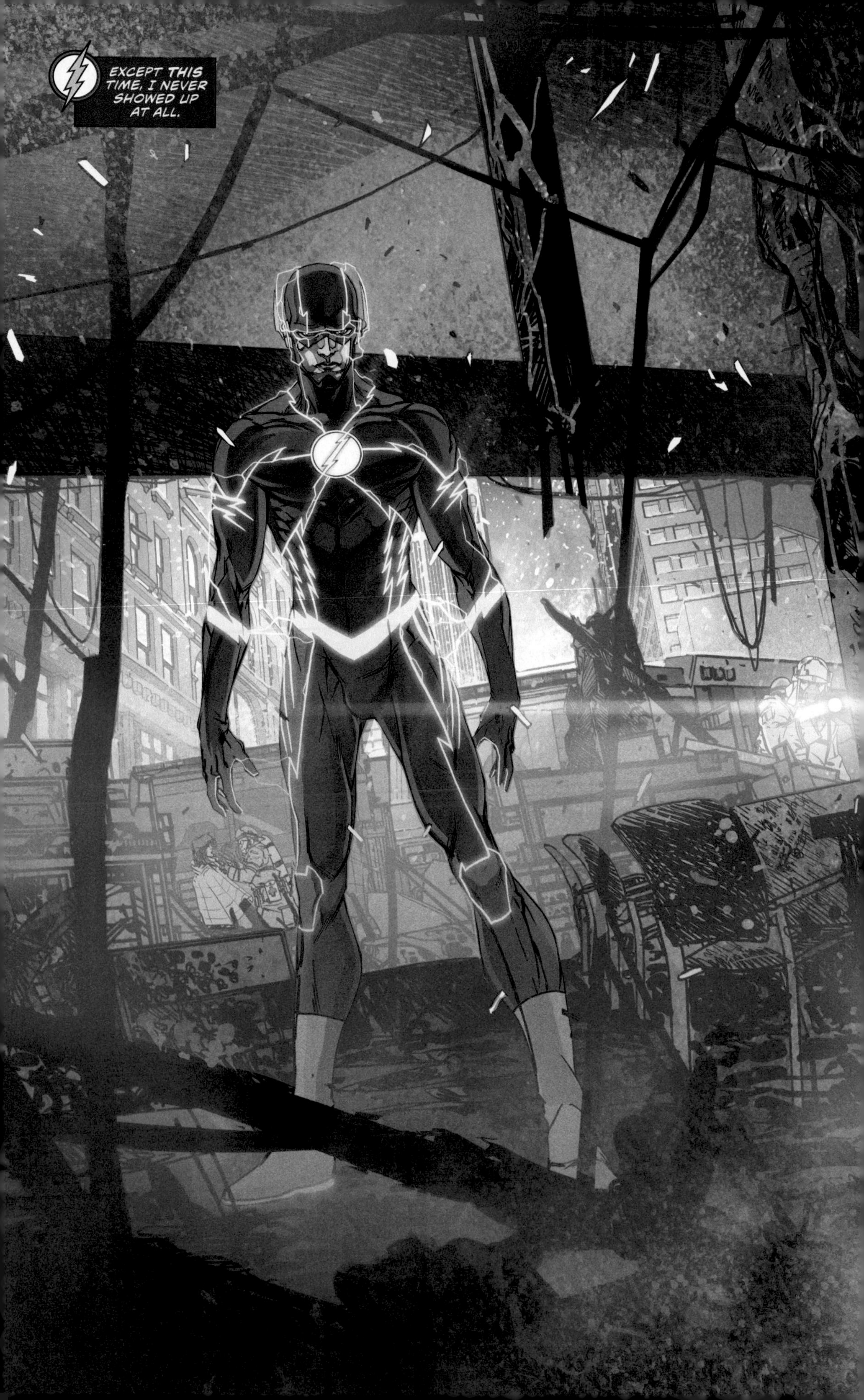
EXCEPT THIS TIME, I NEVER SHOWED UP AT ALL.

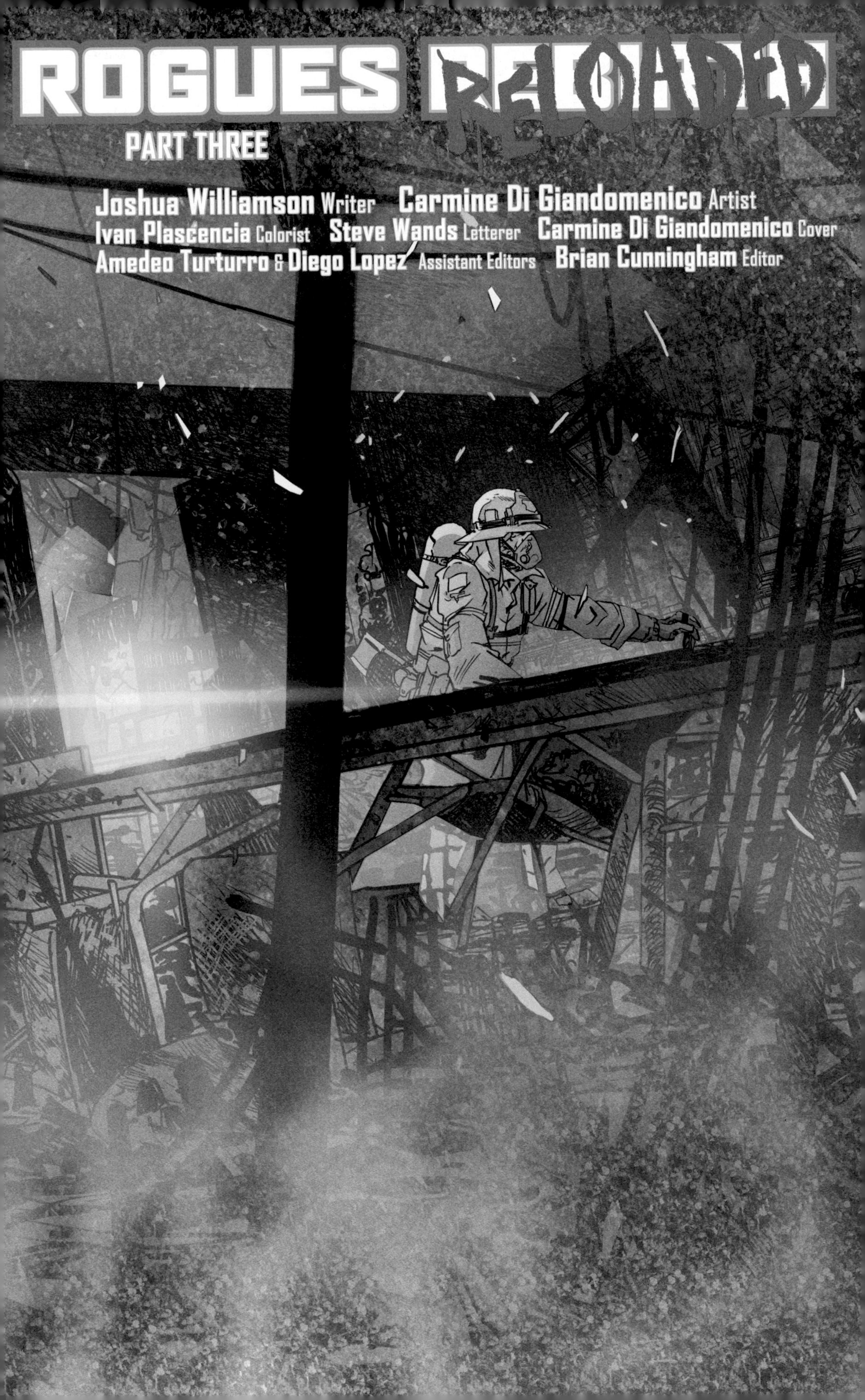
ROGUES RELOADED
PART THREE
Joshua Williamson Writer Carmine Di Giandomenico Artist
Ivan Plascencia Colorist Steve Wands Letterer Carmine Di Giandomenico Cover
Amedeo Turturro & Diego Lopez Assistant Editors Brian Cunningham Editor

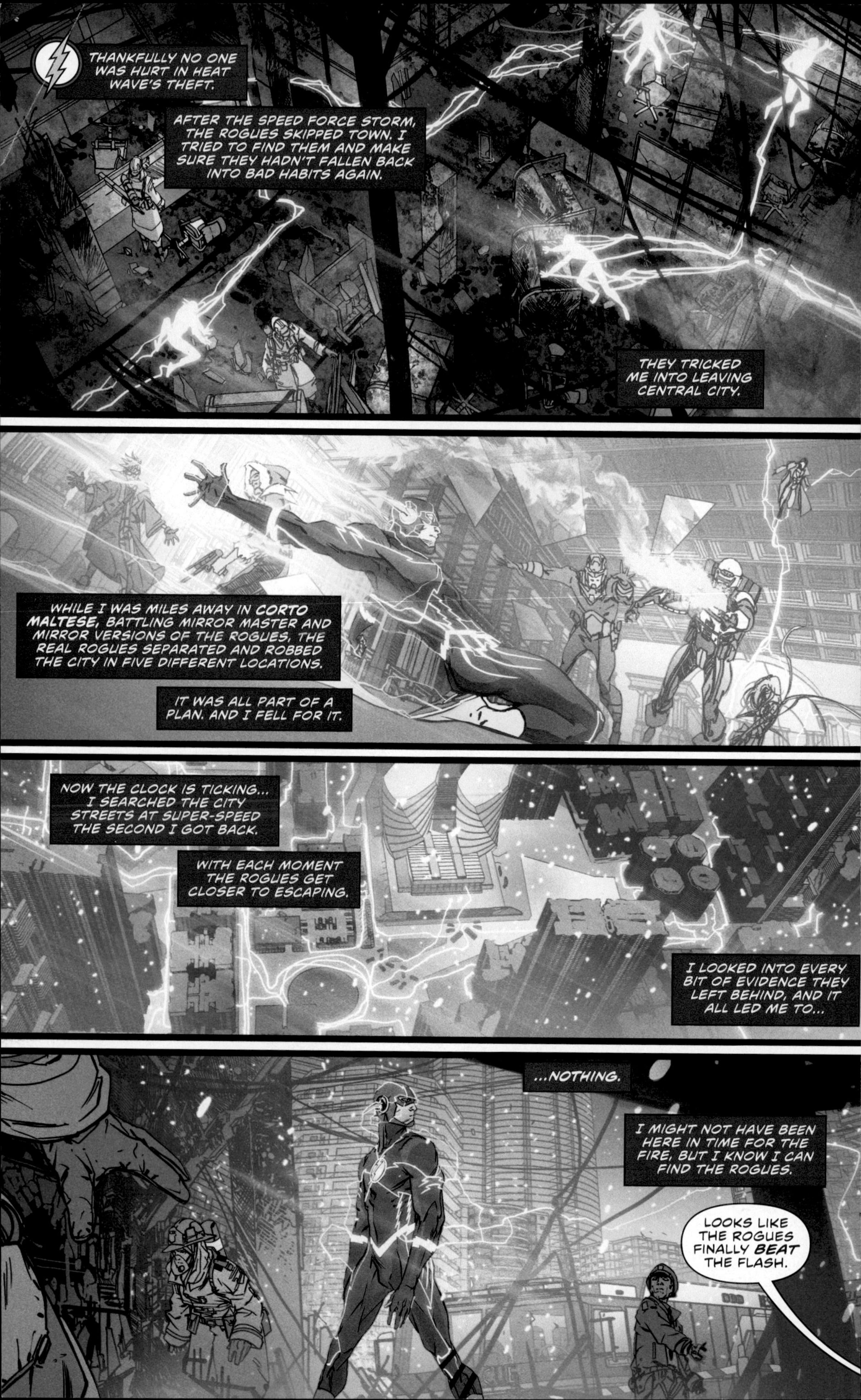
THANKFULLY NO ONE WAS HURT IN HEAT WAVE'S THEFT.
AFTER THE SPEED FORCE STORM, THE ROGUES SKIPPED TOWN. I TRIED TO FIND THEM AND MAKE SURE THEY HADN'T FALLEN BACK INTO BAD HABITS AGAIN.
THEY TRICKED ME INTO LEAVING CENTRAL CITY.
WHILE I WAS MILES AWAY IN CORTO MALTESE, BATTLING MIRROR MASTER AND MIRROR VERSIONS OF THE ROGUES, THE REAL ROGUES SEPARATED AND ROBBED THE CITY IN FIVE DIFFERENT LOCATIONS.
IT WAS ALL PART OF A PLAN. AND I FELL FOR IT.
NOW THE CLOCK IS TICKING... I SEARCHED THE CITY STREETS AT SUPER-SPEED THE SECOND I GOT BACK.
WITH EACH MOMENT THE ROGUES GET CLOSER TO ESCAPING.
I LOOKED INTO EVERY BIT OF EVIDENCE THEY LEFT BEHIND, AND IT ALL LED ME TO...
...NOTHING.
I MIGHT NOT HAVE BEEN HERE IN TIME FOR THE FIRE, BUT I KNOW I CAN FIND THE ROGUES.
LOOKS LIKE THE ROGUES FINALLY BEAT THE FLASH.

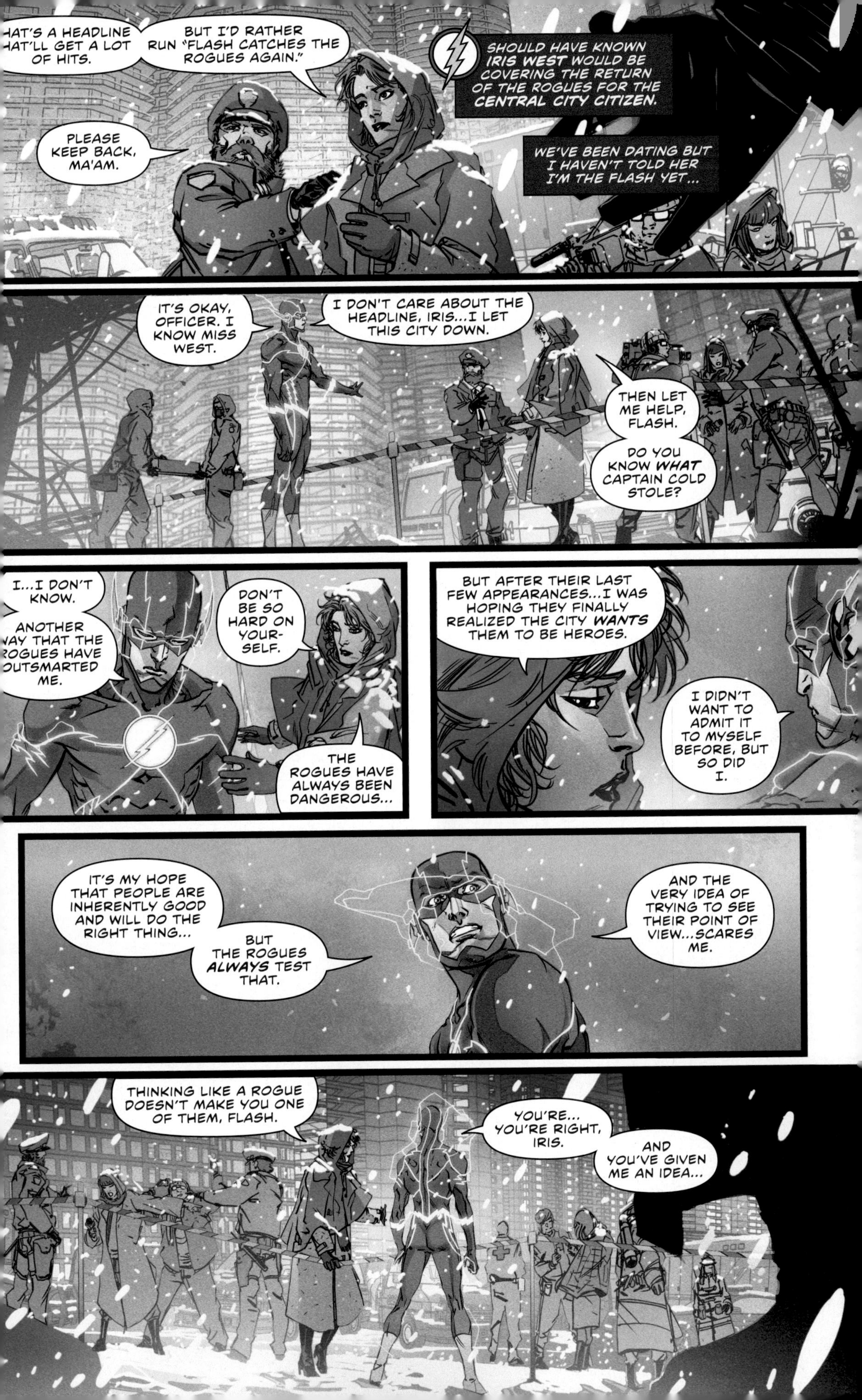

HAT'S A HEADLINE
HAT'LL GET A LOT
OF HITS.
BUT I'D RATHER RUN "FLASH CATCHES THE ROGUES AGAIN."
SHOULD HAVE KNOWN IRIS WEST WOULD BE COVERING THE RETURN OF THE ROGUES FOR THE CENTRAL CITY CITIZEN.
PLEASE KEEP BACK, MA'AM.
WE'VE BEEN DATING BUT I HAVEN'T TOLD HER I'M THE FLASH YET...
IT'S OKAY, OFFICER. I KNOW MISS WEST.
I DON'T CARE ABOUT THE HEADLINE, IRIS...I LET THIS CITY DOWN.
THEN LET ME HELP, FLASH.
DO YOU KNOW WHAT CAPTAIN COLD STOLE?
I...I DON'T KNOW.
ANOTHER
WAY THAT THE
ROGUES HAVE
OUTSMARTED
ME.
DON'T BE SO HARD ON YOUR- SELF.
THE ROGUES HAVE ALWAYS BEEN DANGEROUS...
BUT AFTER THEIR LAST FEW APPEARANCES...I WAS HOPING THEY FINALLY REALIZED THE CITY WANTS THEM TO BE HEROES.
I DIDN'T WANT TO ADMIT IT TO MYSELF BEFORE, BUT SO DID I.
IT'S MY HOPE THAT PEOPLE ARE INHERENTLY GOOD AND WILL DO THE RIGHT THING...
BUT THE ROGUES ALWAYS TEST THAT.
AND THE VERY IDEA OF TRYING TO SEE THEIR POINT OF VIEW...SCARES ME.
THINKING LIKE A ROGUE DOESN'T MAKE YOU ONE OF THEM, FLASH.
YOU'RE... YOU'RE RIGHT, IRIS.
AND YOU'VE GIVEN ME AN IDEA...

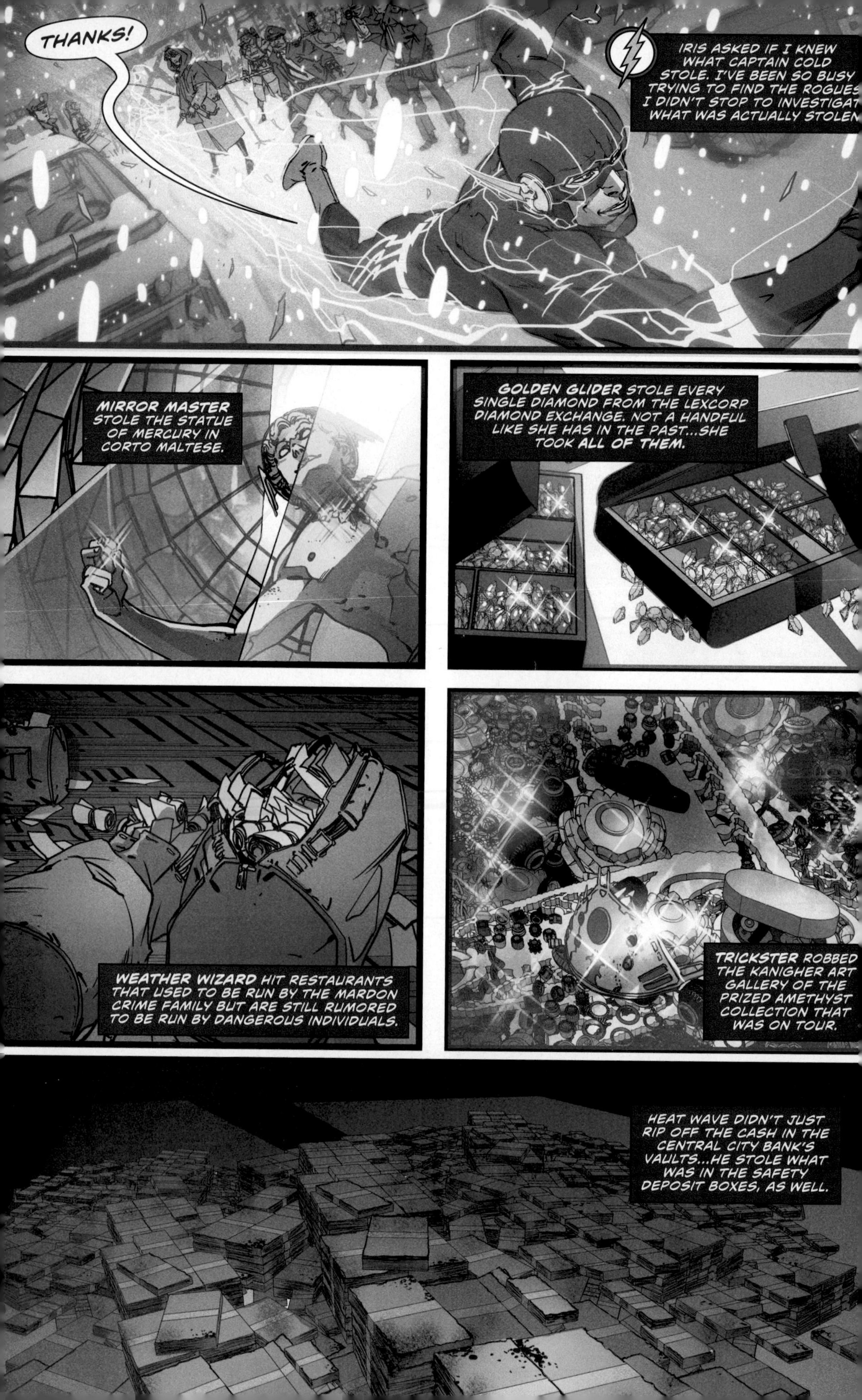
THANKS!
IRIS ASKED IF I KNEW WHAT CAPTAIN COLD STOLE. I'VE BEEN SO BUSY TRYING TO FIND THE ROGUES I DIDN'T STOP TO INVESTIGAT WHAT WAS ACTUALLY STOLEN
MIRROR MASTER STOLE THE STATUE OF MERCURY IN CORTO MALTESE.
GOLDEN GLIDER STOLE EVERY SINGLE DIAMOND FROM THE LEXCORP DIAMOND EXCHANGE. NOT A HANDFUL LIKE SHE HAS IN THE PAST...SHE TOOK ALL OF THEM.
WEATHER WIZARD HIT RESTAURANTS THAT USED TO BE RUN BY THE MARDON CRIME FAMILY BUT ARE STILL RUMORED TO BE RUN BY DANGEROUS INDIVIDUALS.
TRICKSTER ROBBED THE KANIGHER ART GALLERY OF THE PRIZED AMETHYST COLLECTION THAT WAS ON TOUR.
HEAT WAVE DIDN'T JUST RIP OFF THE CASH IN THE CENTRAL CITY BANK'S VAULTS...HE STOLE WHAT WAS IN THE SAFETY DEPOSIT BOXES, AS WELL.

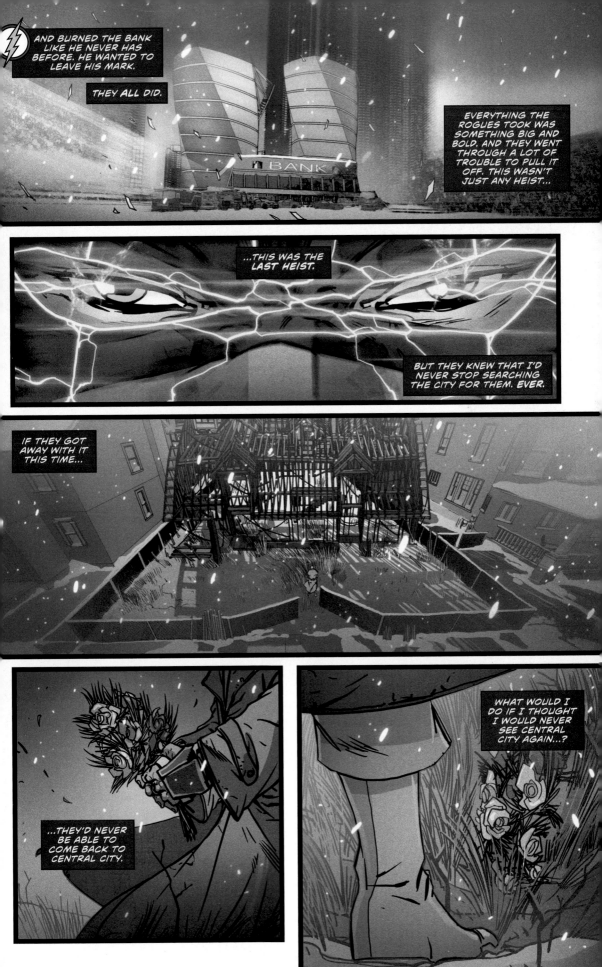

AND BURNED THE BANK LIKE HE NEVER HAS BEFORE. HE WANTED TO LEAVE HIS MARK.

THEY ALL DID.

EVERYTHING THE ROGUES TOOK WAS SOMETHING BIG AND BOLD. AND THEY WENT THROUGH A LOT OF TROUBLE TO PULL IT OFF. THIS WASN'T JUST ANY HEIST...

...THIS WAS THE LAST HEIST.

BUT THEY KNEW THAT I'D NEVER STOP SEARCHING THE CITY FOR THEM. EVER.

IF THEY GOT AWAY WITH IT THIS TIME...

WHAT WOULD I DO IF I THOUGHT I WOULD NEVER SEE CENTRAL CITY AGAIN...?

...THEY'D NEVER BE ABLE TO COME BACK TO CENTRAL CITY.

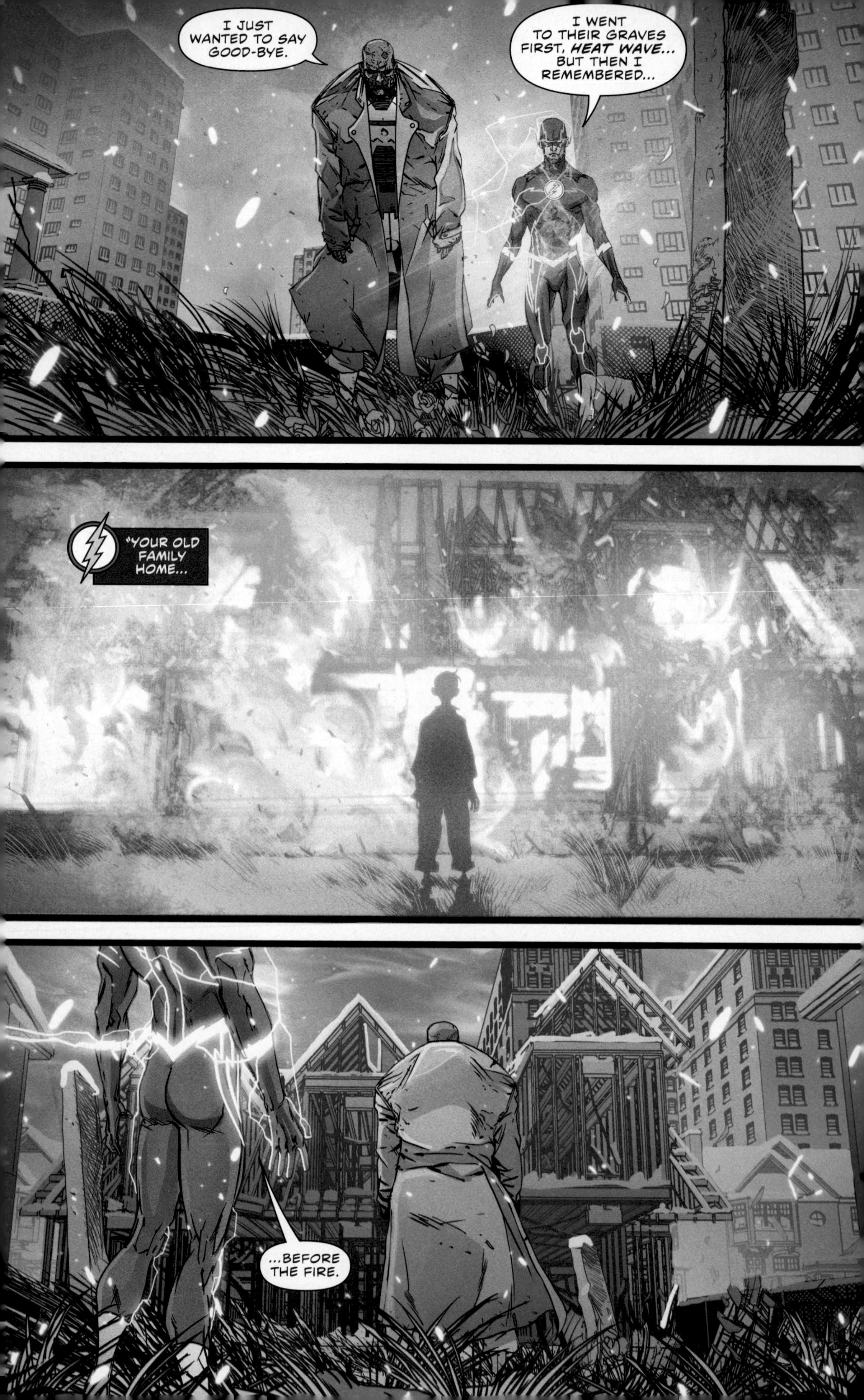
I JUST WANTED TO SAY GOOD-BYE.
I WENT TO THEIR GRAVES FIRST, HEAT WAVE... BUT THEN I REMEMBERED...
"YOUR OLD FAMILY HOME...
...BEFORE THE FIRE.

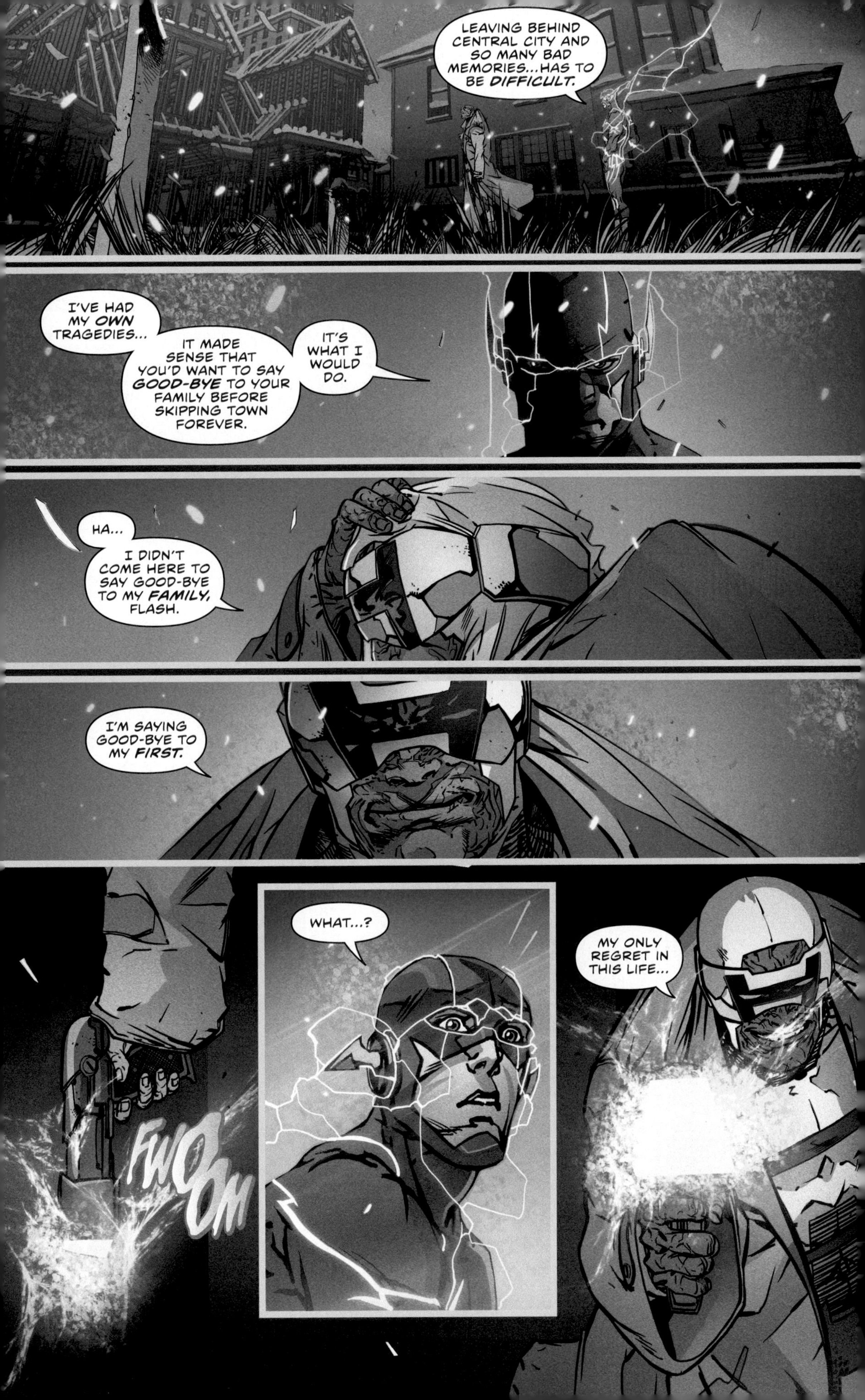
LEAVING BEHIND CENTRAL CITY AND SO MANY BAD MEMORIES...HAS TO BE DIFFICULT.
I'VE HAD MY OWN TRAGEDIES...
IT MADE SENSE THAT YOU'D WANT TO SAY GOOD-BYE TO YOUR FAMILY BEFORE SKIPPING TOWN FOREVER.
IT'S WHAT I WOULD DO.
HA...
I DIDN'T COME HERE TO SAY GOOD-BYE TO MY FAMILY, FLASH.
I'M SAYING GOOD-BYE TO MY FIRST.
FWOOM
WHAT...?
MY ONLY REGRET IN THIS LIFE...

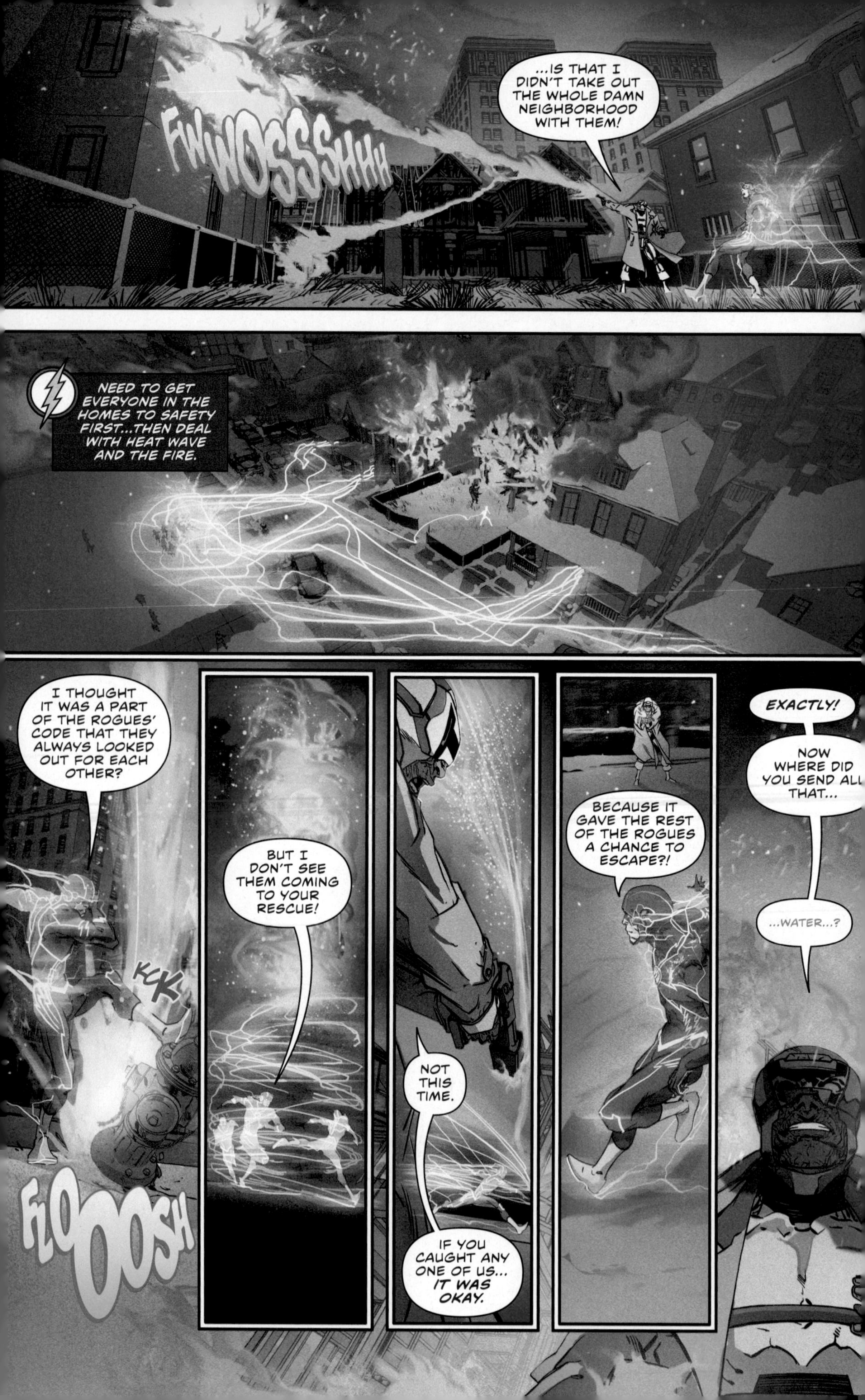
FWWOSSSHHH
...IS THAT I DIDN'T TAKE OUT THE WHOLE DAMN NEIGHBORHOOD WITH THEM!
NEED TO GET EVERYONE IN THE HOMES TO SAFETY FIRST...THEN DEAL WITH HEAT WAVE AND THE FIRE.
I THOUGHT IT WAS A PART OF THE ROGUES' CODE THAT THEY ALWAYS LOOKED OUT FOR EACH OTHER?
KCK
FLOOOSH
BUT I DON'T SEE THEM COMING TO YOUR RESCUE!
NOT THIS TIME.
IF YOU CAUGHT ANY ONE OF US... IT WAS OKAY.
BECAUSE IT GAVE THE REST OF THE ROGUES A CHANCE TO ESCAPE?!
EXACTLY!
NOW WHERE DID YOU SEND ALL THAT...
...WATER...?

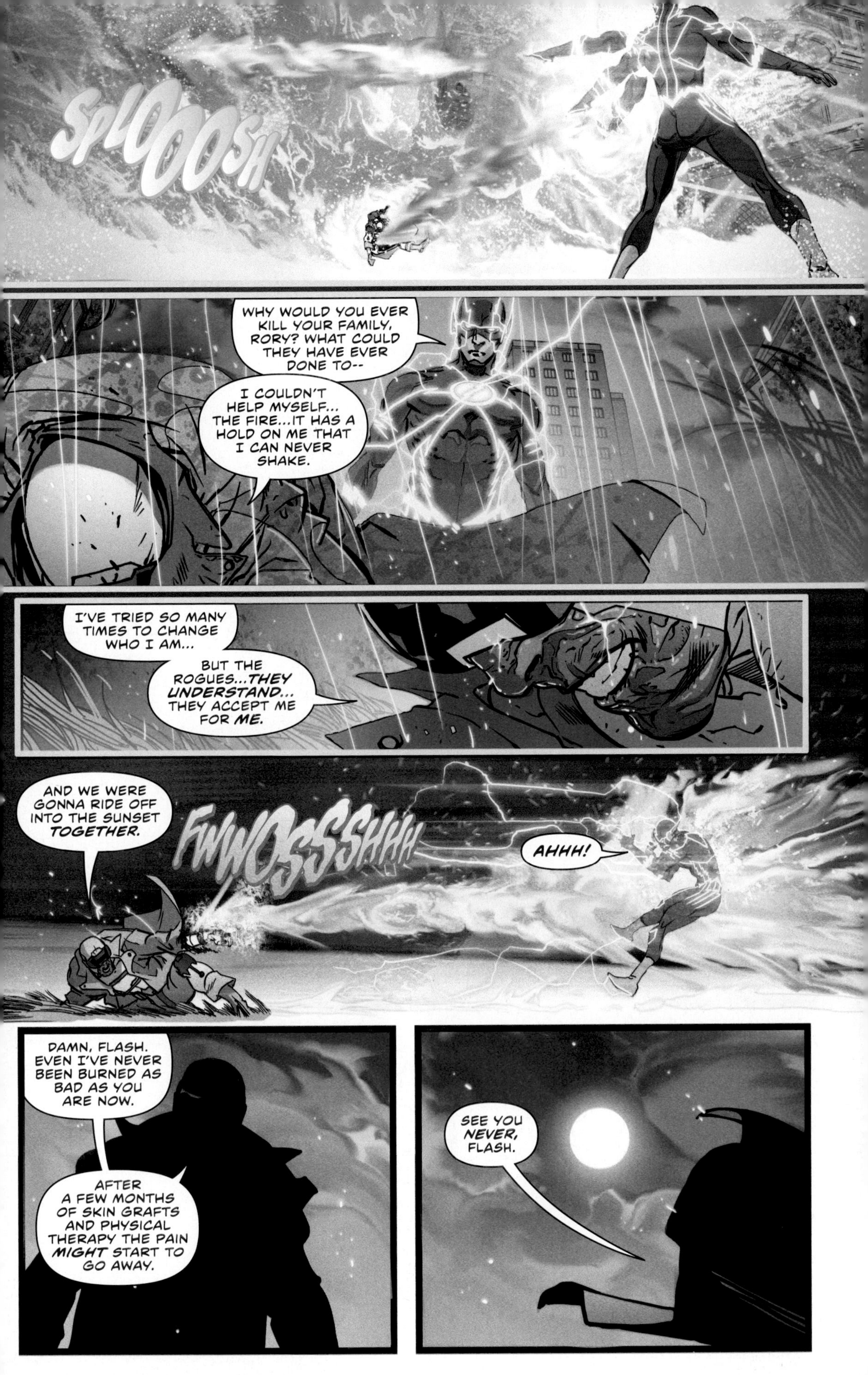
SPLOOOSH
WHY WOULD YOU EVER KILL YOUR FAMILY, RORY? WHAT COULD THEY HAVE EVER DONE TO--
I COULDN'T HELP MYSELF... THE FIRE...IT HAS A HOLD ON ME THAT I CAN NEVER SHAKE.
I'VE TRIED SO MANY TIMES TO CHANGE WHO I AM...
BUT THE ROGUES...*THEY UNDERSTAND*... THEY ACCEPT ME FOR *ME.*
AND WE WERE GONNA RIDE OFF INTO THE SUNSET *TOGETHER.*
FWWOSSSHHH
AHHH!
DAMN, FLASH. EVEN I'VE NEVER BEEN BURNED AS BAD AS YOU ARE NOW.
AFTER A FEW MONTHS OF SKIN GRAFTS AND PHYSICAL THERAPY THE PAIN *MIGHT* START TO GO AWAY.
SEE YOU *NEVER,* FLASH.

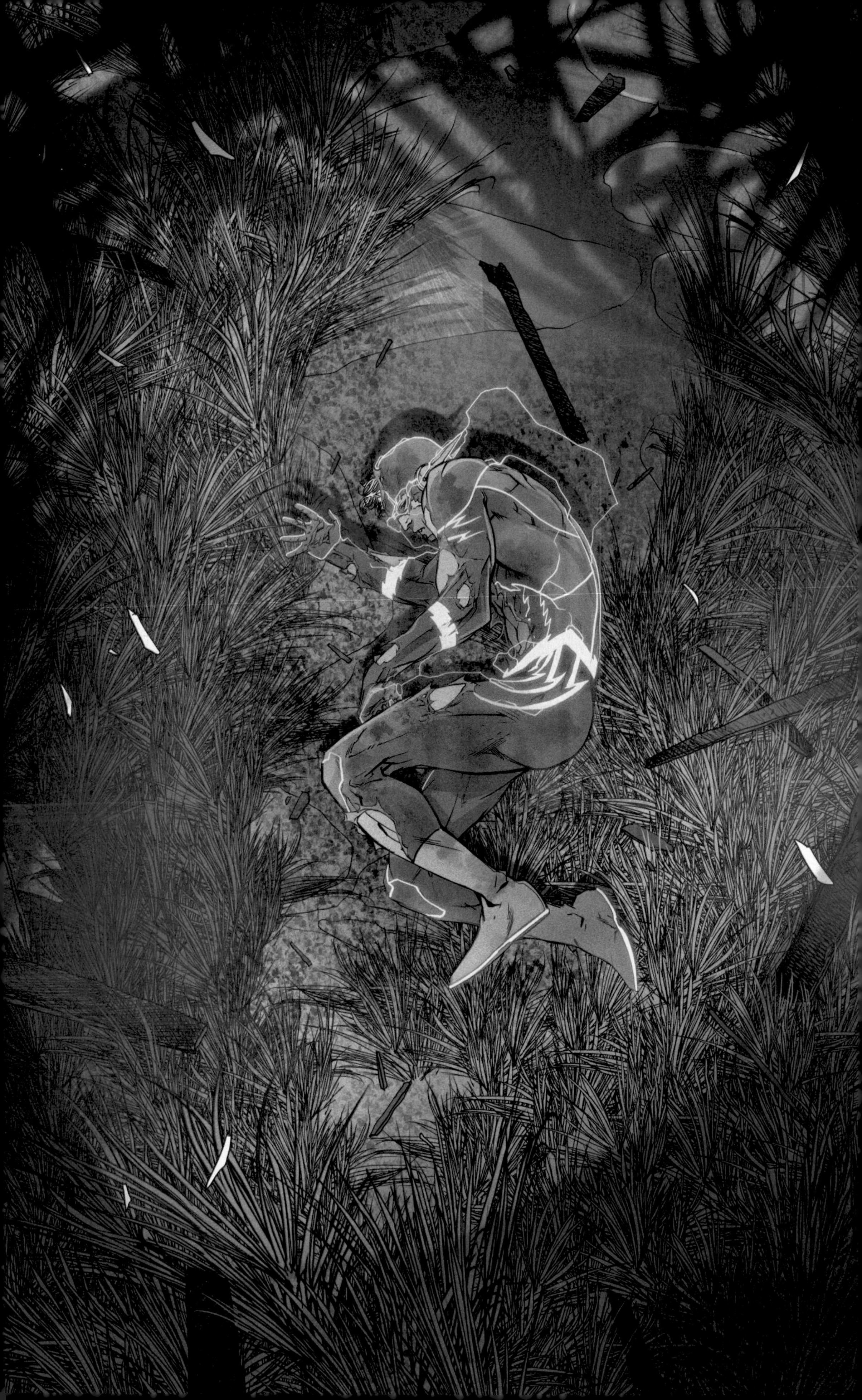

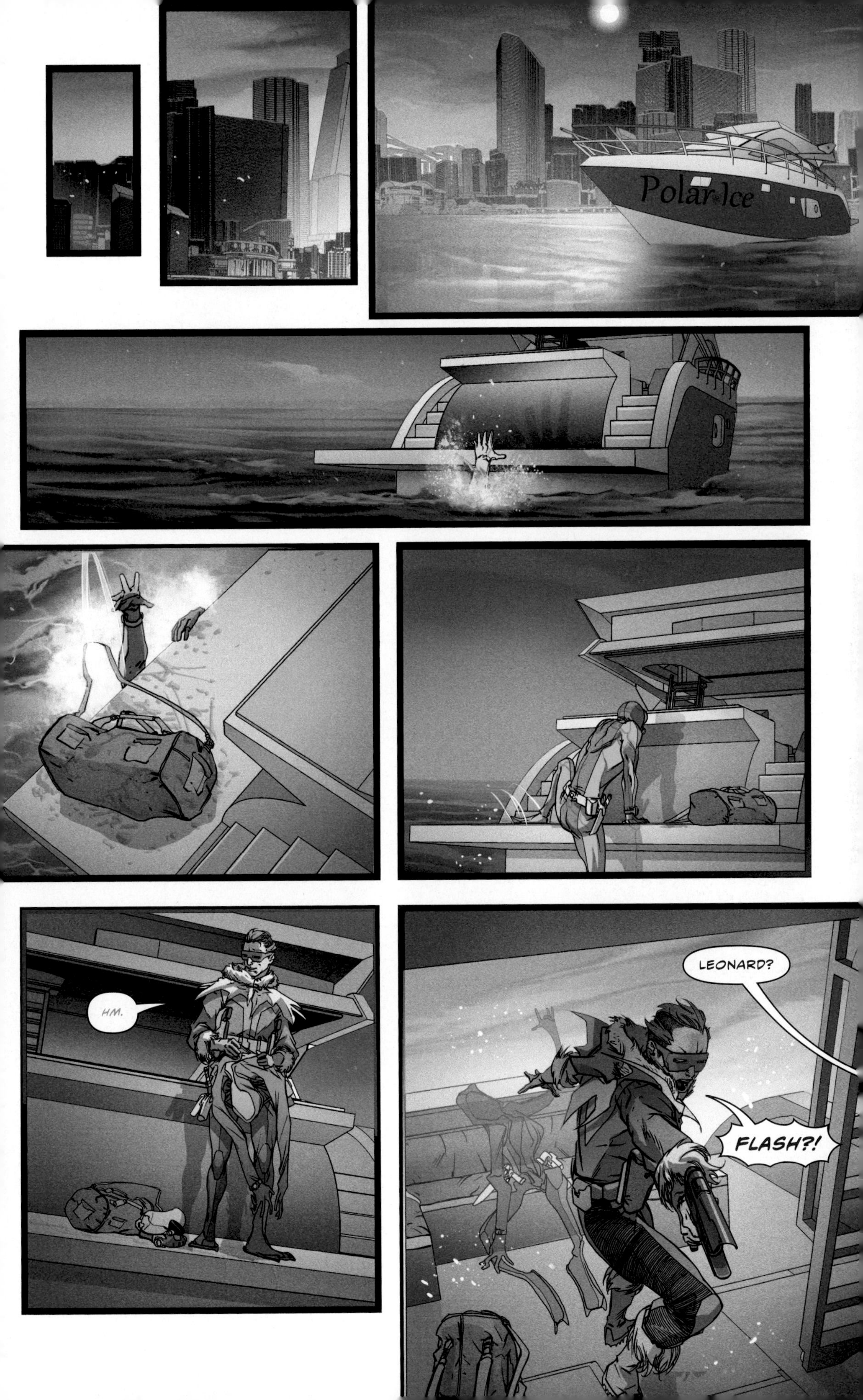
Polar Ice
HM.
LEONARD?
FLASH?!

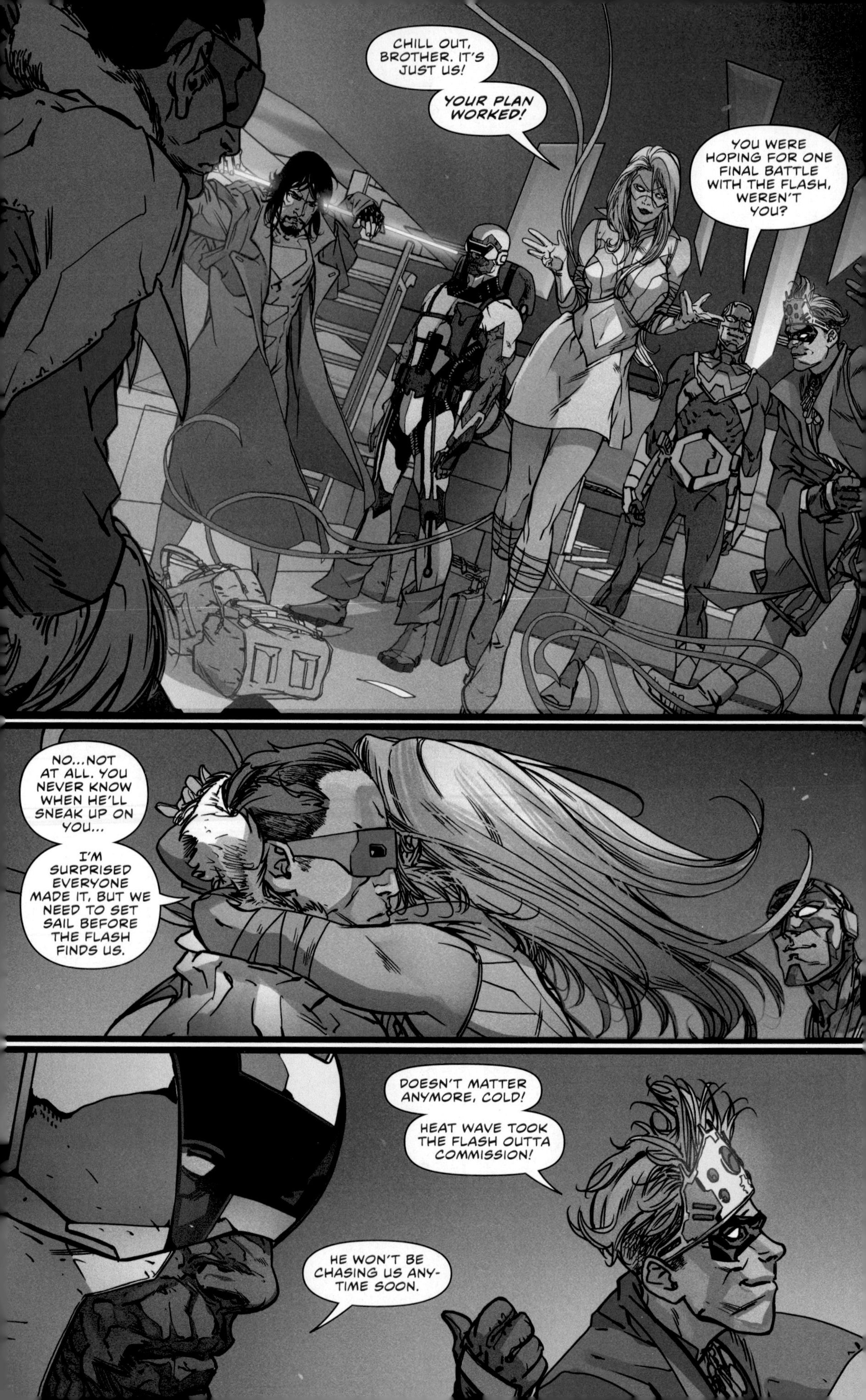
CHILL OUT, BROTHER. IT'S JUST US!
YOUR PLAN WORKED!
YOU WERE HOPING FOR ONE FINAL BATTLE WITH THE FLASH, WEREN'T YOU?
NO...NOT AT ALL. YOU NEVER KNOW WHEN HE'LL SNEAK UP ON YOU...
I'M SURPRISED EVERYONE MADE IT, BUT WE NEED TO SET SAIL BEFORE THE FLASH FINDS US.
DOESN'T MATTER ANYMORE, COLD!
HEAT WAVE TOOK THE FLASH OUTTA COMMISSION!
HE WON'T BE CHASING US ANY-TIME SOON.

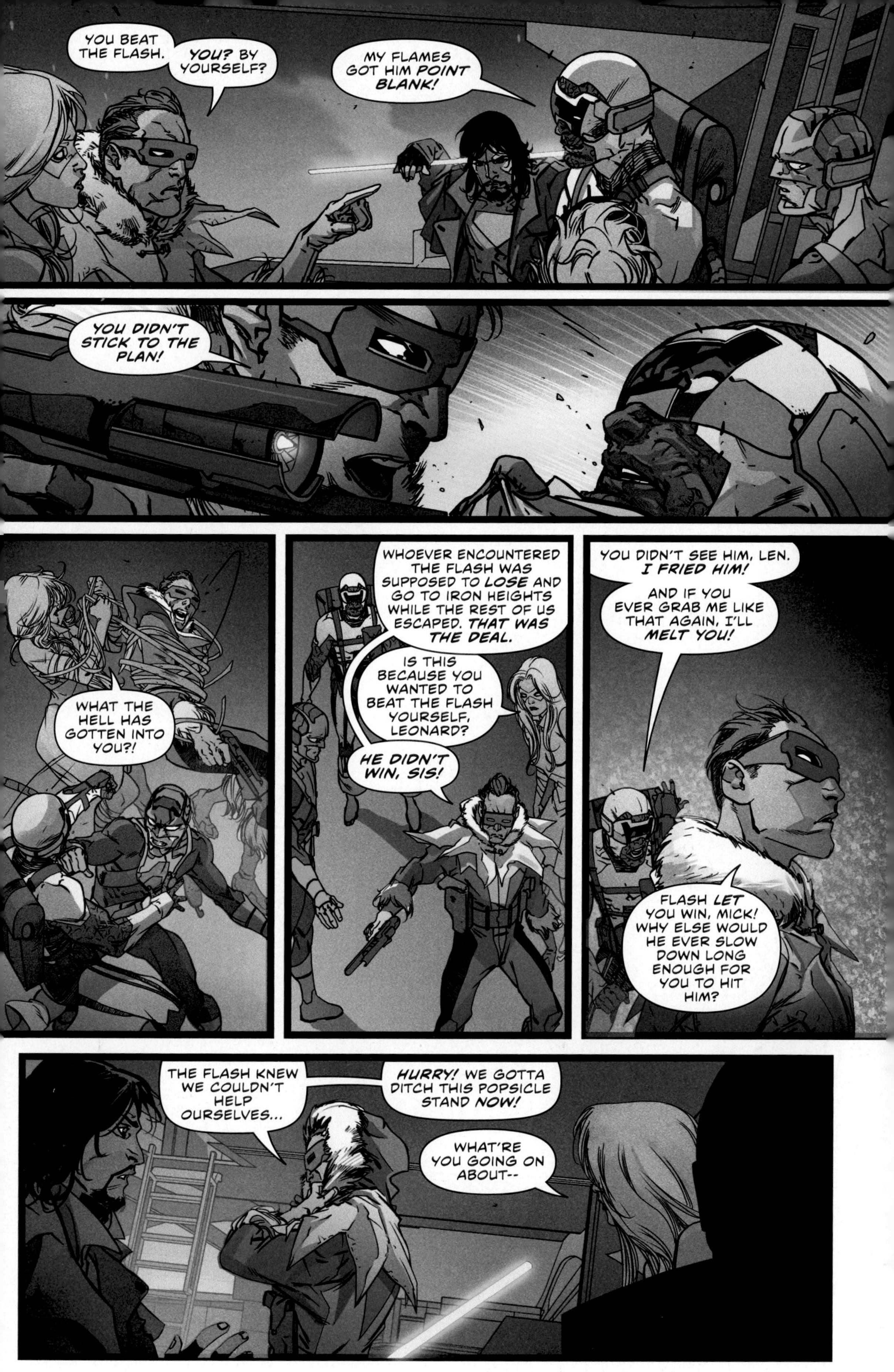
YOU BEAT THE FLASH.
YOU? BY YOURSELF?
MY FLAMES GOT HIM POINT BLANK!
YOU DIDN'T STICK TO THE PLAN!
WHAT THE HELL HAS GOTTEN INTO YOU?!
WHOEVER ENCOUNTERED THE FLASH WAS SUPPOSED TO LOSE AND GO TO IRON HEIGHTS WHILE THE REST OF US ESCAPED. THAT WAS THE DEAL.
IS THIS BECAUSE YOU WANTED TO BEAT THE FLASH YOURSELF, LEONARD?
HE DIDN'T WIN, SIS!
YOU DIDN'T SEE HIM, LEN. I FRIED HIM!
AND IF YOU EVER GRAB ME LIKE THAT AGAIN, I'LL MELT YOU!
FLASH LET YOU WIN, MICK! WHY ELSE WOULD HE EVER SLOW DOWN LONG ENOUGH FOR YOU TO HIT HIM?
THE FLASH KNEW WE COULDN'T HELP OURSELVES...
HURRY! WE GOTTA DITCH THIS POPSICLE STAND NOW!
WHAT'RE YOU GOING ON ABOUT--

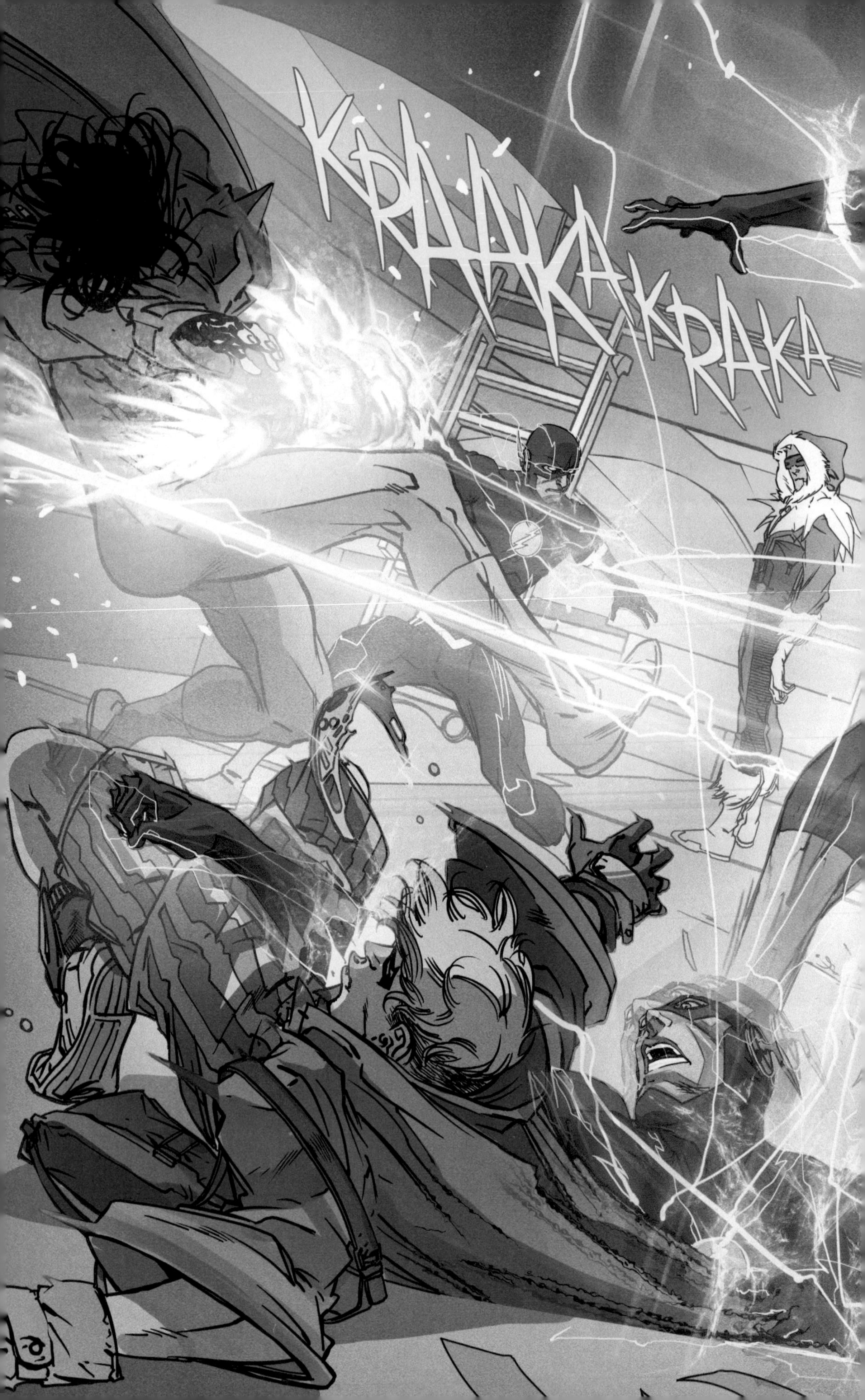
KRAAKAKRAKA

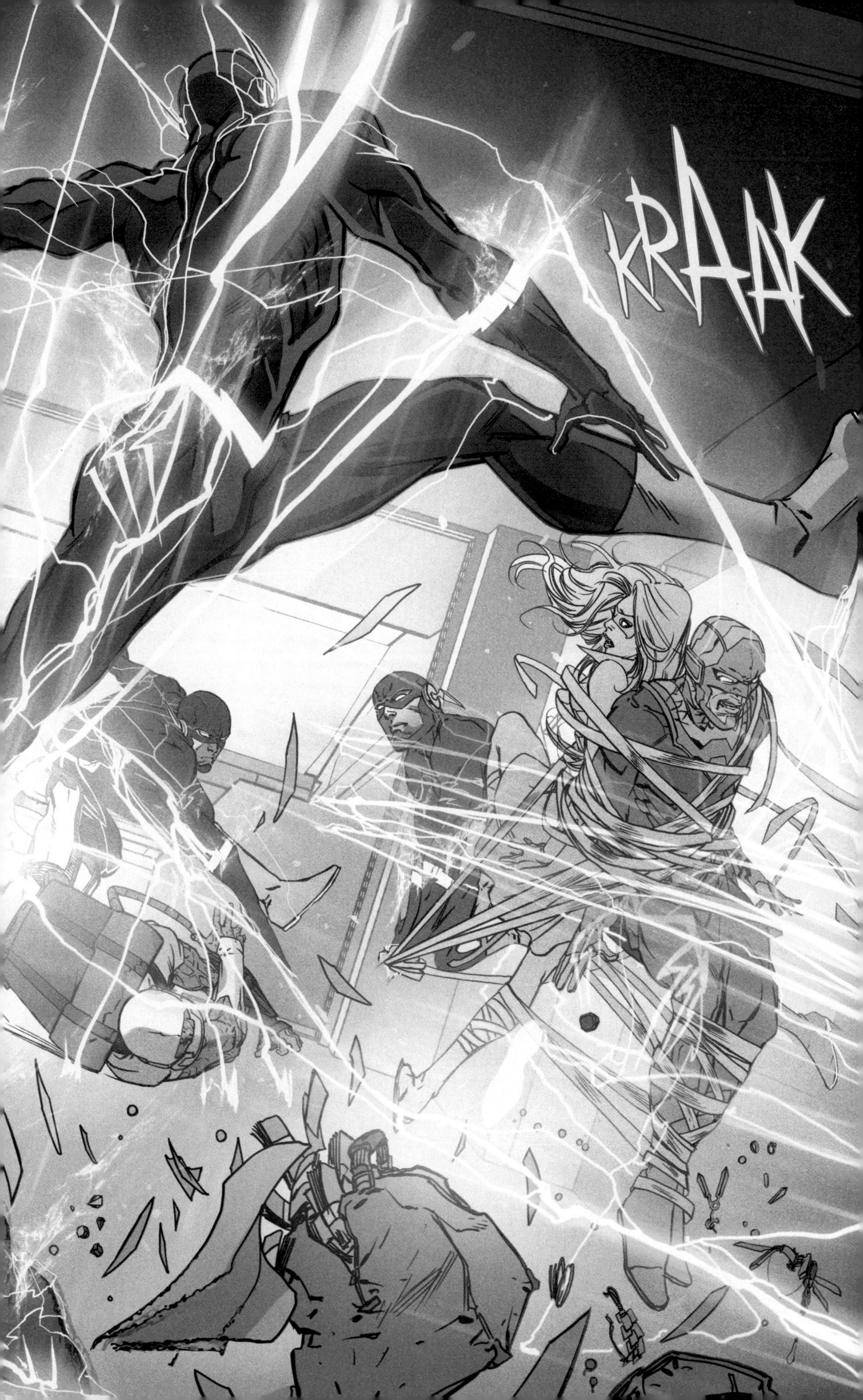
KRAAK

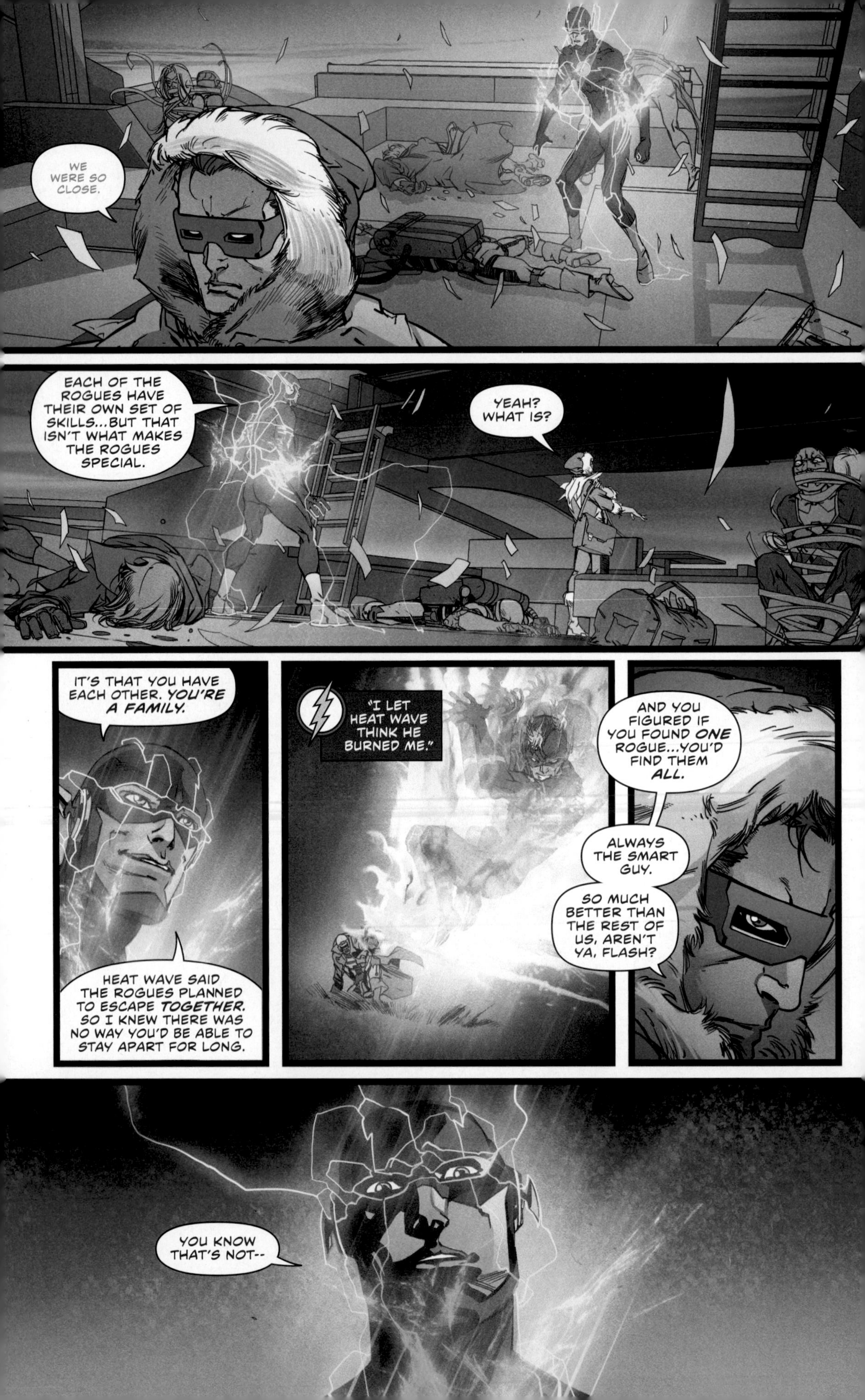
WE WERE SO CLOSE.
EACH OF THE ROGUES HAVE THEIR OWN SET OF SKILLS...BUT THAT ISN'T WHAT MAKES THE ROGUES SPECIAL.
YEAH? WHAT IS?
IT'S THAT YOU HAVE EACH OTHER. *YOU'RE A FAMILY.*
HEAT WAVE SAID THE ROGUES PLANNED TO ESCAPE *TOGETHER.* SO I KNEW THERE WAS NO WAY YOU'D BE ABLE TO STAY APART FOR LONG.
"I LET HEAT WAVE THINK HE BURNED ME."
AND YOU FIGURED IF YOU FOUND *ONE* ROGUE...YOU'D FIND THEM *ALL.*
ALWAYS THE SMART GUY.
SO MUCH BETTER THAN THE REST OF US, AREN'T YA, FLASH?
YOU KNOW THAT'S NOT--

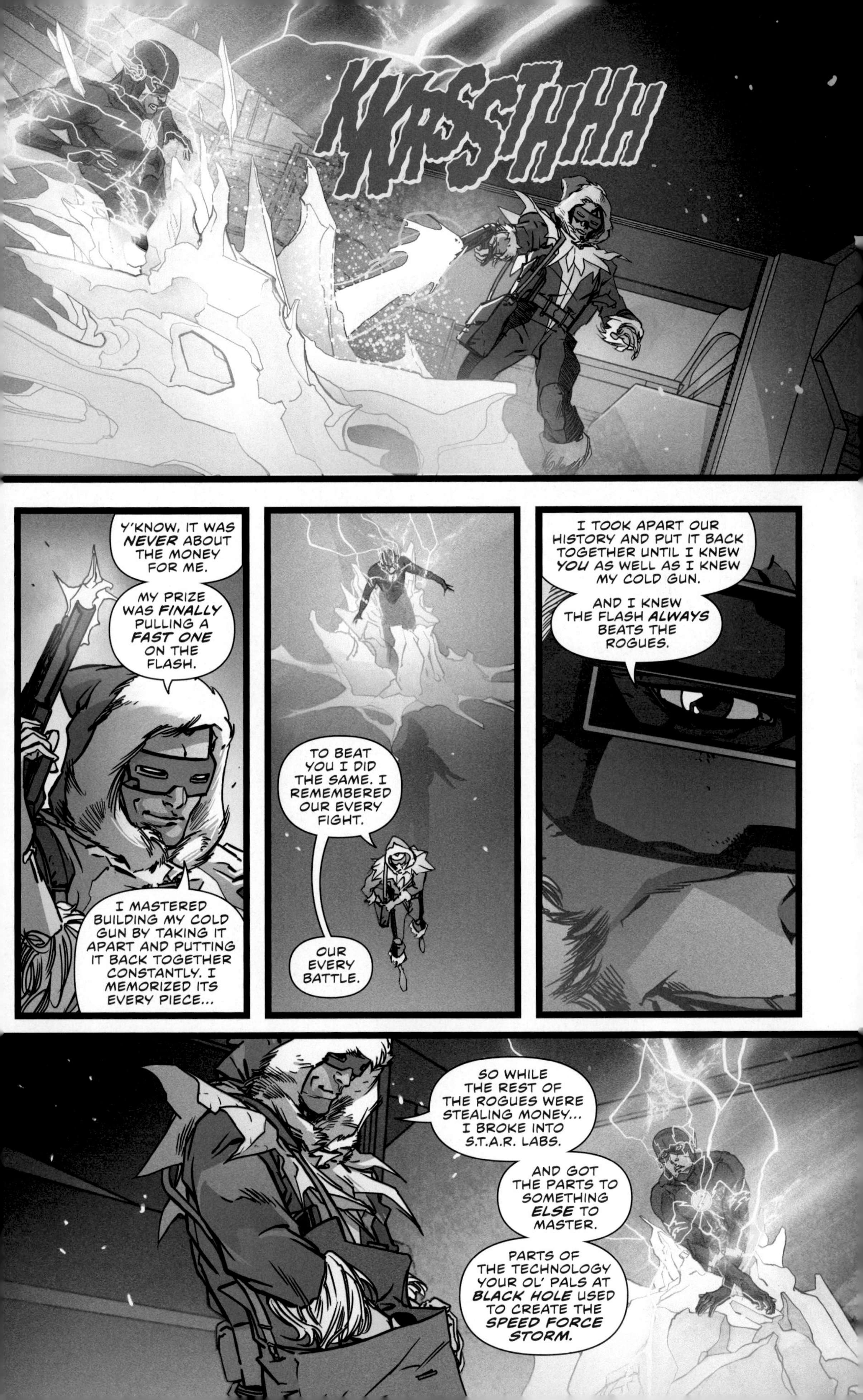
KKRSSTHHH
Y'KNOW, IT WAS NEVER ABOUT THE MONEY FOR ME.
MY PRIZE WAS FINALLY PULLING A FAST ONE ON THE FLASH.
I MASTERED BUILDING MY COLD GUN BY TAKING IT APART AND PUTTING IT BACK TOGETHER CONSTANTLY. I MEMORIZED ITS EVERY PIECE...
TO BEAT YOU I DID THE SAME. I REMEMBERED OUR EVERY FIGHT.
OUR EVERY BATTLE.
I TOOK APART OUR HISTORY AND PUT IT BACK TOGETHER UNTIL I KNEW YOU AS WELL AS I KNEW MY COLD GUN.
AND I KNEW THE FLASH ALWAYS BEATS THE ROGUES.
SO WHILE THE REST OF THE ROGUES WERE STEALING MONEY... I BROKE INTO S.T.A.R. LABS.
AND GOT THE PARTS TO SOMETHING ELSE TO MASTER.
PARTS OF THE TECHNOLOGY YOUR OL' PALS AT BLACK HOLE USED TO CREATE THE SPEED FORCE STORM.

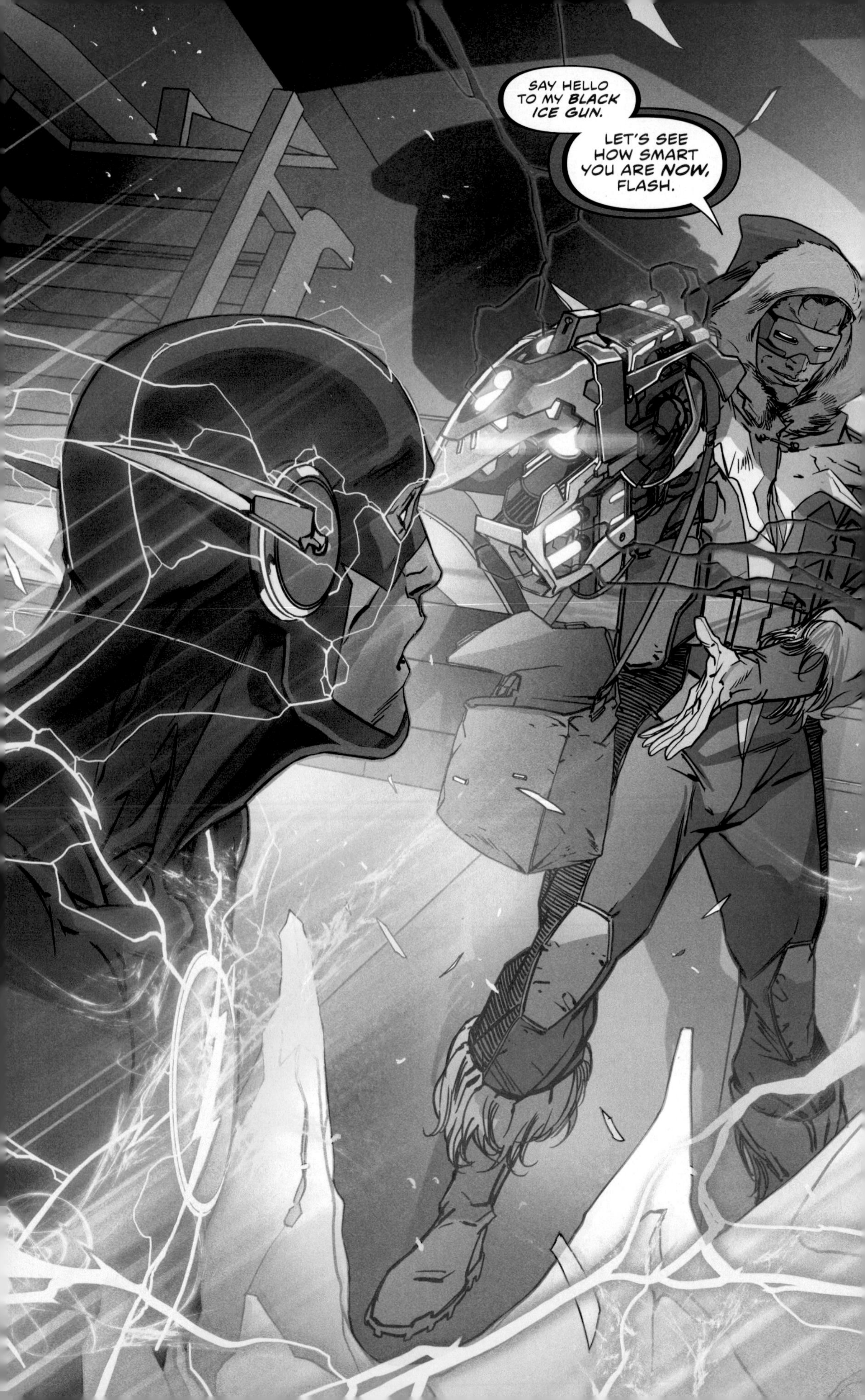
SAY HELLO TO MY BLACK ICE GUN.
LET'S SEE HOW SMART YOU ARE NOW, FLASH.

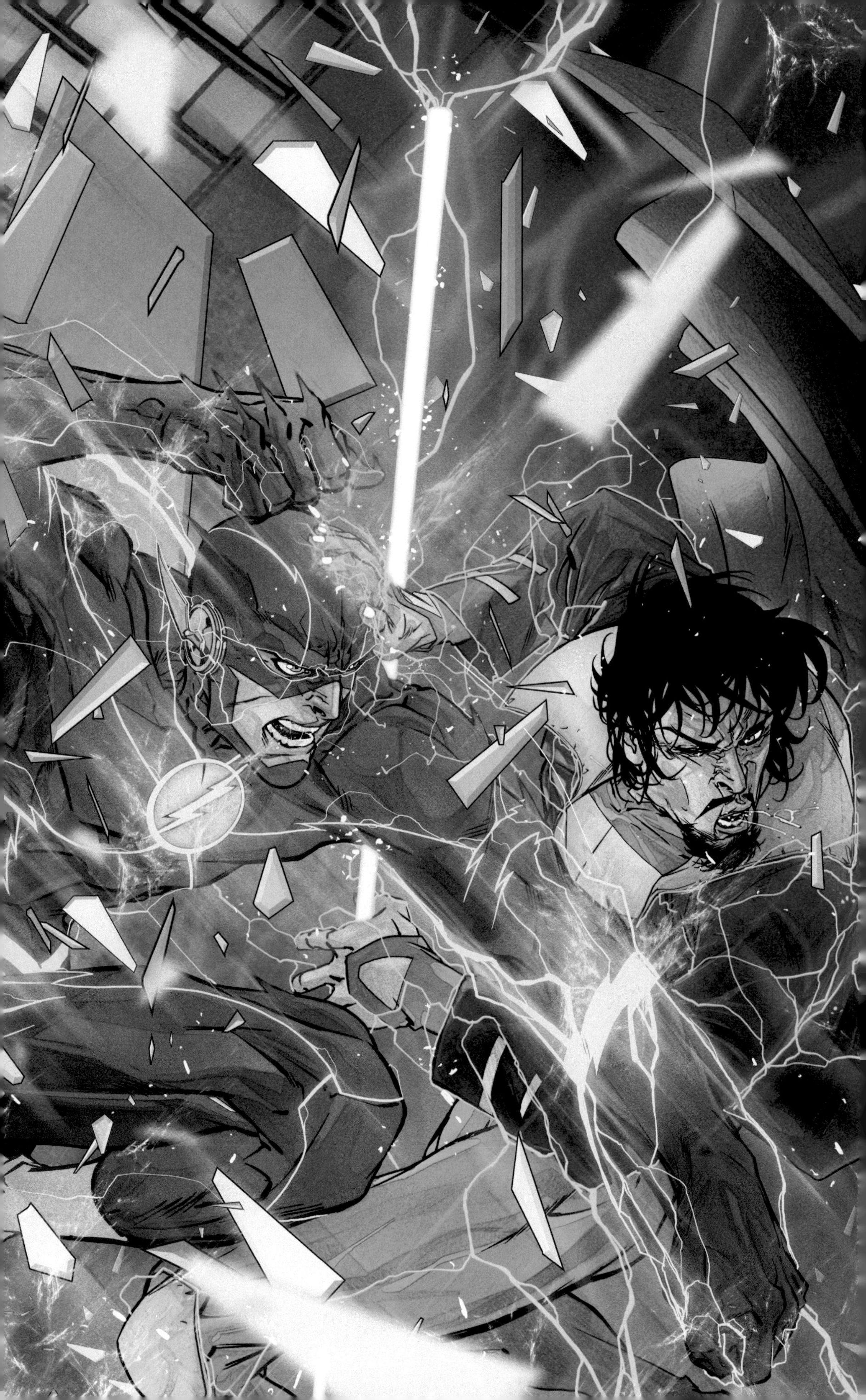

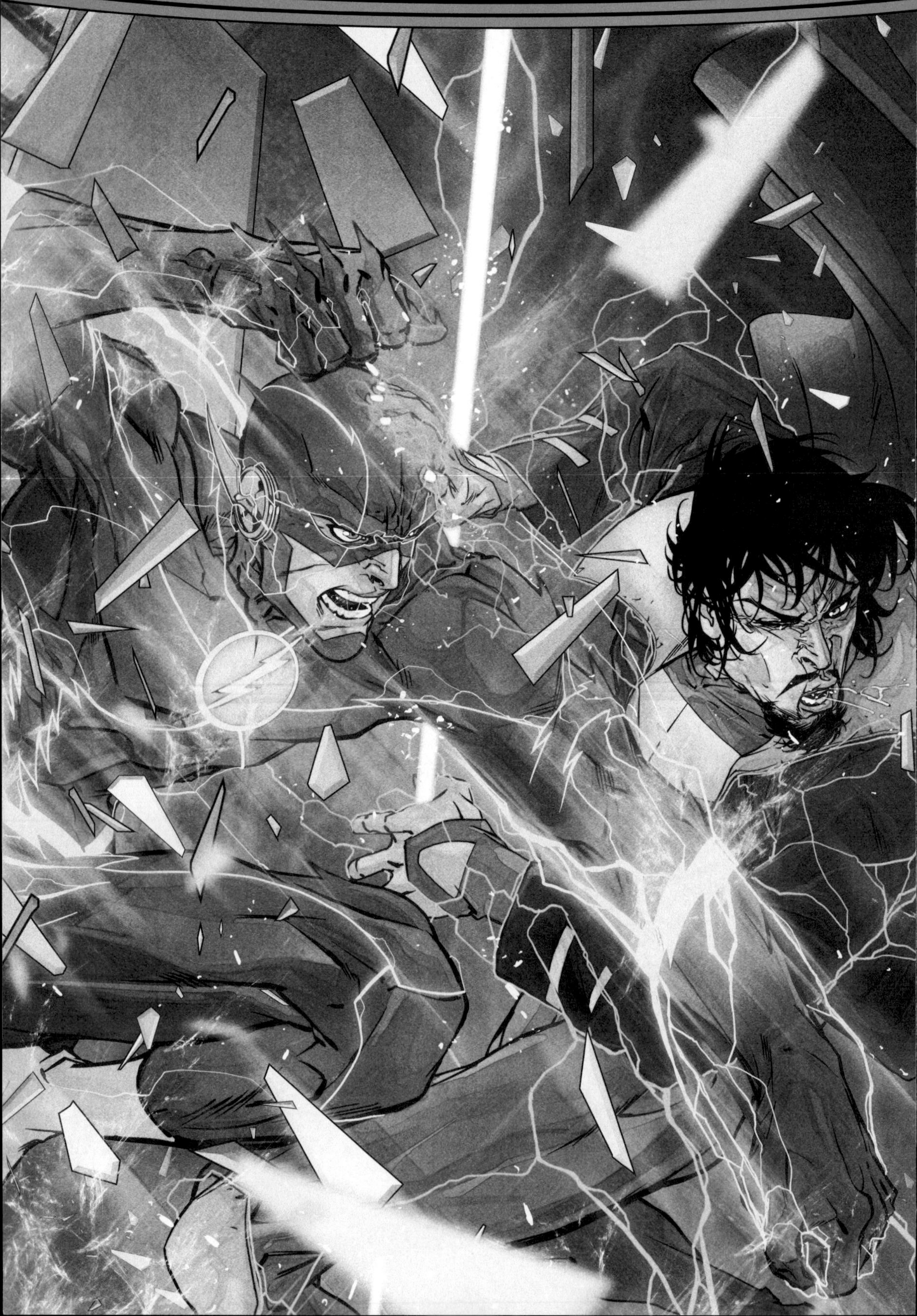

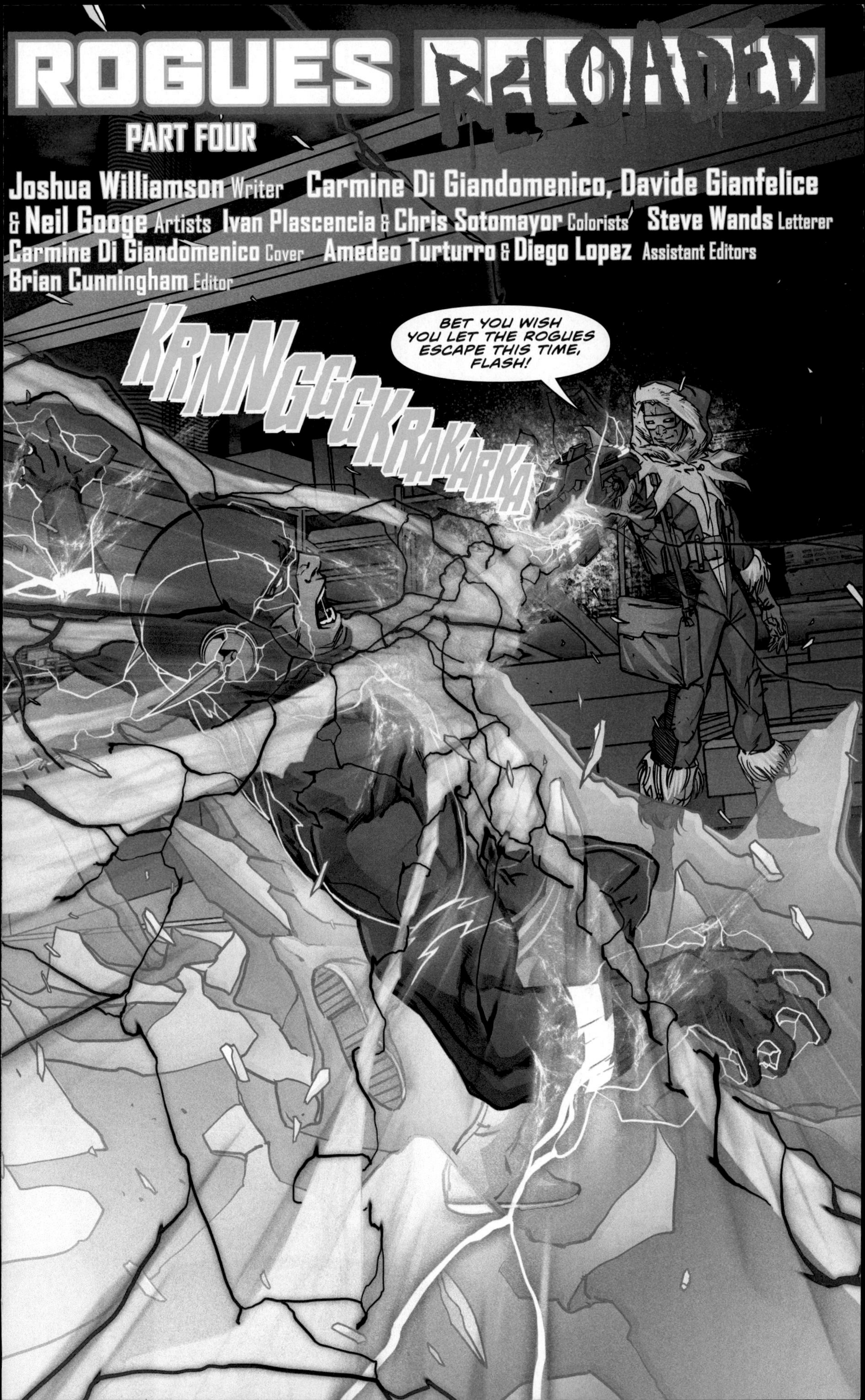
ROGUES RELOADED
PART FOUR
Joshua Williamson Writer Carmine Di Giandomenico, Davide Gianfelice & Neil Googe Artists Ivan Plascencia & Chris Sotomayor Colorists Steve Wands Letterer Carmine Di Giandomenico Cover Amedeo Turturro & Diego Lopez Assistant Editors Brian Cunningham Editor
KRNNGGGKRAKARKA
BET YOU WISH YOU LET THE ROGUES ESCAPE THIS TIME, FLASH!

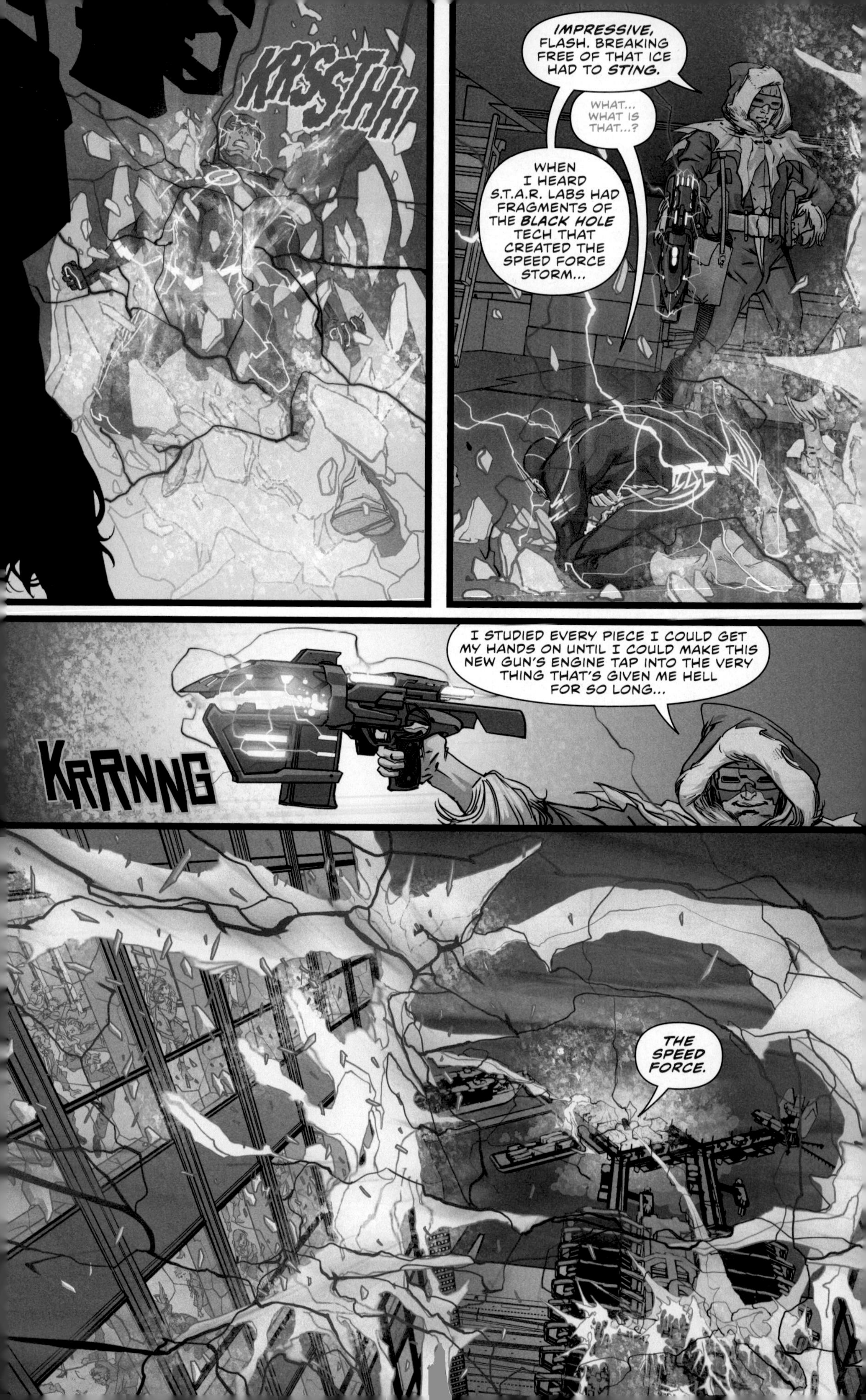
KRSTHH
IMPRESSIVE, FLASH. BREAKING FREE OF THAT ICE HAD TO STING.
WHAT... WHAT IS THAT...?
WHEN I HEARD S.T.A.R. LABS HAD FRAGMENTS OF THE BLACK HOLE TECH THAT CREATED THE SPEED FORCE STORM...
I STUDIED EVERY PIECE I COULD GET MY HANDS ON UNTIL I COULD MAKE THIS NEW GUN'S ENGINE TAP INTO THE VERY THING THAT'S GIVEN ME HELL FOR SO LONG...
KRRNNG
THE SPEED FORCE.

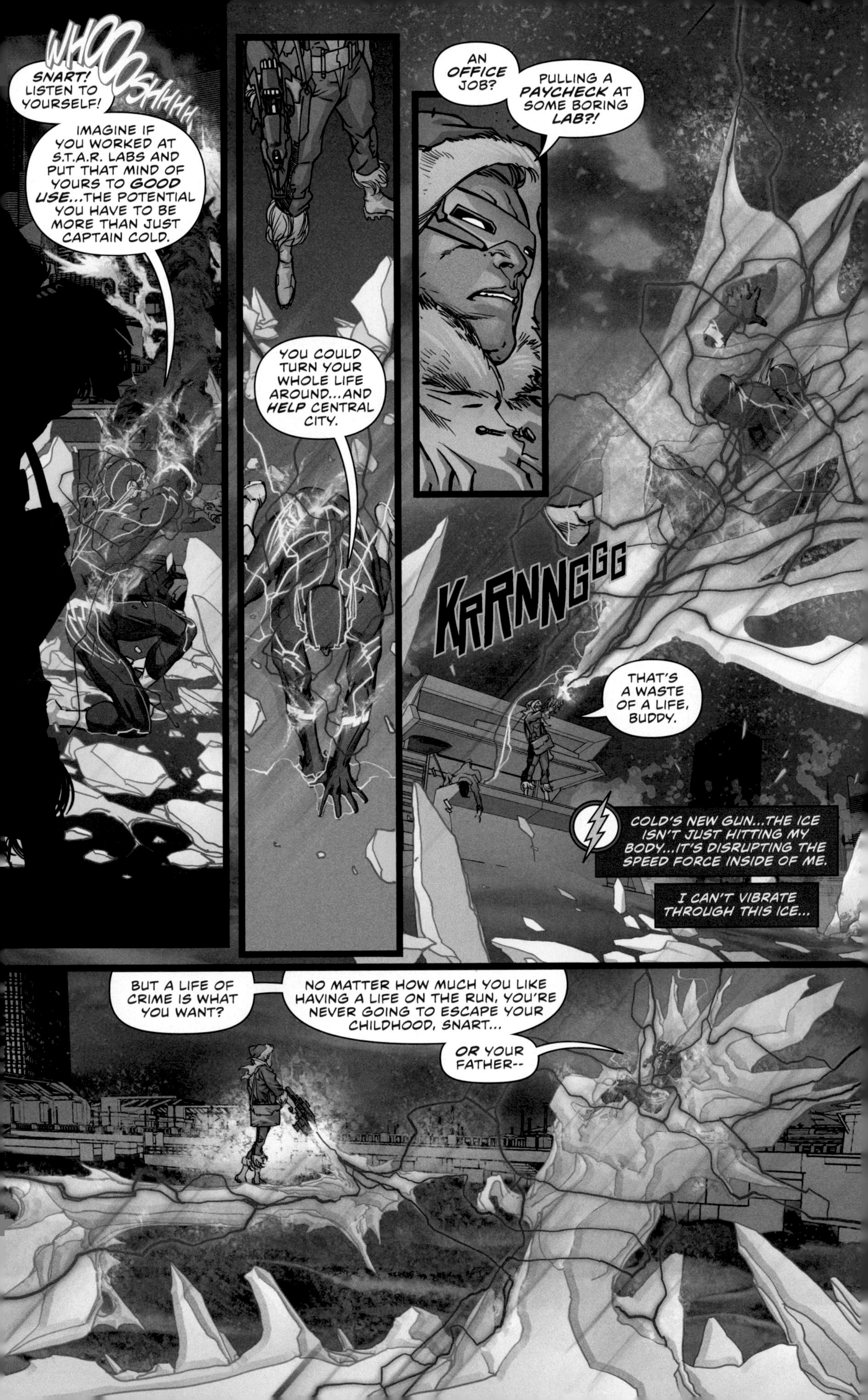
WHOOOOSHHHH
SNART! LISTEN TO YOURSELF!
IMAGINE IF YOU WORKED AT S.T.A.R. LABS AND PUT THAT MIND OF YOURS TO GOOD USE...THE POTENTIAL YOU HAVE TO BE MORE THAN JUST CAPTAIN COLD.
YOU COULD TURN YOUR WHOLE LIFE AROUND...AND HELP CENTRAL CITY.
AN OFFICE JOB?
PULLING A PAYCHECK AT SOME BORING LAB?!
KRRNNGGG
THAT'S A WASTE OF A LIFE, BUDDY.
COLD'S NEW GUN...THE ICE ISN'T JUST HITTING MY BODY...IT'S DISRUPTING THE SPEED FORCE INSIDE OF ME.
I CAN'T VIBRATE THROUGH THIS ICE...
BUT A LIFE OF CRIME IS WHAT YOU WANT?
NO MATTER HOW MUCH YOU LIKE HAVING A LIFE ON THE RUN, YOU'RE NEVER GOING TO ESCAPE YOUR CHILDHOOD, SNART...
OR YOUR FATHER--

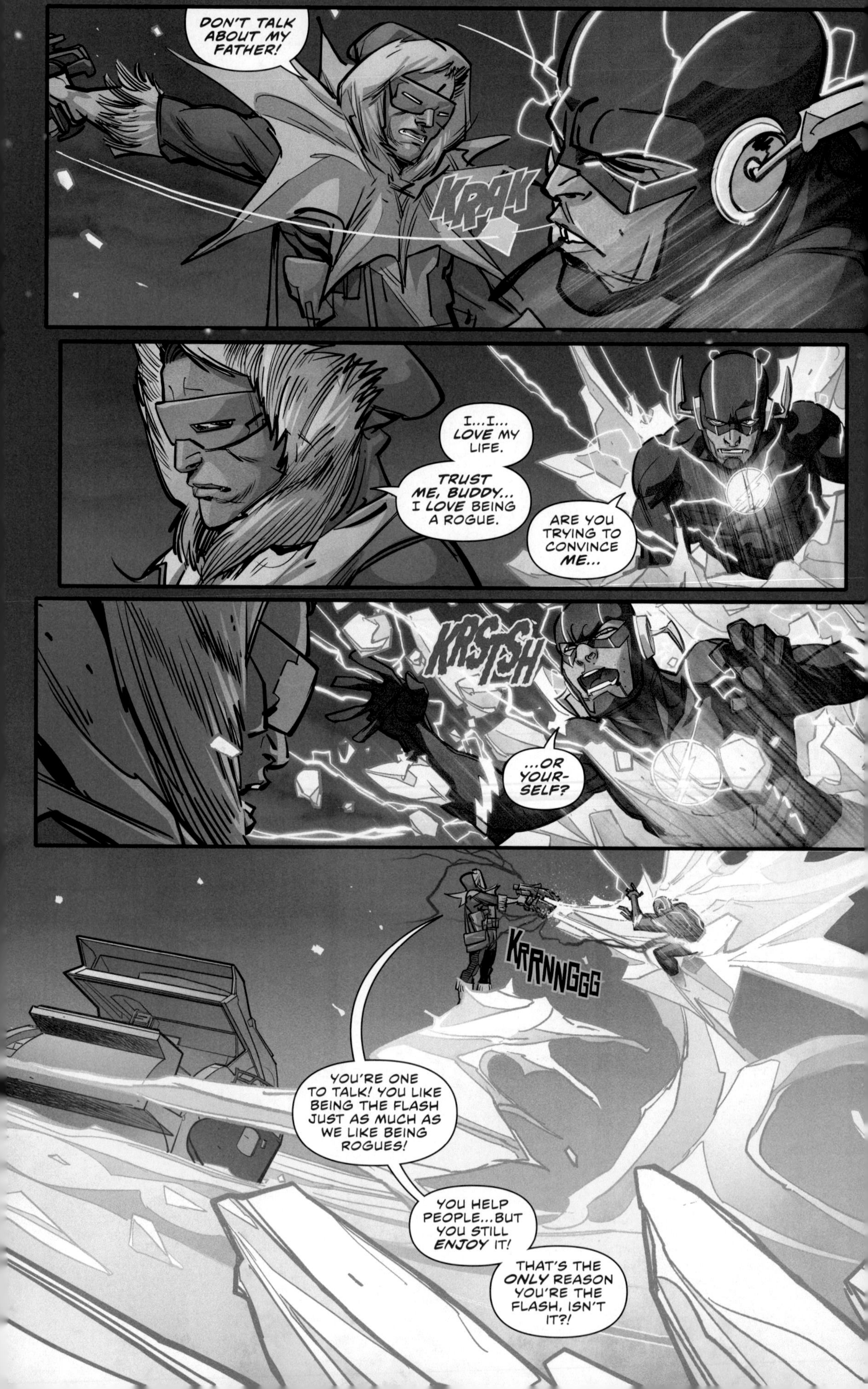
DON'T TALK ABOUT MY FATHER!
KRAK
I...I... LOVE MY LIFE.
TRUST ME, BUDDY... I LOVE BEING A ROGUE.
ARE YOU TRYING TO CONVINCE ME...
KRSTSH
...OR YOUR-SELF?
KRRNNGGG
YOU'RE ONE TO TALK! YOU LIKE BEING THE FLASH JUST AS MUCH AS WE LIKE BEING ROGUES!
YOU HELP PEOPLE...BUT YOU STILL ENJOY IT!
THAT'S THE ONLY REASON YOU'RE THE FLASH, ISN'T IT?!

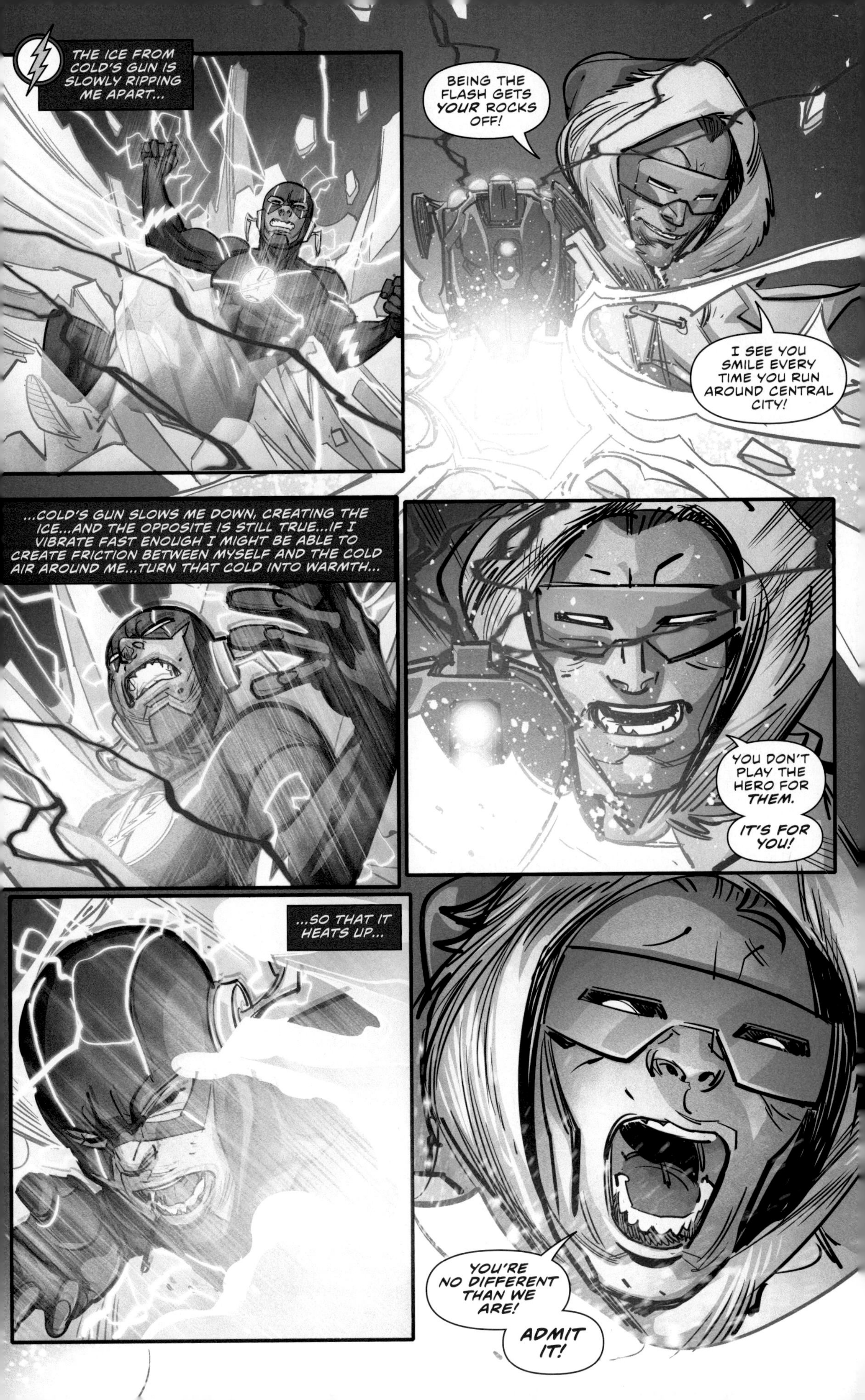
THE ICE FROM COLD'S GUN IS SLOWLY RIPPING ME APART...
BEING THE FLASH GETS YOUR ROCKS OFF!
I SEE YOU SMILE EVERY TIME YOU RUN AROUND CENTRAL CITY!
...COLD'S GUN SLOWS ME DOWN, CREATING THE ICE...AND THE OPPOSITE IS STILL TRUE...IF I VIBRATE FAST ENOUGH I MIGHT BE ABLE TO CREATE FRICTION BETWEEN MYSELF AND THE COLD AIR AROUND ME...TURN THAT COLD INTO WARMTH...
YOU DON'T PLAY THE HERO FOR THEM.
IT'S FOR YOU!
...SO THAT IT HEATS UP...
YOU'RE NO DIFFERENT THAN WE ARE!
ADMIT IT!

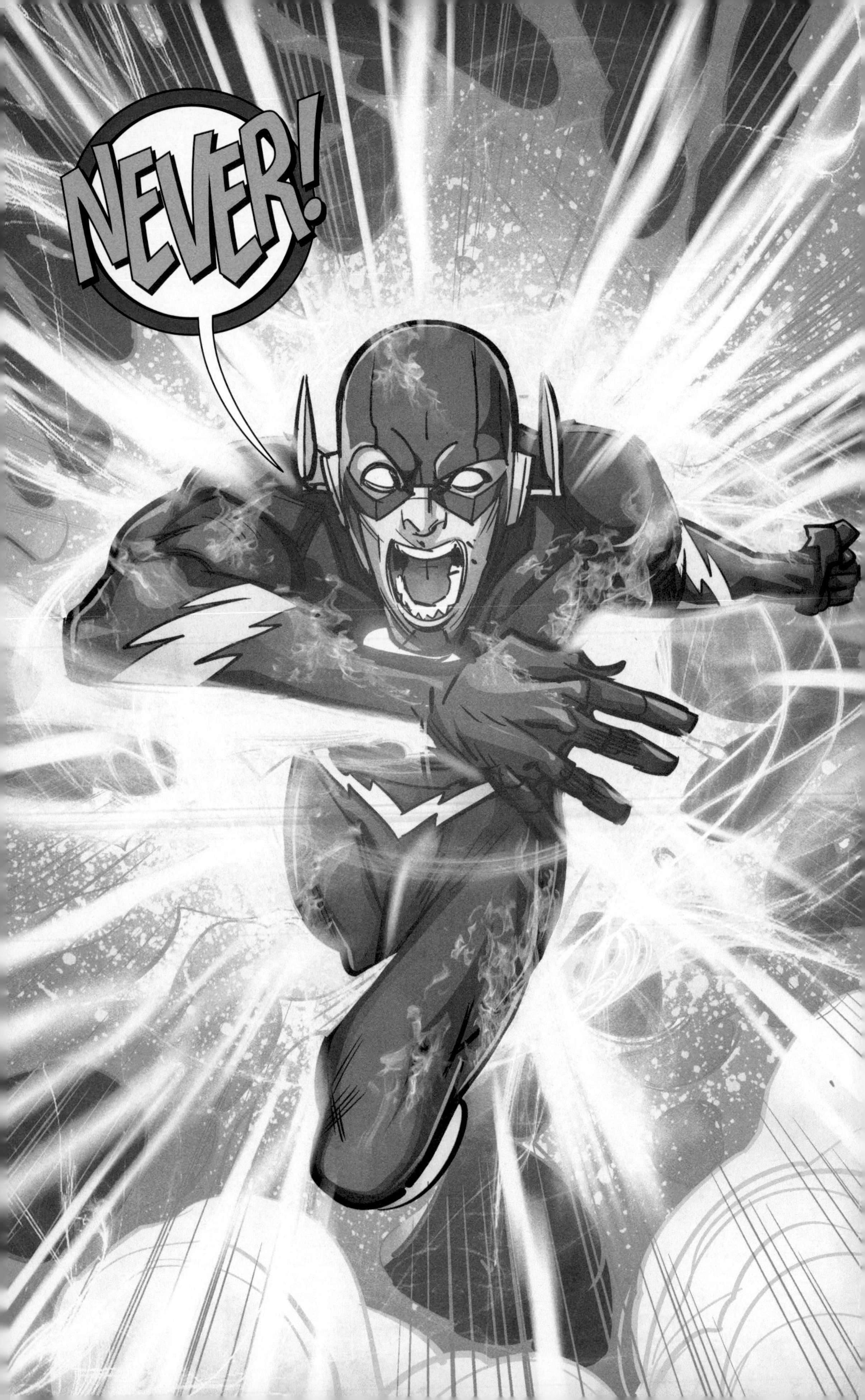
NEVER!

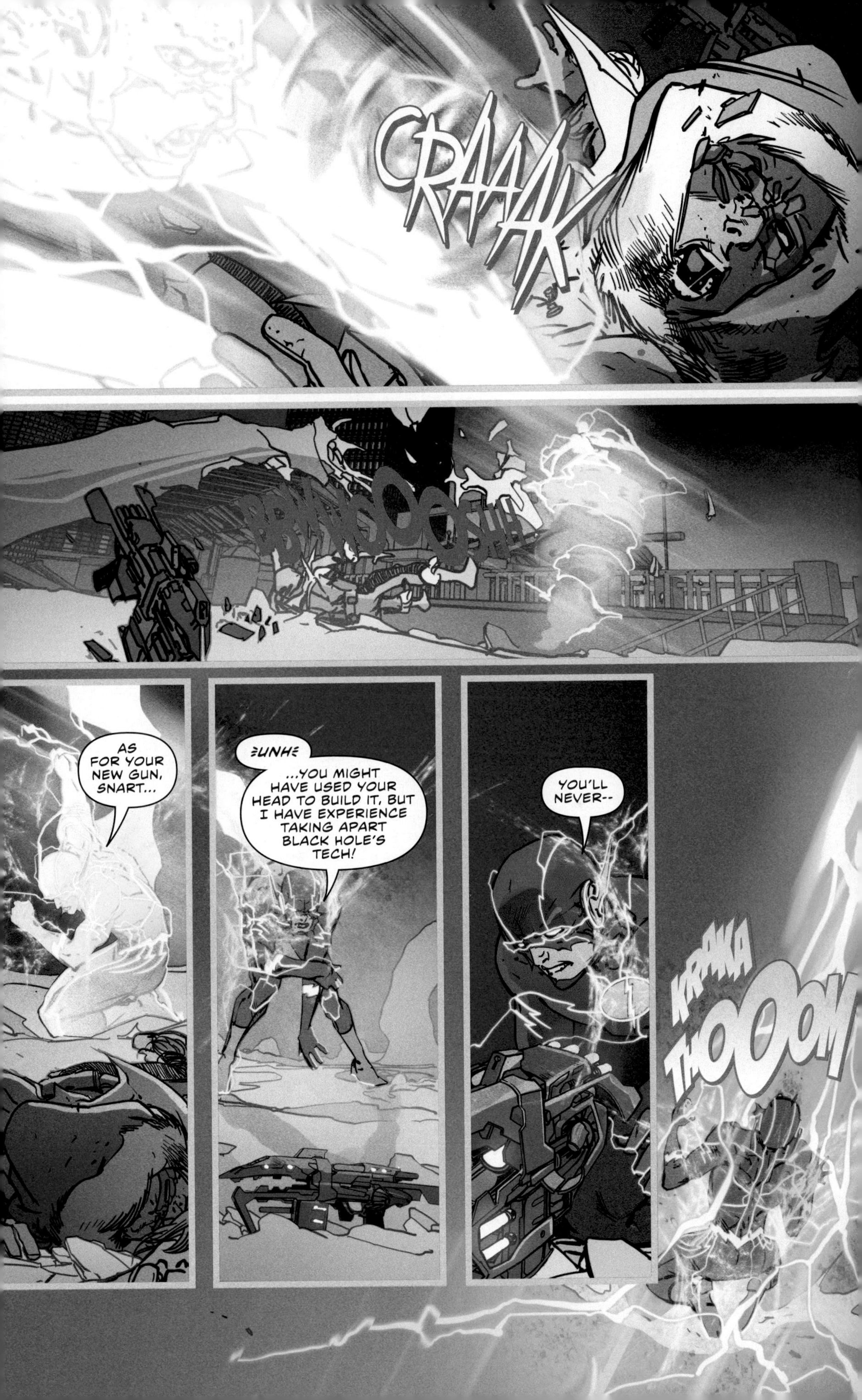
CRAAAK
BRWOOOSHH
AS FOR YOUR NEW GUN, SNART...
UNH
...YOU MIGHT HAVE USED YOUR HEAD TO BUILD IT, BUT I HAVE EXPERIENCE TAKING APART BLACK HOLE'S TECH!
YOU'LL NEVER--
KRAKA THOOOM

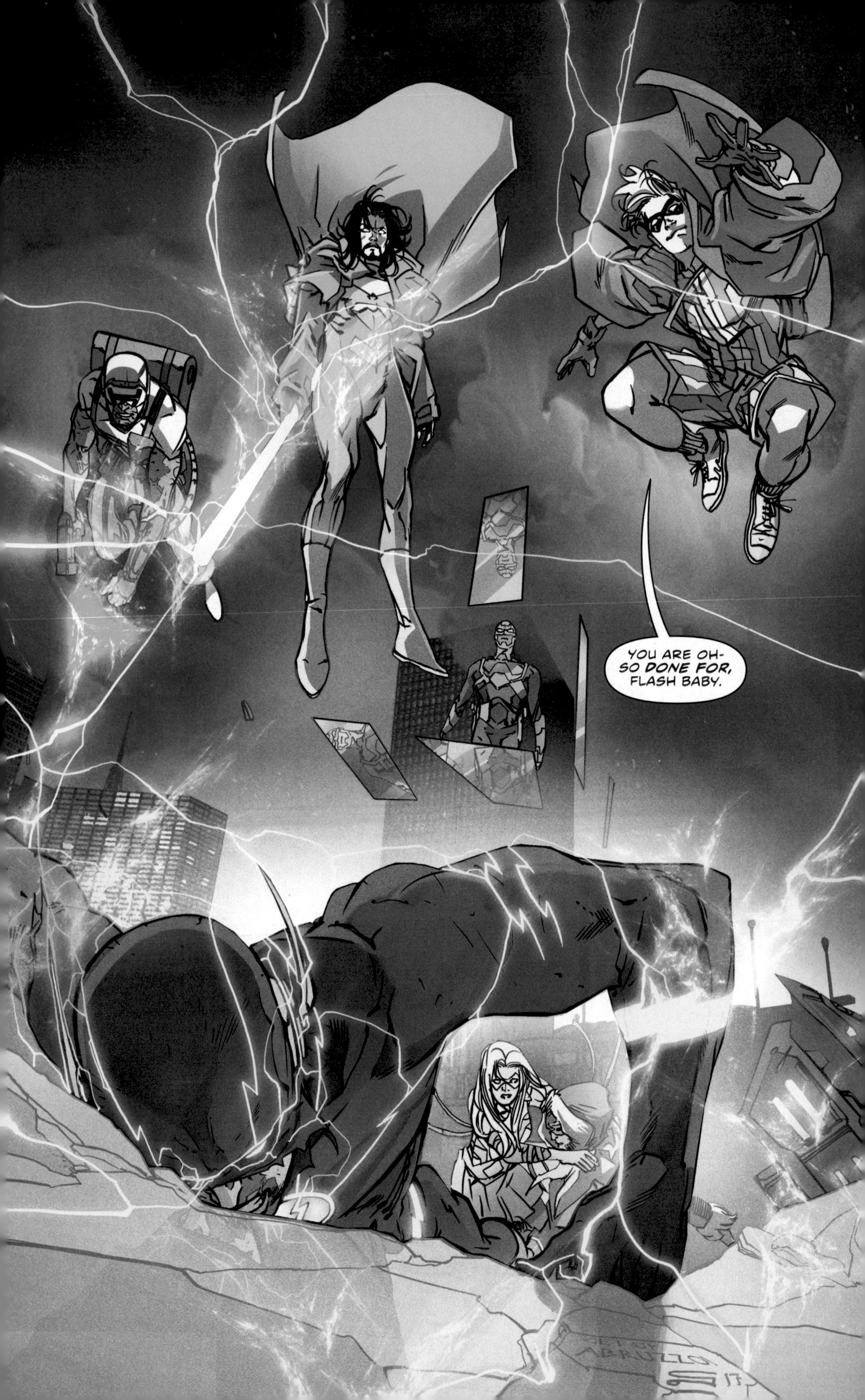
YOU ARE OH-SO DONE FOR, FLASH BABY.

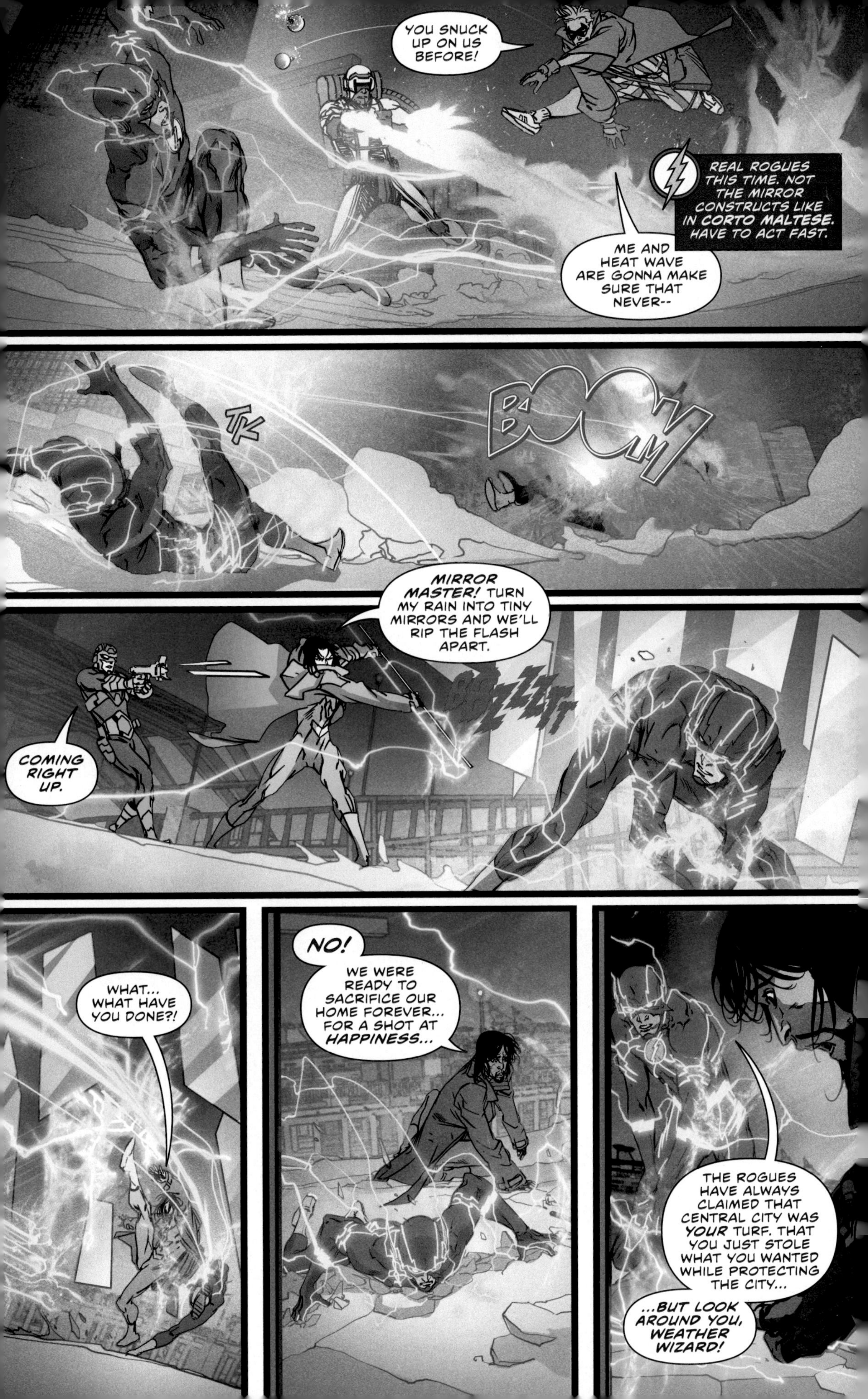
YOU SNUCK UP ON US BEFORE!
REAL ROGUES THIS TIME. NOT THE MIRROR CONSTRUCTS LIKE IN CORTO MALTESE. HAVE TO ACT FAST.
ME AND HEAT WAVE ARE GONNA MAKE SURE THAT NEVER--
TK
BOOM
MIRROR MASTER! TURN MY RAIN INTO TINY MIRRORS AND WE'LL RIP THE FLASH APART.
COMING RIGHT UP.
BZZZZT
WHAT... WHAT HAVE YOU DONE?!
NO!
WE WERE READY TO SACRIFICE OUR HOME FOREVER... FOR A SHOT AT HAPPINESS...
THE ROGUES HAVE ALWAYS CLAIMED THAT CENTRAL CITY WAS YOUR TURF. THAT YOU JUST STOLE WHAT YOU WANTED WHILE PROTECTING THE CITY...
...BUT LOOK AROUND YOU, WEATHER WIZARD!

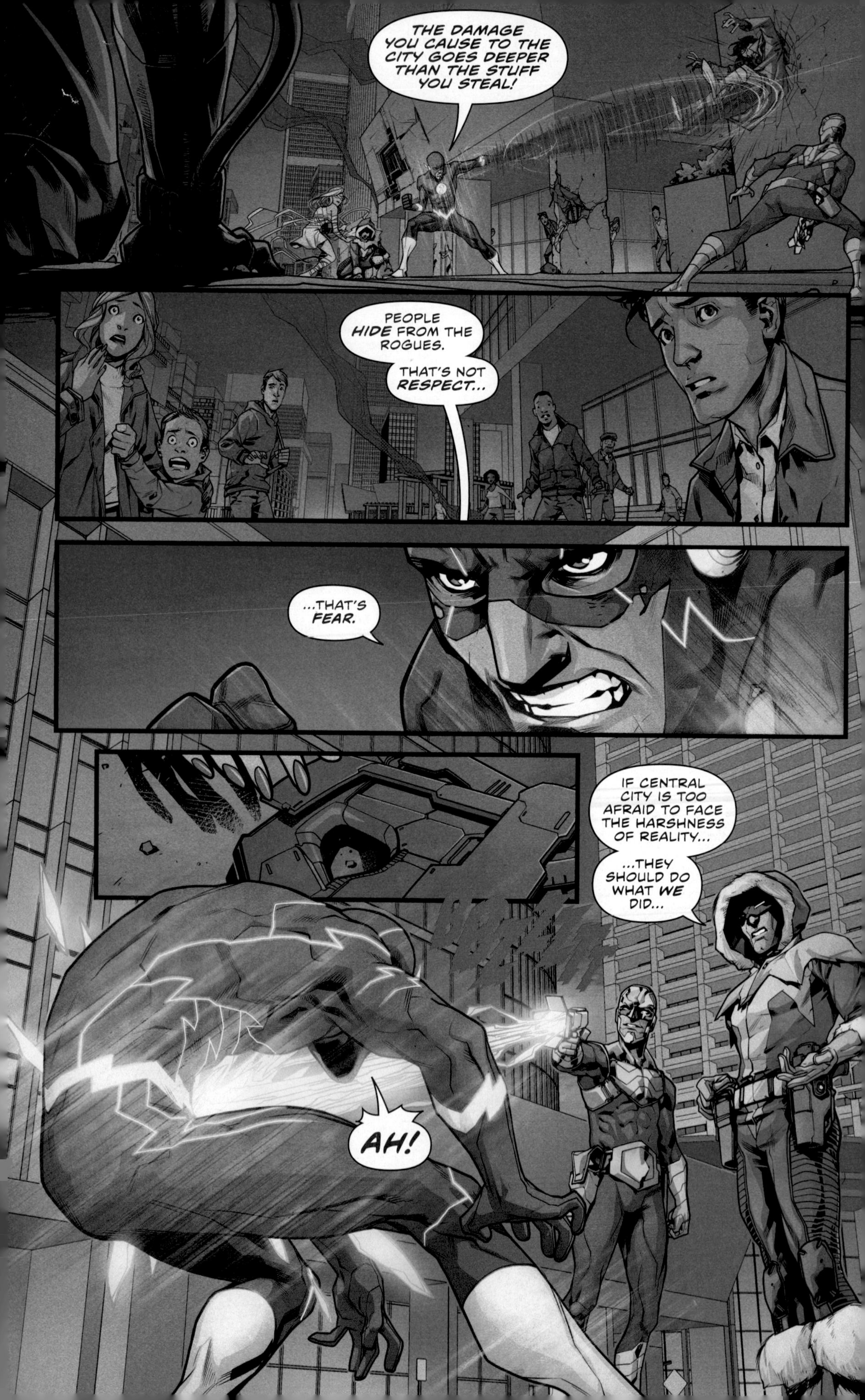
THE DAMAGE YOU CAUSE TO THE CITY GOES DEEPER THAN THE STUFF YOU STEAL!
PEOPLE HIDE FROM THE ROGUES.
THAT'S NOT RESPECT...
...THAT'S FEAR.
IF CENTRAL CITY IS TOO AFRAID TO FACE THE HARSHNESS OF REALITY...
...THEY SHOULD DO WHAT WE DID...
AH!

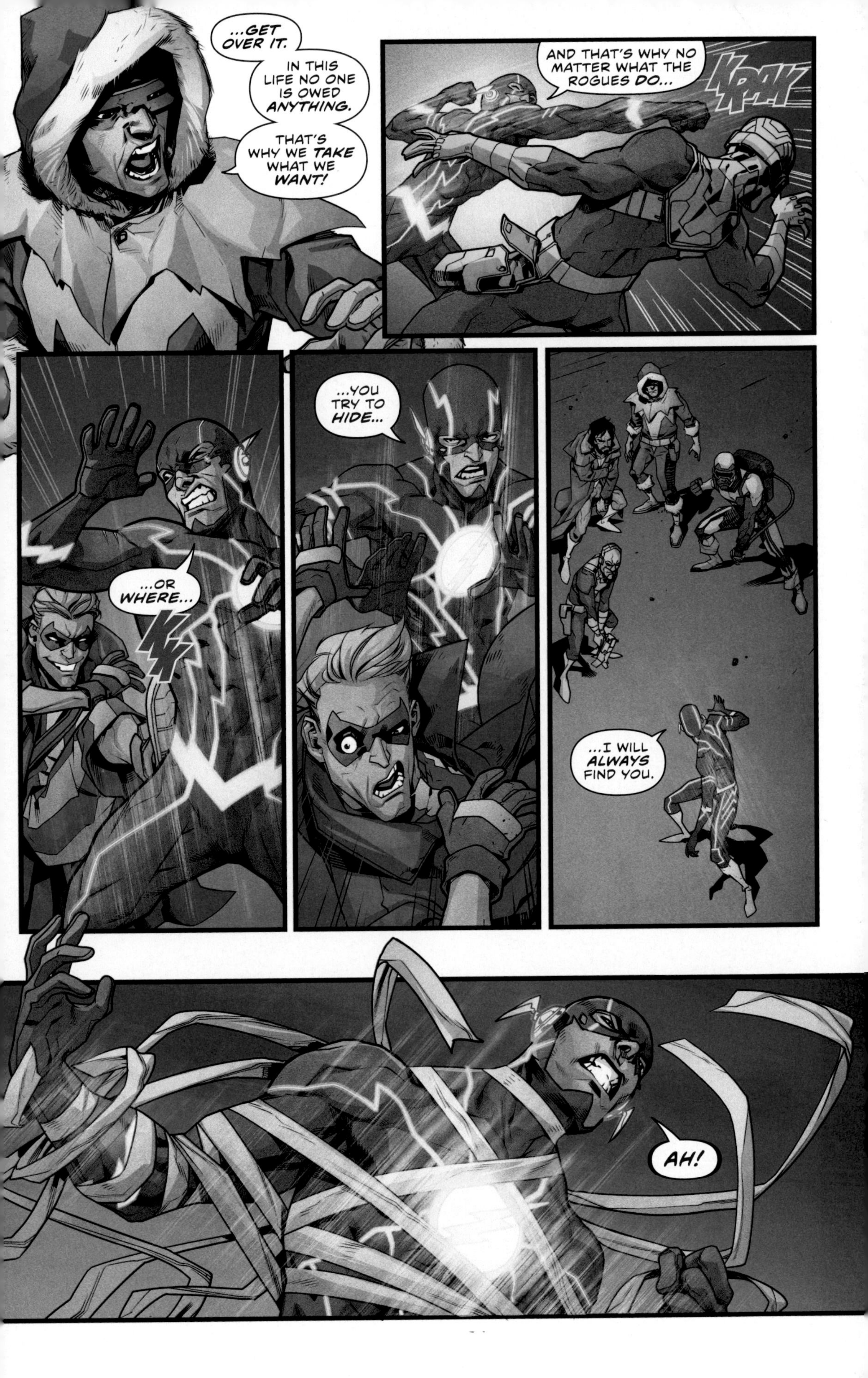
...GET OVER IT.
IN THIS LIFE NO ONE IS OWED ANYTHING.
THAT'S WHY WE TAKE WHAT WE WANT!
AND THAT'S WHY NO MATTER WHAT THE ROGUES DO...
KRAK
...OR WHERE...
KK
...YOU TRY TO HIDE...
...I WILL ALWAYS FIND YOU.
AH!

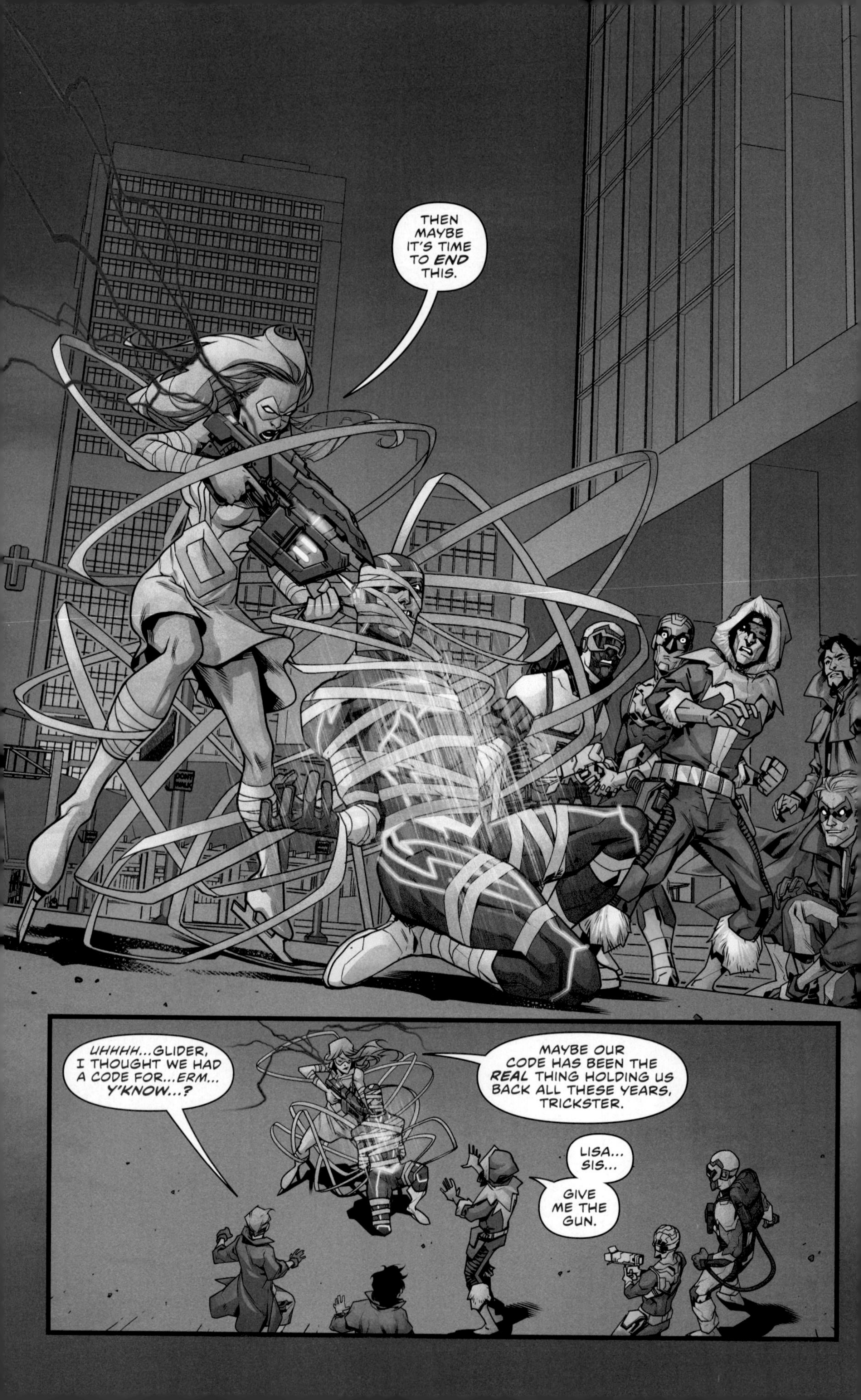
THEN MAYBE IT'S TIME TO *END* THIS.
UHHHH...GLIDER, I THOUGHT WE HAD A CODE FOR...ERM... *Y'KNOW...?*
MAYBE OUR CODE HAS BEEN THE *REAL* THING HOLDING US BACK ALL THESE YEARS, TRICKSTER.
LISA... SIS...
GIVE ME THE GUN.

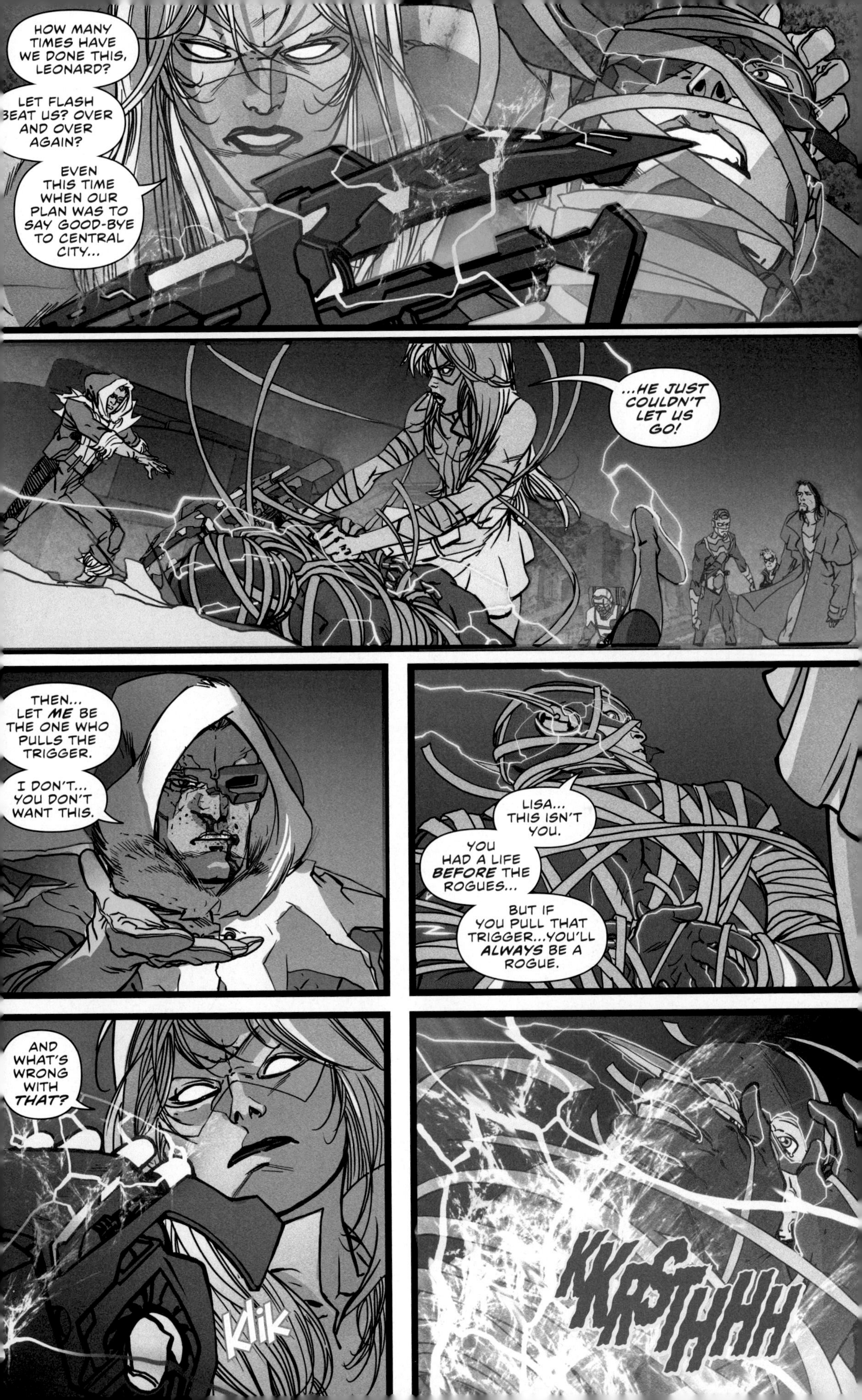
HOW MANY TIMES HAVE WE DONE THIS, LEONARD?
LET FLASH BEAT US? OVER AND OVER AGAIN?
EVEN THIS TIME WHEN OUR PLAN WAS TO SAY GOOD-BYE TO CENTRAL CITY...
...HE JUST COULDN'T LET US GO!
THEN... LET ME BE THE ONE WHO PULLS THE TRIGGER.
I DON'T... YOU DON'T WANT THIS.
LISA... THIS ISN'T YOU.
YOU HAD A LIFE BEFORE THE ROGUES...
BUT IF YOU PULL THAT TRIGGER...YOU'LL ALWAYS BE A ROGUE.
AND WHAT'S WRONG WITH THAT?
KLIK
KKRSTHHH

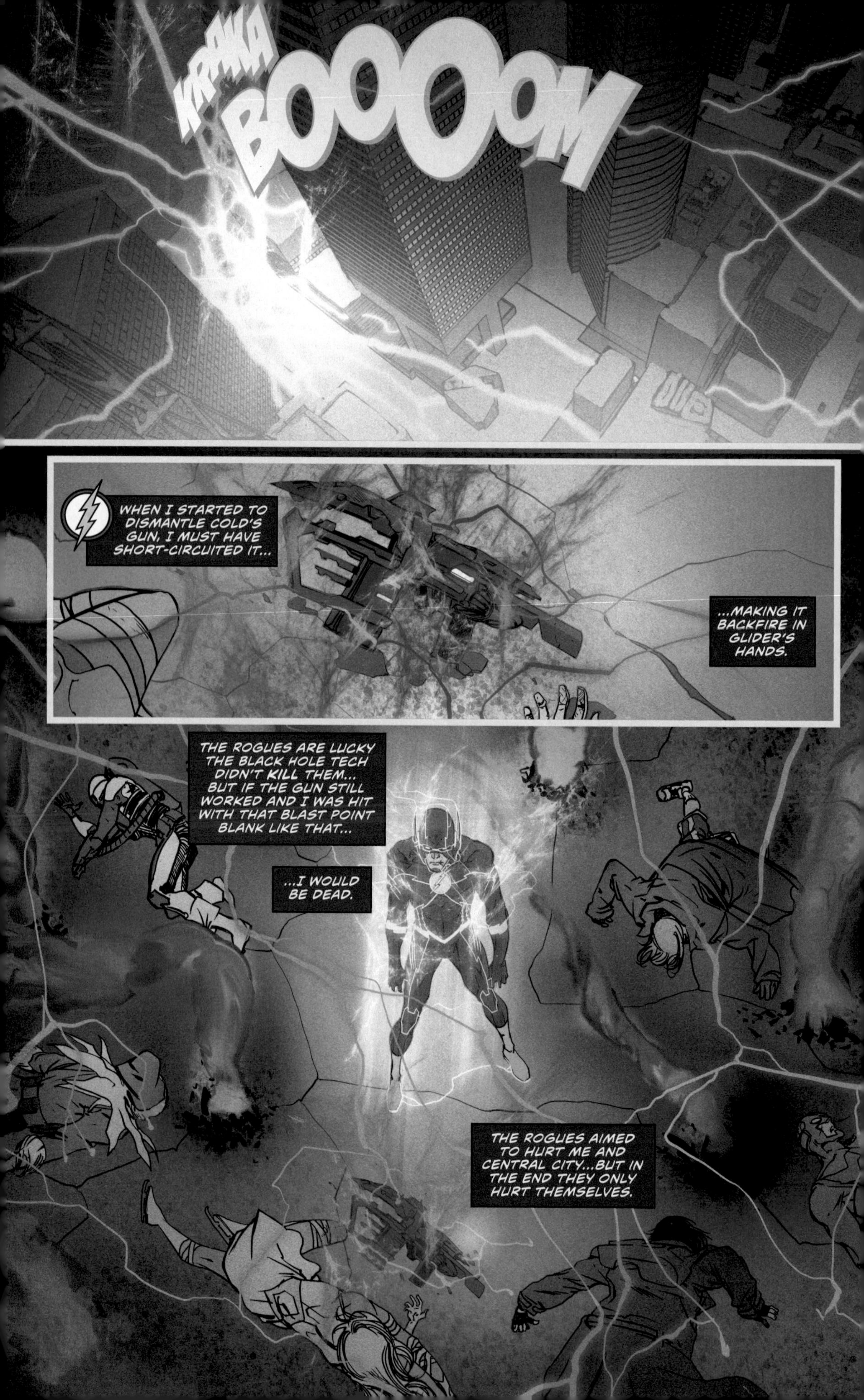
KRAKA BOOOOOM
WHEN I STARTED TO DISMANTLE COLD'S GUN, I MUST HAVE SHORT-CIRCUITED IT...
...MAKING IT BACKFIRE IN GLIDER'S HANDS.
THE ROGUES ARE LUCKY THE BLACK HOLE TECH DIDN'T KILL THEM... BUT IF THE GUN STILL WORKED AND I WAS HIT WITH THAT BLAST POINT BLANK LIKE THAT...
...I WOULD BE DEAD.
THE ROGUES AIMED TO HURT ME AND CENTRAL CITY...BUT IN THE END THEY ONLY HURT THEMSELVES.

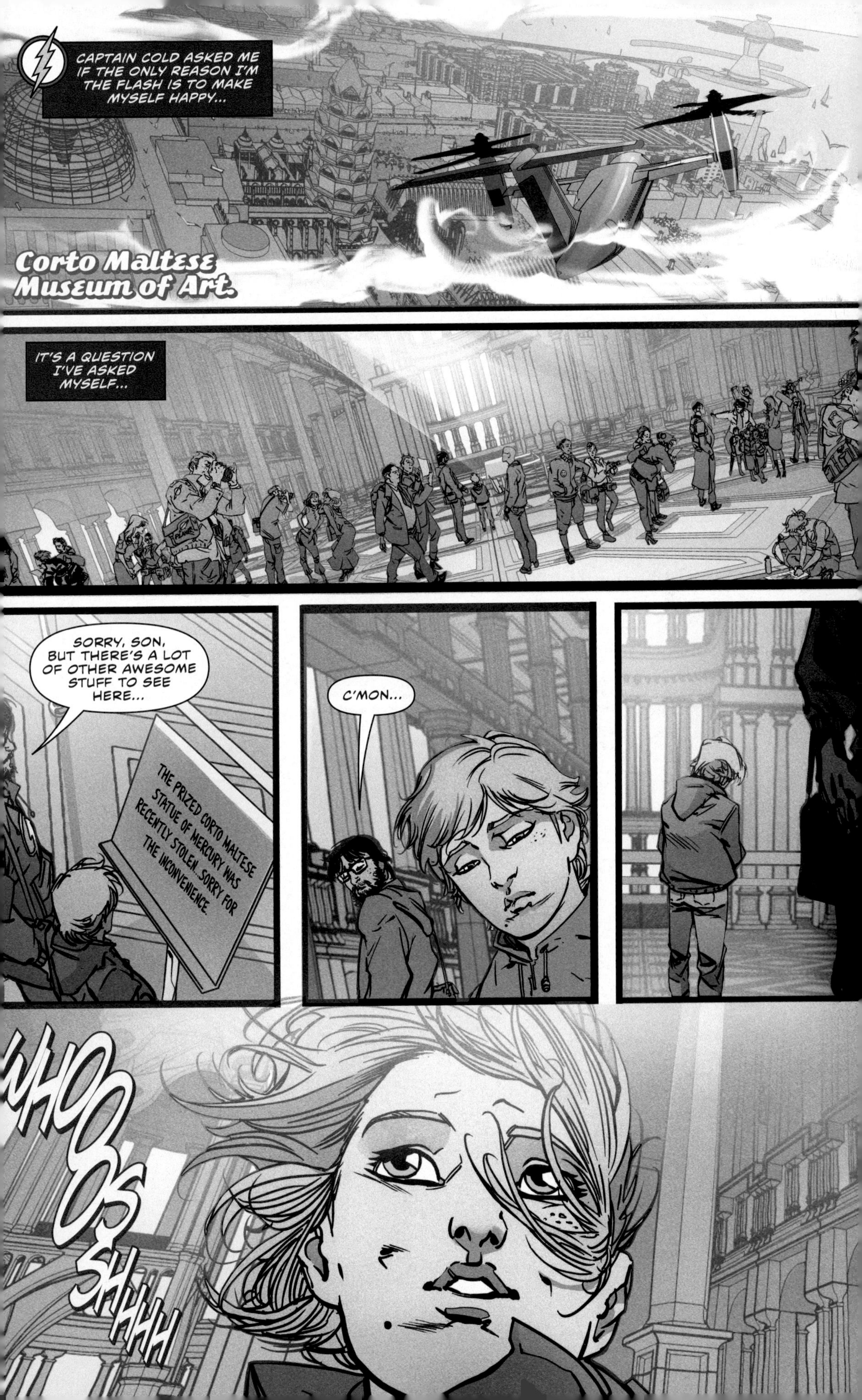
CAPTAIN COLD ASKED ME IF THE ONLY REASON I'M THE FLASH IS TO MAKE MYSELF HAPPY...
Corto Maltese Museum of Art.
IT'S A QUESTION I'VE ASKED MYSELF...
SORRY, SON, BUT THERE'S A LOT OF OTHER AWESOME STUFF TO SEE HERE...
THE PRIZED CORTO MALTESE STATUE OF MERCURY WAS RECENTLY STOLEN...SORRY FOR THE INCONVENIENCE.
C'MON...
WHOOOSHHHH

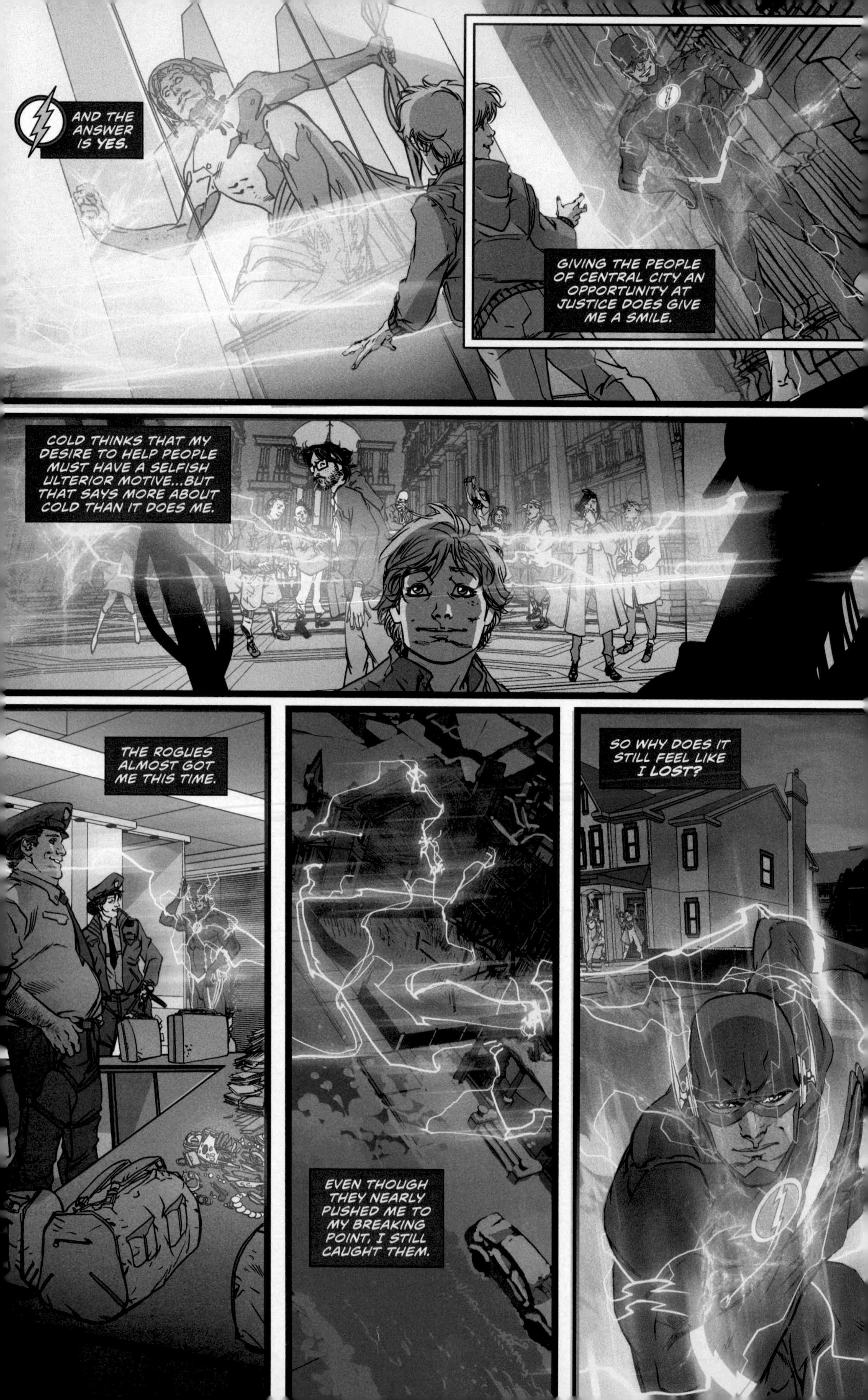
AND THE ANSWER IS YES.
GIVING THE PEOPLE OF CENTRAL CITY AN OPPORTUNITY AT JUSTICE DOES GIVE ME A SMILE.
COLD THINKS THAT MY DESIRE TO HELP PEOPLE MUST HAVE A SELFISH ULTERIOR MOTIVE...BUT THAT SAYS MORE ABOUT COLD THAN IT DOES ME.
THE ROGUES ALMOST GOT ME THIS TIME.
EVEN THOUGH THEY NEARLY PUSHED ME TO MY BREAKING POINT, I STILL CAUGHT THEM.
SO WHY DOES IT STILL FEEL LIKE I LOST?

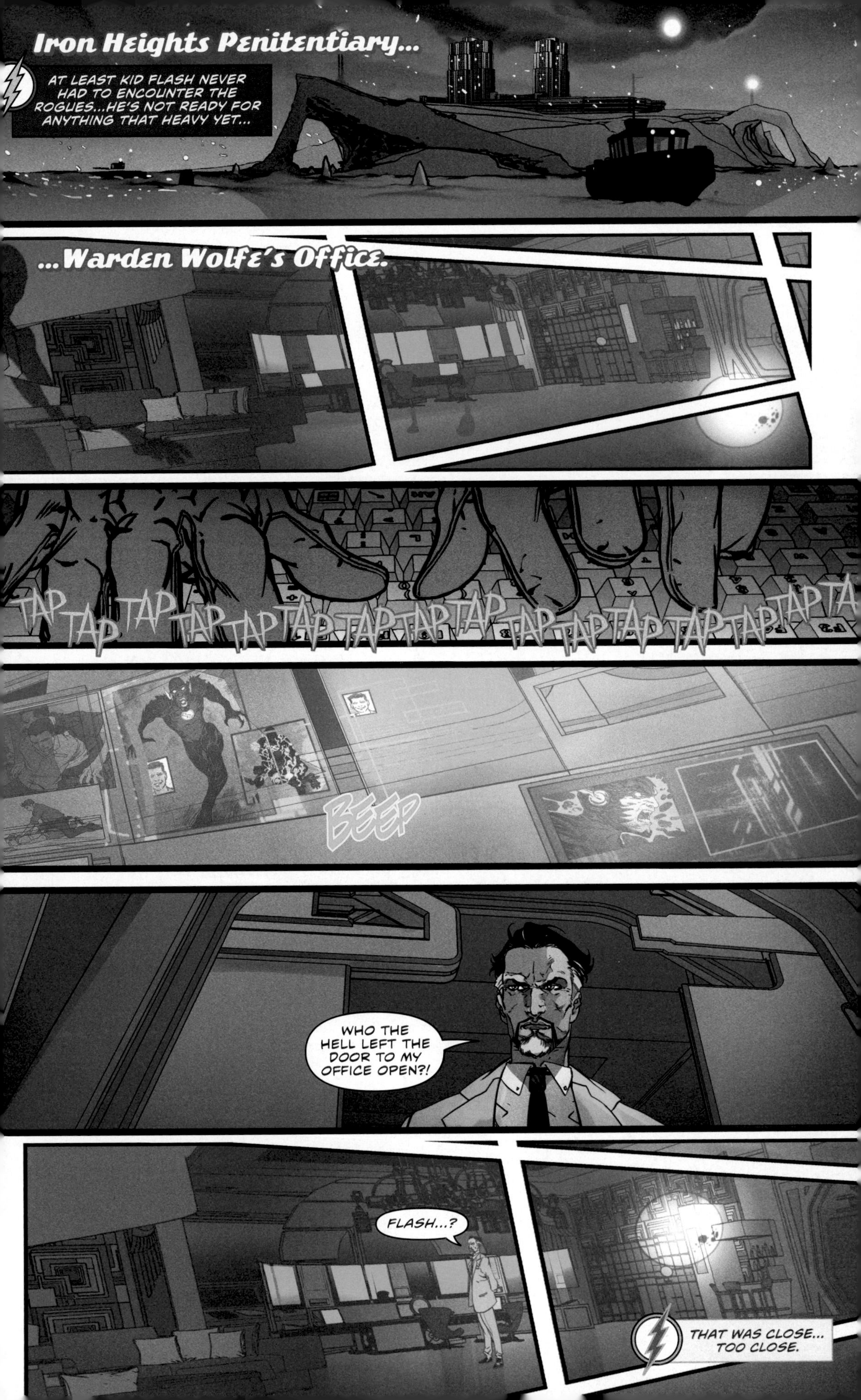
Iron Heights Penitentiary...
AT LEAST KID FLASH NEVER HAD TO ENCOUNTER THE ROGUES...HE'S NOT READY FOR ANYTHING THAT HEAVY YET...
...Warden Wolfe's Office.
TAP TAP TAP TAP TAP TAP TAP TAP TAP TAP TAP TAP TAP TAP TAP TA
BEEP
WHO THE HELL LEFT THE DOOR TO MY OFFICE OPEN?!
FLASH...?
THAT WAS CLOSE... TOO CLOSE.

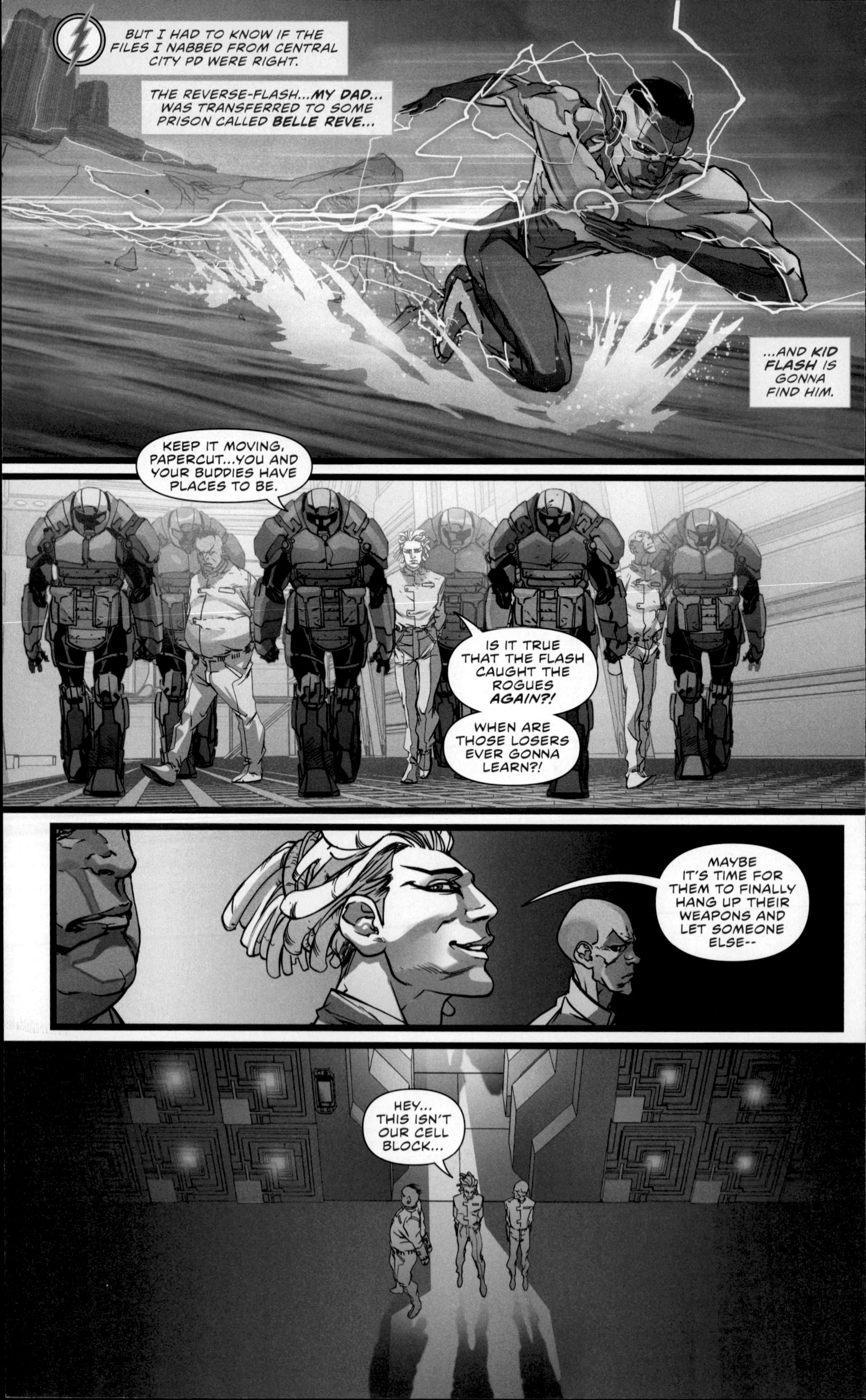
BUT I HAD TO KNOW IF THE FILES I NABBED FROM CENTRAL CITY PD WERE RIGHT.
THE REVERSE-FLASH...MY DAD... WAS TRANSFERRED TO SOME PRISON CALLED BELLE REVE...
...AND KID FLASH IS GONNA FIND HIM.
KEEP IT MOVING, PAPERCUT...YOU AND YOUR BUDDIES HAVE PLACES TO BE.
IS IT TRUE THAT THE FLASH CAUGHT THE ROGUES AGAIN?!
WHEN ARE THOSE LOSERS EVER GONNA LEARN?!
MAYBE IT'S TIME FOR THEM TO FINALLY HANG UP THEIR WEAPONS AND LET SOMEONE ELSE--
HEY... THIS ISN'T OUR CELL BLOCK...

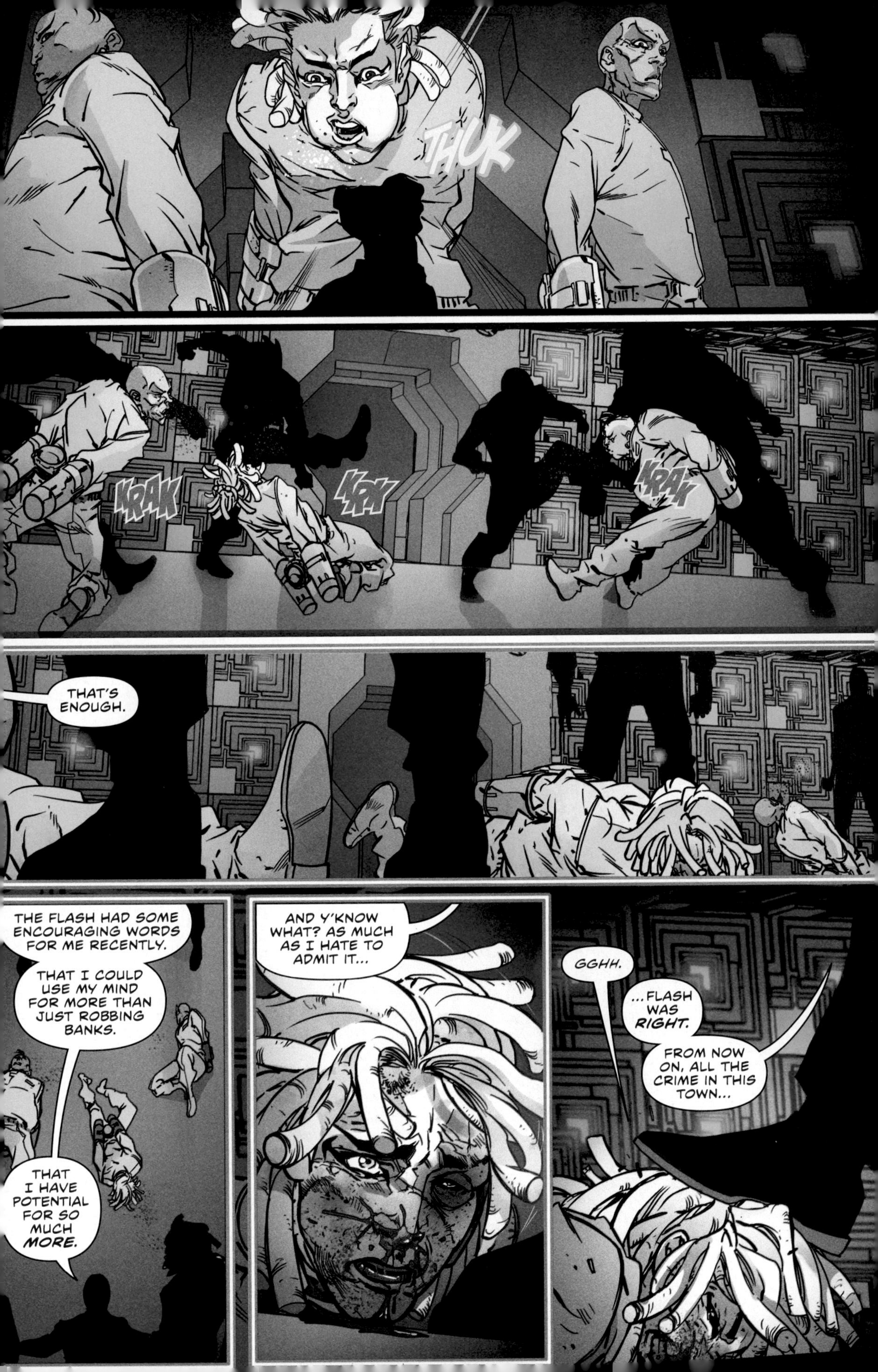
THUK
KRAK
KRAK
KRAK
THAT'S ENOUGH.
THE FLASH HAD SOME ENCOURAGING WORDS FOR ME RECENTLY.
THAT I COULD USE MY MIND FOR MORE THAN JUST ROBBING BANKS.
THAT I HAVE POTENTIAL FOR SO MUCH MORE.
AND Y'KNOW WHAT? AS MUCH AS I HATE TO ADMIT IT...
GGHH.
...FLASH WAS RIGHT.
FROM NOW ON, ALL THE CRIME IN THIS TOWN...

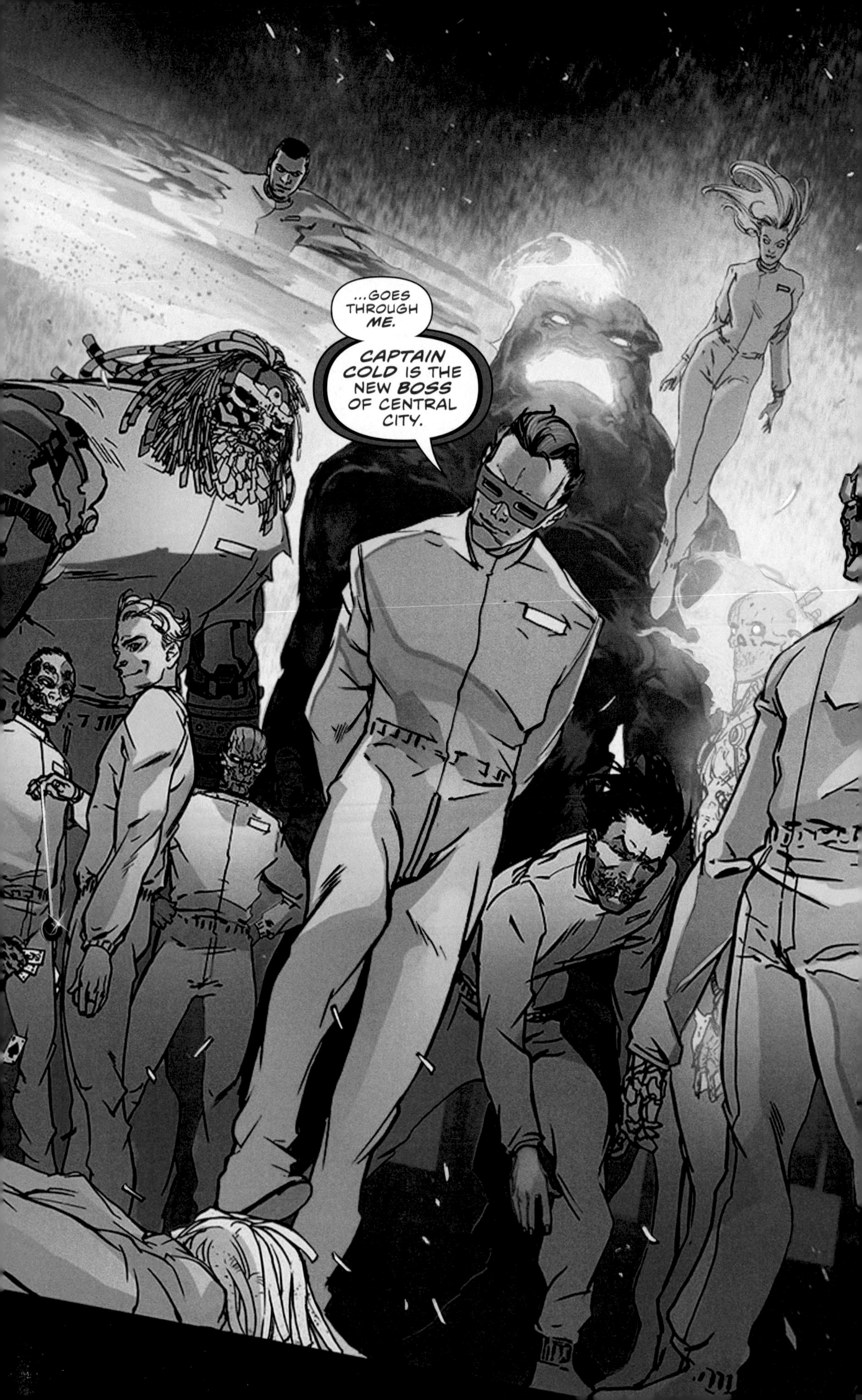
...GOES THROUGH ME.
CAPTAIN COLD IS THE NEW BOSS OF CENTRAL CITY.

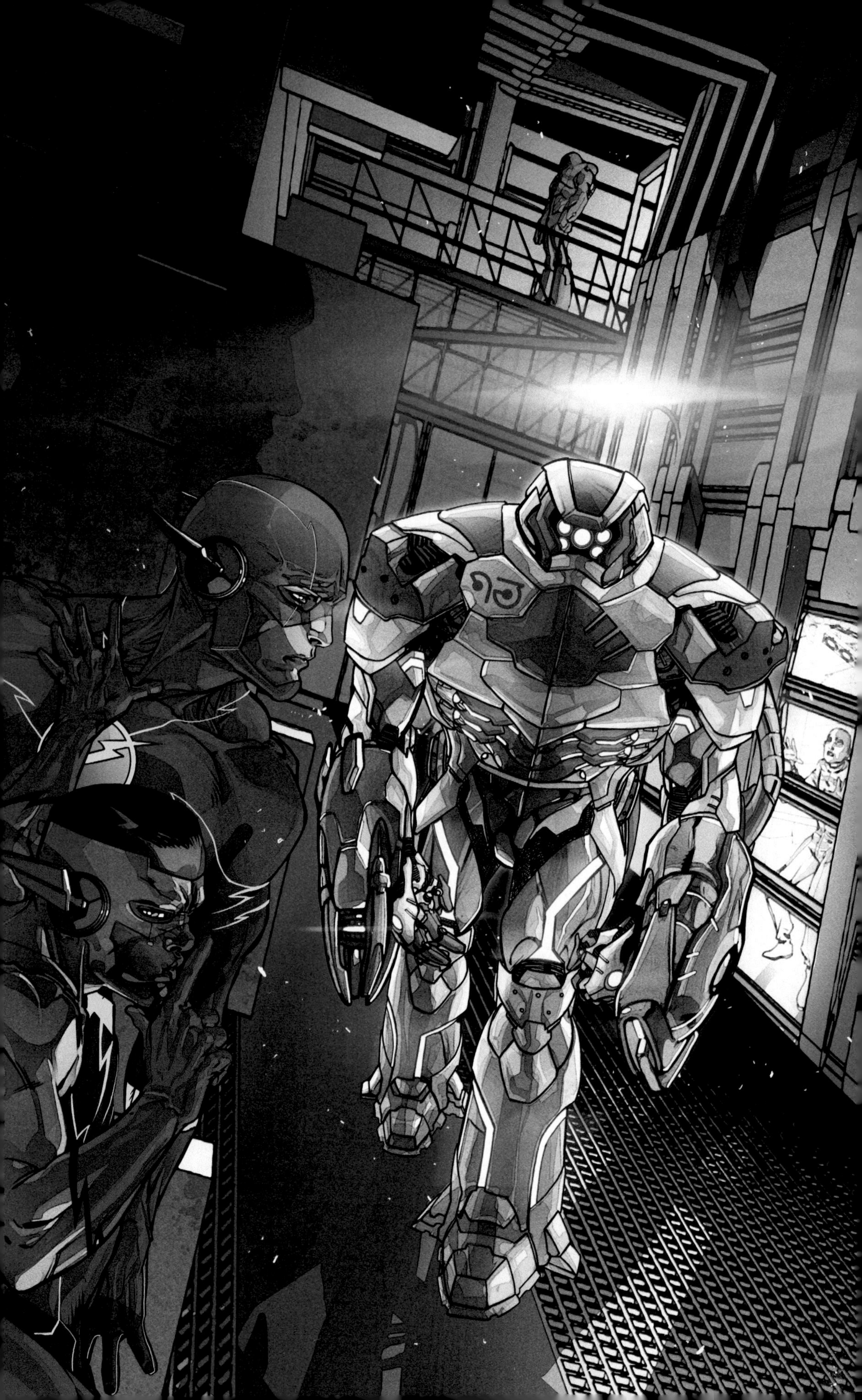

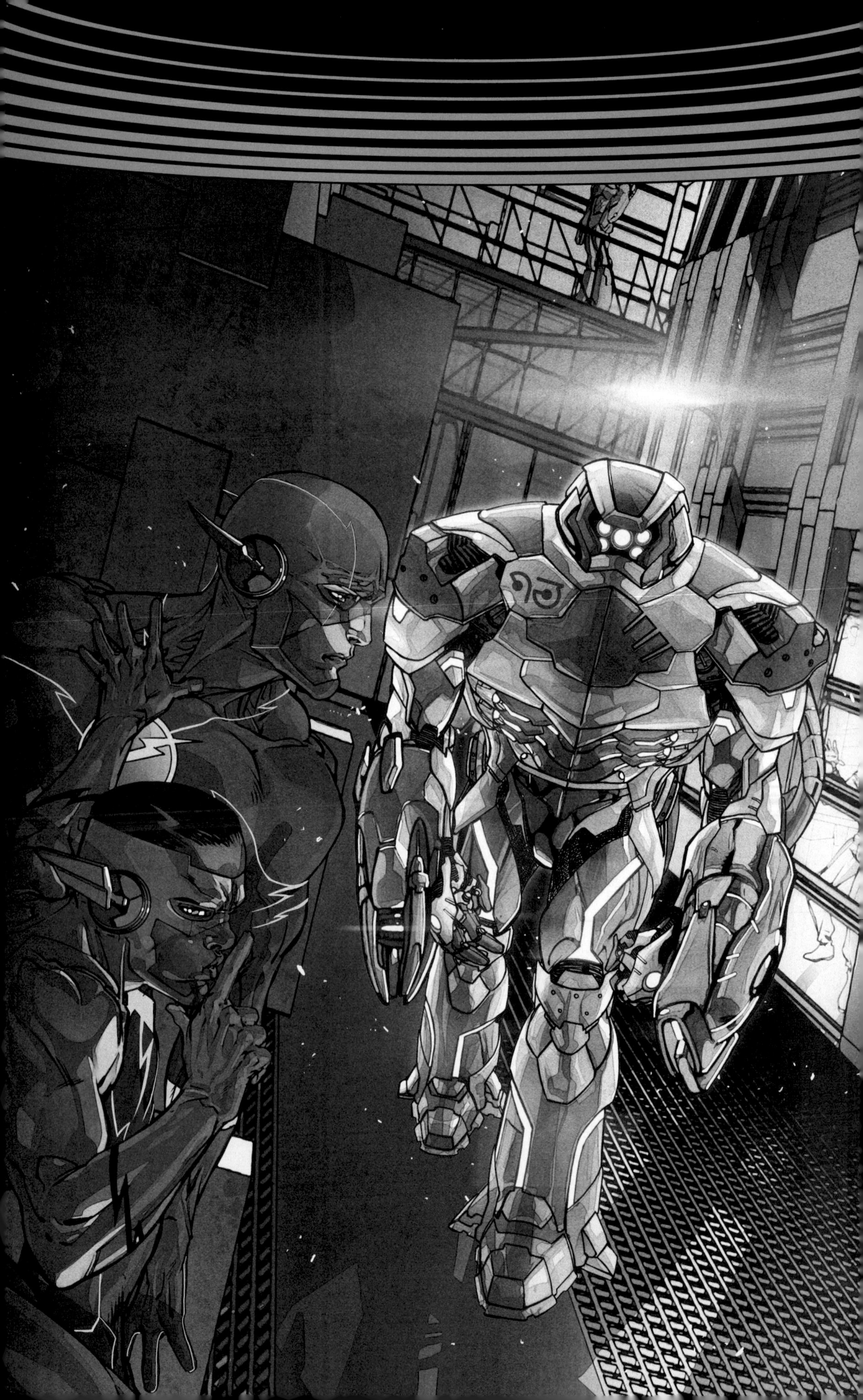

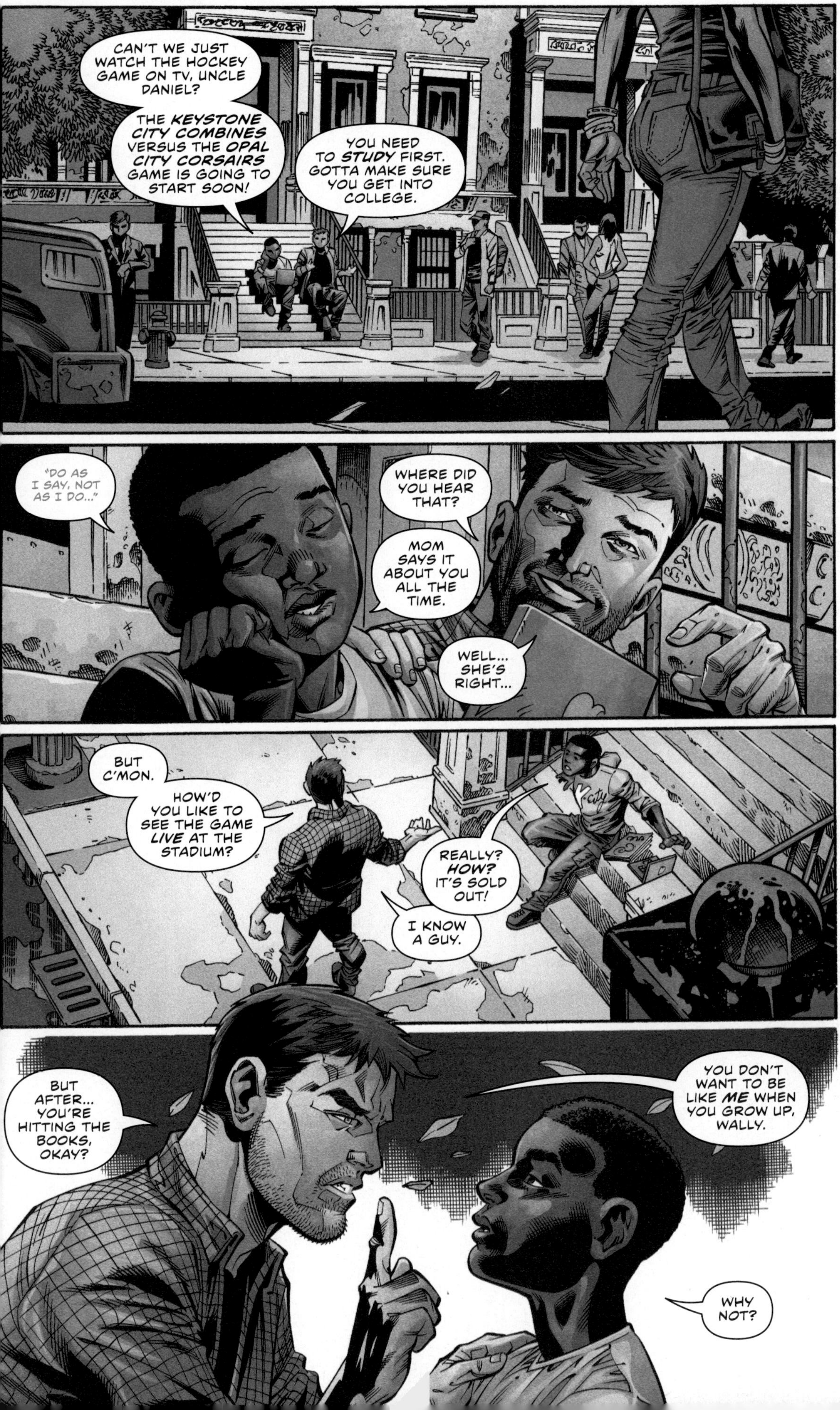
CAN'T WE JUST WATCH THE HOCKEY GAME ON TV, UNCLE DANIEL?
THE KEYSTONE CITY COMBINES VERSUS THE OPAL CITY CORSAIRS GAME IS GOING TO START SOON!
YOU NEED TO STUDY FIRST. GOTTA MAKE SURE YOU GET INTO COLLEGE.
"DO AS I SAY, NOT AS I DO..."
WHERE DID YOU HEAR THAT?
MOM SAYS IT ABOUT YOU ALL THE TIME.
WELL... SHE'S RIGHT...
BUT C'MON.
HOW'D YOU LIKE TO SEE THE GAME LIVE AT THE STADIUM?
REALLY? HOW? IT'S SOLD OUT!
I KNOW A GUY.
BUT AFTER... YOU'RE HITTING THE BOOKS, OKAY?
YOU DON'T WANT TO BE LIKE ME WHEN YOU GROW UP, WALLY.
WHY NOT?

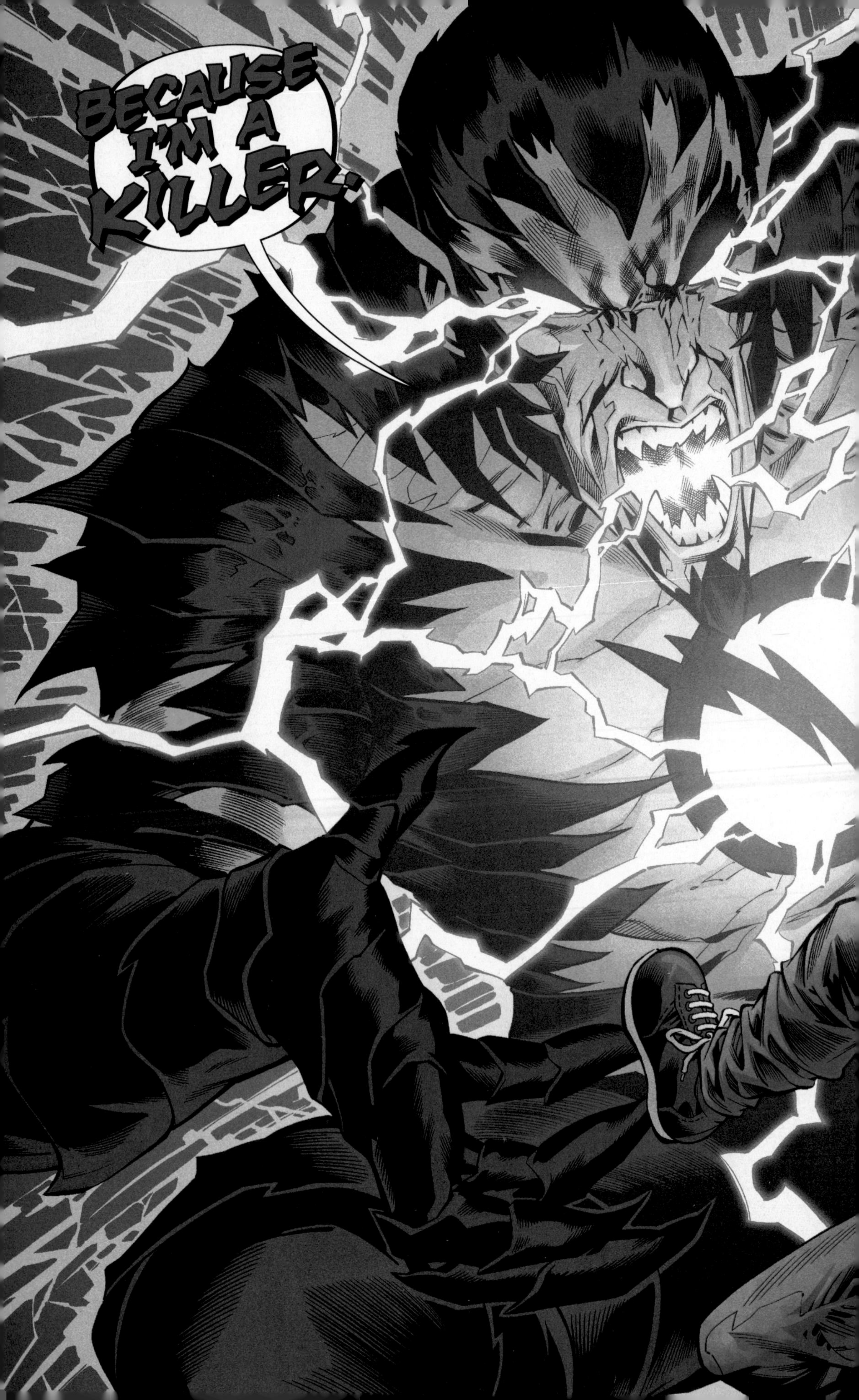
BECAUSE I'M A KILLER.

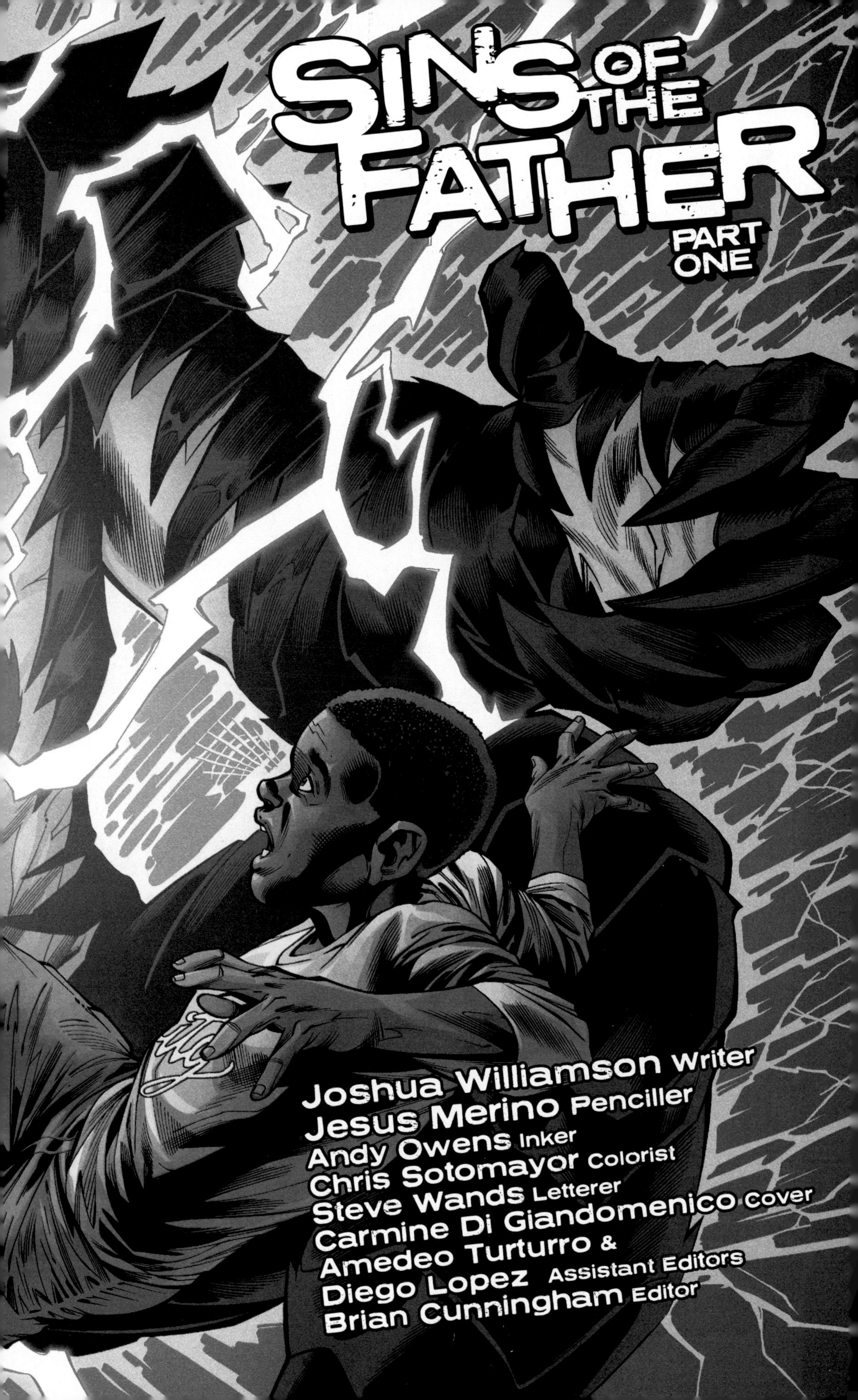
SINS OF THE FATHER
PART ONE
Joshua Williamson Writer
Jesus Merino Penciller
Andy Owens Inker
Chris Sotomayor Colorist
Steve Wands Letterer
Carmine Di Giandomenico Cover
Amedeo Turturro &
Diego Lopez Assistant Editors
Brian Cunningham Editor

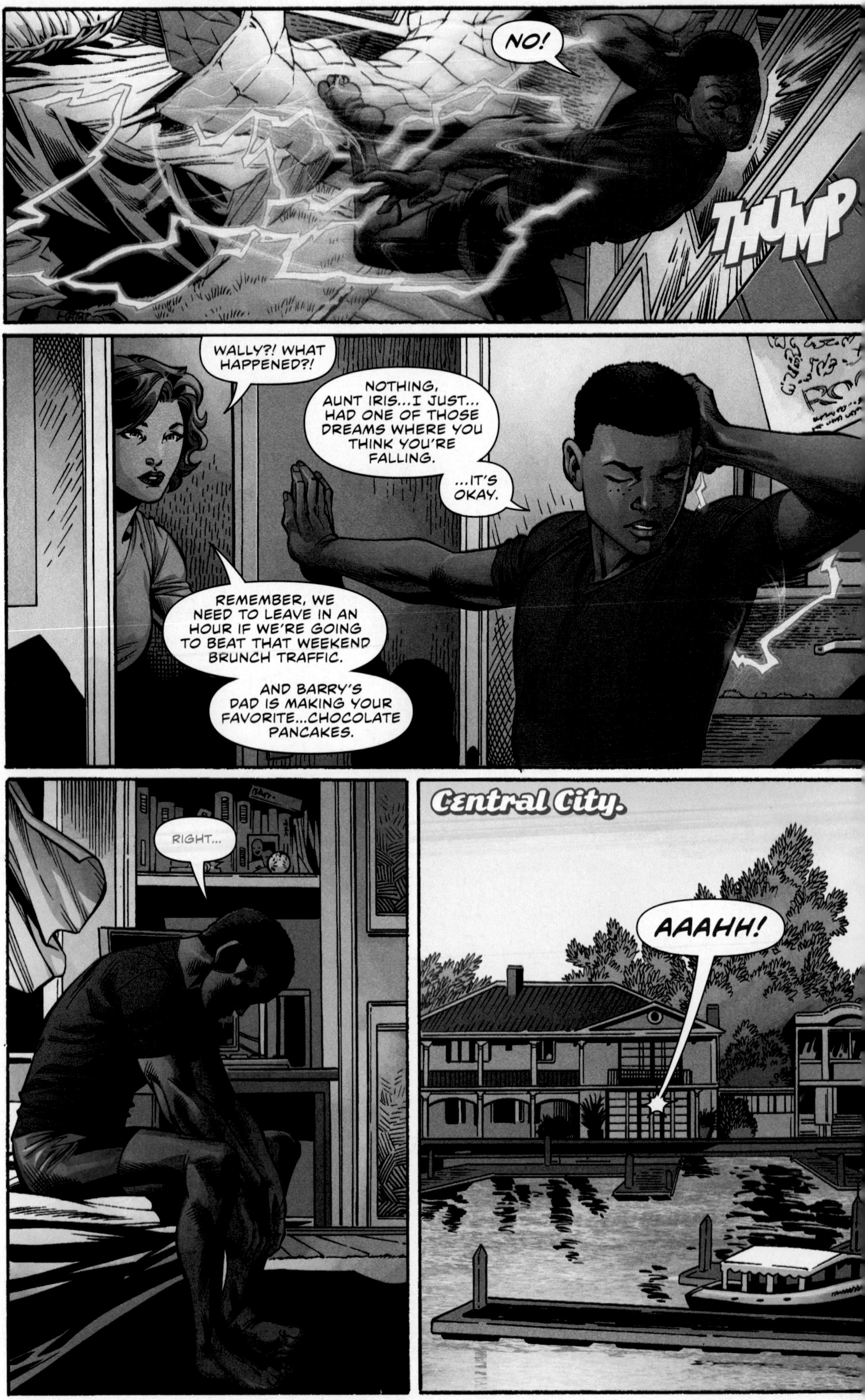
NO!
THUMP
WALLY?! WHAT HAPPENED?!
NOTHING, AUNT IRIS...I JUST... HAD ONE OF THOSE DREAMS WHERE YOU THINK YOU'RE FALLING.
...IT'S OKAY.
REMEMBER, WE NEED TO LEAVE IN AN HOUR IF WE'RE GOING TO BEAT THAT WEEKEND BRUNCH TRAFFIC.
AND BARRY'S DAD IS MAKING YOUR FAVORITE...CHOCOLATE PANCAKES.
RIGHT...
Central City.
AAAHH!

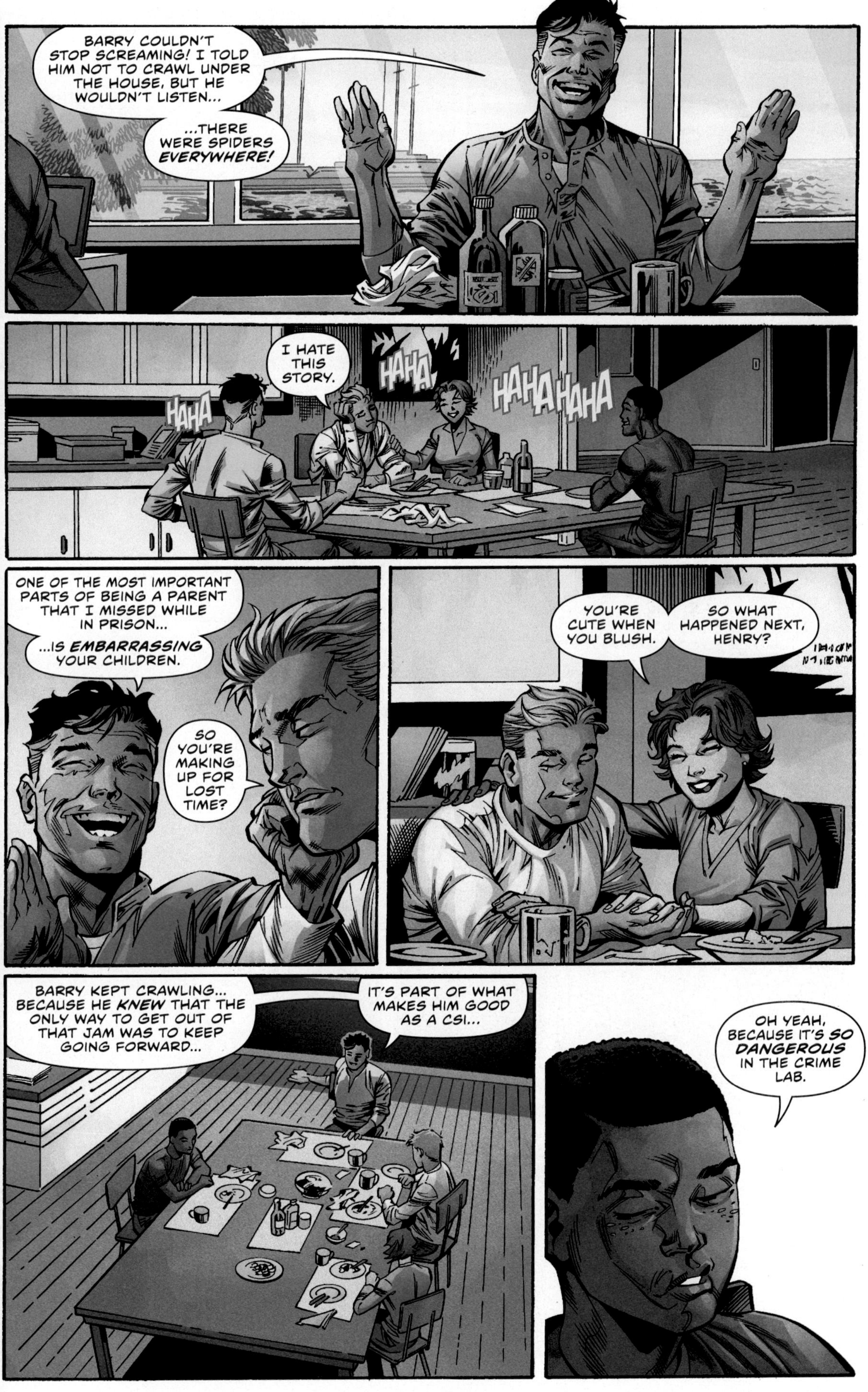
BARRY COULDN'T STOP SCREAMING! I TOLD HIM NOT TO CRAWL UNDER THE HOUSE, BUT HE WOULDN'T LISTEN...
...THERE WERE SPIDERS *EVERYWHERE!*
I HATE THIS STORY.
HAHA
HAHA
HAHAHAHA
ONE OF THE MOST IMPORTANT PARTS OF BEING A PARENT THAT I MISSED WHILE IN PRISON...
...IS *EMBARRASSING* YOUR CHILDREN.
SO YOU'RE MAKING UP FOR LOST TIME?
YOU'RE CUTE WHEN YOU BLUSH.
SO WHAT HAPPENED NEXT, HENRY?
BARRY KEPT CRAWLING... BECAUSE HE *KNEW* THAT THE ONLY WAY TO GET OUT OF THAT JAM WAS TO KEEP GOING FORWARD...
IT'S PART OF WHAT MAKES HIM GOOD AS A CSI...
OH YEAH, BECAUSE IT'S *SO DANGEROUS* IN THE CRIME LAB.

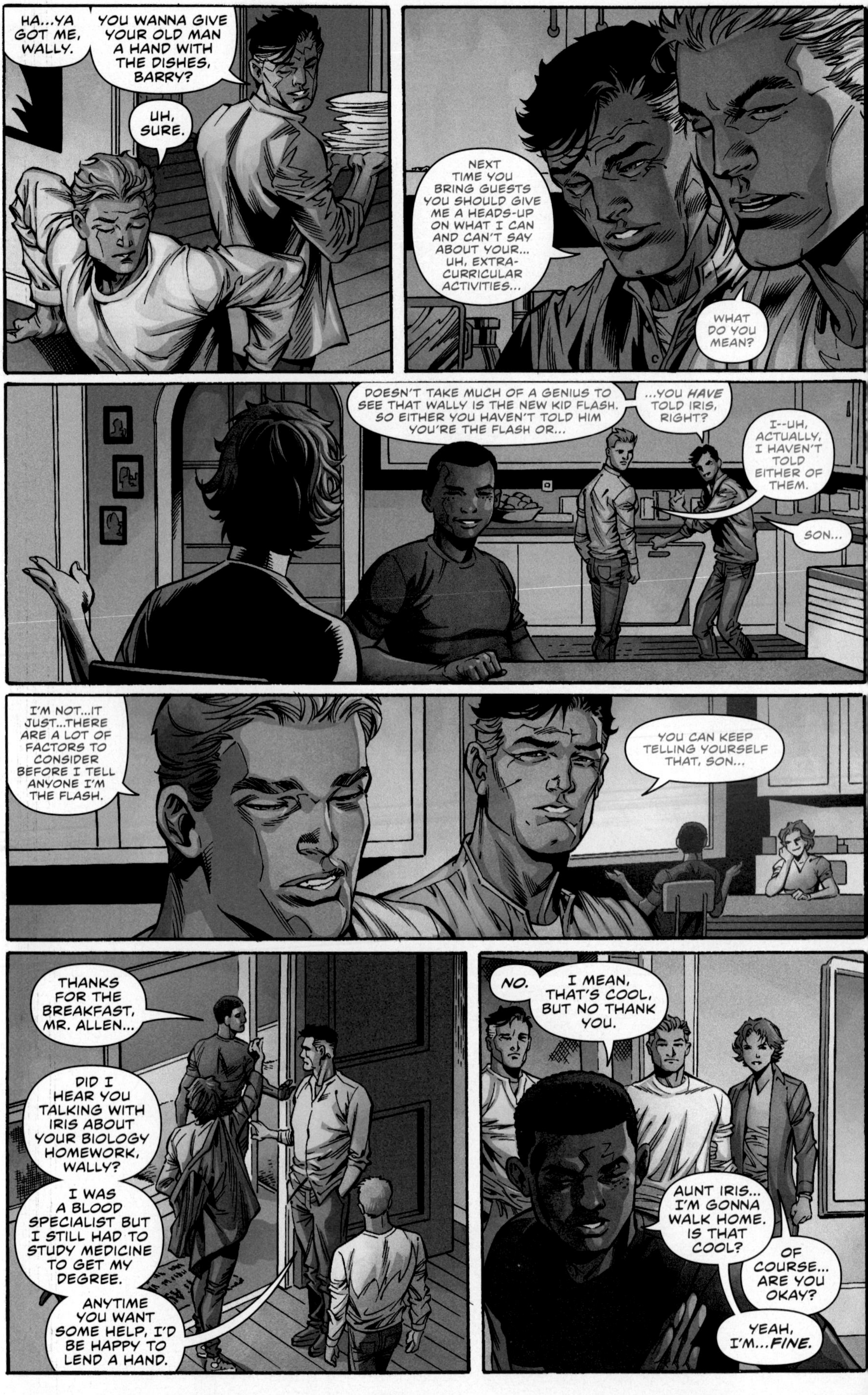
HA...YA GOT ME, WALLY.
YOU WANNA GIVE YOUR OLD MAN A HAND WITH THE DISHES, BARRY?
UH, SURE.
NEXT TIME YOU BRING GUESTS YOU SHOULD GIVE ME A HEADS-UP ON WHAT I CAN AND CAN'T SAY ABOUT YOUR...UH, EXTRA-CURRICULAR ACTIVITIES...
WHAT DO YOU MEAN?
DOESN'T TAKE MUCH OF A GENIUS TO SEE THAT WALLY IS THE NEW KID FLASH. SO EITHER YOU HAVEN'T TOLD HIM YOU'RE THE FLASH OR...
...YOU *HAVE* TOLD IRIS, RIGHT?
I--UH, ACTUALLY, I HAVEN'T TOLD EITHER OF THEM.
SON...
I'M NOT...IT JUST...THERE ARE A LOT OF FACTORS TO CONSIDER BEFORE I TELL ANYONE I'M THE FLASH.
YOU CAN KEEP TELLING YOURSELF THAT, SON...
THANKS FOR THE BREAKFAST, MR. ALLEN...
DID I HEAR YOU TALKING WITH IRIS ABOUT YOUR BIOLOGY HOMEWORK, WALLY?
I WAS A BLOOD SPECIALIST BUT I STILL HAD TO STUDY MEDICINE TO GET MY DEGREE.
ANYTIME YOU WANT SOME HELP, I'D BE HAPPY TO LEND A HAND.
NO.
I MEAN, THAT'S COOL, BUT NO THANK YOU.
AUNT IRIS... I'M GONNA WALK HOME. IS THAT COOL?
OF COURSE... ARE YOU OKAY?
YEAH, I'M...*FINE*.

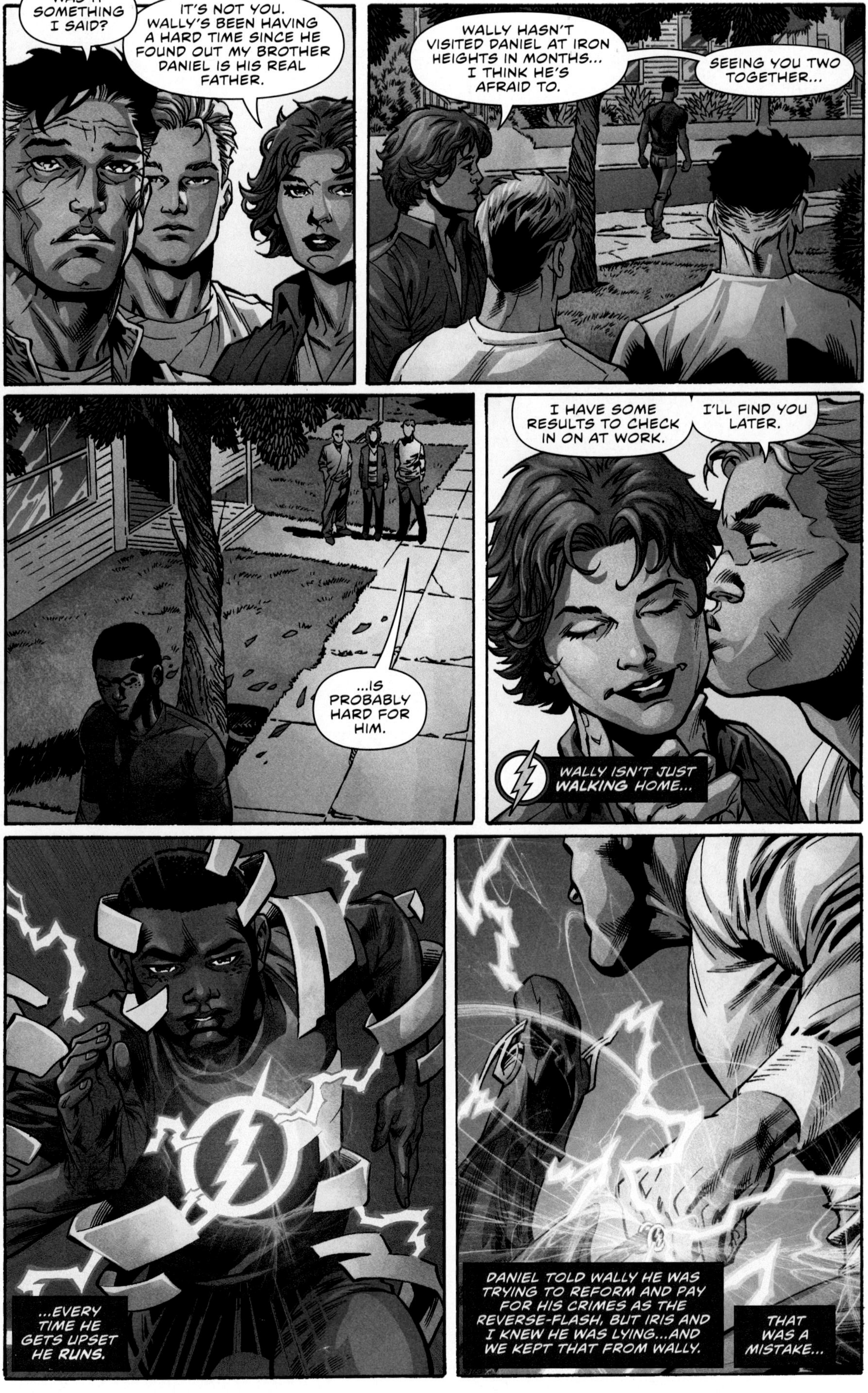
WAS IT SOMETHING I SAID?
IT'S NOT YOU. WALLY'S BEEN HAVING A HARD TIME SINCE HE FOUND OUT MY BROTHER DANIEL IS HIS REAL FATHER.
WALLY HASN'T VISITED DANIEL AT IRON HEIGHTS IN MONTHS... I THINK HE'S AFRAID TO.
SEEING YOU TWO TOGETHER...
...IS PROBABLY HARD FOR HIM.
I HAVE SOME RESULTS TO CHECK IN ON AT WORK.
I'LL FIND YOU LATER.
WALLY ISN'T JUST WALKING HOME...
...EVERY TIME HE GETS UPSET HE RUNS.
DANIEL TOLD WALLY HE WAS TRYING TO REFORM AND PAY FOR HIS CRIMES AS THE REVERSE-FLASH, BUT IRIS AND I KNEW HE WAS LYING...AND WE KEPT THAT FROM WALLY.
THAT WAS A MISTAKE...

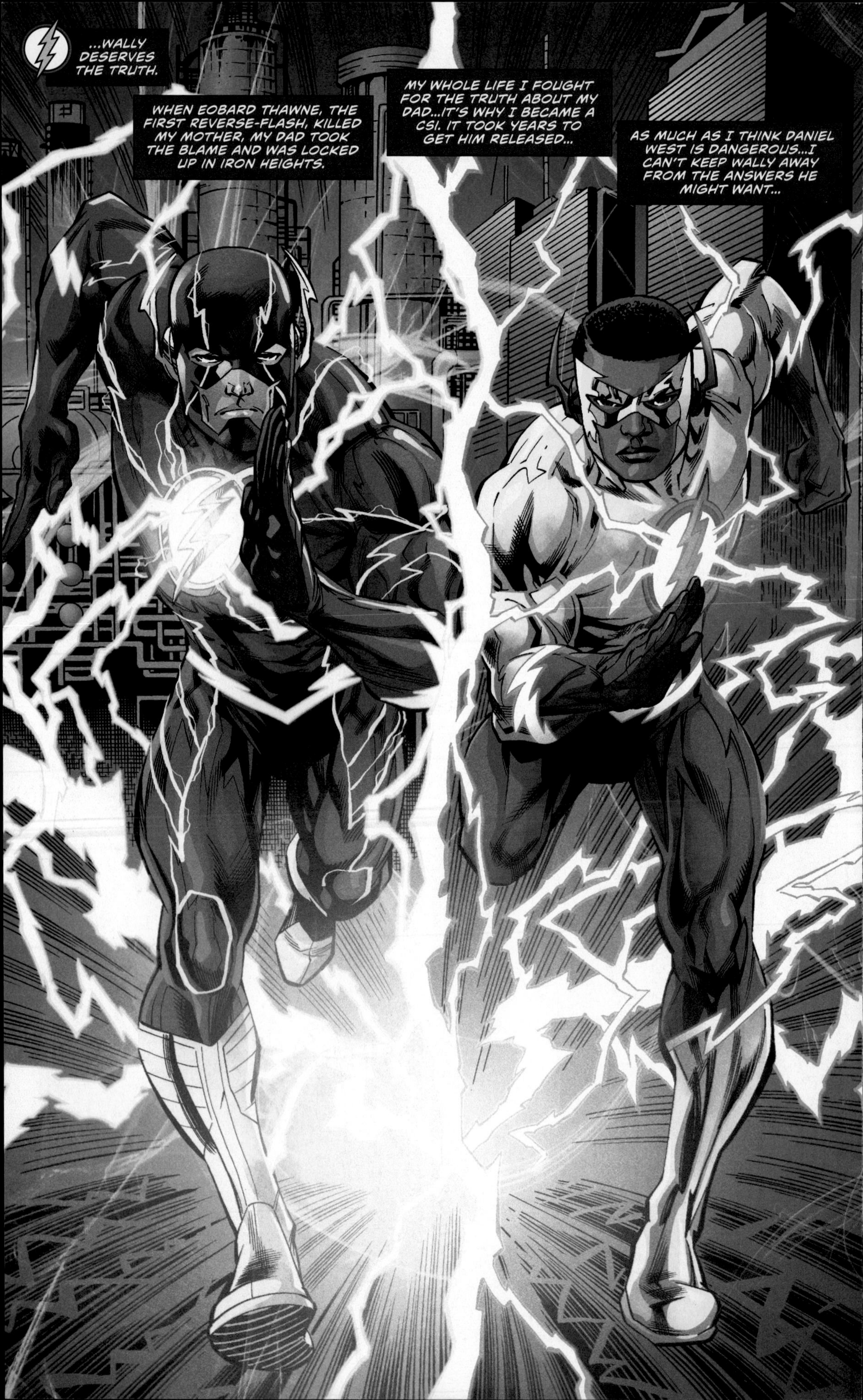
...WALLY DESERVES THE TRUTH.
WHEN EOBARD THAWNE, THE FIRST REVERSE-FLASH, KILLED MY MOTHER, MY DAD TOOK THE BLAME AND WAS LOCKED UP IN IRON HEIGHTS.
MY WHOLE LIFE I FOUGHT FOR THE TRUTH ABOUT MY DAD...IT'S WHY I BECAME A CSI. IT TOOK YEARS TO GET HIM RELEASED...
AS MUCH AS I THINK DANIEL WEST IS DANGEROUS...I CAN'T KEEP WALLY AWAY FROM THE ANSWERS HE MIGHT WANT...

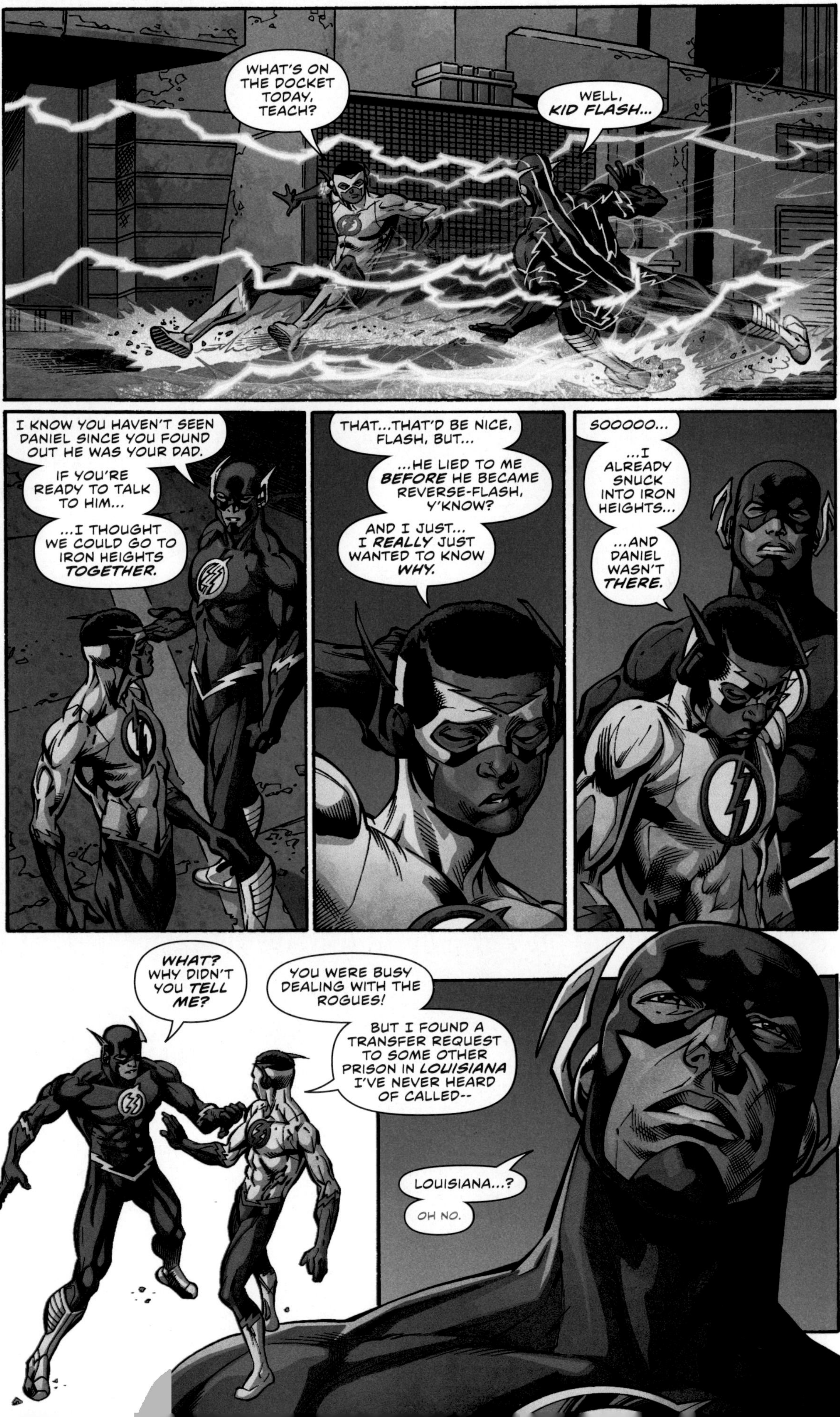
WHAT'S ON THE DOCKET TODAY, TEACH?
WELL, KID FLASH...
I KNOW YOU HAVEN'T SEEN DANIEL SINCE YOU FOUND OUT HE WAS YOUR DAD.
IF YOU'RE READY TO TALK TO HIM...
...I THOUGHT WE COULD GO TO IRON HEIGHTS TOGETHER.
THAT...THAT'D BE NICE, FLASH, BUT...
...HE LIED TO ME BEFORE HE BECAME REVERSE-FLASH, Y'KNOW?
AND I JUST... I REALLY JUST WANTED TO KNOW WHY.
SOOOOO...
...I ALREADY SNUCK INTO IRON HEIGHTS...
...AND DANIEL WASN'T THERE.
WHAT? WHY DIDN'T YOU TELL ME?
YOU WERE BUSY DEALING WITH THE ROGUES!
BUT I FOUND A TRANSFER REQUEST TO SOME OTHER PRISON IN LOUISIANA I'VE NEVER HEARD OF CALLED--
LOUISIANA...?
OH NO.

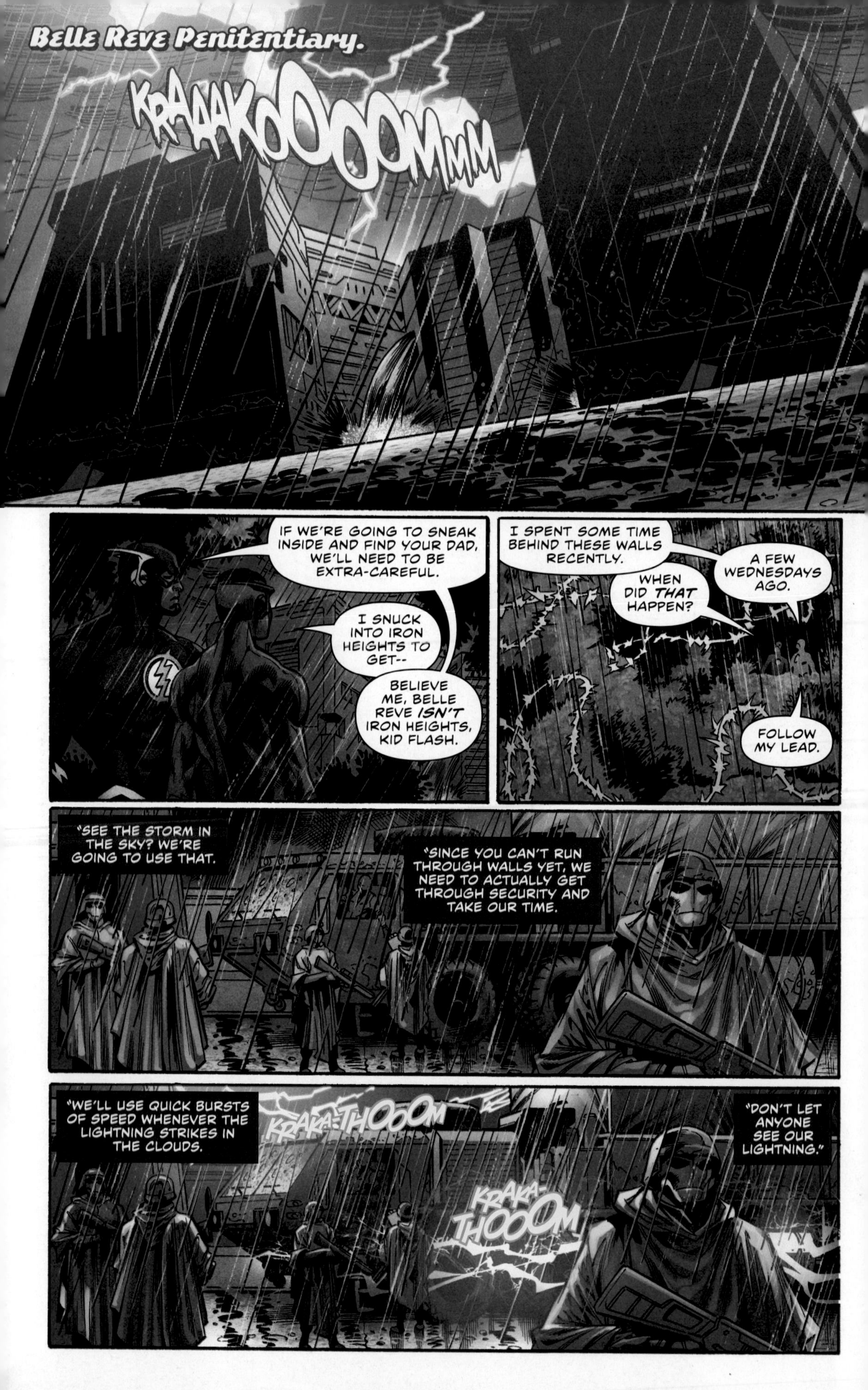
Belle Reve Penitentiary.
KRAAAKOOOOMMM
IF WE'RE GOING TO SNEAK INSIDE AND FIND YOUR DAD, WE'LL NEED TO BE EXTRA-CAREFUL.
I SNUCK INTO IRON HEIGHTS TO GET--
BELIEVE ME, BELLE REVE ISN'T IRON HEIGHTS, KID FLASH.
I SPENT SOME TIME BEHIND THESE WALLS RECENTLY.
WHEN DID THAT HAPPEN?
A FEW WEDNESDAYS AGO.
FOLLOW MY LEAD.
"SEE THE STORM IN THE SKY? WE'RE GOING TO USE THAT.
"SINCE YOU CAN'T RUN THROUGH WALLS YET, WE NEED TO ACTUALLY GET THROUGH SECURITY AND TAKE OUR TIME.
"WE'LL USE QUICK BURSTS OF SPEED WHENEVER THE LIGHTNING STRIKES IN THE CLOUDS.
KRAKA-THOOOM
KRAKA-THOOOM
"DON'T LET ANYONE SEE OUR LIGHTNING."

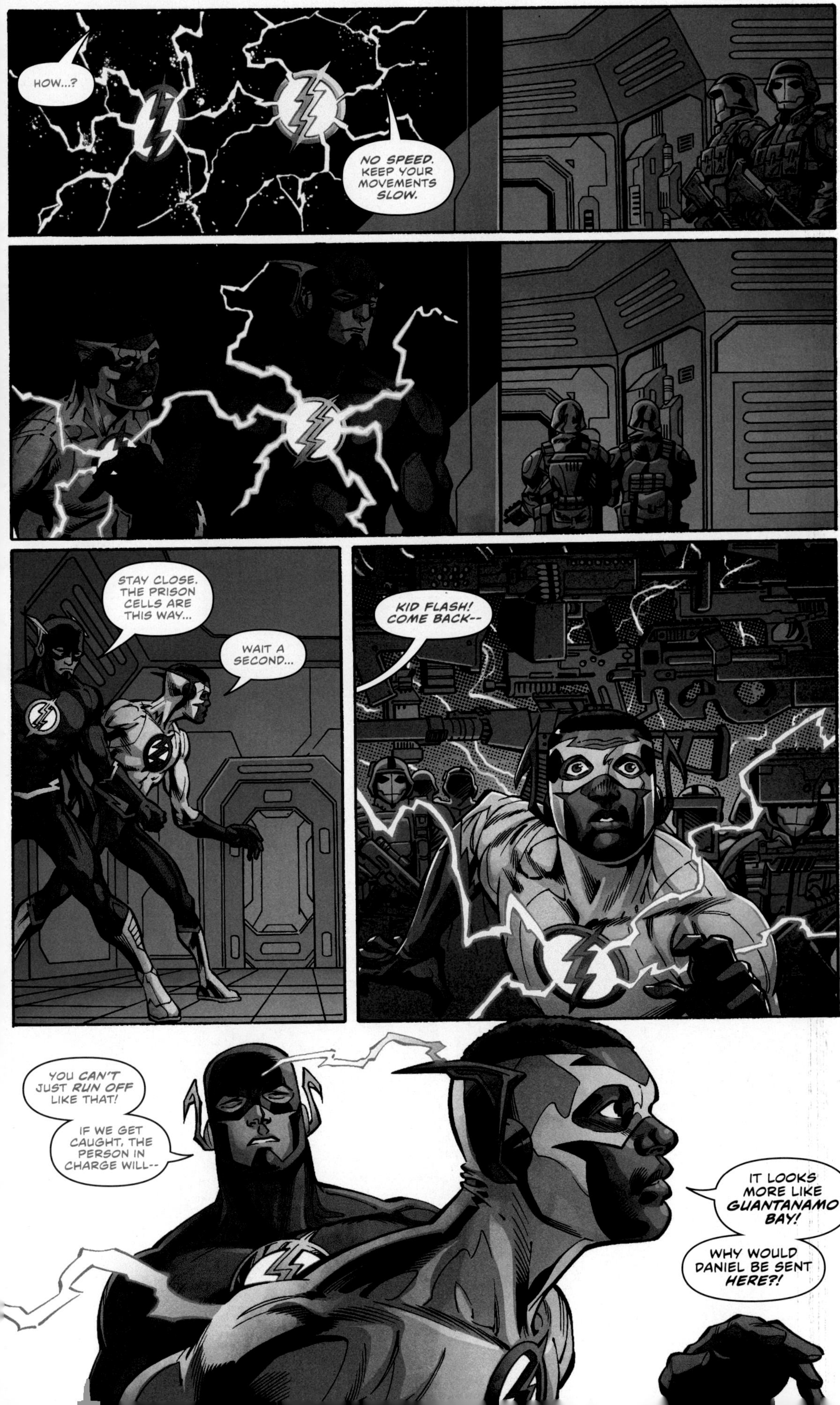
HOW...?
NO SPEED. KEEP YOUR MOVEMENTS SLOW.
STAY CLOSE. THE PRISON CELLS ARE THIS WAY...
WAIT A SECOND...
KID FLASH! COME BACK--
YOU CAN'T JUST RUN OFF LIKE THAT!
IF WE GET CAUGHT, THE PERSON IN CHARGE WILL--
IT LOOKS MORE LIKE GUANTANAMO BAY!
WHY WOULD DANIEL BE SENT HERE?!

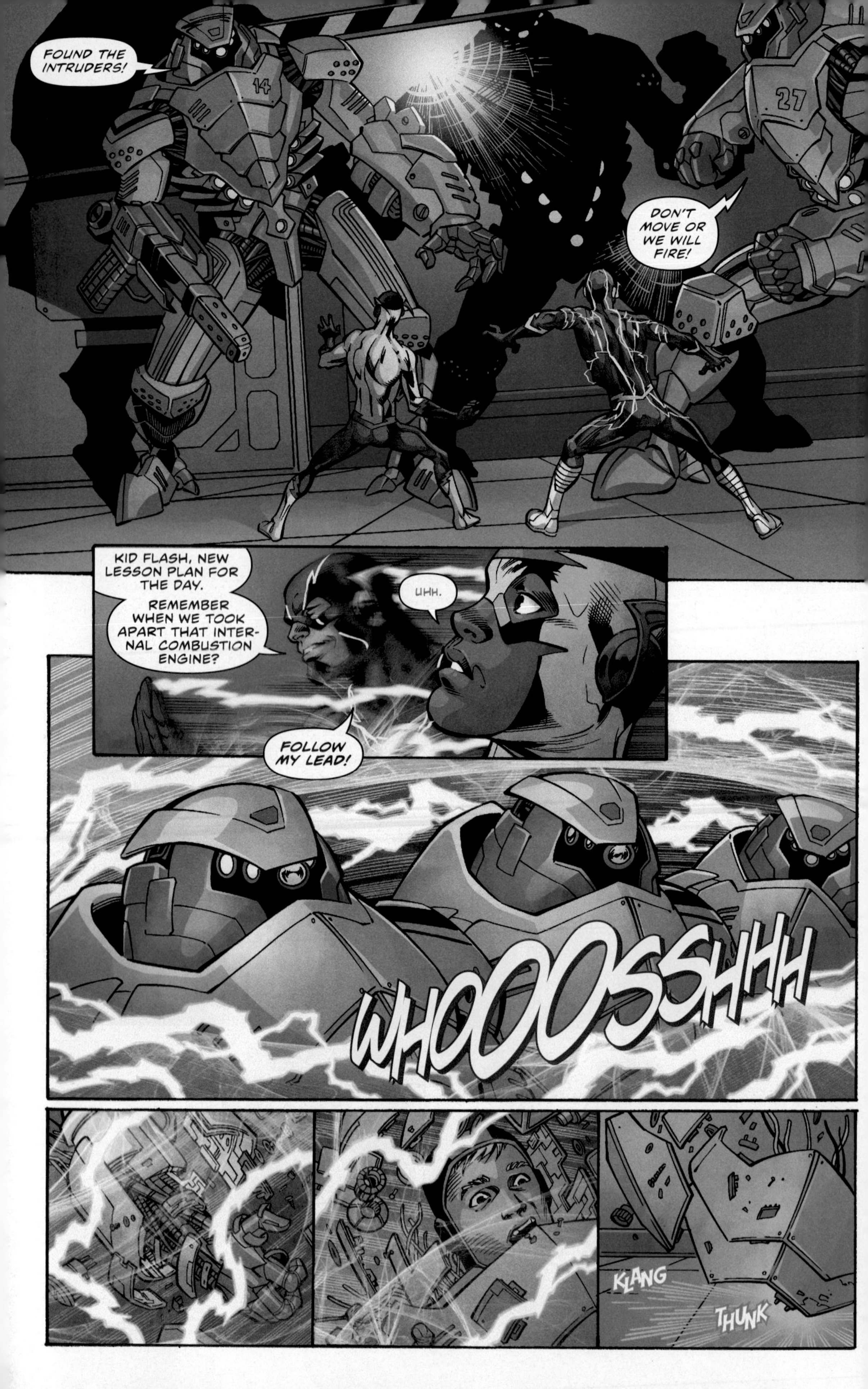
FOUND THE INTRUDERS!
DON'T MOVE OR WE WILL FIRE!
KID FLASH, NEW LESSON PLAN FOR THE DAY.
REMEMBER WHEN WE TOOK APART THAT INTERNAL COMBUSTION ENGINE?
UHH.
FOLLOW MY LEAD!
WHOOOOSSHHH
KLANG
THUNK

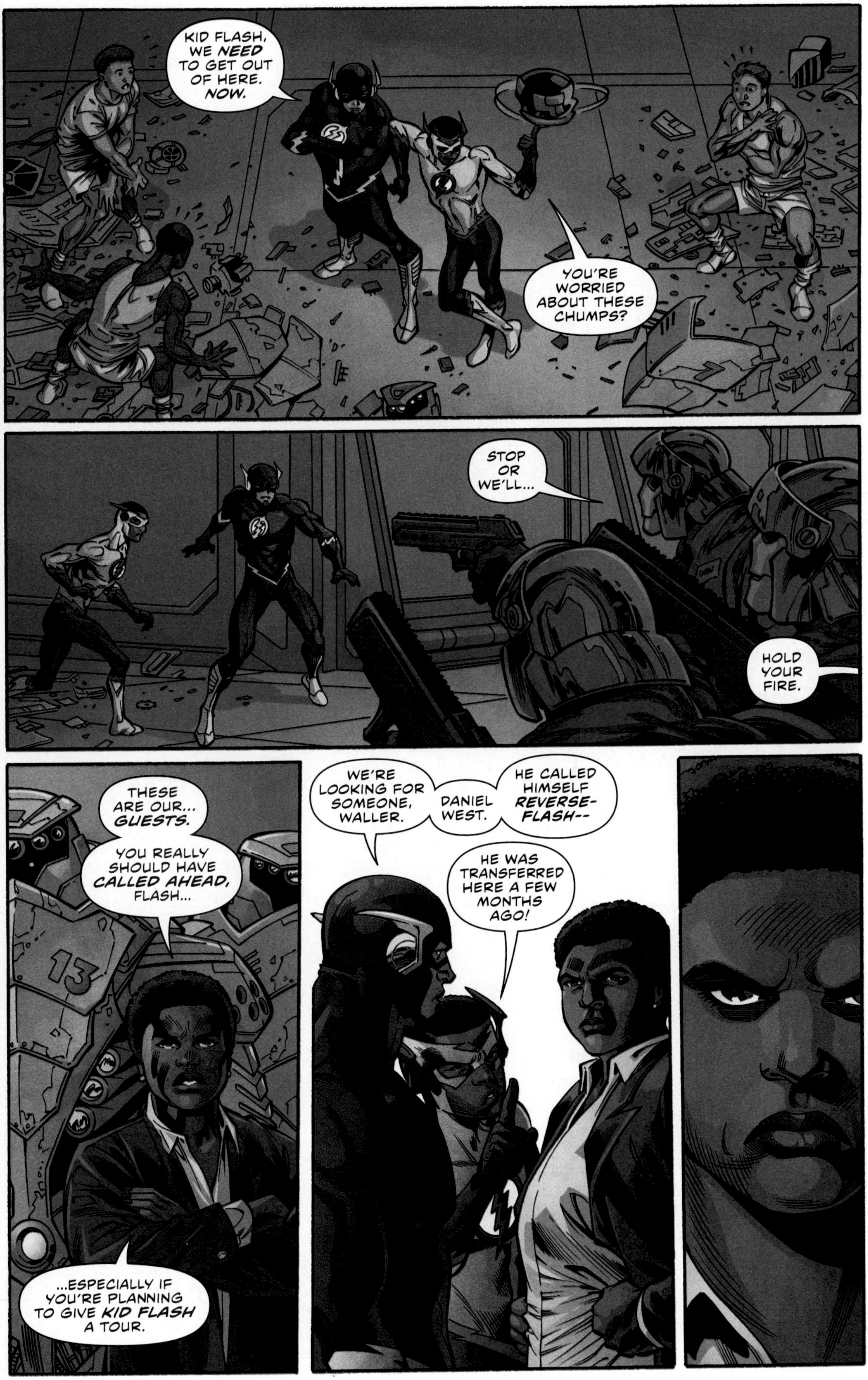
KID FLASH, WE *NEED* TO GET OUT OF HERE. *NOW.*
YOU'RE WORRIED ABOUT THESE CHUMPS?
STOP OR WE'LL...
HOLD YOUR FIRE.
THESE ARE OUR... *GUESTS.*
YOU REALLY SHOULD HAVE *CALLED AHEAD,* FLASH...
...ESPECIALLY IF YOU'RE PLANNING TO GIVE *KID FLASH* A TOUR.
WE'RE LOOKING FOR SOMEONE, WALLER.
DANIEL WEST.
HE CALLED HIMSELF *REVERSE-FLASH--*
HE WAS TRANSFERRED HERE A FEW MONTHS AGO!
13

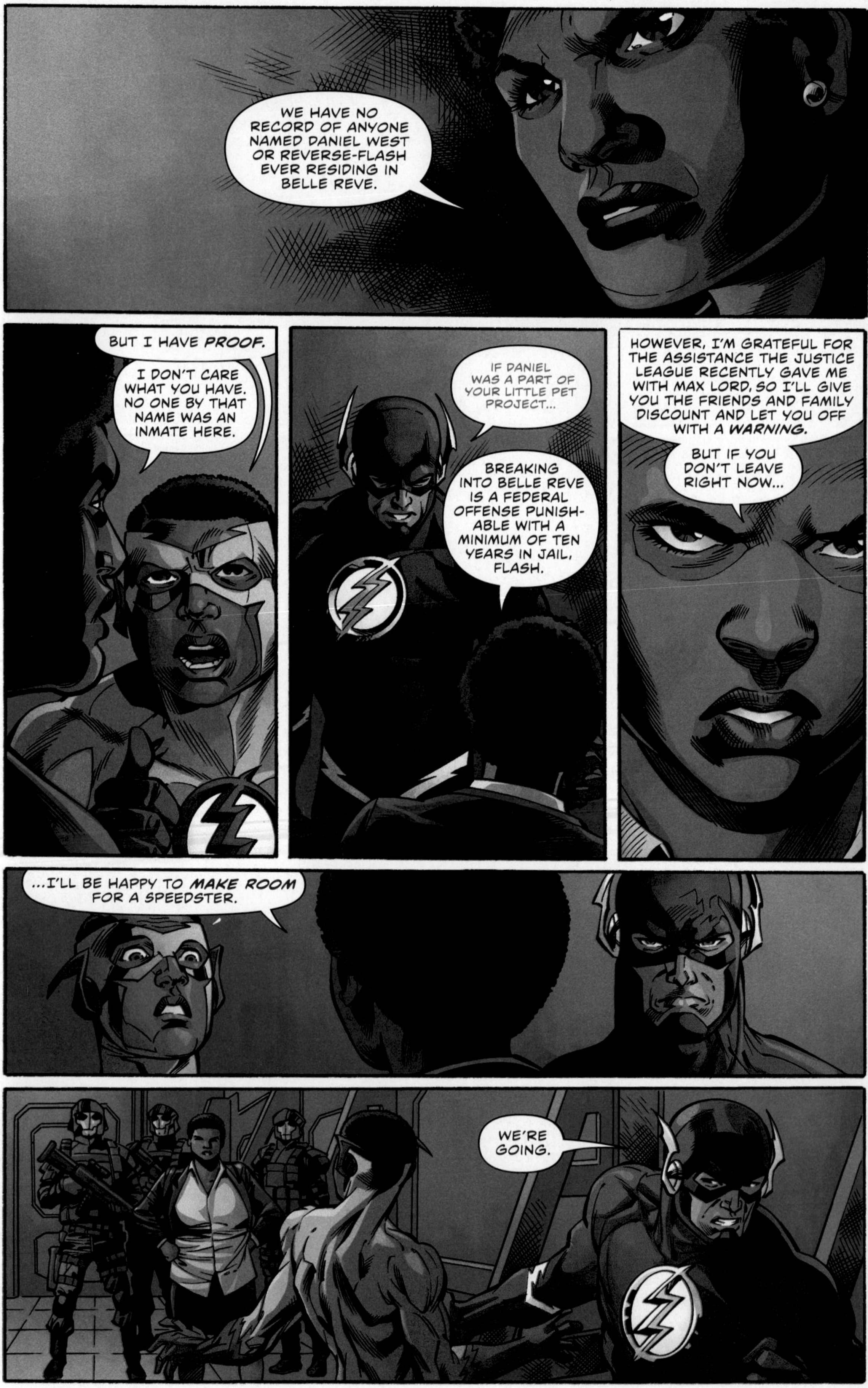
WE HAVE NO RECORD OF ANYONE NAMED DANIEL WEST OR REVERSE-FLASH EVER RESIDING IN BELLE REVE.
BUT I HAVE PROOF.
I DON'T CARE WHAT YOU HAVE. NO ONE BY THAT NAME WAS AN INMATE HERE.
IF DANIEL WAS A PART OF YOUR LITTLE PET PROJECT...
BREAKING INTO BELLE REVE IS A FEDERAL OFFENSE PUNISH-ABLE WITH A MINIMUM OF TEN YEARS IN JAIL, FLASH.
HOWEVER, I'M GRATEFUL FOR THE ASSISTANCE THE JUSTICE LEAGUE RECENTLY GAVE ME WITH MAX LORD, SO I'LL GIVE YOU THE FRIENDS AND FAMILY DISCOUNT AND LET YOU OFF WITH A WARNING.
BUT IF YOU DON'T LEAVE RIGHT NOW...
...I'LL BE HAPPY TO MAKE ROOM FOR A SPEEDSTER.
WE'RE GOING.

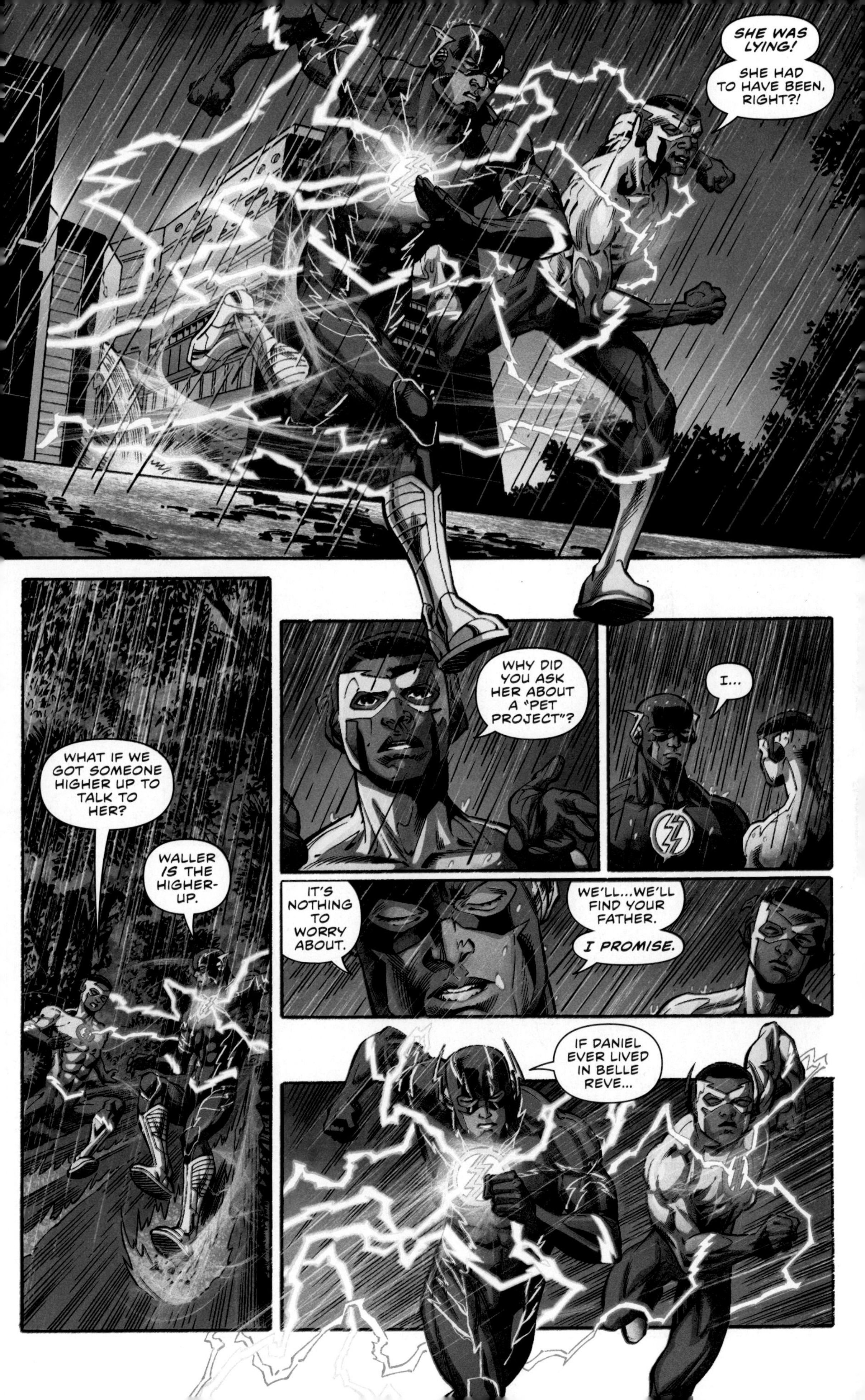
SHE WAS LYING!
SHE HAD TO HAVE BEEN, RIGHT?!
WHAT IF WE GOT SOMEONE HIGHER UP TO TALK TO HER?
WALLER *IS* THE HIGHER-UP.
WHY DID YOU ASK HER ABOUT A "PET PROJECT"?
I...
IT'S NOTHING TO WORRY ABOUT.
WE'LL...WE'LL FIND YOUR FATHER.
I PROMISE.
IF DANIEL EVER LIVED IN BELLE REVE...

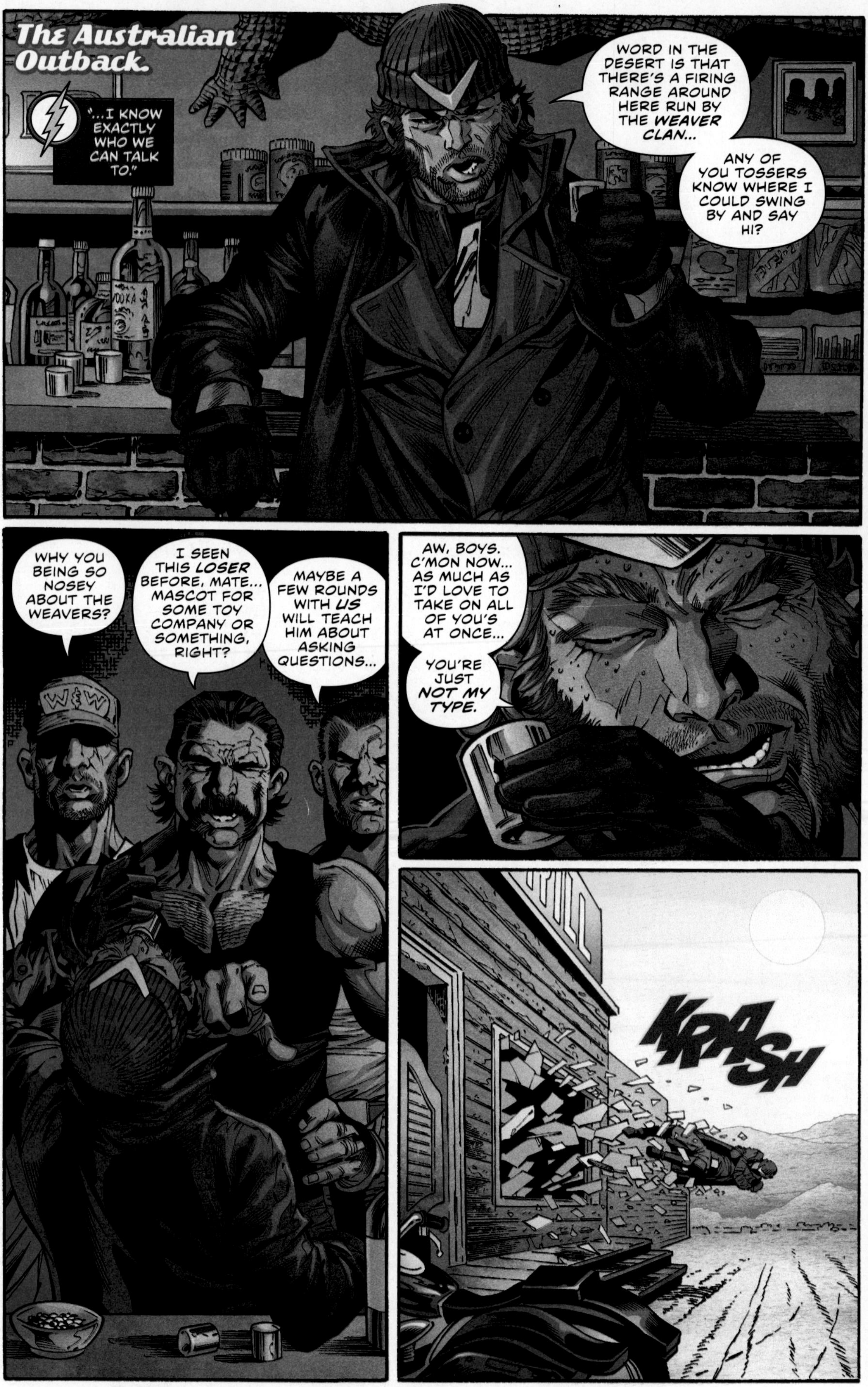
The Australian Outback.
"...I KNOW EXACTLY WHO WE CAN TALK TO."
WORD IN THE DESERT IS THAT THERE'S A FIRING RANGE AROUND HERE RUN BY THE WEAVER CLAN...
ANY OF YOU TOSSERS KNOW WHERE I COULD SWING BY AND SAY HI?
WHY YOU BEING SO NOSEY ABOUT THE WEAVERS?
I SEEN THIS LOSER BEFORE, MATE... MASCOT FOR SOME TOY COMPANY OR SOMETHING, RIGHT?
MAYBE A FEW ROUNDS WITH US WILL TEACH HIM ABOUT ASKING QUESTIONS...
AW, BOYS. C'MON NOW... AS MUCH AS I'D LOVE TO TAKE ON ALL OF YOU'S AT ONCE...
YOU'RE JUST NOT MY TYPE.
KRASH

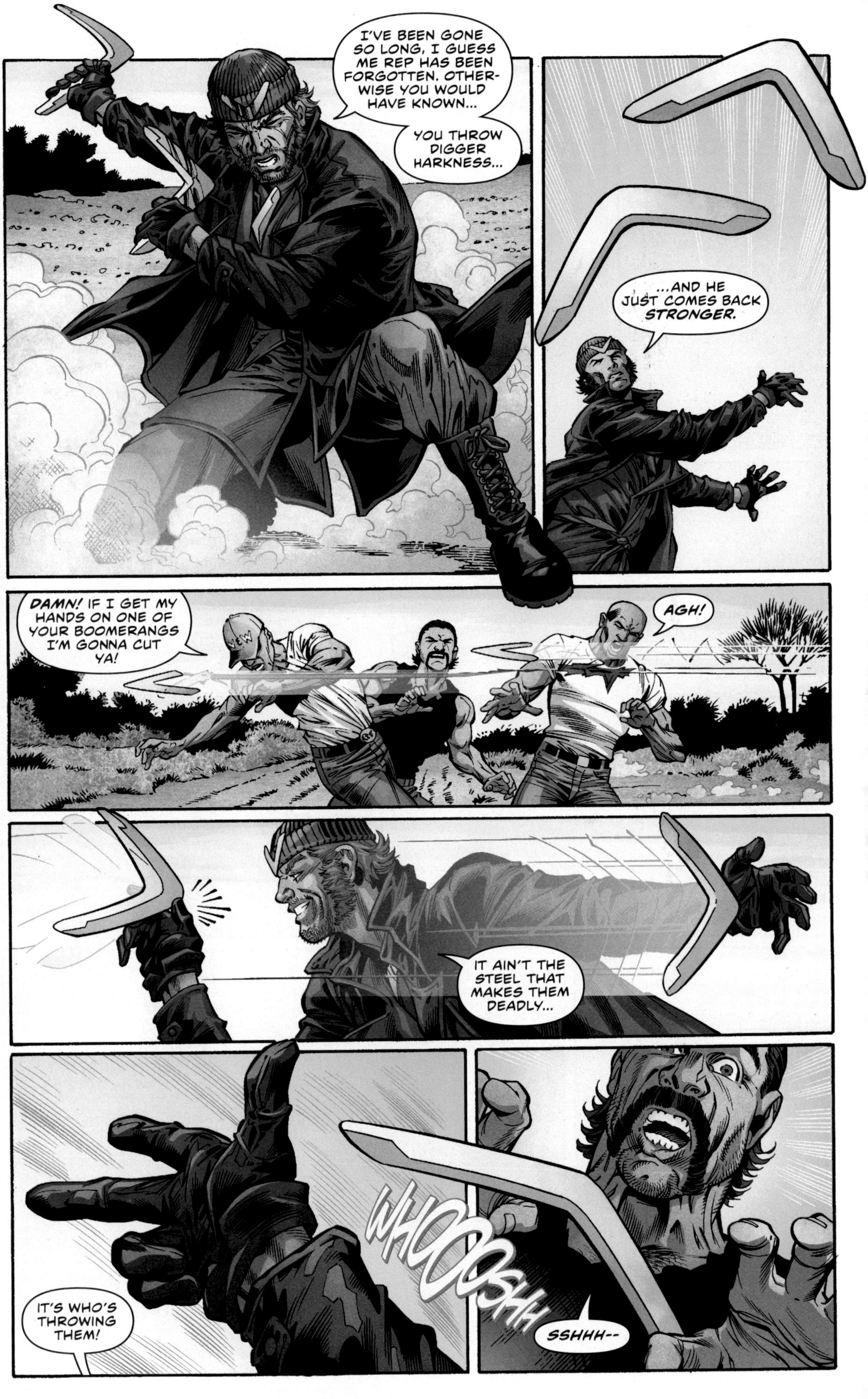

I'VE BEEN GONE SO LONG, I GUESS ME REP HAS BEEN FORGOTTEN. OTHER-WISE YOU WOULD HAVE KNOWN...
YOU THROW DIGGER HARKNESS...
...AND HE JUST COMES BACK STRONGER.
DAMN! IF I GET MY HANDS ON ONE OF YOUR BOOMERANGS I'M GONNA CUT YA!
AGH!
IT AIN'T THE STEEL THAT MAKES THEM DEADLY...
WHOOOSHH
IT'S WHO'S THROWING THEM!
SSHHH--

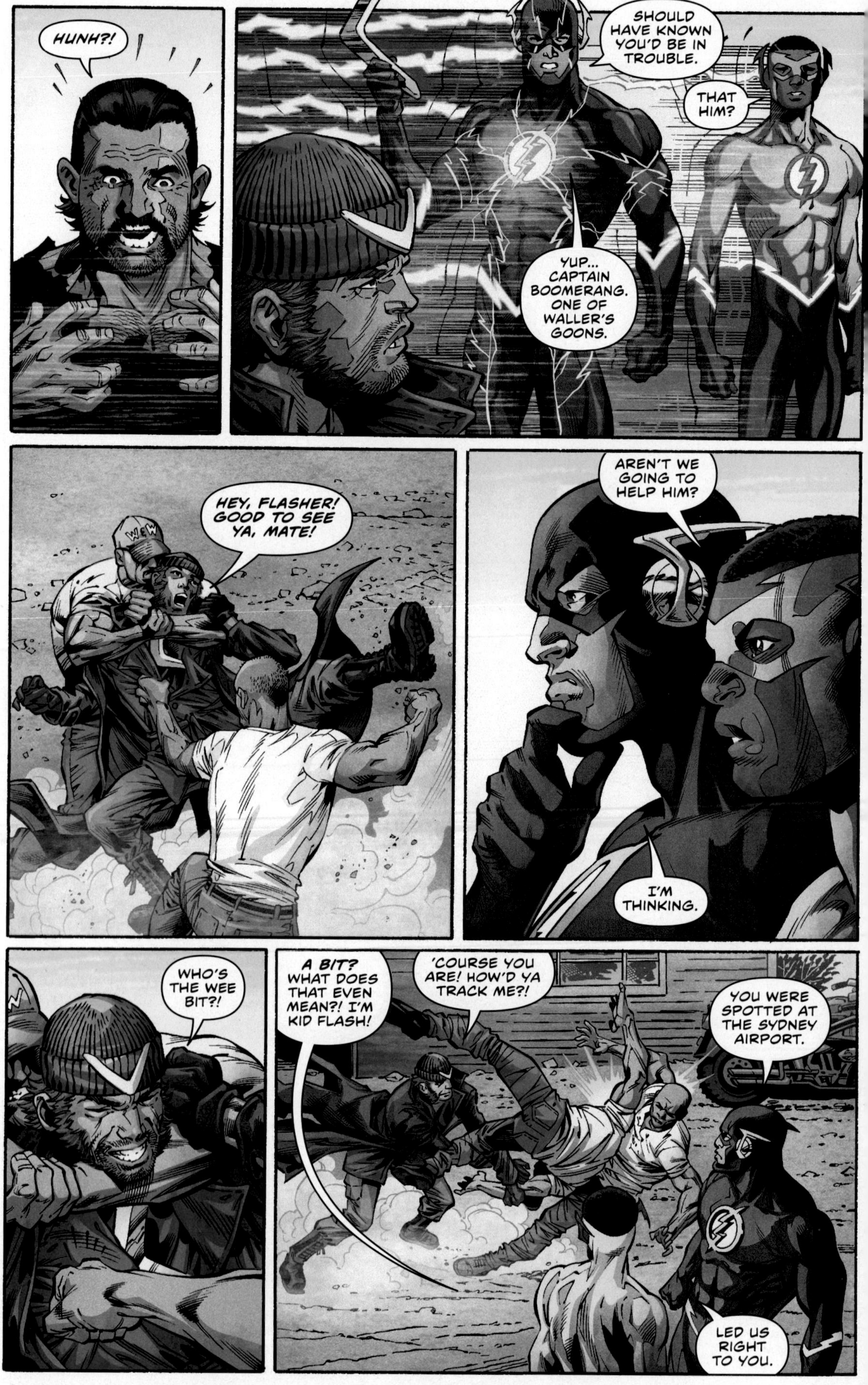
HUNH?!
SHOULD HAVE KNOWN YOU'D BE IN TROUBLE.
THAT HIM?
YUP... CAPTAIN BOOMERANG. ONE OF WALLER'S GOONS.
HEY, FLASHER! GOOD TO SEE YA, MATE!
AREN'T WE GOING TO HELP HIM?
I'M THINKING.
WHO'S THE WEE BIT?!
A BIT? WHAT DOES THAT EVEN MEAN?! I'M KID FLASH!
'COURSE YOU ARE! HOW'D YA TRACK ME?!
YOU WERE SPOTTED AT THE SYDNEY AIRPORT.
LED US RIGHT TO YOU.

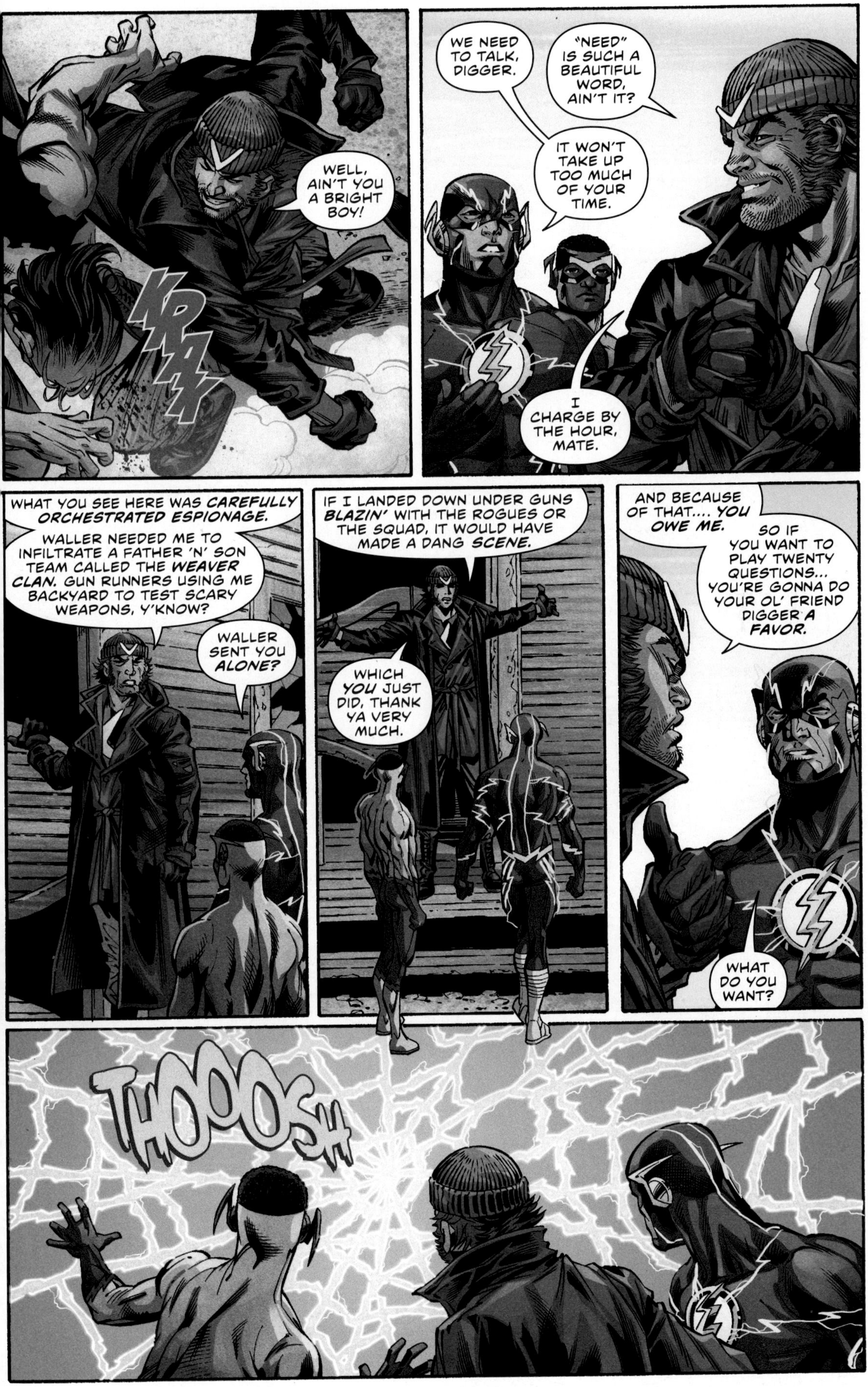

WELL, AIN'T YOU A BRIGHT BOY!
KRAK
WE NEED TO TALK, DIGGER.
"NEED" IS SUCH A BEAUTIFUL WORD, AIN'T IT?
IT WON'T TAKE UP TOO MUCH OF YOUR TIME.
I CHARGE BY THE HOUR, MATE.
WHAT YOU SEE HERE WAS CAREFULLY ORCHESTRATED ESPIONAGE.
WALLER NEEDED ME TO INFILTRATE A FATHER 'N' SON TEAM CALLED THE WEAVER CLAN. GUN RUNNERS USING ME BACKYARD TO TEST SCARY WEAPONS, Y'KNOW?
WALLER SENT YOU ALONE?
IF I LANDED DOWN UNDER GUNS BLAZIN' WITH THE ROGUES OR THE SQUAD, IT WOULD HAVE MADE A DANG SCENE.
WHICH YOU JUST DID, THANK YA VERY MUCH.
AND BECAUSE OF THAT.... YOU OWE ME.
SO IF YOU WANT TO PLAY TWENTY QUESTIONS... YOU'RE GONNA DO YOUR OL' FRIEND DIGGER A FAVOR.
WHAT DO YOU WANT?
THOOOSH

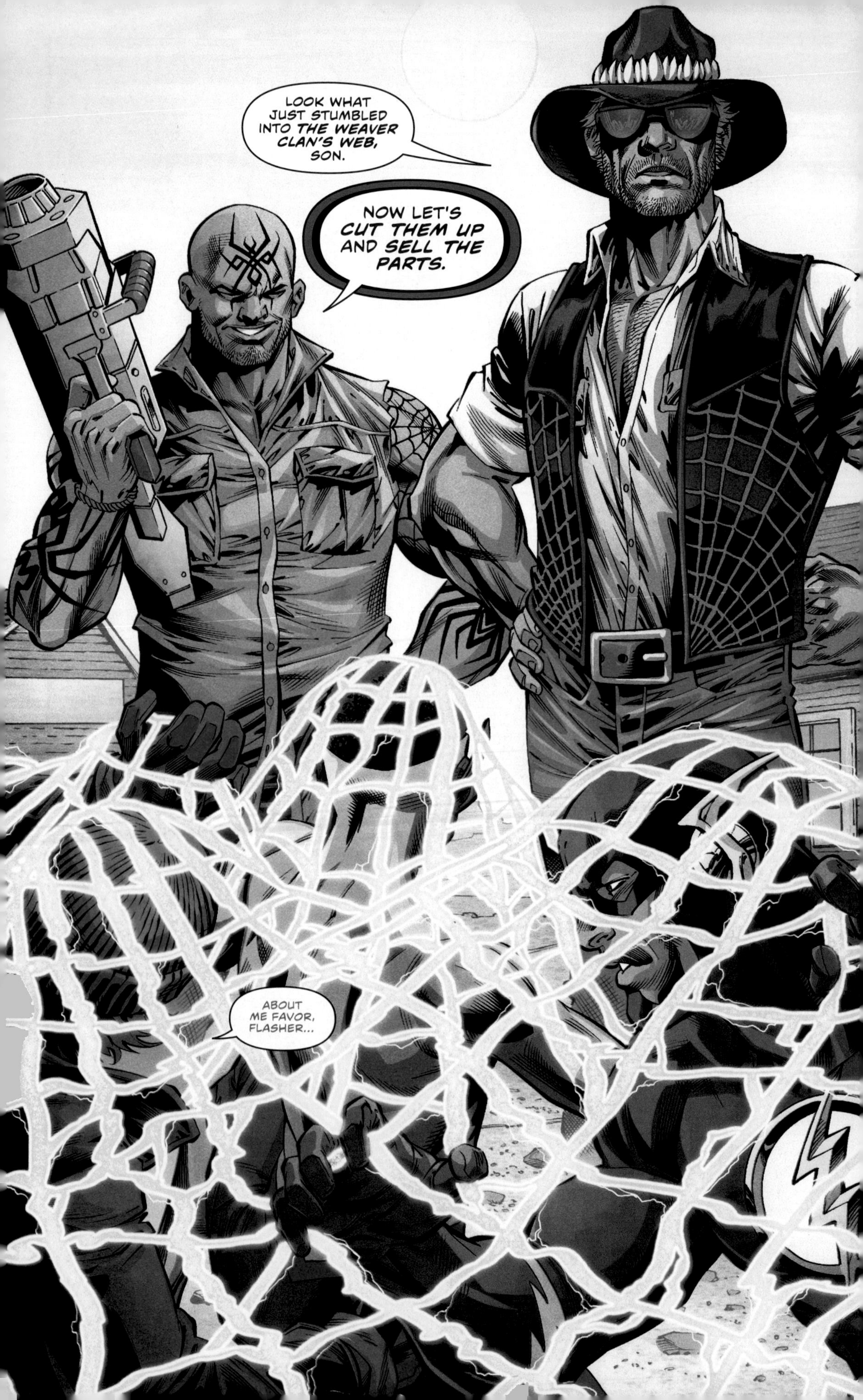
LOOK WHAT JUST STUMBLED INTO THE WEAVER CLAN'S WEB, SON.
NOW LET'S CUT THEM UP AND SELL THE PARTS.
ABOUT ME FAVOR, FLASHER...

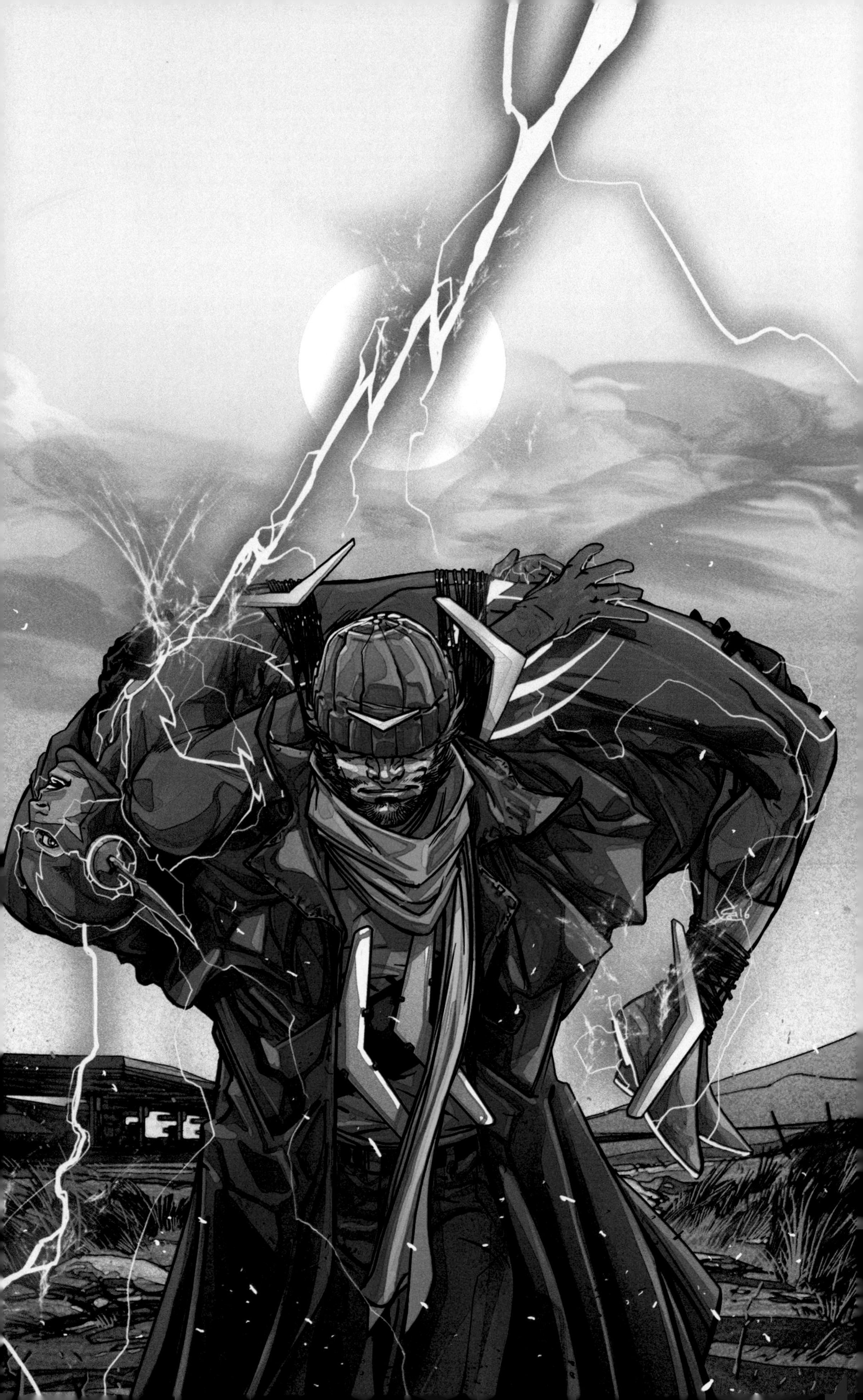

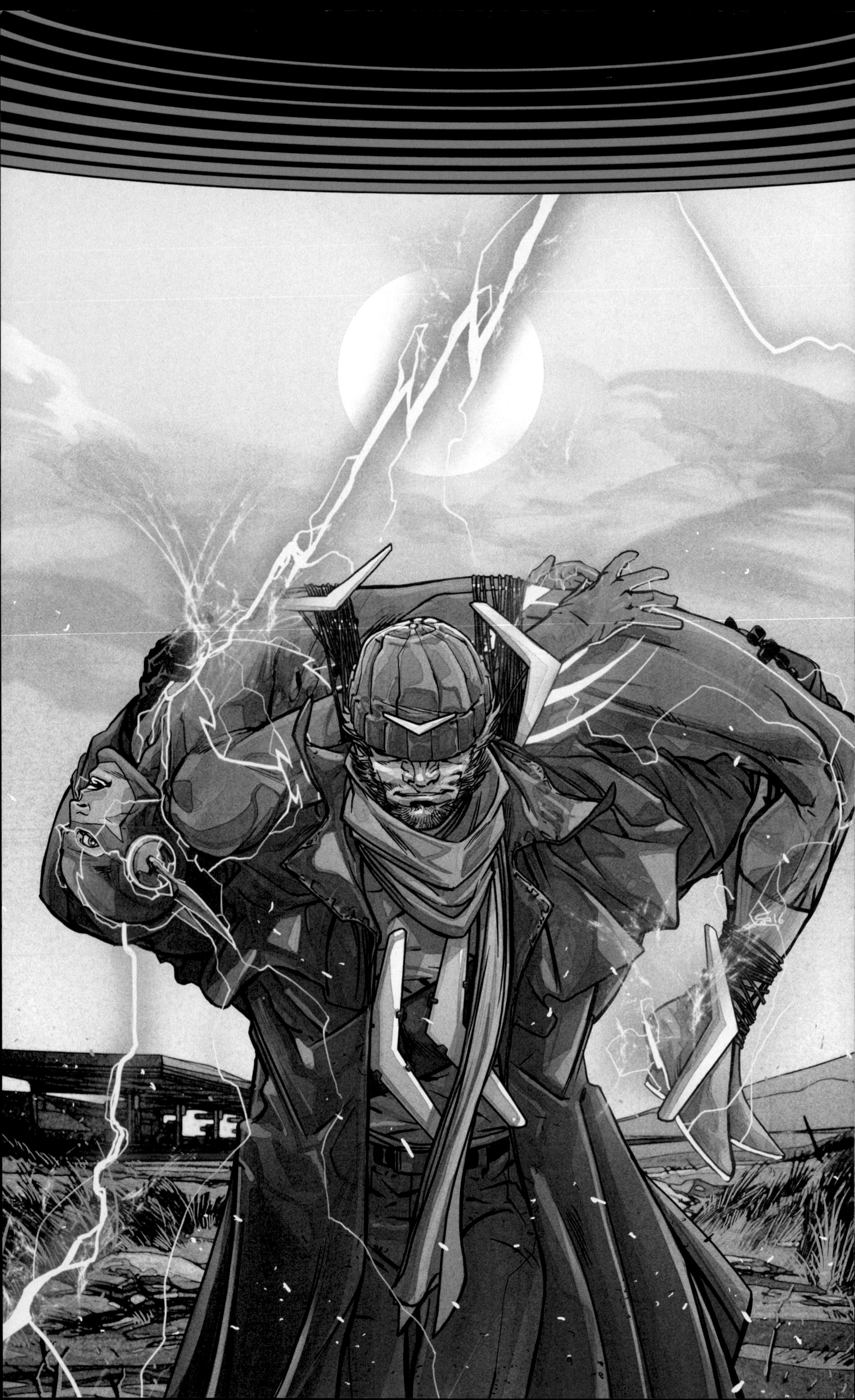

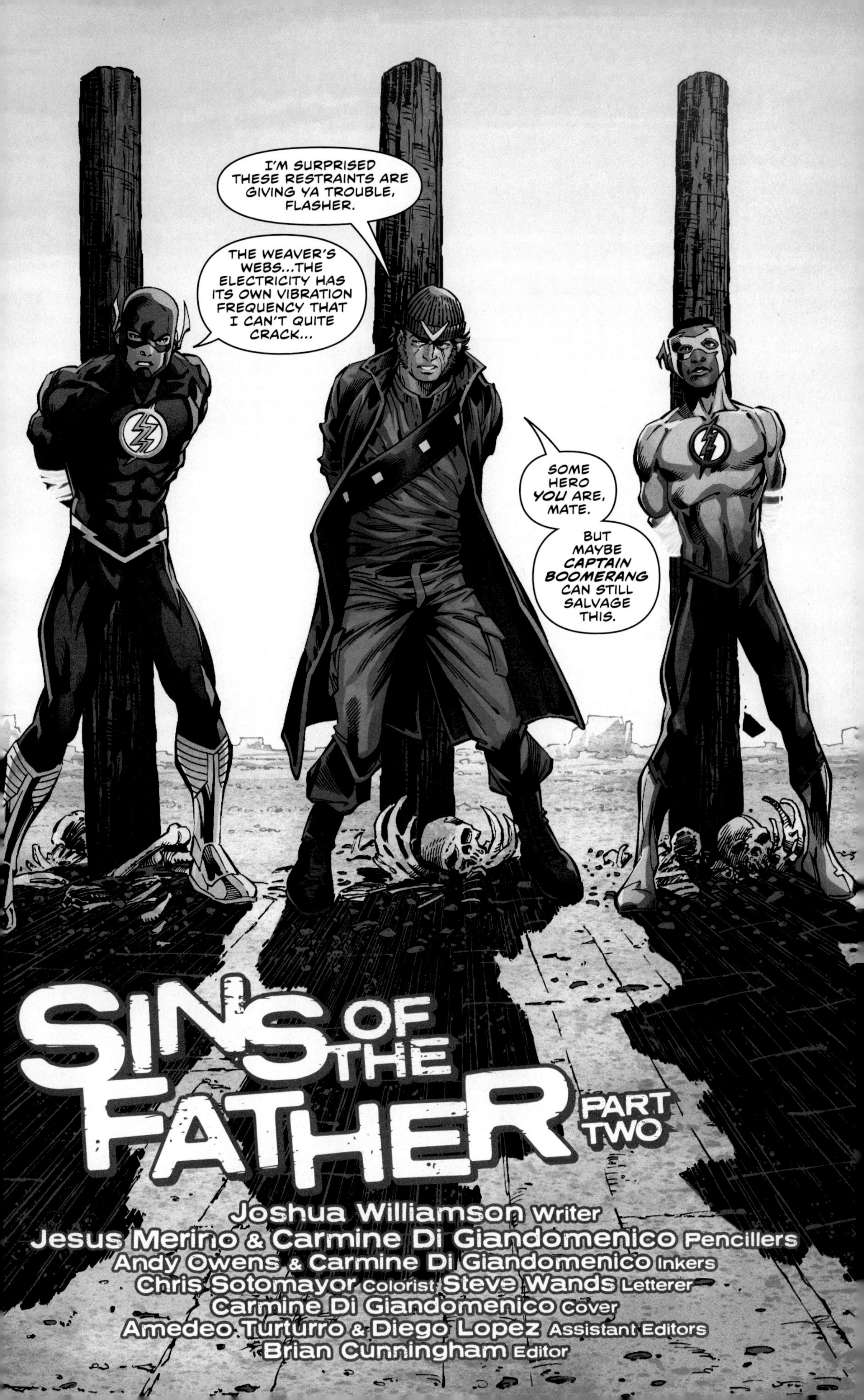
I'M SURPRISED THESE RESTRAINTS ARE GIVING YA TROUBLE, FLASHER.
THE WEAVER'S WEBS...THE ELECTRICITY HAS ITS OWN VIBRATION FREQUENCY THAT I CAN'T QUITE CRACK...
SOME HERO YOU ARE, MATE.
BUT MAYBE CAPTAIN BOOMERANG CAN STILL SALVAGE THIS.
SINS OF THE FATHER PART TWO
Joshua Williamson Writer
Jesus Merino & Carmine Di Giandomenico Pencillers
Andy Owens & Carmine Di Giandomenico Inkers
Chris Sotomayor Colorist Steve Wands Letterer
Carmine Di Giandomenico Cover
Amedeo Turturro & Diego Lopez Assistant Editors
Brian Cunningham Editor

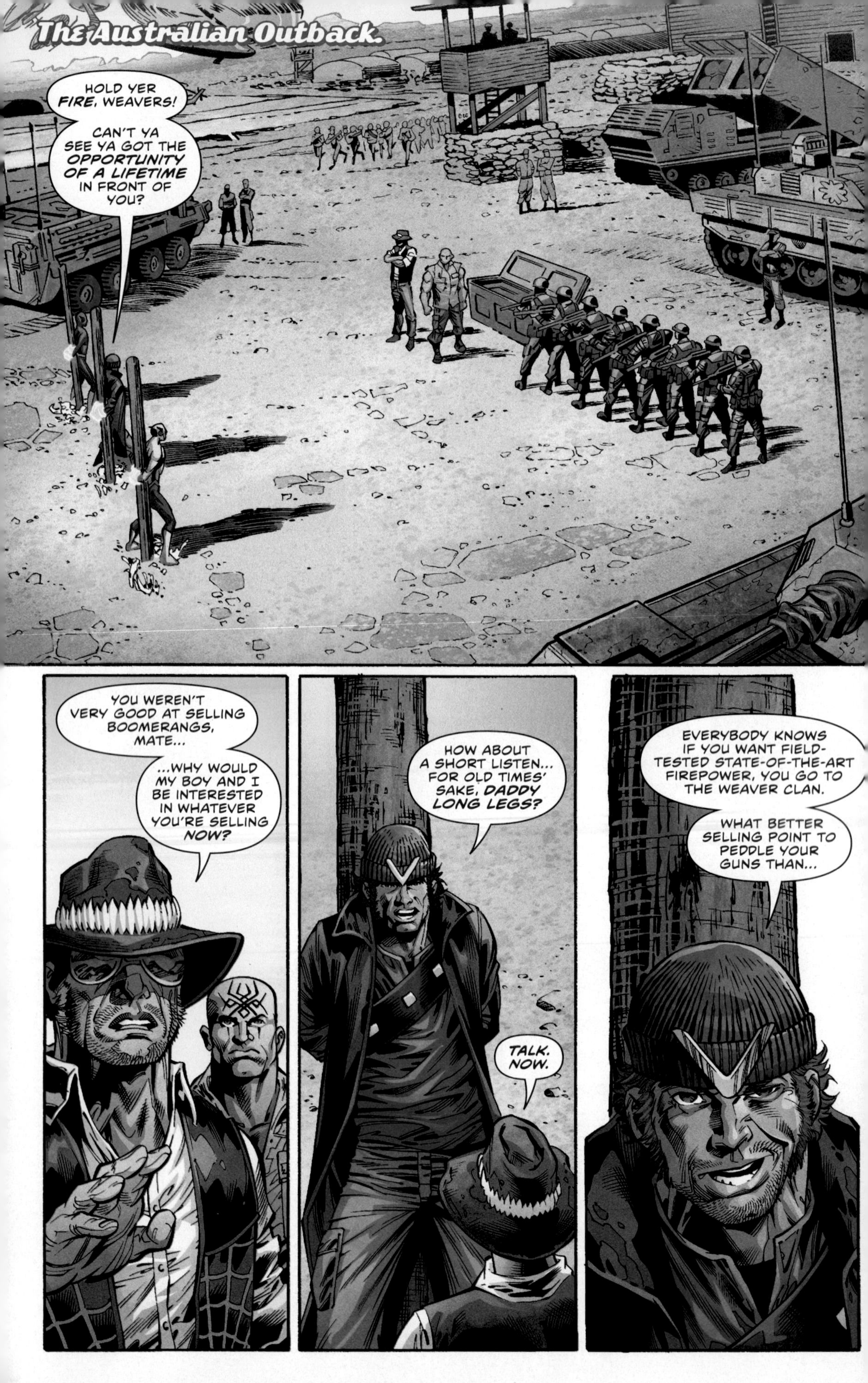
The Australian Outback.
HOLD YER FIRE, WEAVERS!
CAN'T YA SEE YA GOT THE OPPORTUNITY OF A LIFETIME IN FRONT OF YOU?
YOU WEREN'T VERY GOOD AT SELLING BOOMERANGS, MATE...
...WHY WOULD MY BOY AND I BE INTERESTED IN WHATEVER YOU'RE SELLING NOW?
HOW ABOUT A SHORT LISTEN... FOR OLD TIMES' SAKE, DADDY LONG LEGS?
TALK. NOW.
EVERYBODY KNOWS IF YOU WANT FIELD-TESTED STATE-OF-THE-ART FIREPOWER, YOU GO TO THE WEAVER CLAN.
WHAT BETTER SELLING POINT TO PEDDLE YOUR GUNS THAN...

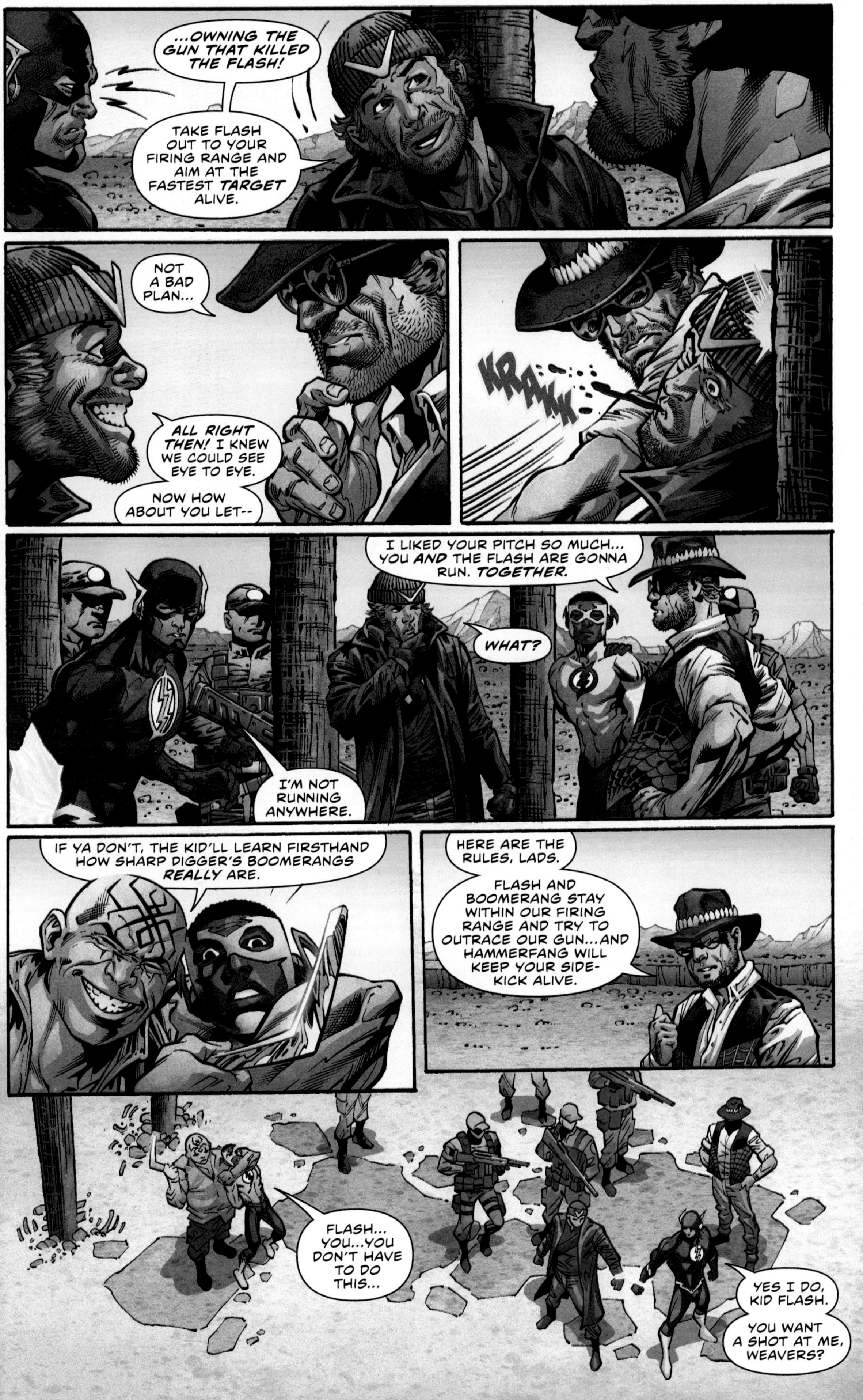
...OWNING THE GUN THAT KILLED THE FLASH!
TAKE FLASH OUT TO YOUR FIRING RANGE AND AIM AT THE FASTEST TARGET ALIVE.
NOT A BAD PLAN...
ALL RIGHT THEN! I KNEW WE COULD SEE EYE TO EYE.
NOW HOW ABOUT YOU LET--
KRAKK
I LIKED YOUR PITCH SO MUCH... YOU AND THE FLASH ARE GONNA RUN. TOGETHER.
WHAT?
I'M NOT RUNNING ANYWHERE.
IF YA DON'T, THE KID'LL LEARN FIRSTHAND HOW SHARP DIGGER'S BOOMERANGS REALLY ARE.
HERE ARE THE RULES, LADS.
FLASH AND BOOMERANG STAY WITHIN OUR FIRING RANGE AND TRY TO OUTRACE OUR GUN...AND HAMMERFANG WILL KEEP YOUR SIDE-KICK ALIVE.
FLASH... YOU...YOU DON'T HAVE TO DO THIS...
YES I DO, KID FLASH.
YOU WANT A SHOT AT ME, WEAVERS?

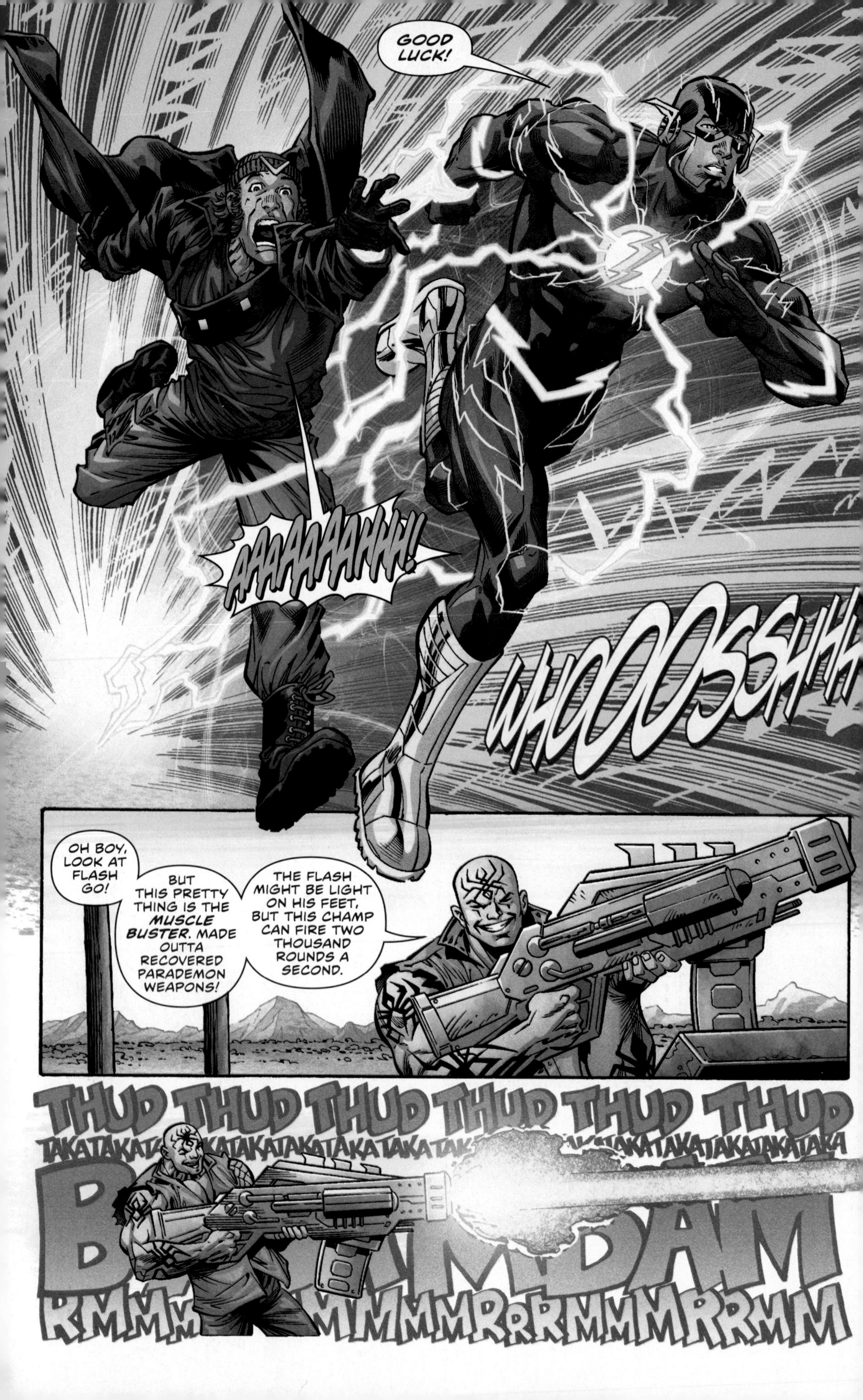
GOOD LUCK!
AAAAAAAHHH!
WHOOOOSSHH
OH BOY, LOOK AT FLASH GO!
BUT THIS PRETTY THING IS THE *MUSCLE BUSTER*. MADE OUTTA RECOVERED PARADEMON WEAPONS!
THE FLASH MIGHT BE LIGHT ON HIS FEET, BUT THIS CHAMP CAN FIRE TWO THOUSAND ROUNDS A SECOND.
THUD THUD THUD THUD THUD THUD
TAKATAKATAKATAKATAKATAKATAKATAK
TAKATAKATAKATAKATAKA
DAM
MMMMRRMMMMRRMM

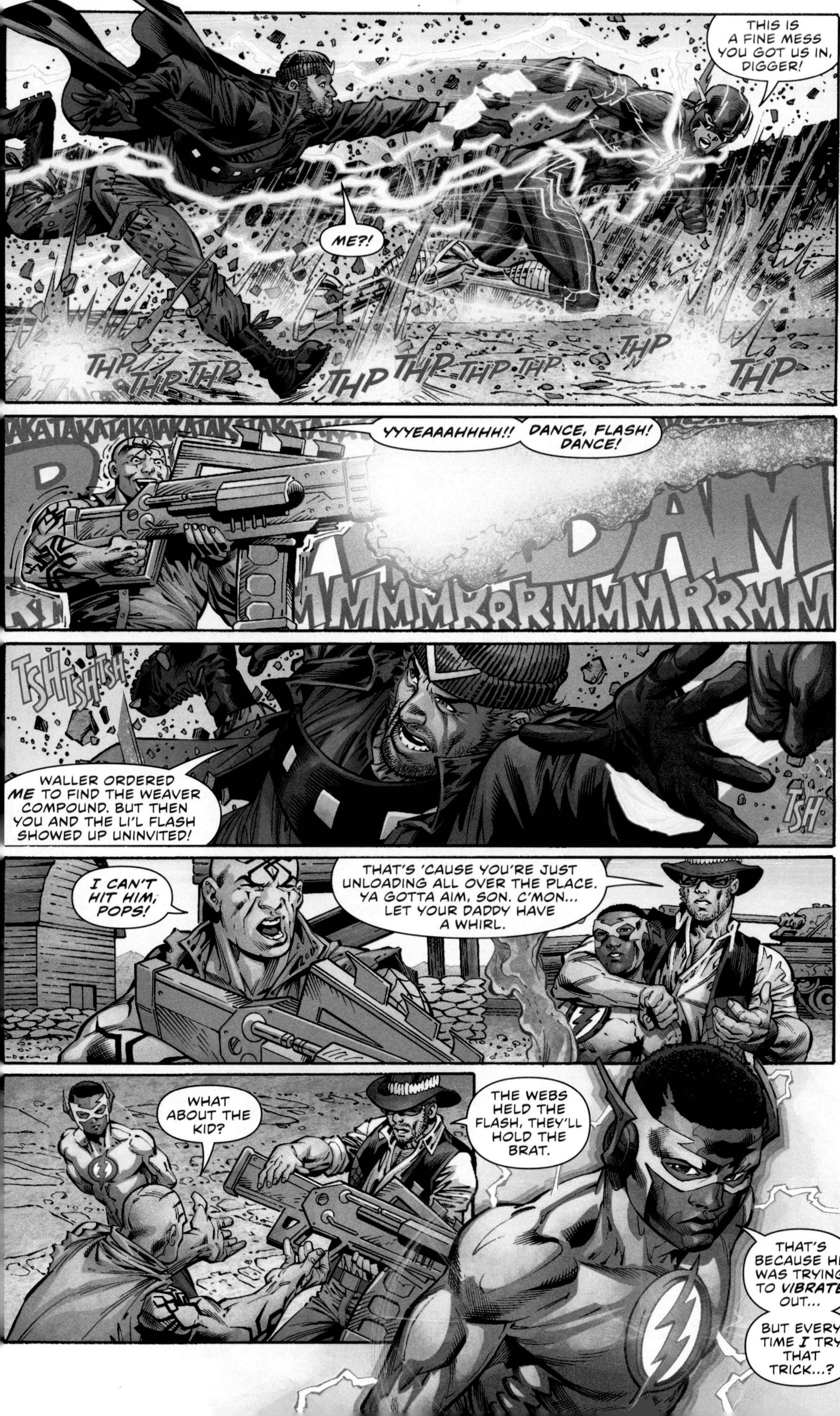
THIS IS A FINE MESS YOU GOT US IN, DIGGER!
ME?!
THP THP THP THP THP THP THP THP THP
TAKATAKATAKATAKATAKA
YYYEAAAHHHH!!
DANCE, FLASH! DANCE!
MMMMRRMMMMRRMM
TSHTSHTSH
WALLER ORDERED ME TO FIND THE WEAVER COMPOUND. BUT THEN YOU AND THE LI'L FLASH SHOWED UP UNINVITED!
TSH
I CAN'T HIT HIM, POPS!
THAT'S 'CAUSE YOU'RE JUST UNLOADING ALL OVER THE PLACE. YA GOTTA AIM, SON. C'MON... LET YOUR DADDY HAVE A WHIRL.
WHAT ABOUT THE KID?
THE WEBS HELD THE FLASH, THEY'LL HOLD THE BRAT.
THAT'S BECAUSE HE WAS TRYING TO VIBRATE OUT...
BUT EVERY TIME I TRY THAT TRICK...?

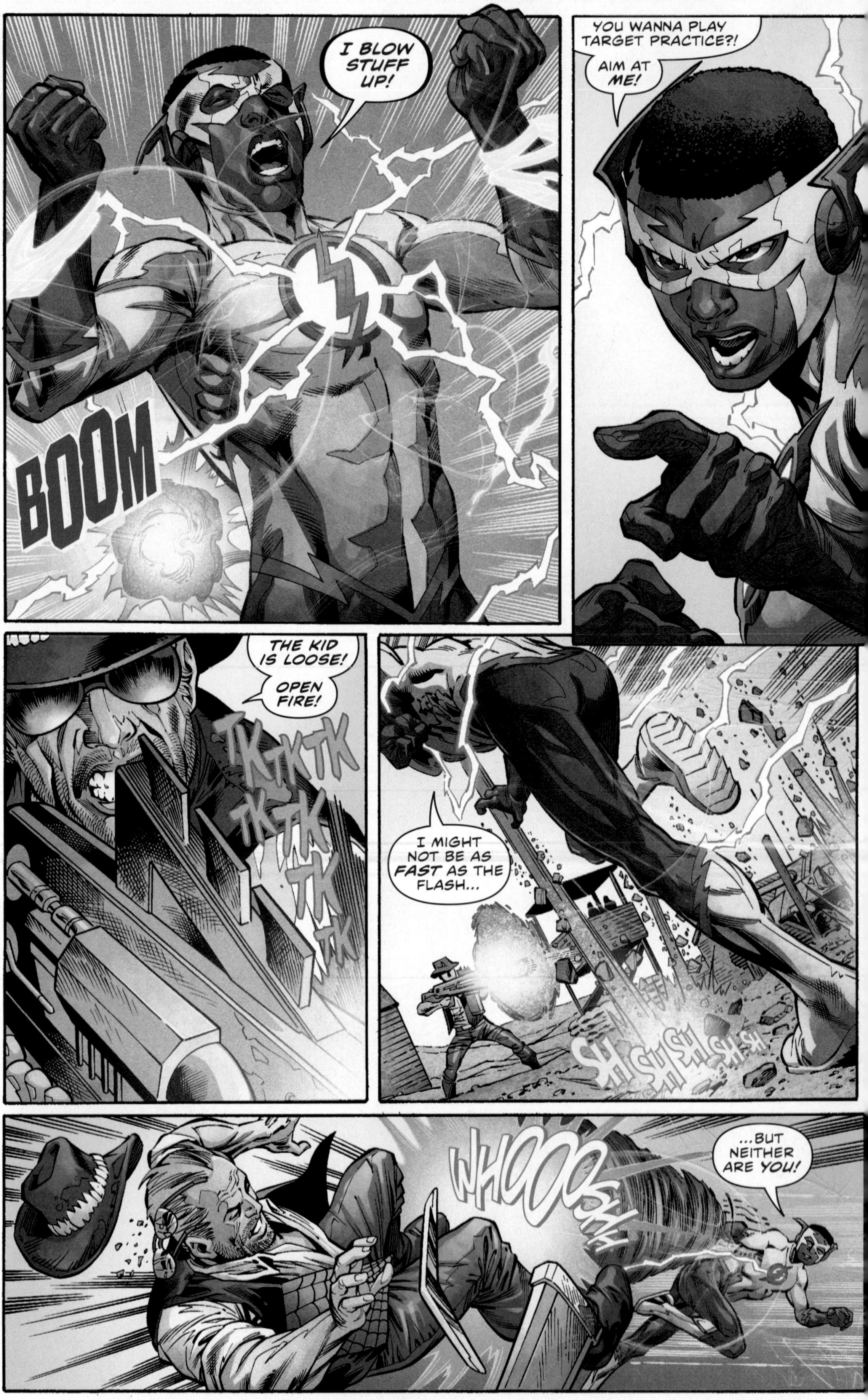
I BLOW STUFF UP!
BOOM
YOU WANNA PLAY TARGET PRACTICE?!
AIM AT ME!
THE KID IS LOOSE!
OPEN FIRE!
TKTKTK TKTK TK TK TK
I MIGHT NOT BE AS *FAST* AS THE FLASH...
...BUT NEITHER ARE *YOU!*

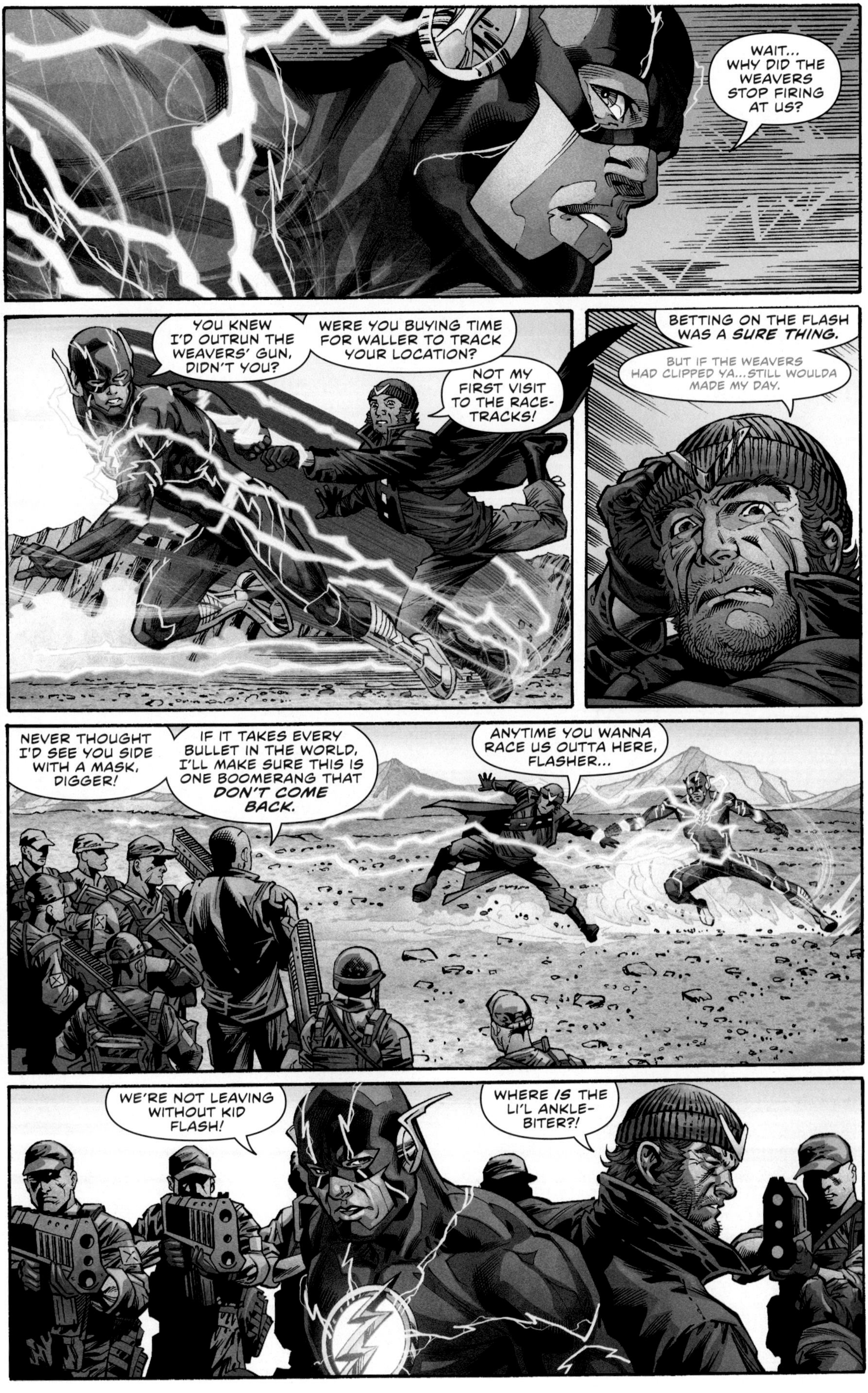
WAIT... WHY DID THE WEAVERS STOP FIRING AT US?
YOU KNEW I'D OUTRUN THE WEAVERS' GUN, DIDN'T YOU?
WERE YOU BUYING TIME FOR WALLER TO TRACK YOUR LOCATION?
NOT MY FIRST VISIT TO THE RACE-TRACKS!
BETTING ON THE FLASH WAS A *SURE THING.*
BUT IF THE WEAVERS HAD CLIPPED YA...STILL WOULDA MADE MY DAY.
NEVER THOUGHT I'D SEE YOU SIDE WITH A MASK, DIGGER!
IF IT TAKES EVERY BULLET IN THE WORLD, I'LL MAKE SURE THIS IS ONE BOOMERANG THAT *DON'T COME BACK.*
ANYTIME YOU WANNA RACE US OUTTA HERE, FLASHER...
WE'RE NOT LEAVING WITHOUT KID FLASH!
WHERE *IS* THE LI'L ANKLE-BITER?!

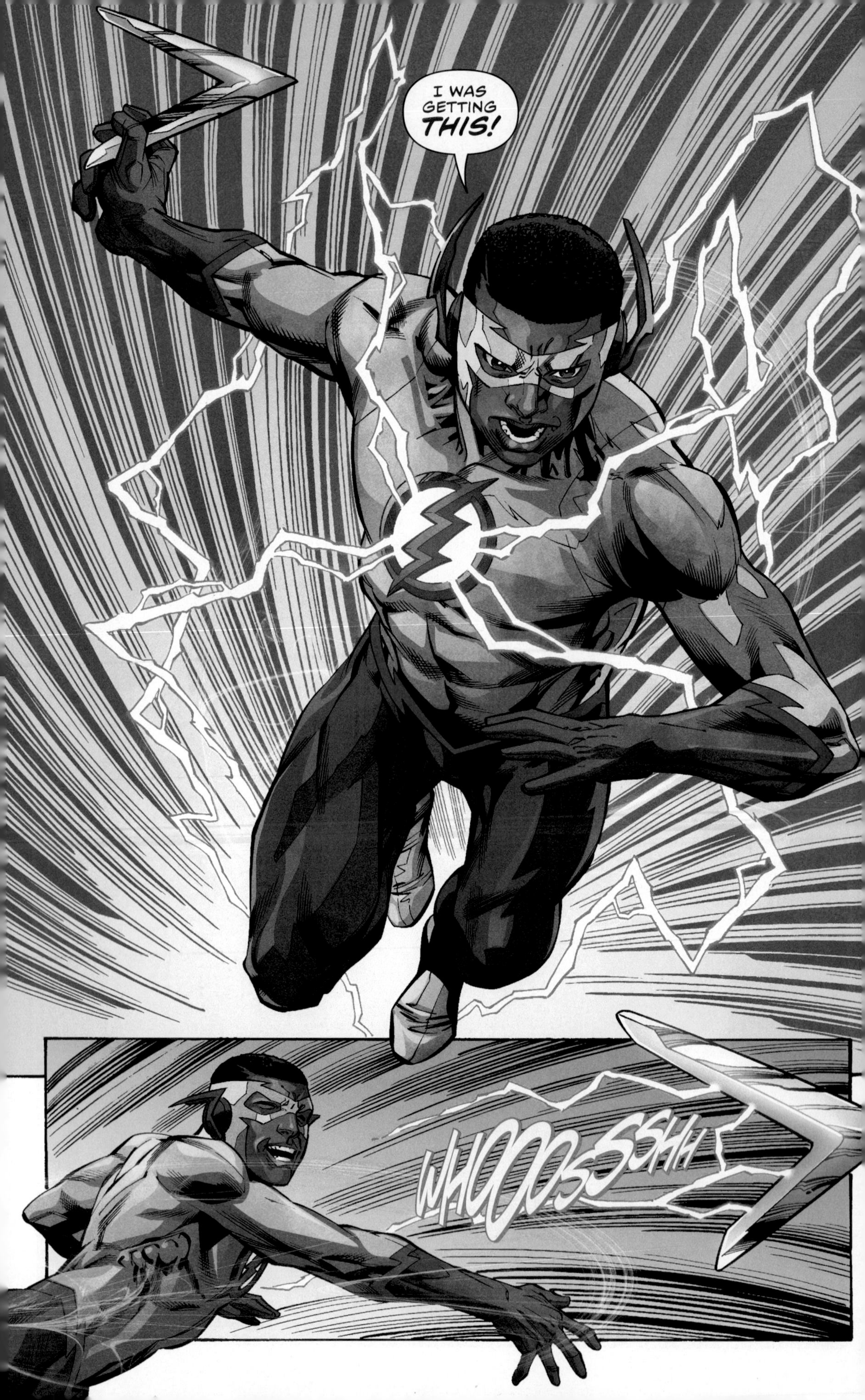
I WAS GETTING THIS!
WHOOOSSSHH

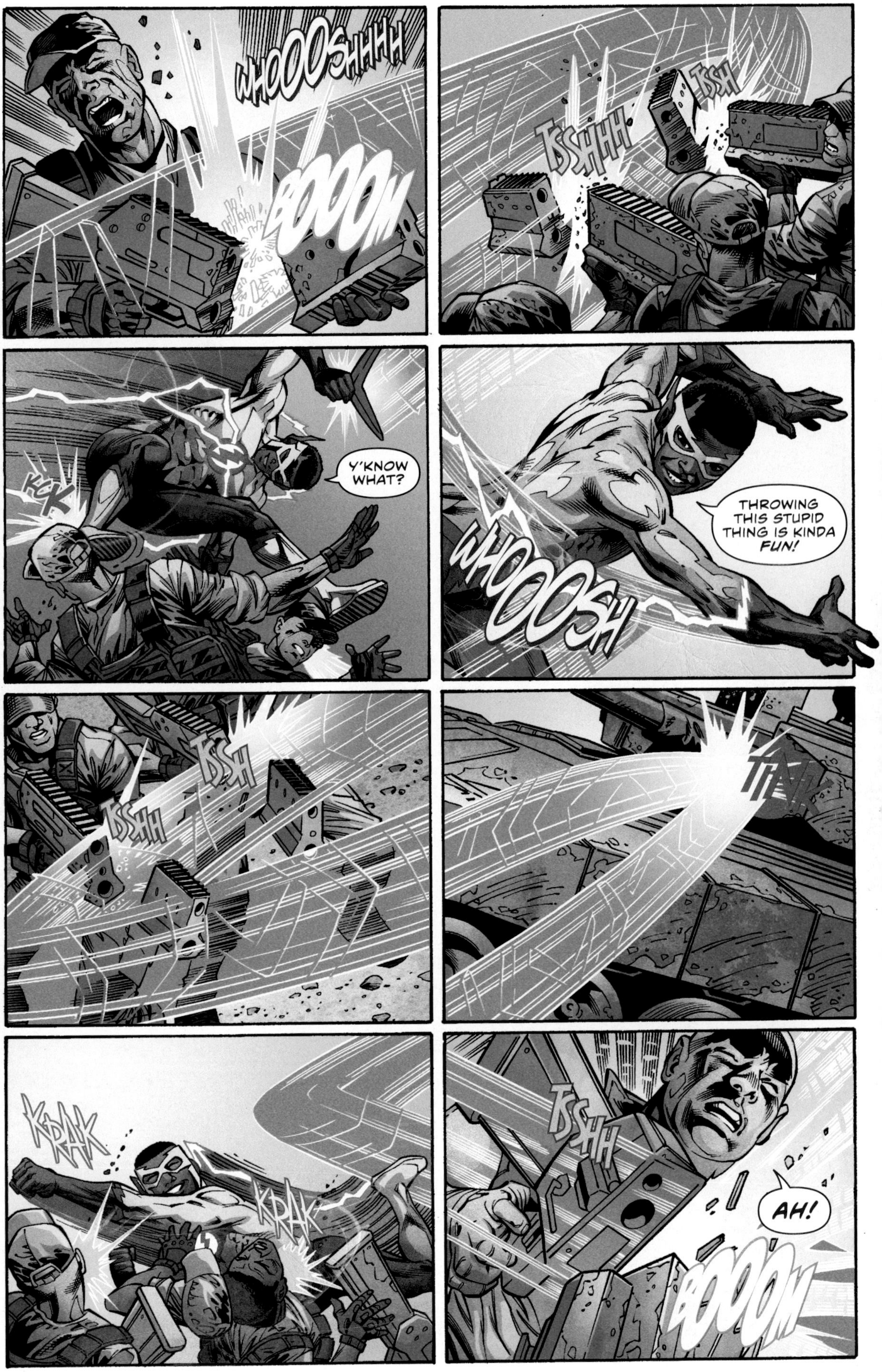
WHOOOSHHHH
BOOOOM
TSSHHH
TSSH
KCK
Y'KNOW WHAT?
THROWING THIS STUPID THING IS KINDA FUN!
WHOOOOSH
TSSH
TSSHH
TINK
KRAK
KRAK
TSSHH
AH!
BOOOM

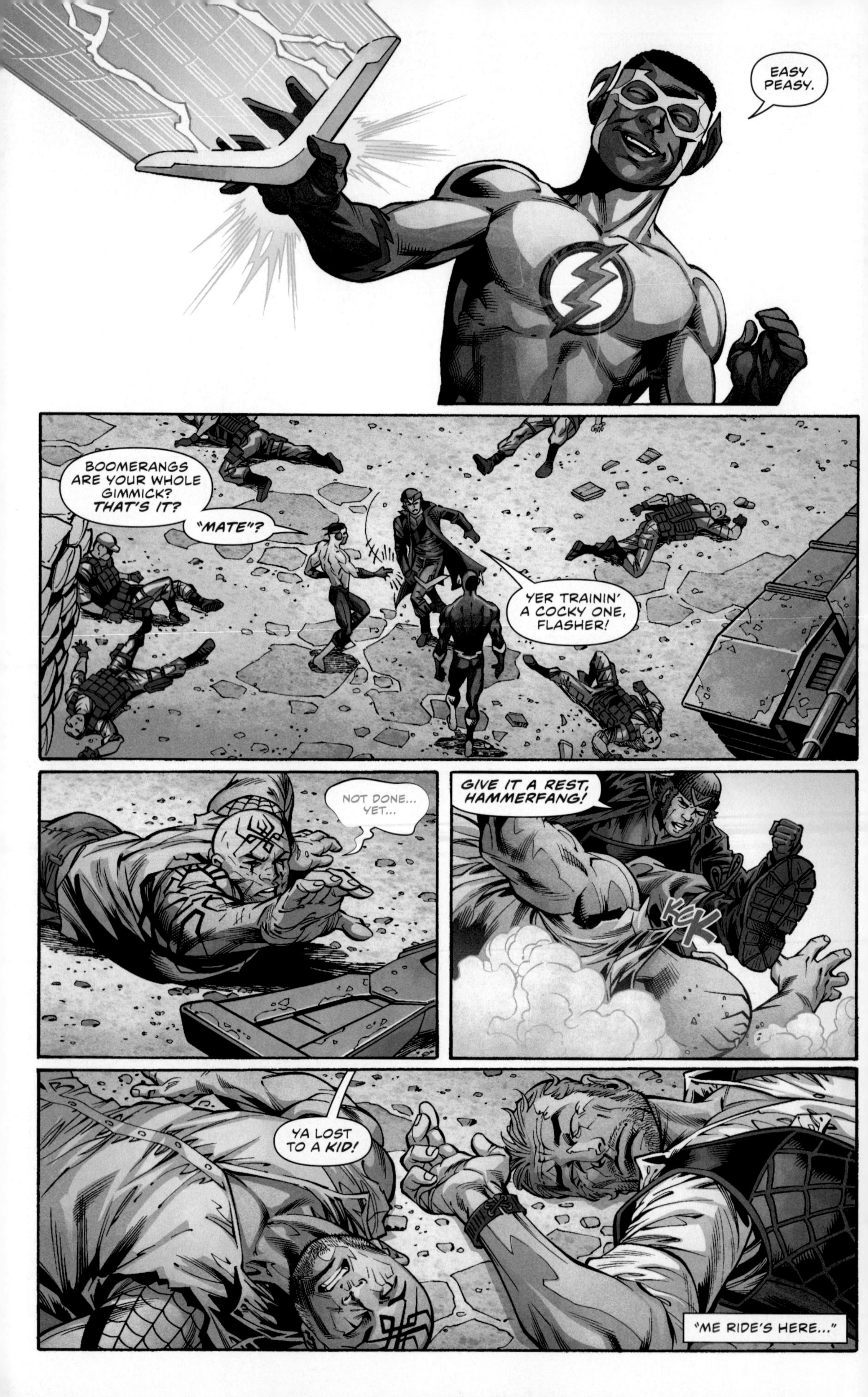
EASY PEASY.
BOOMERANGS ARE YOUR WHOLE GIMMICK? THAT'S IT?
"MATE"?
YER TRAININ' A COCKY ONE, FLASHER!
NOT DONE... YET...
GIVE IT A REST, HAMMERFANG!
KCK
YA LOST TO A KID!
"ME RIDE'S HERE..."

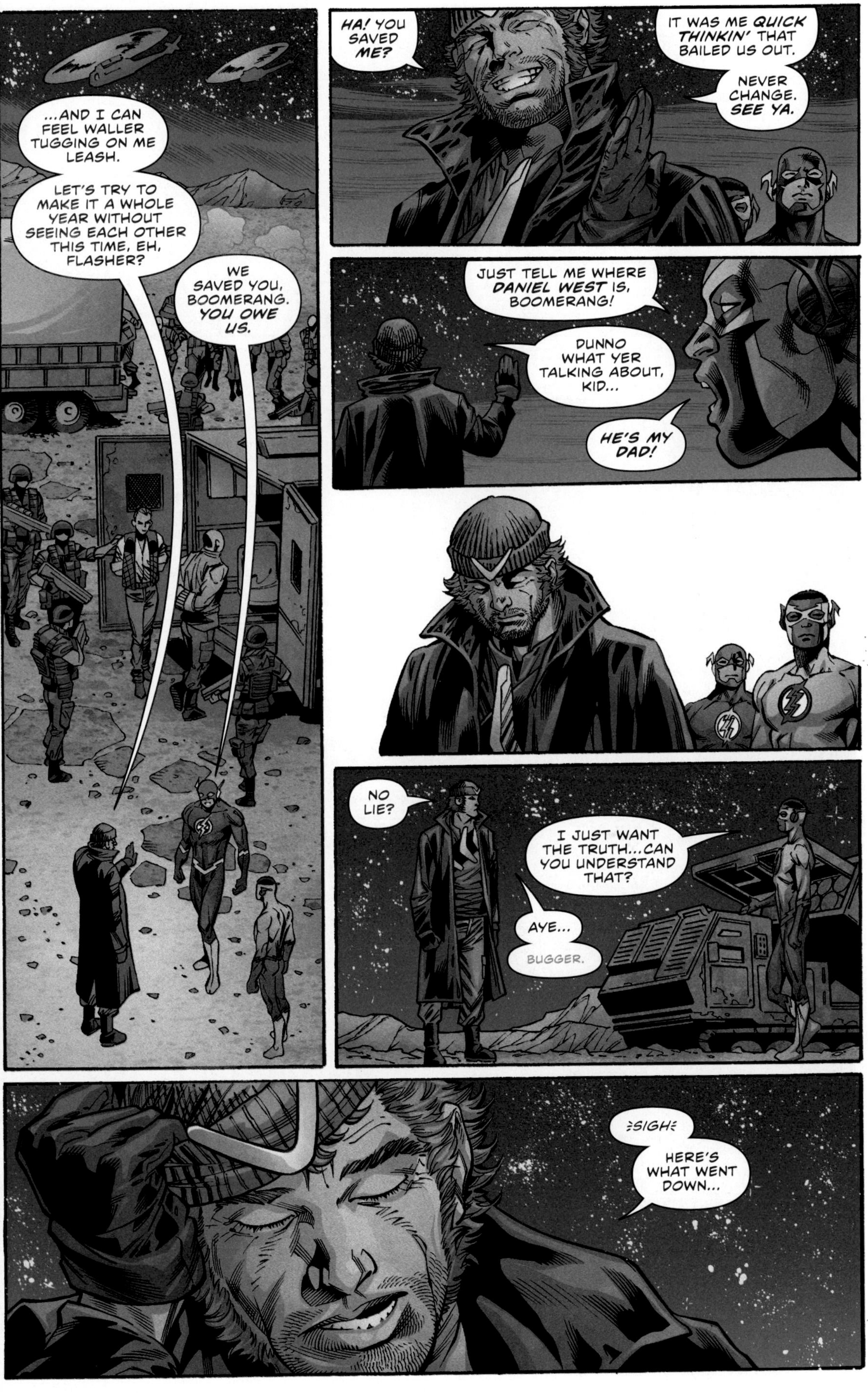
...AND I CAN FEEL WALLER TUGGING ON ME LEASH.
LET'S TRY TO MAKE IT A WHOLE YEAR WITHOUT SEEING EACH OTHER THIS TIME, EH, FLASHER?
WE SAVED YOU, BOOMERANG. YOU OWE US.
HA! YOU SAVED ME?
IT WAS ME QUICK THINKIN' THAT BAILED US OUT.
NEVER CHANGE. SEE YA.
JUST TELL ME WHERE DANIEL WEST IS, BOOMERANG!
DUNNO WHAT YER TALKING ABOUT, KID...
HE'S MY DAD!
NO LIE?
I JUST WANT THE TRUTH...CAN YOU UNDERSTAND THAT?
AYE...
BUGGER.
=SIGH=
HERE'S WHAT WENT DOWN...

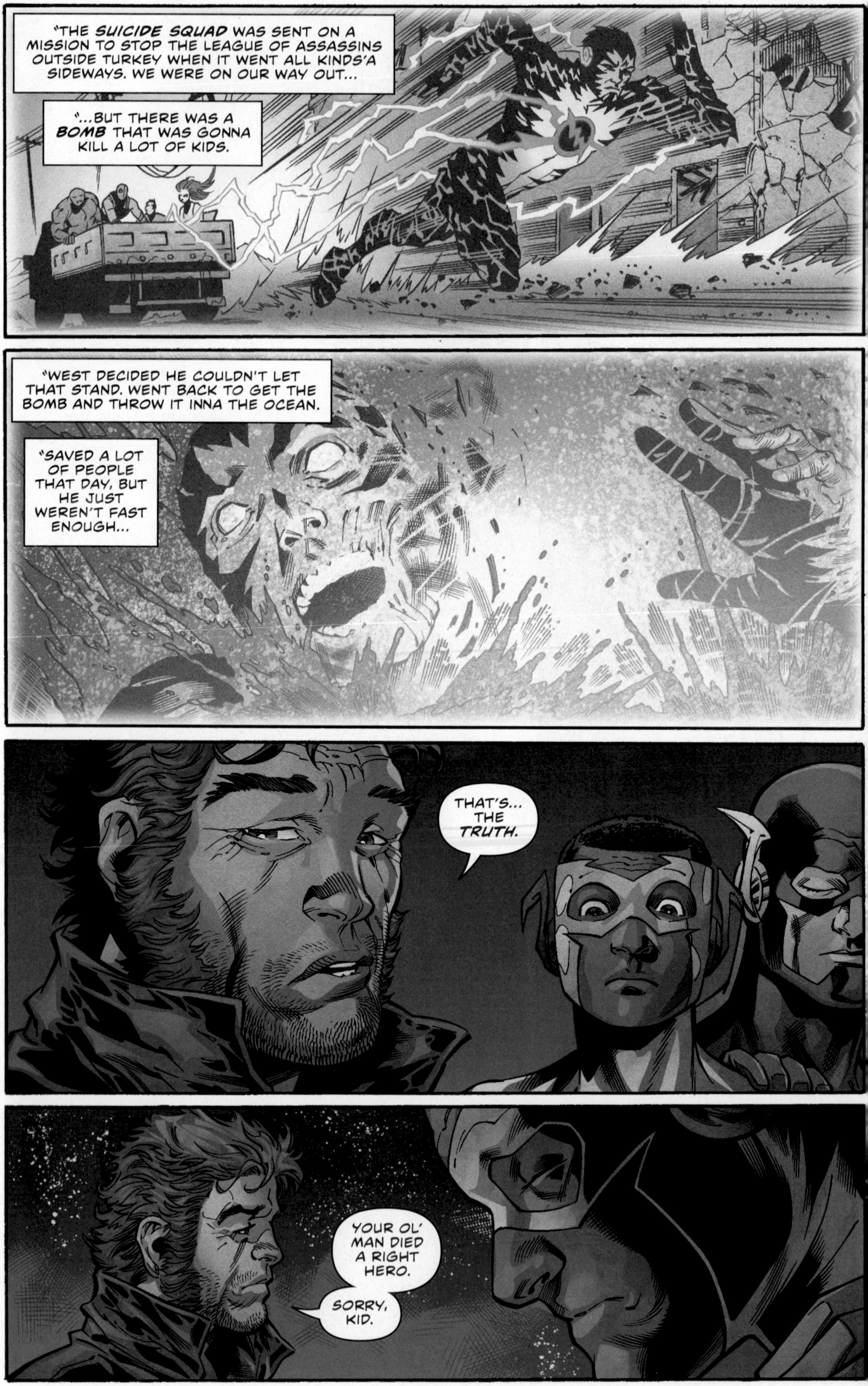
"THE *SUICIDE SQUAD* WAS SENT ON A MISSION TO STOP THE LEAGUE OF ASSASSINS OUTSIDE TURKEY WHEN IT WENT ALL KINDS'A SIDEWAYS. WE WERE ON OUR WAY OUT...
"...BUT THERE WAS A *BOMB* THAT WAS GONNA KILL A LOT OF KIDS.
"WEST DECIDED HE COULDN'T LET THAT STAND. WENT BACK TO GET THE BOMB AND THROW IT INNA THE OCEAN.
"SAVED A LOT OF PEOPLE THAT DAY, BUT HE JUST WEREN'T FAST ENOUGH...
THAT'S... THE *TRUTH*.
YOUR OL' MAN DIED A RIGHT HERO.
SORRY, KID.

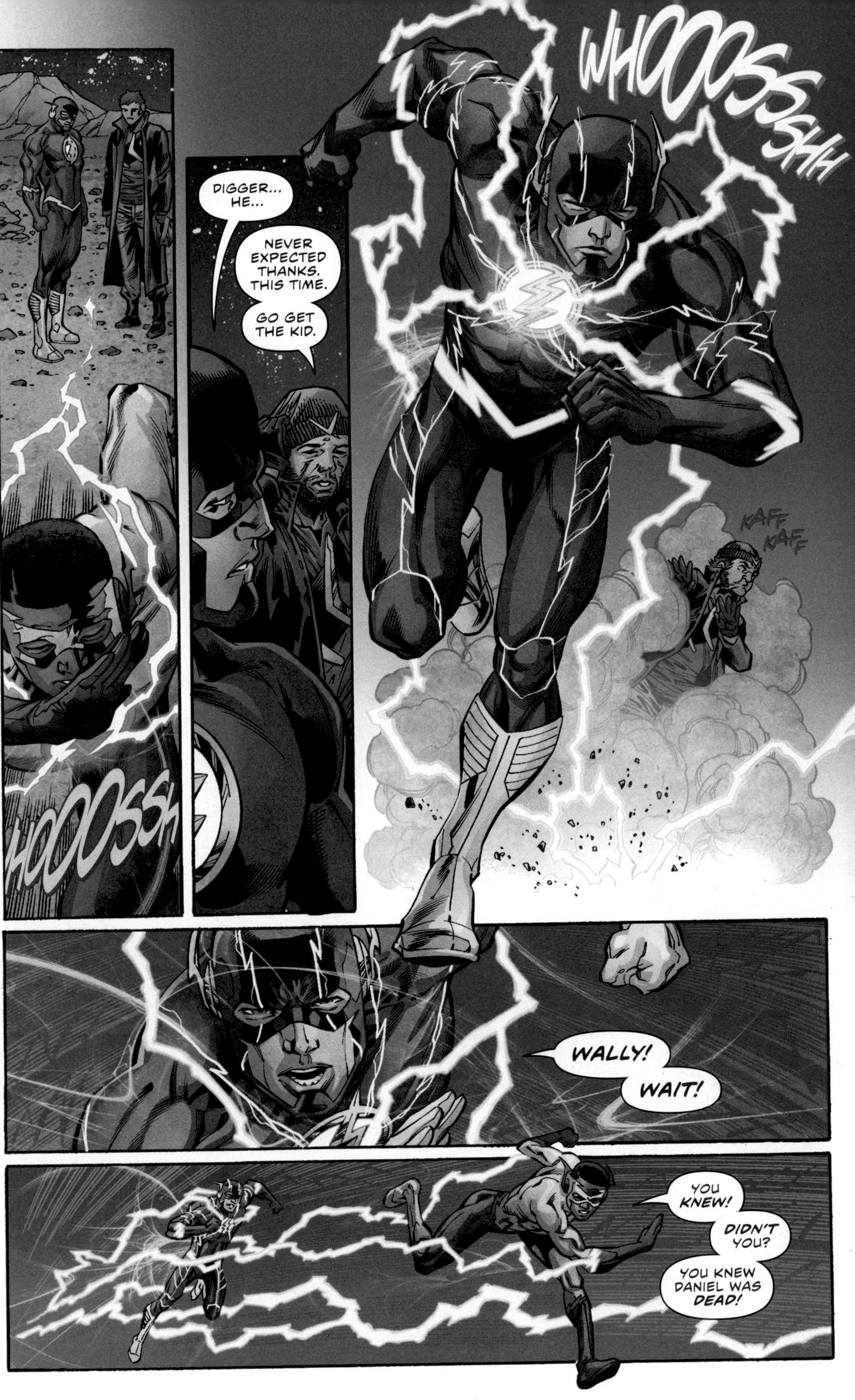
DIGGER... HE...
NEVER EXPECTED THANKS. THIS TIME.
GO GET THE KID.
WHOOOSSH
WHOOOSSHH
KAFF KAFF
WALLY!
WAIT!
YOU KNEW!
DIDN'T YOU?
YOU KNEW DANIEL WAS DEAD!

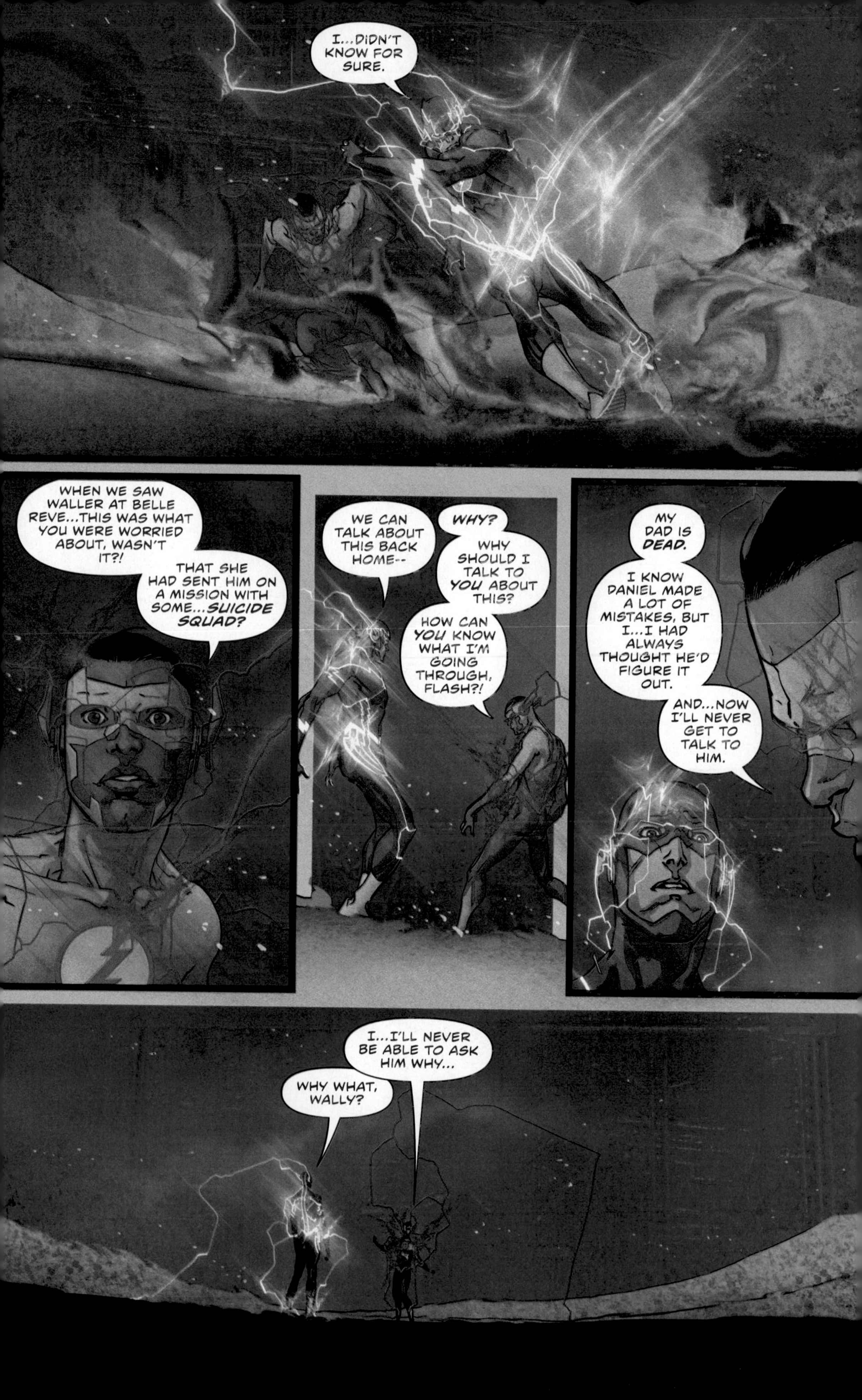
I...DIDN'T KNOW FOR SURE.
WHEN WE SAW WALLER AT BELLE REVE...THIS WAS WHAT YOU WERE WORRIED ABOUT, WASN'T IT?!
THAT SHE HAD SENT HIM ON A MISSION WITH SOME...SUICIDE SQUAD?
WE CAN TALK ABOUT THIS BACK HOME--
WHY?
WHY SHOULD I TALK TO YOU ABOUT THIS?
HOW CAN YOU KNOW WHAT I'M GOING THROUGH, FLASH?!
MY DAD IS DEAD.
I KNOW DANIEL MADE A LOT OF MISTAKES, BUT I...I HAD ALWAYS THOUGHT HE'D FIGURE IT OUT.
AND...NOW I'LL NEVER GET TO TALK TO HIM.
I...I'LL NEVER BE ABLE TO ASK HIM WHY...
WHY WHAT, WALLY?

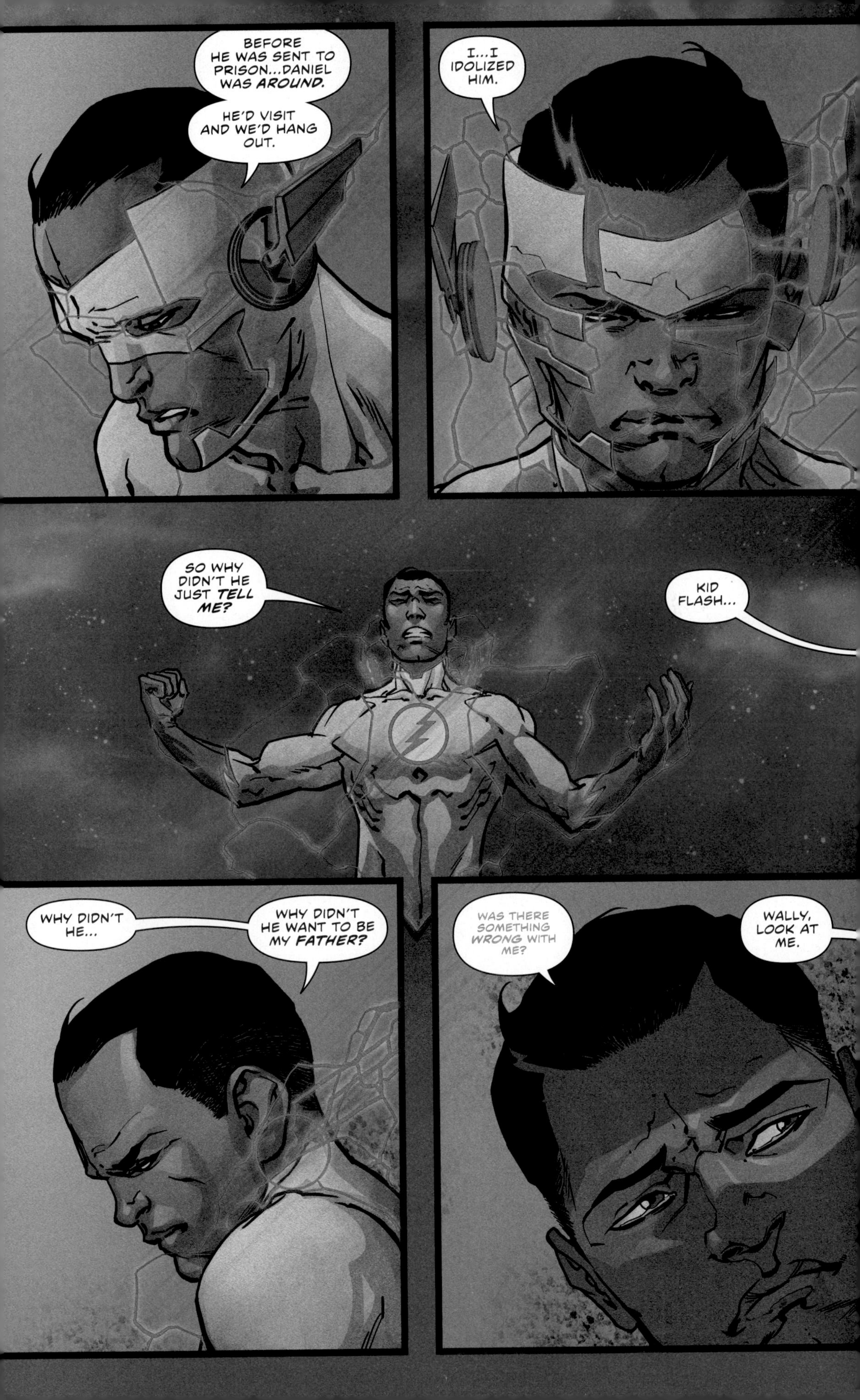
BEFORE HE WAS SENT TO PRISON...DANIEL WAS *AROUND.*
HE'D VISIT AND WE'D HANG OUT.
I...I IDOLIZED HIM.
SO WHY DIDN'T HE JUST *TELL ME?*
KID FLASH...
WHY DIDN'T HE...
WHY DIDN'T HE WANT TO BE MY *FATHER?*
WAS THERE SOMETHING *WRONG* WITH ME?
WALLY, LOOK AT ME.

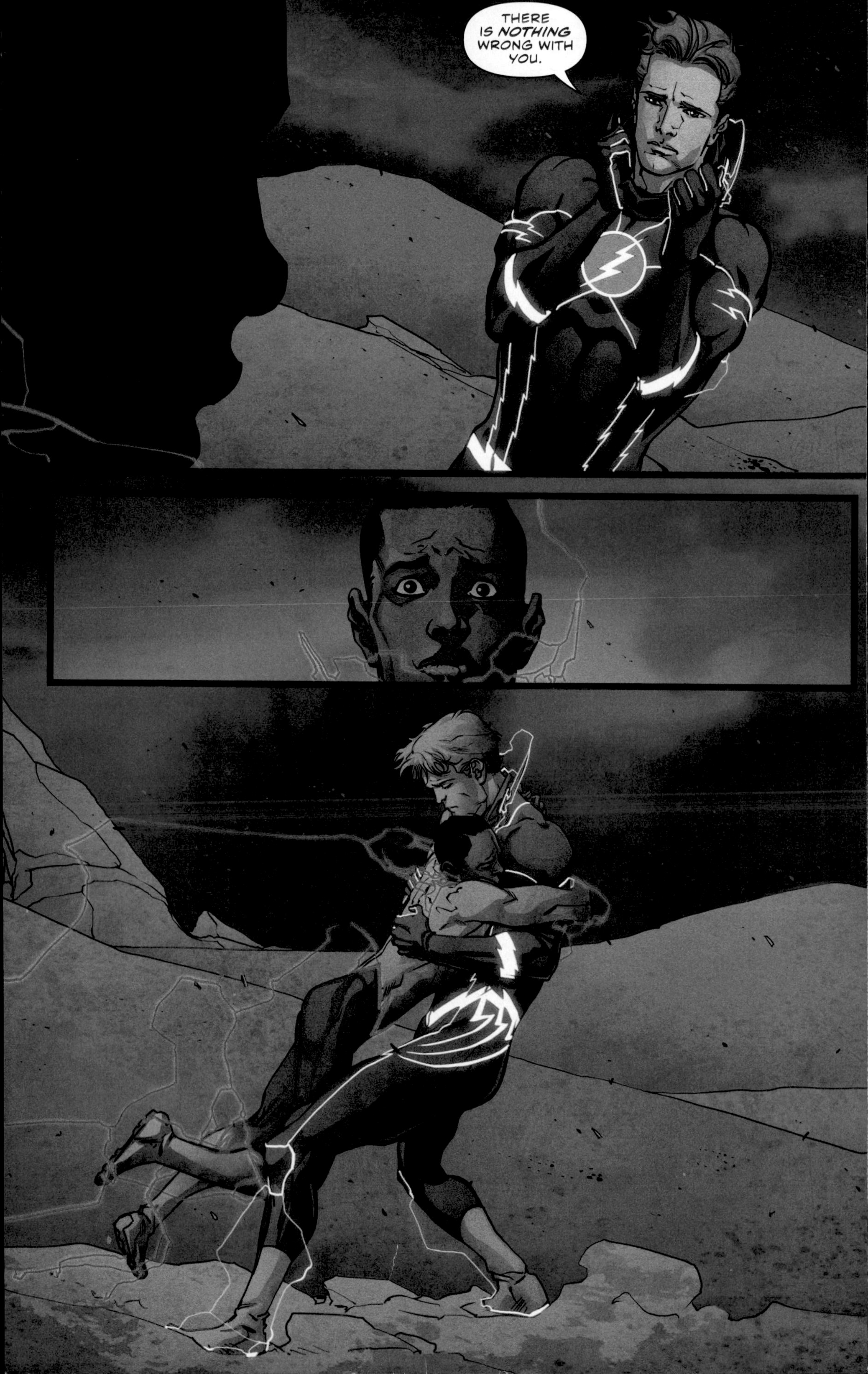
THERE IS *NOTHING* WRONG WITH YOU.

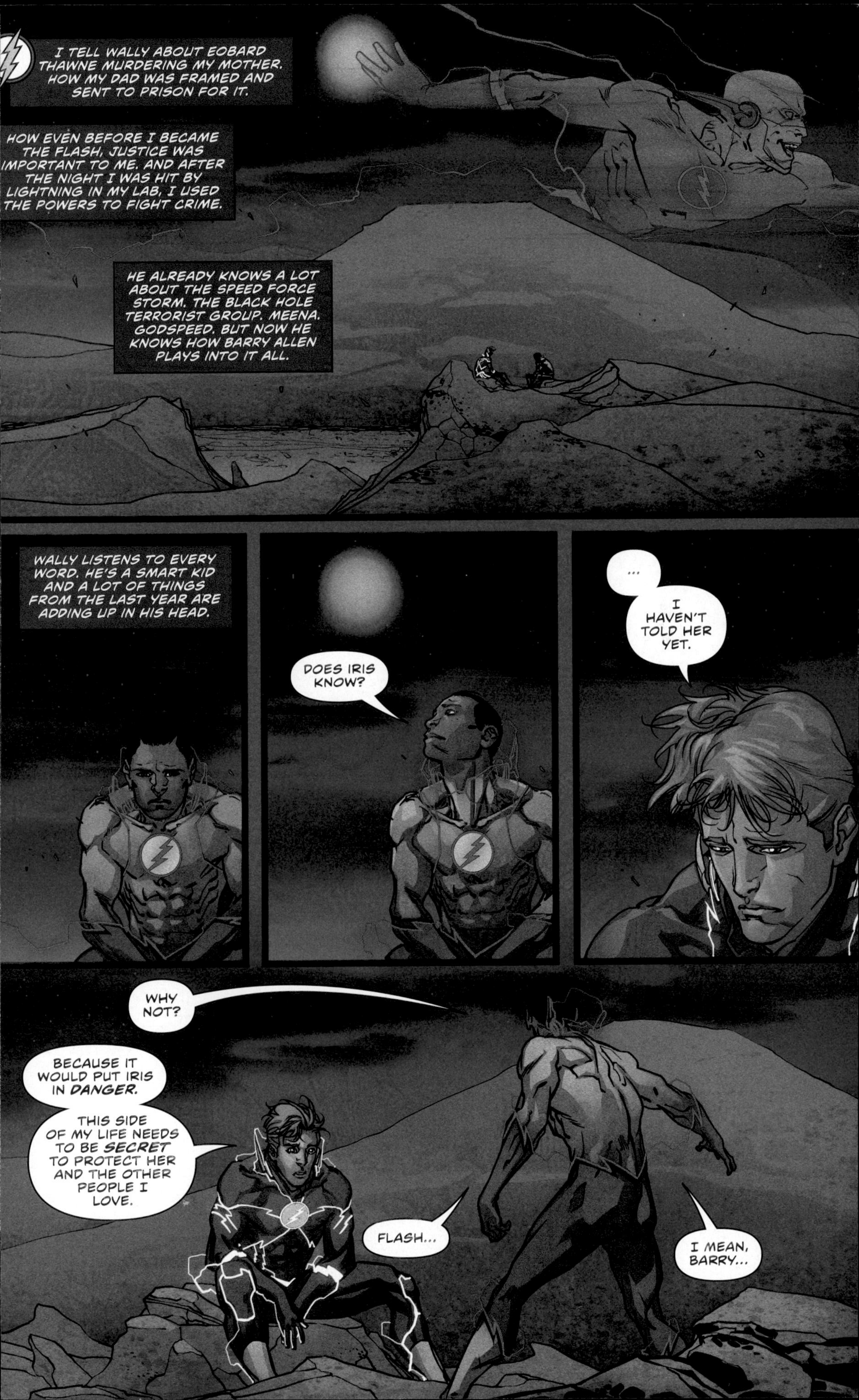
I TELL WALLY ABOUT EOBARD THAWNE MURDERING MY MOTHER. HOW MY DAD WAS FRAMED AND SENT TO PRISON FOR IT.
HOW EVEN BEFORE I BECAME THE FLASH, JUSTICE WAS IMPORTANT TO ME. AND AFTER THE NIGHT I WAS HIT BY LIGHTNING IN MY LAB, I USED THE POWERS TO FIGHT CRIME.
HE ALREADY KNOWS A LOT ABOUT THE SPEED FORCE STORM. THE BLACK HOLE TERRORIST GROUP. MEENA. GODSPEED. BUT NOW HE KNOWS HOW BARRY ALLEN PLAYS INTO IT ALL.
WALLY LISTENS TO EVERY WORD. HE'S A SMART KID AND A LOT OF THINGS FROM THE LAST YEAR ARE ADDING UP IN HIS HEAD.
DOES IRIS KNOW?
...
I HAVEN'T TOLD HER YET.
WHY NOT?
BECAUSE IT WOULD PUT IRIS IN *DANGER.*
THIS SIDE OF MY LIFE NEEDS TO BE *SECRET* TO PROTECT HER AND THE OTHER PEOPLE I LOVE.
FLASH...
I MEAN, BARRY...

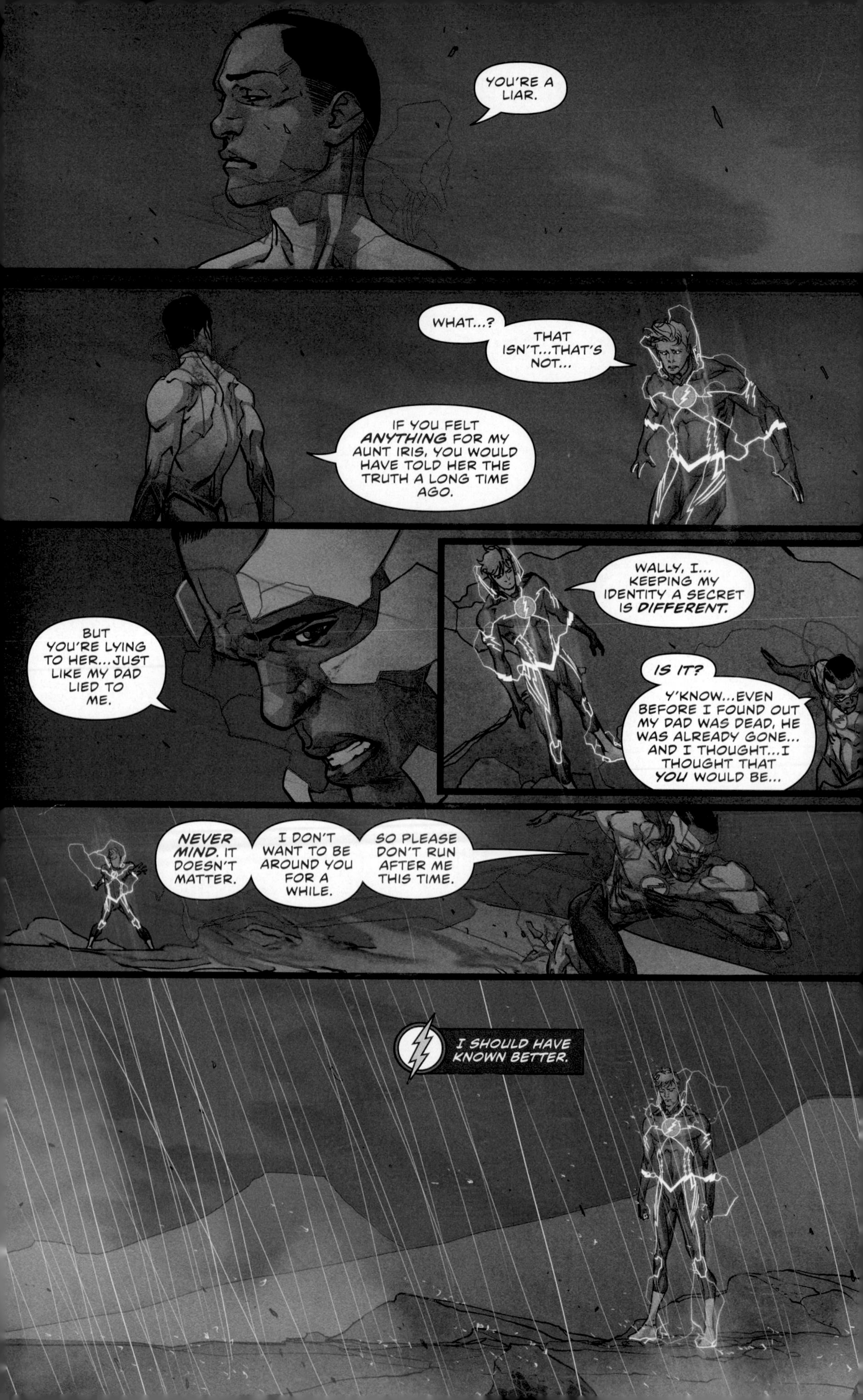
YOU'RE A LIAR.
WHAT...?
THAT ISN'T...THAT'S NOT...
IF YOU FELT ANYTHING FOR MY AUNT IRIS, YOU WOULD HAVE TOLD HER THE TRUTH A LONG TIME AGO.
BUT YOU'RE LYING TO HER...JUST LIKE MY DAD LIED TO ME.
WALLY, I... KEEPING MY IDENTITY A SECRET IS DIFFERENT.
IS IT?
Y'KNOW...EVEN BEFORE I FOUND OUT MY DAD WAS DEAD, HE WAS ALREADY GONE... AND I THOUGHT...I THOUGHT THAT YOU WOULD BE...
NEVER MIND. IT DOESN'T MATTER.
I DON'T WANT TO BE AROUND YOU FOR A WHILE.
SO PLEASE DON'T RUN AFTER ME THIS TIME.
I SHOULD HAVE KNOWN BETTER.

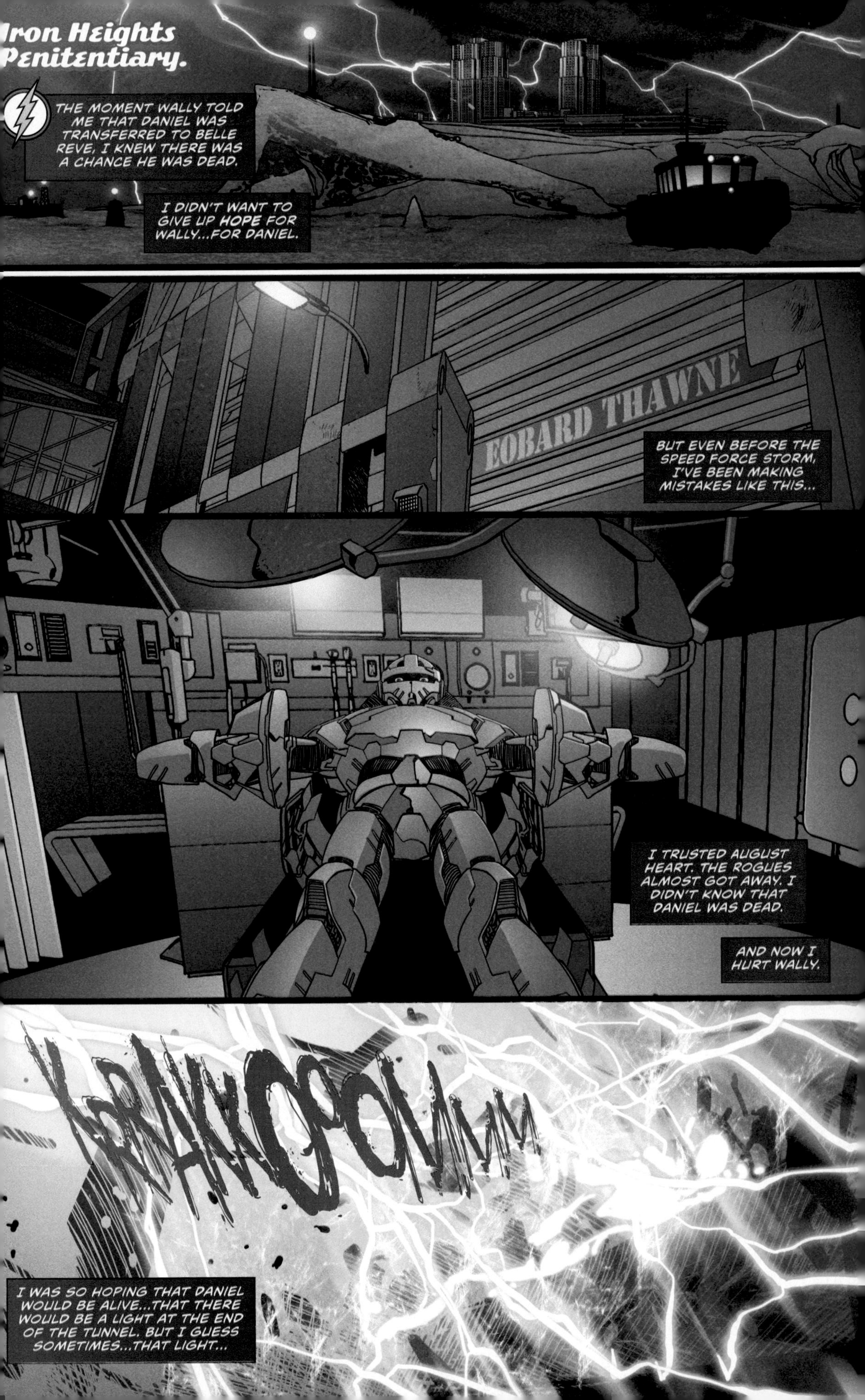
Iron Heights Penitentiary.
THE MOMENT WALLY TOLD ME THAT DANIEL WAS TRANSFERRED TO BELLE REVE, I KNEW THERE WAS A CHANCE HE WAS DEAD.
I DIDN'T WANT TO GIVE UP HOPE FOR WALLY...FOR DANIEL.
EOBARD THAWNE
BUT EVEN BEFORE THE SPEED FORCE STORM, I'VE BEEN MAKING MISTAKES LIKE THIS...
I TRUSTED AUGUST HEART. THE ROGUES ALMOST GOT AWAY. I DIDN'T KNOW THAT DANIEL WAS DEAD.
AND NOW I HURT WALLY.
KRAKOOMM
I WAS SO HOPING THAT DANIEL WOULD BE ALIVE...THAT THERE WOULD BE A LIGHT AT THE END OF THE TUNNEL. BUT I GUESS SOMETIMES...THAT LIGHT...

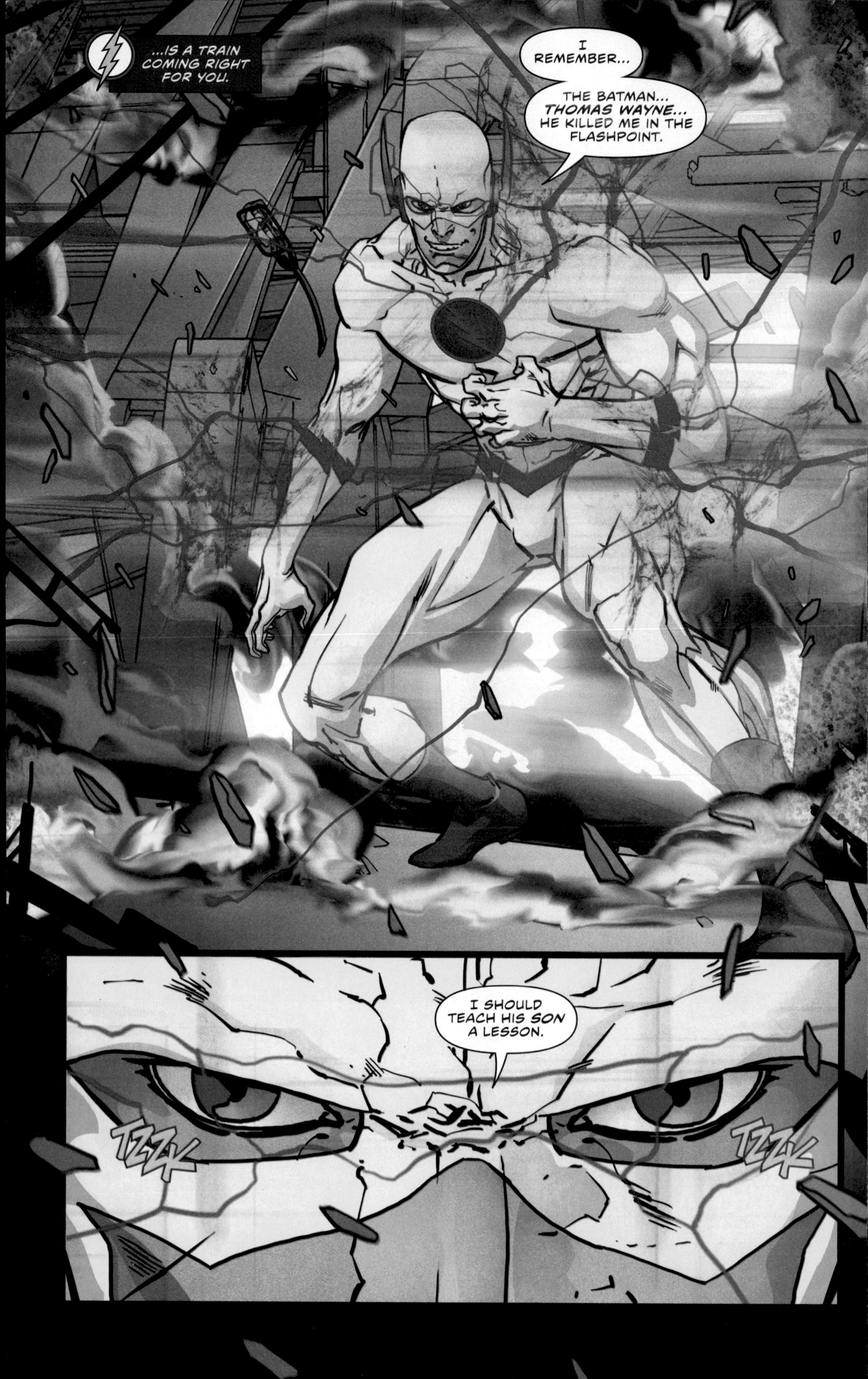

...IS A TRAIN COMING RIGHT FOR YOU.
I REMEMBER...
THE BATMAN... THOMAS WAYNE... HE KILLED ME IN THE FLASHPOINT.
I SHOULD TEACH HIS SON A LESSON.
TZZK
TZZK

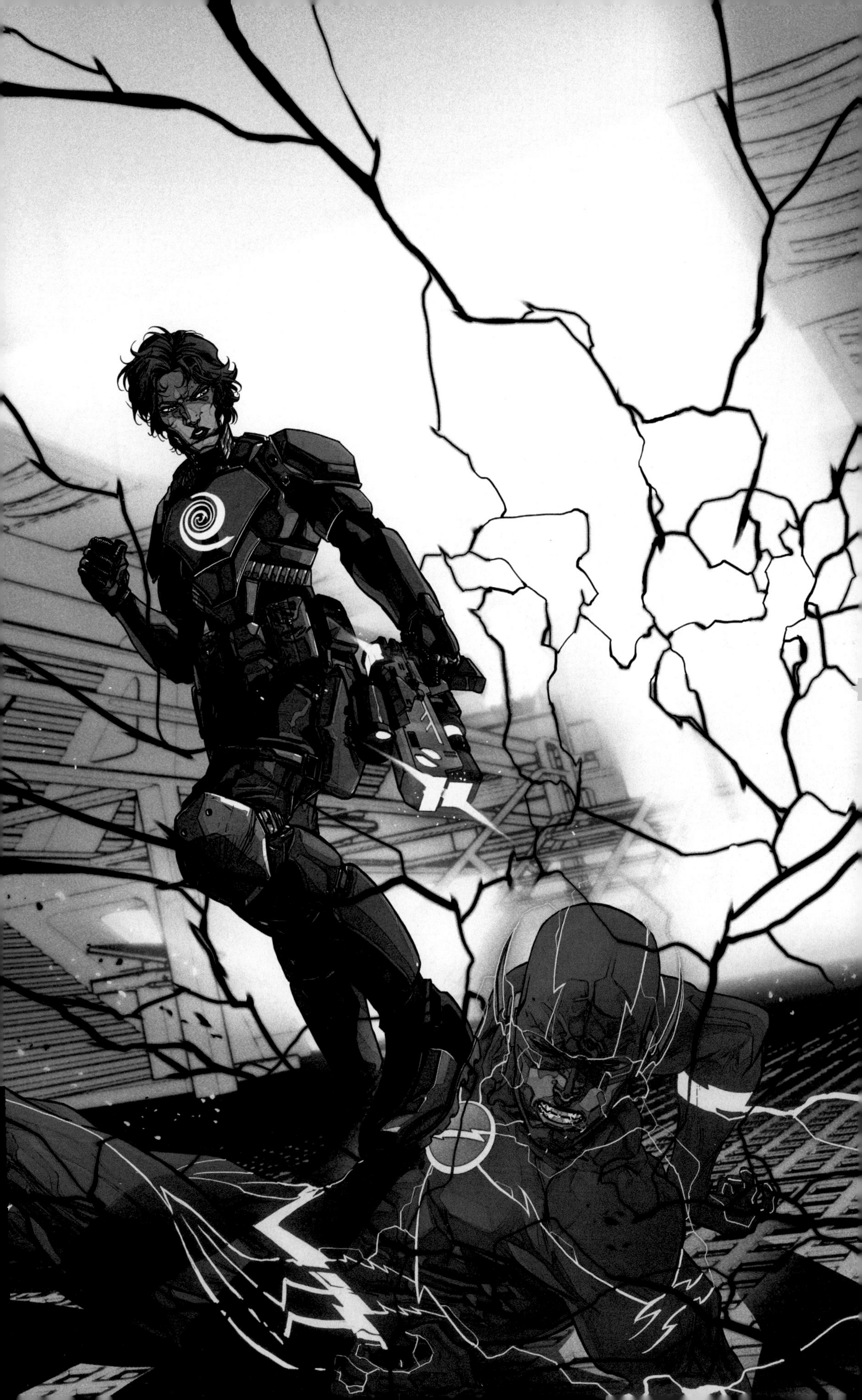

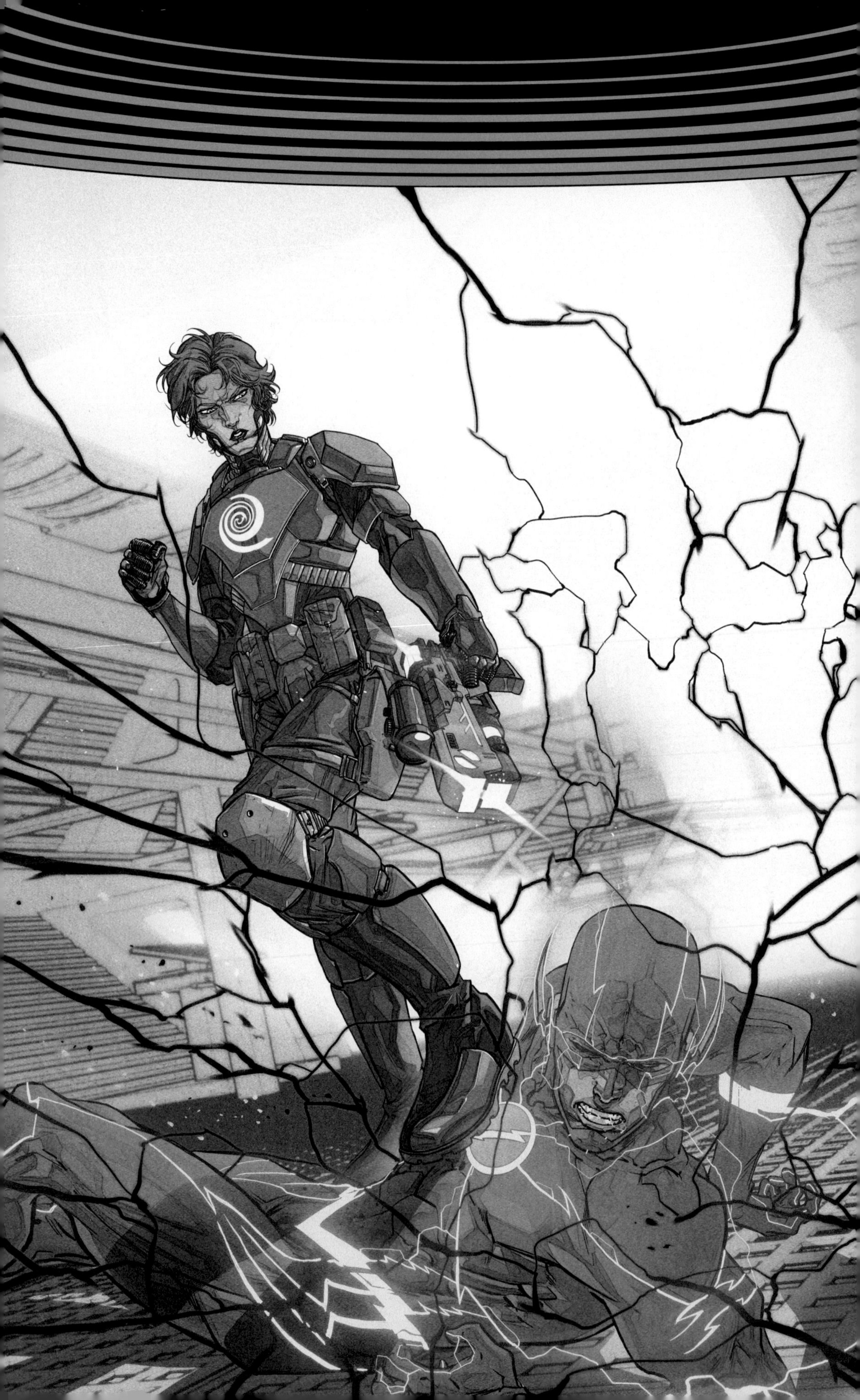

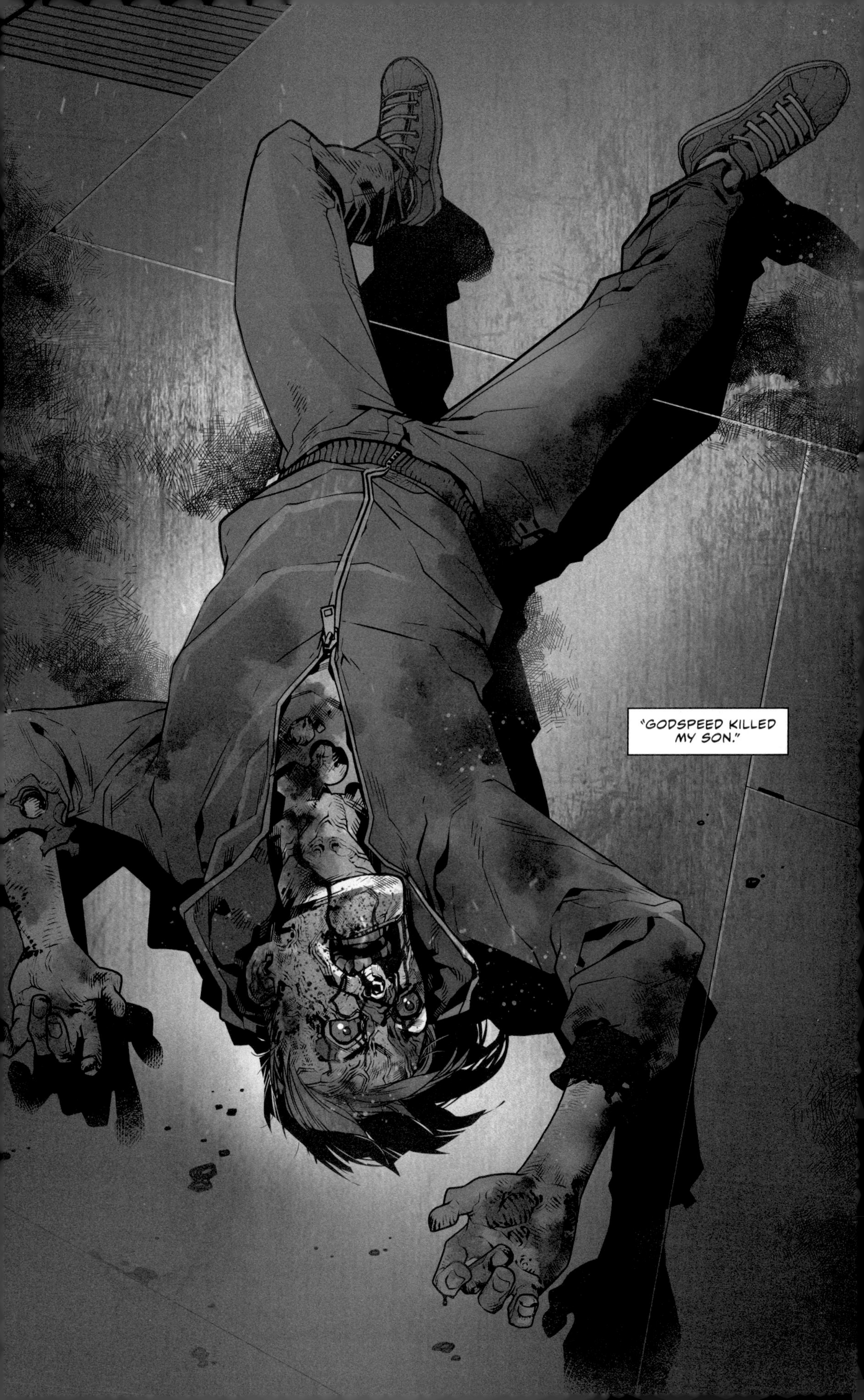
"GODSPEED KILLED MY SON."

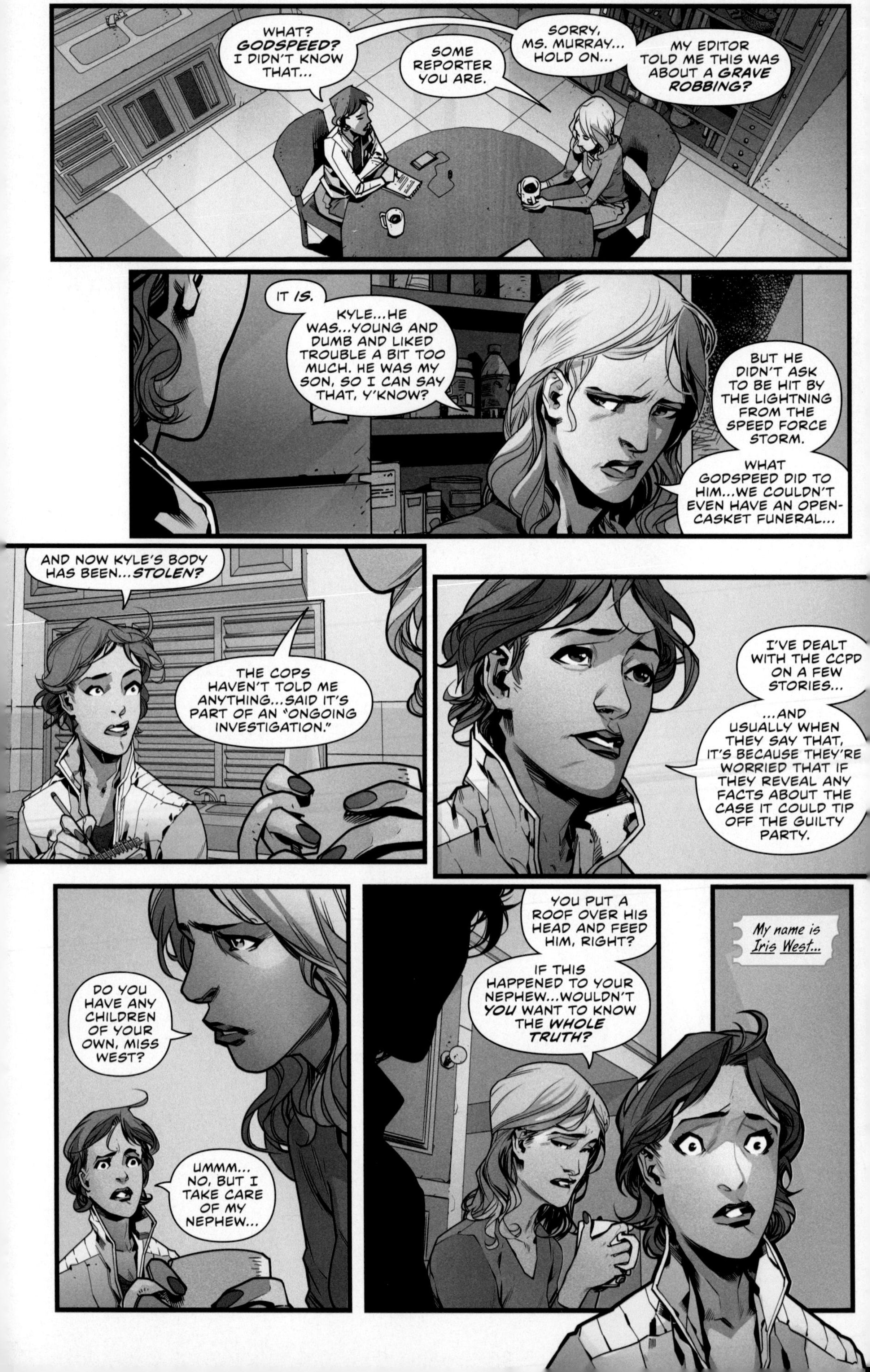
WHAT? GODSPEED? I DIDN'T KNOW THAT...
SOME REPORTER YOU ARE.
SORRY, MS. MURRAY... HOLD ON...
MY EDITOR TOLD ME THIS WAS ABOUT A GRAVE ROBBING?
IT IS.
KYLE...HE WAS...YOUNG AND DUMB AND LIKED TROUBLE A BIT TOO MUCH. HE WAS MY SON, SO I CAN SAY THAT, Y'KNOW?
BUT HE DIDN'T ASK TO BE HIT BY THE LIGHTNING FROM THE SPEED FORCE STORM.
WHAT GODSPEED DID TO HIM...WE COULDN'T EVEN HAVE AN OPEN-CASKET FUNERAL...
AND NOW KYLE'S BODY HAS BEEN...STOLEN?
THE COPS HAVEN'T TOLD ME ANYTHING...SAID IT'S PART OF AN "ONGOING INVESTIGATION."
I'VE DEALT WITH THE CCPD ON A FEW STORIES...
...AND USUALLY WHEN THEY SAY THAT, IT'S BECAUSE THEY'RE WORRIED THAT IF THEY REVEAL ANY FACTS ABOUT THE CASE IT COULD TIP OFF THE GUILTY PARTY.
DO YOU HAVE ANY CHILDREN OF YOUR OWN, MISS WEST?
UMMM... NO, BUT I TAKE CARE OF MY NEPHEW...
YOU PUT A ROOF OVER HIS HEAD AND FEED HIM, RIGHT?
IF THIS HAPPENED TO YOUR NEPHEW...WOULDN'T YOU WANT TO KNOW THE WHOLE TRUTH?
My name is Iris West...

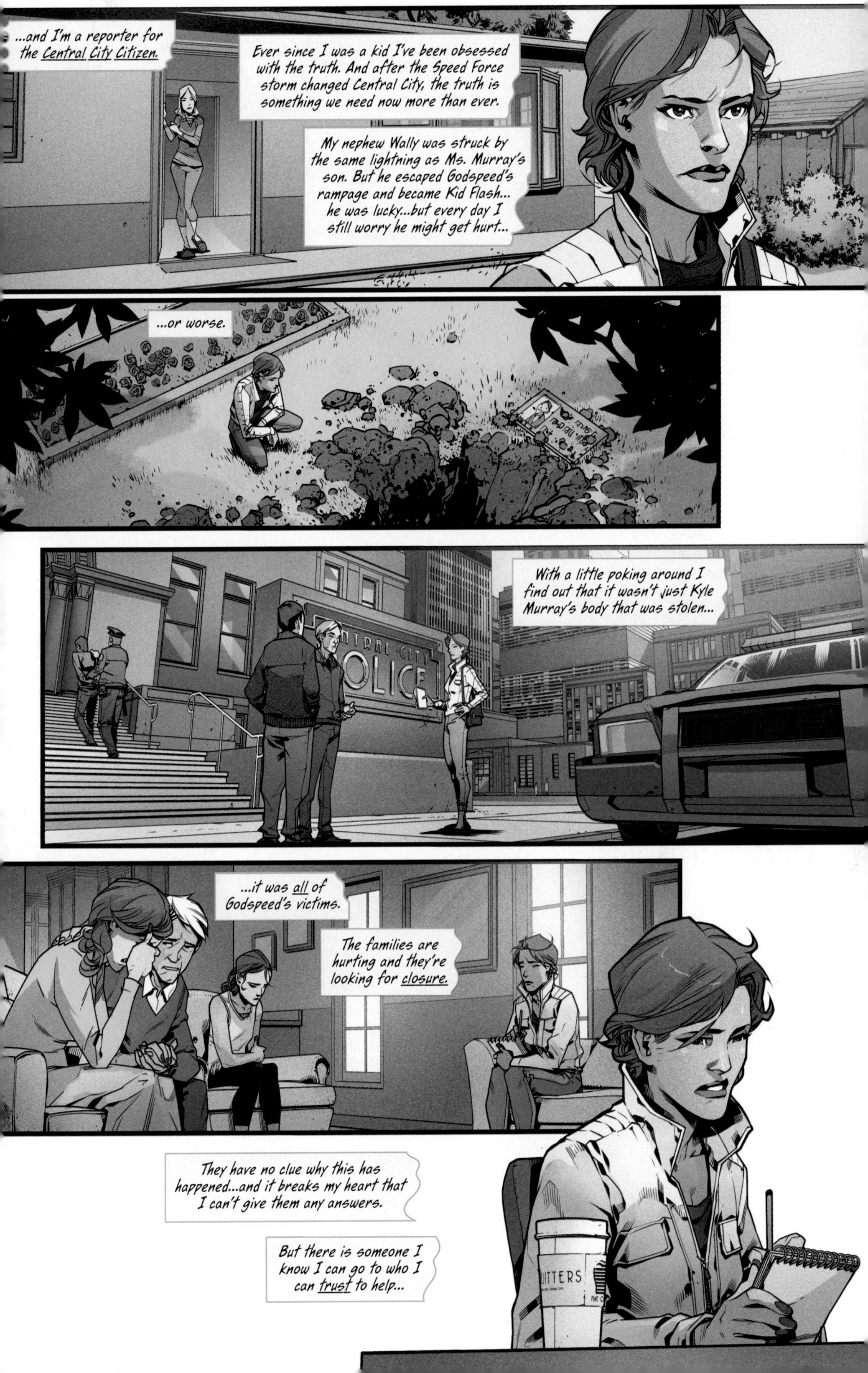
...and I'm a reporter for the Central City Citizen.
Ever since I was a kid I've been obsessed with the truth. And after the Speed Force storm changed Central City, the truth is something we need now more than ever.
My nephew Wally was struck by the same lightning as Ms. Murray's son. But he escaped Godspeed's rampage and became Kid Flash... he was lucky...but every day I still worry he might get hurt...
...or worse.
With a little poking around I find out that it wasn't just Kyle Murray's body that was stolen...
...it was all of Godspeed's victims.
The families are hurting and they're looking for closure.
They have no clue why this has happened...and it breaks my heart that I can't give them any answers.
But there is someone I know I can go to who I can trust to help...

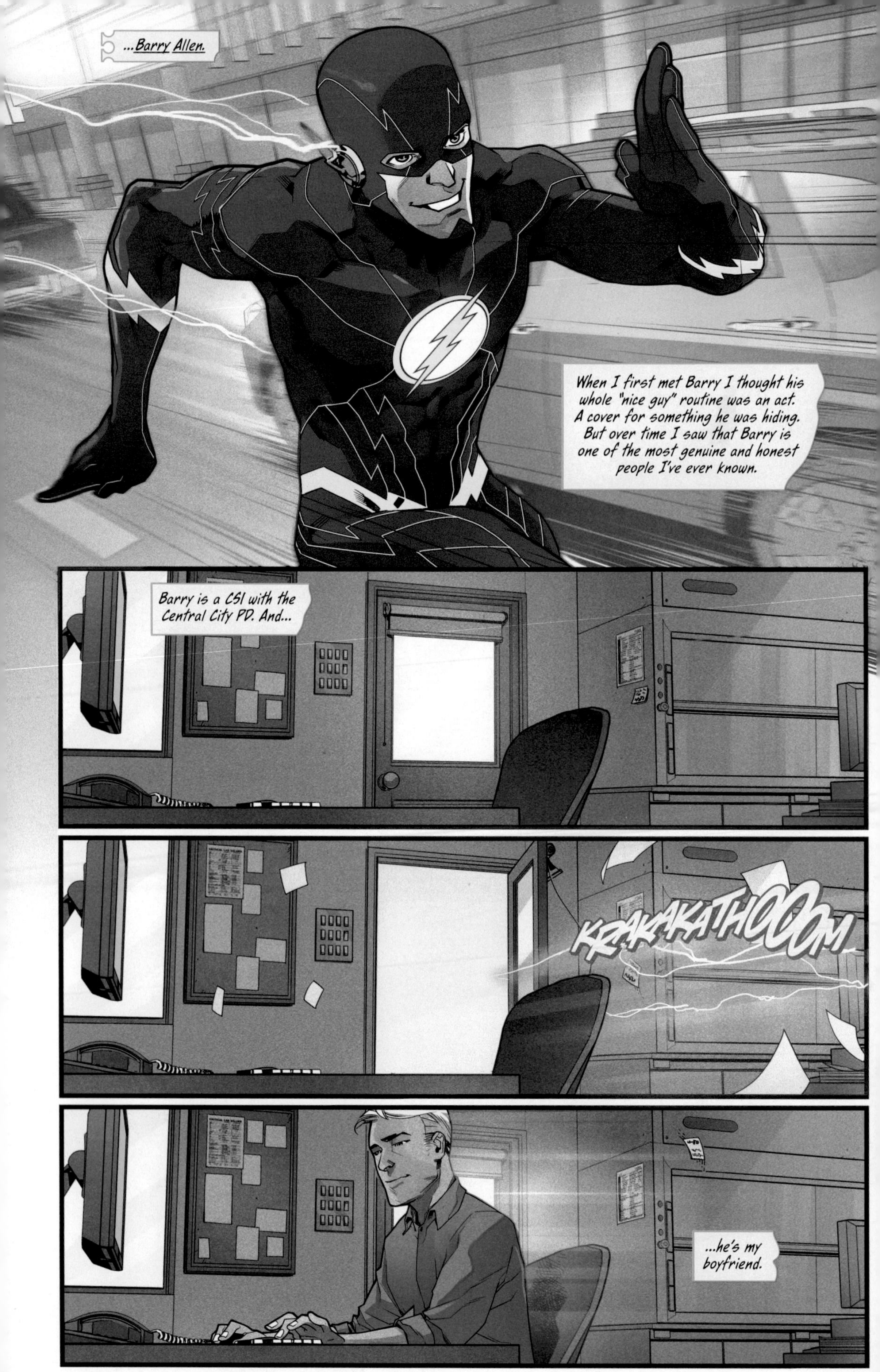
...Barry Allen.
When I first met Barry I thought his whole "nice guy" routine was an act. A cover for something he was hiding. But over time I saw that Barry is one of the most genuine and honest people I've ever known.
Barry is a CSI with the Central City PD. And...
KRAKAKATHOOOM
...he's my boyfriend.

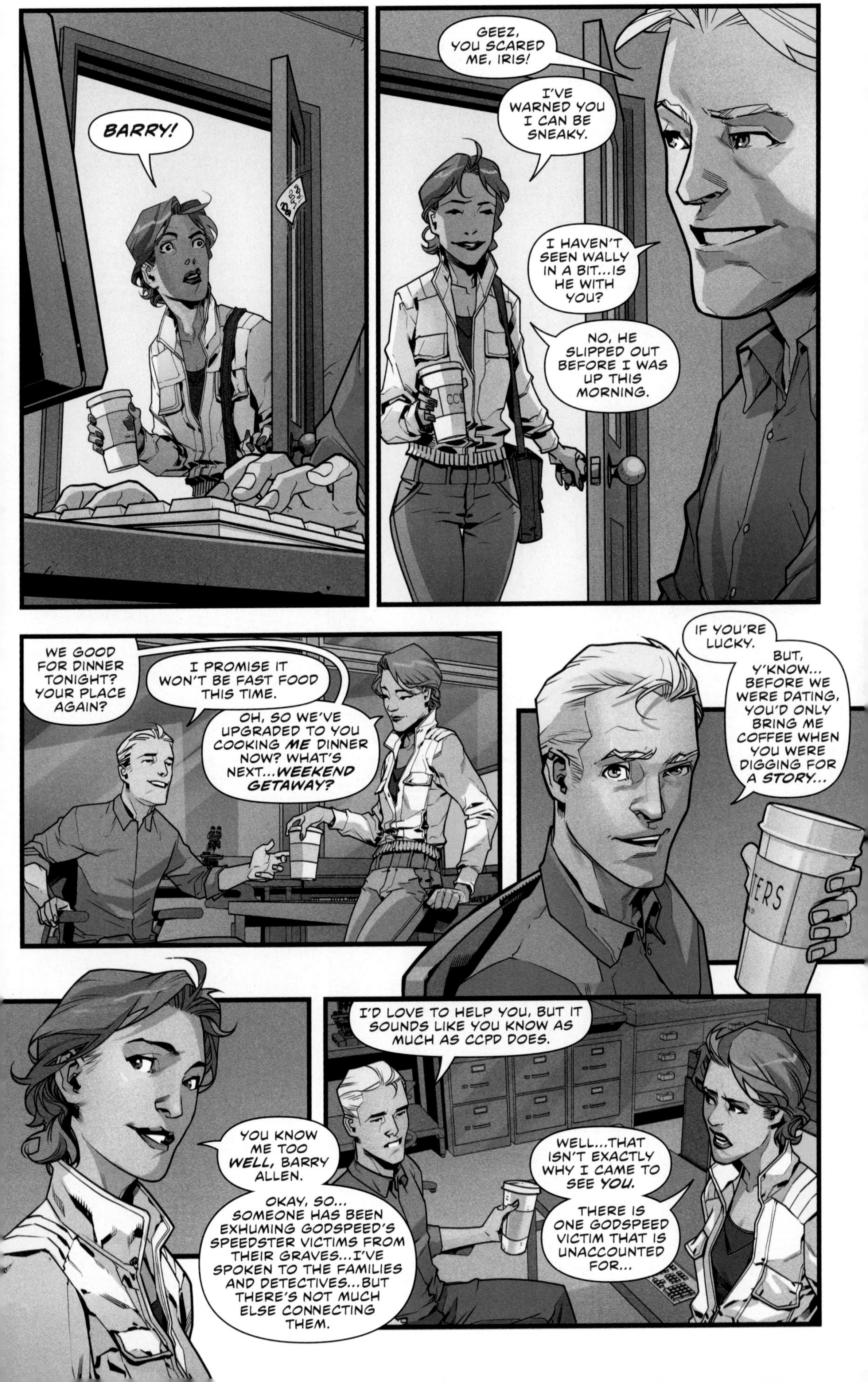
BARRY!
GEEZ, YOU SCARED ME, IRIS!
I'VE WARNED YOU I CAN BE SNEAKY.
I HAVEN'T SEEN WALLY IN A BIT...IS HE WITH YOU?
NO, HE SLIPPED OUT BEFORE I WAS UP THIS MORNING.
WE GOOD FOR DINNER TONIGHT? YOUR PLACE AGAIN?
I PROMISE IT WON'T BE FAST FOOD THIS TIME.
OH, SO WE'VE UPGRADED TO YOU COOKING ME DINNER NOW? WHAT'S NEXT...WEEKEND GETAWAY?
IF YOU'RE LUCKY.
BUT, Y'KNOW... BEFORE WE WERE DATING, YOU'D ONLY BRING ME COFFEE WHEN YOU WERE DIGGING FOR A STORY...
YOU KNOW ME TOO WELL, BARRY ALLEN.
OKAY, SO... SOMEONE HAS BEEN EXHUMING GODSPEED'S SPEEDSTER VICTIMS FROM THEIR GRAVES...I'VE SPOKEN TO THE FAMILIES AND DETECTIVES...BUT THERE'S NOT MUCH ELSE CONNECTING THEM.
I'D LOVE TO HELP YOU, BUT IT SOUNDS LIKE YOU KNOW AS MUCH AS CCPD DOES.
WELL...THAT ISN'T EXACTLY WHY I CAME TO SEE YOU.
THERE IS ONE GODSPEED VICTIM THAT IS UNACCOUNTED FOR...

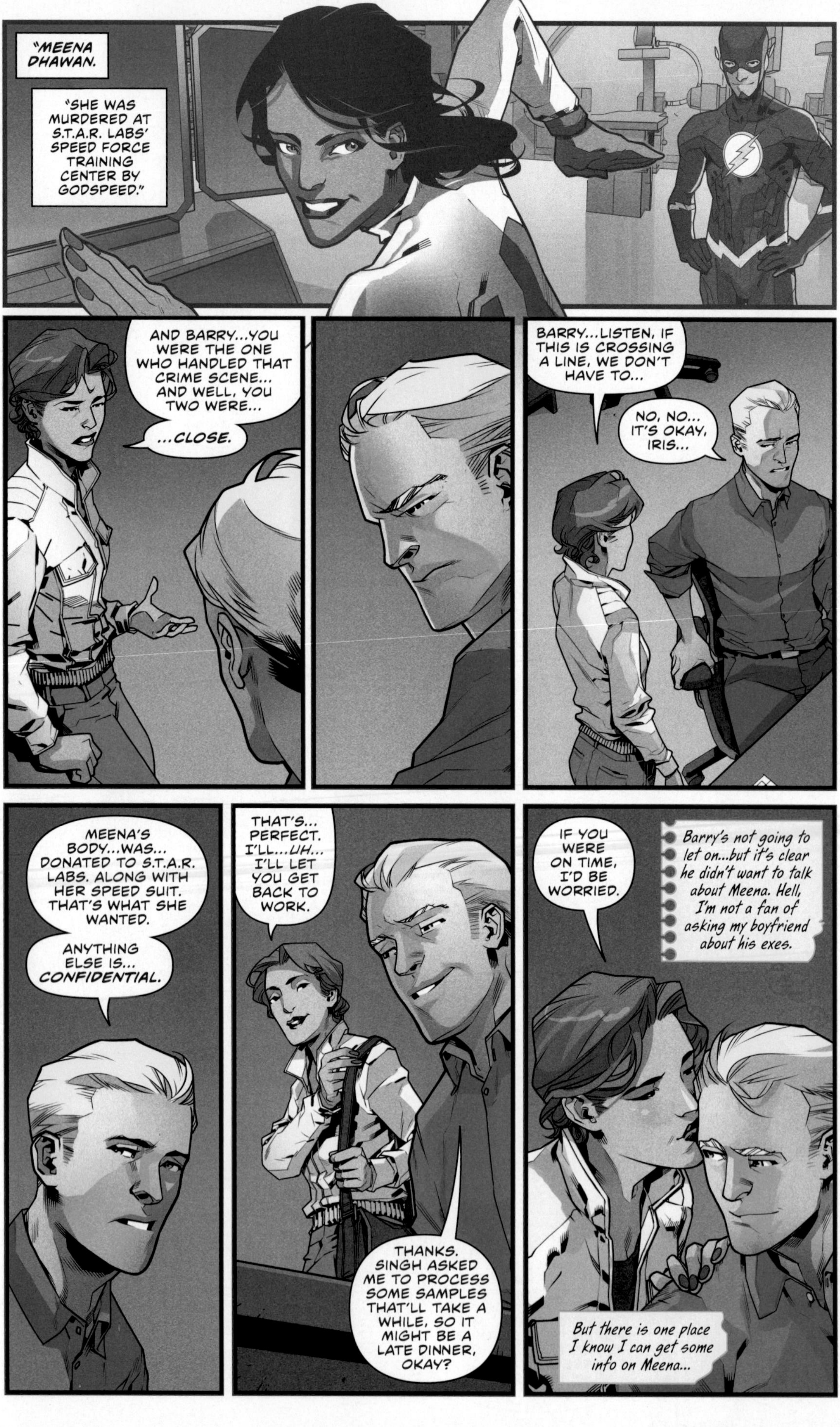
"MEENA DHAWAN.
"SHE WAS MURDERED AT S.T.A.R. LABS' SPEED FORCE TRAINING CENTER BY GODSPEED."
AND BARRY...YOU WERE THE ONE WHO HANDLED THAT CRIME SCENE... AND WELL, YOU TWO WERE...
...CLOSE.
BARRY...LISTEN, IF THIS IS CROSSING A LINE, WE DON'T HAVE TO...
NO, NO... IT'S OKAY, IRIS...
MEENA'S BODY...WAS... DONATED TO S.T.A.R. LABS. ALONG WITH HER SPEED SUIT. THAT'S WHAT SHE WANTED.
ANYTHING ELSE IS... CONFIDENTIAL.
THAT'S... PERFECT. I'LL...UH... I'LL LET YOU GET BACK TO WORK.
THANKS. SINGH ASKED ME TO PROCESS SOME SAMPLES THAT'LL TAKE A WHILE, SO IT MIGHT BE A LATE DINNER, OKAY?
IF YOU WERE ON TIME, I'D BE WORRIED.
Barry's not going to let on...but it's clear he didn't want to talk about Meena. Hell, I'm not a fan of asking my boyfriend about his exes.
But there is one place I know I can get some info on Meena...

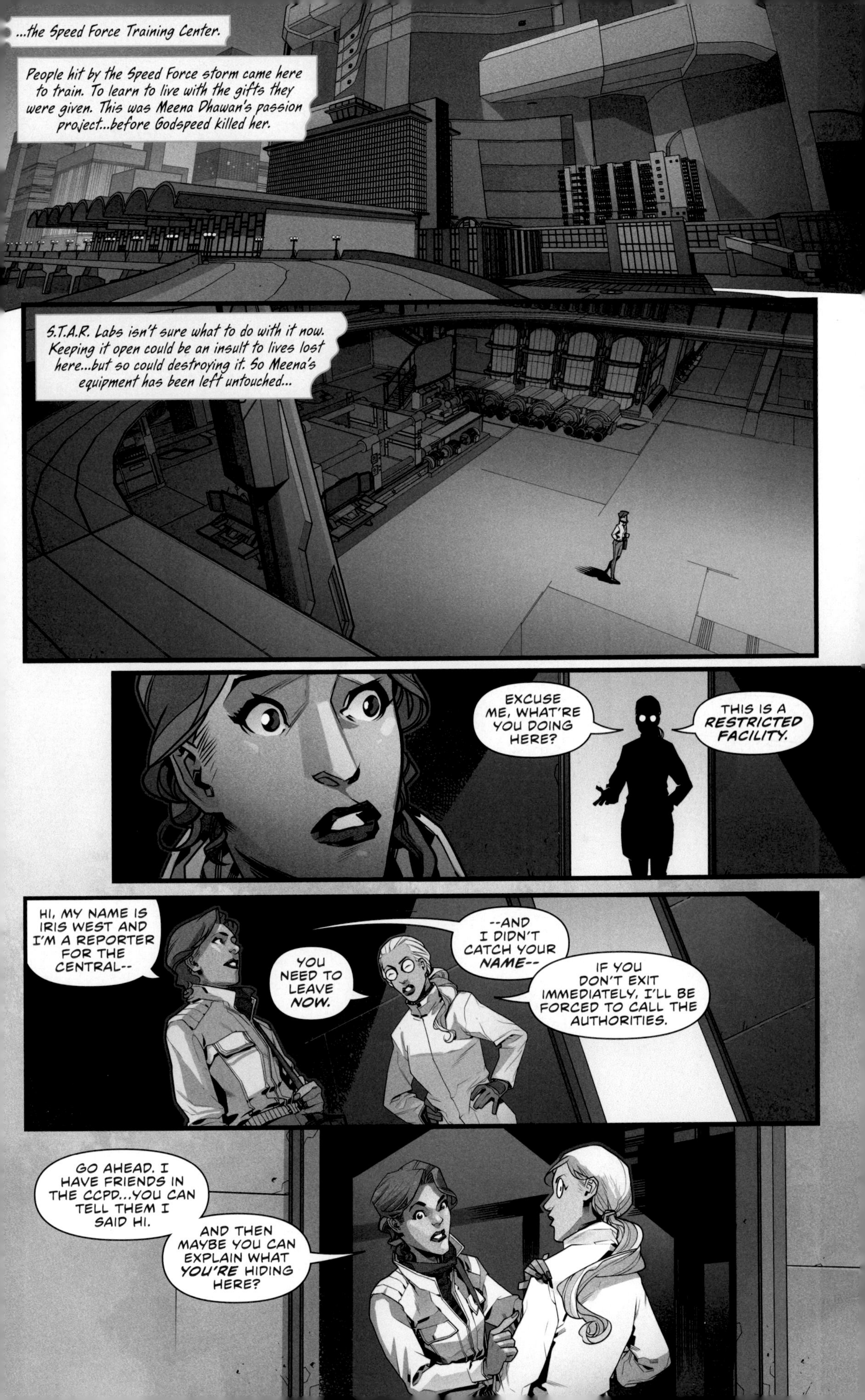
...the Speed Force Training Center.
People hit by the Speed Force storm came here to train. To learn to live with the gifts they were given. This was Meena Dhawan's passion project...before Godspeed killed her.
S.T.A.R. Labs isn't sure what to do with it now. Keeping it open could be an insult to lives lost here...but so could destroying it. So Meena's equipment has been left untouched...
EXCUSE ME, WHAT'RE YOU DOING HERE?
THIS IS A RESTRICTED FACILITY.
HI, MY NAME IS IRIS WEST AND I'M A REPORTER FOR THE CENTRAL--
YOU NEED TO LEAVE NOW.
--AND I DIDN'T CATCH YOUR NAME--
IF YOU DON'T EXIT IMMEDIATELY, I'LL BE FORCED TO CALL THE AUTHORITIES.
GO AHEAD. I HAVE FRIENDS IN THE CCPD...YOU CAN TELL THEM I SAID HI.
AND THEN MAYBE YOU CAN EXPLAIN WHAT YOU'RE HIDING HERE?

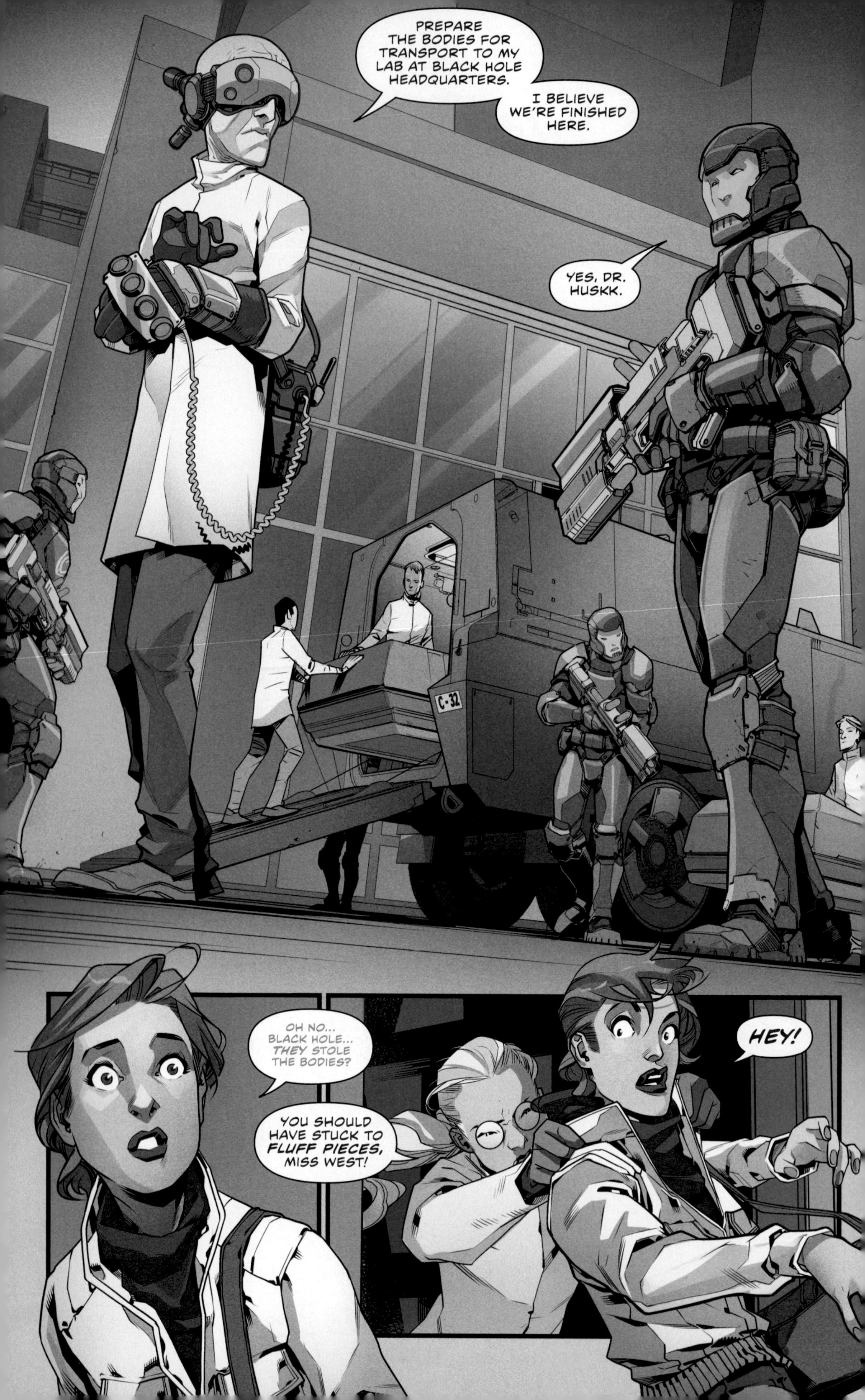
PREPARE THE BODIES FOR TRANSPORT TO MY LAB AT BLACK HOLE HEADQUARTERS.
I BELIEVE WE'RE FINISHED HERE.
YES, DR. HUSKK.
C-32
OH NO... BLACK HOLE... *THEY* STOLE THE BODIES?
YOU SHOULD HAVE STUCK TO **FLUFF PIECES,** MISS WEST!
HEY!

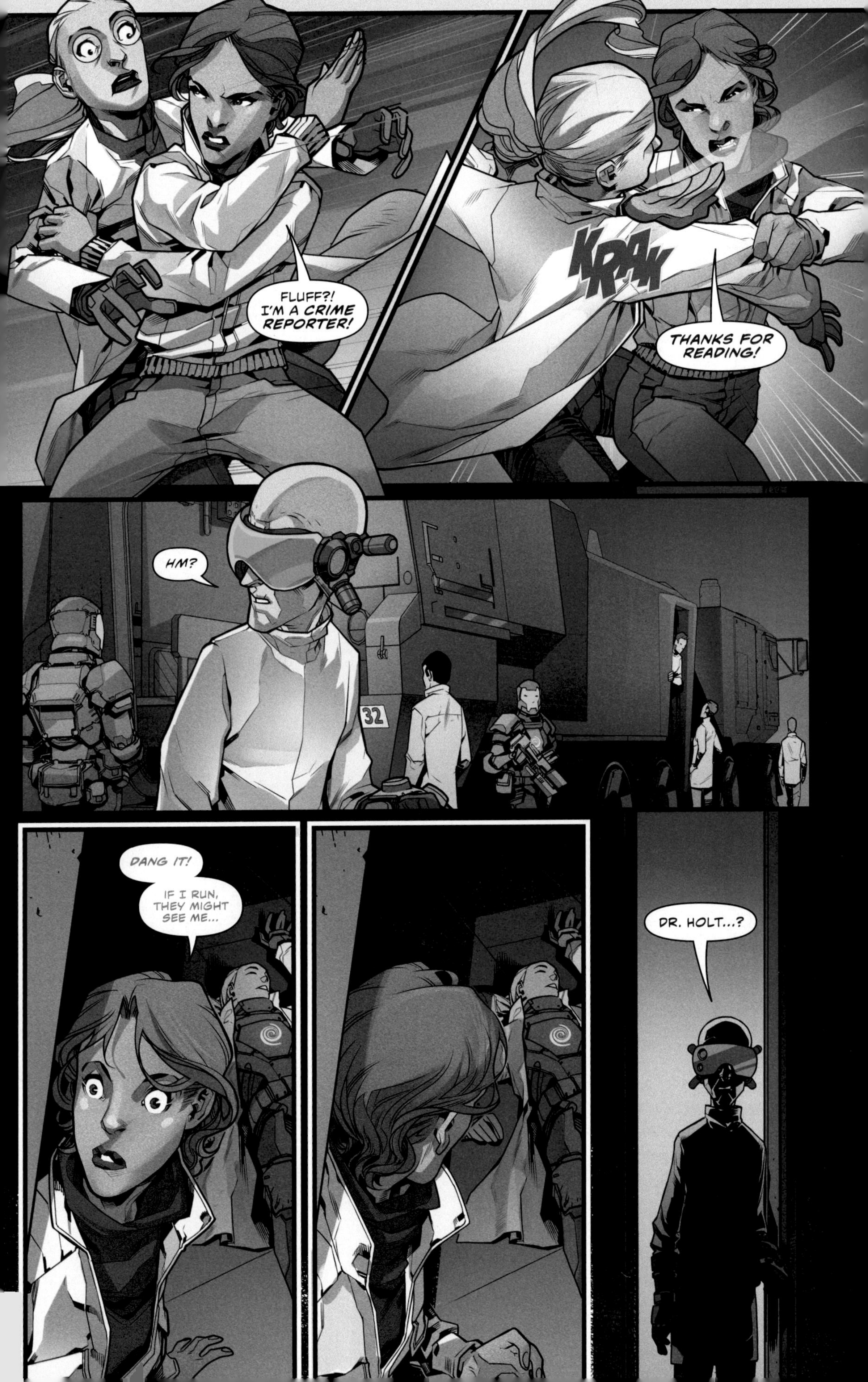
FLUFF?! I'M A CRIME REPORTER!
KRAK
THANKS FOR READING!
HM?
32
DANG IT!
IF I RUN, THEY MIGHT SEE ME...
DR. HOLT...?

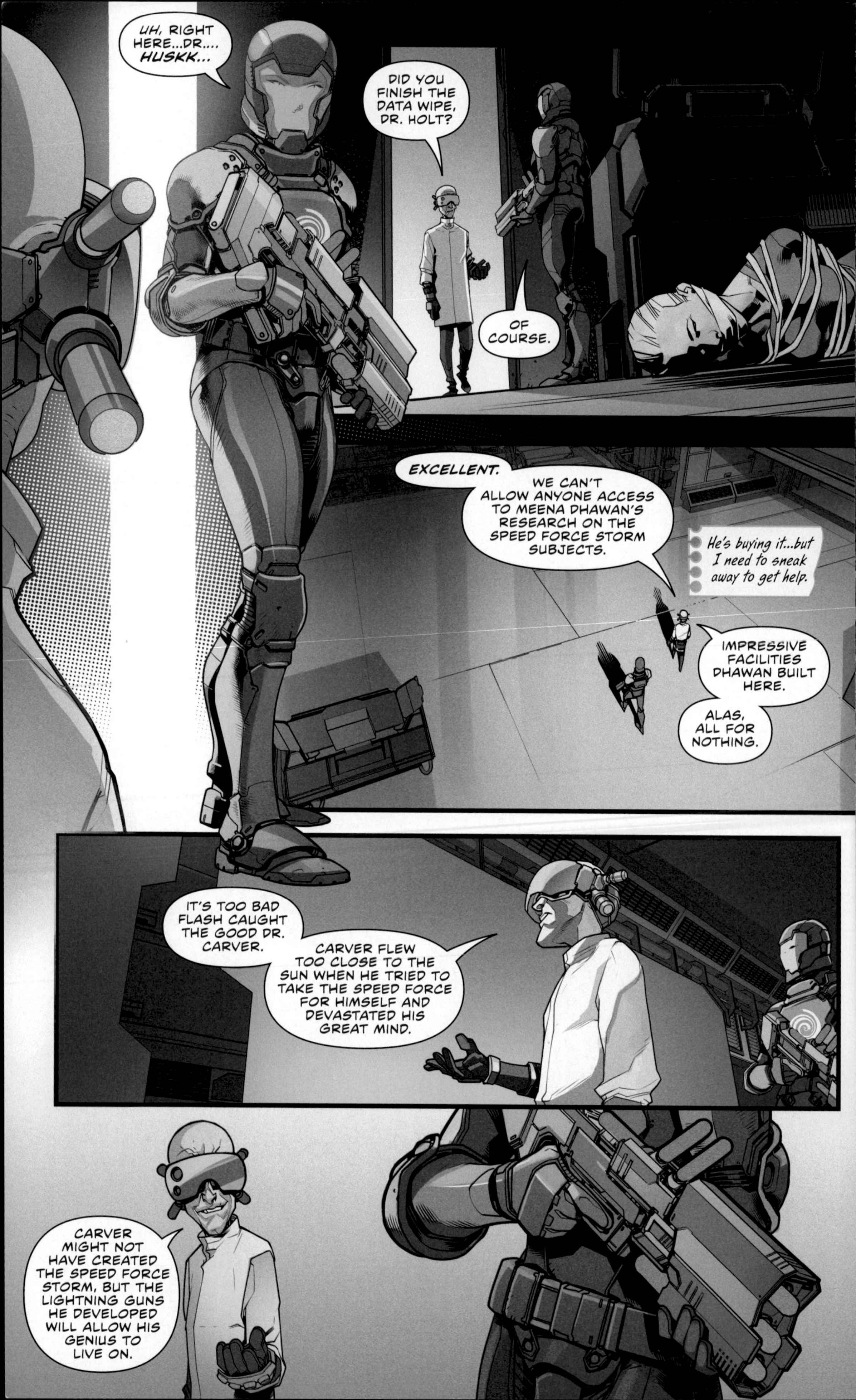
UH, RIGHT HERE...DR.... HUSKK...
DID YOU FINISH THE DATA WIPE, DR. HOLT?
OF COURSE.
EXCELLENT.
WE CAN'T ALLOW ANYONE ACCESS TO MEENA DHAWAN'S RESEARCH ON THE SPEED FORCE STORM SUBJECTS.
He's buying it...but I need to sneak away to get help.
IMPRESSIVE FACILITIES DHAWAN BUILT HERE.
ALAS, ALL FOR NOTHING.
IT'S TOO BAD FLASH CAUGHT THE GOOD DR. CARVER.
CARVER FLEW TOO CLOSE TO THE SUN WHEN HE TRIED TO TAKE THE SPEED FORCE FOR HIMSELF AND DEVASTATED HIS GREAT MIND.
CARVER MIGHT NOT HAVE CREATED THE SPEED FORCE STORM, BUT THE LIGHTNING GUNS HE DEVELOPED WILL ALLOW HIS GENIUS TO LIVE ON.

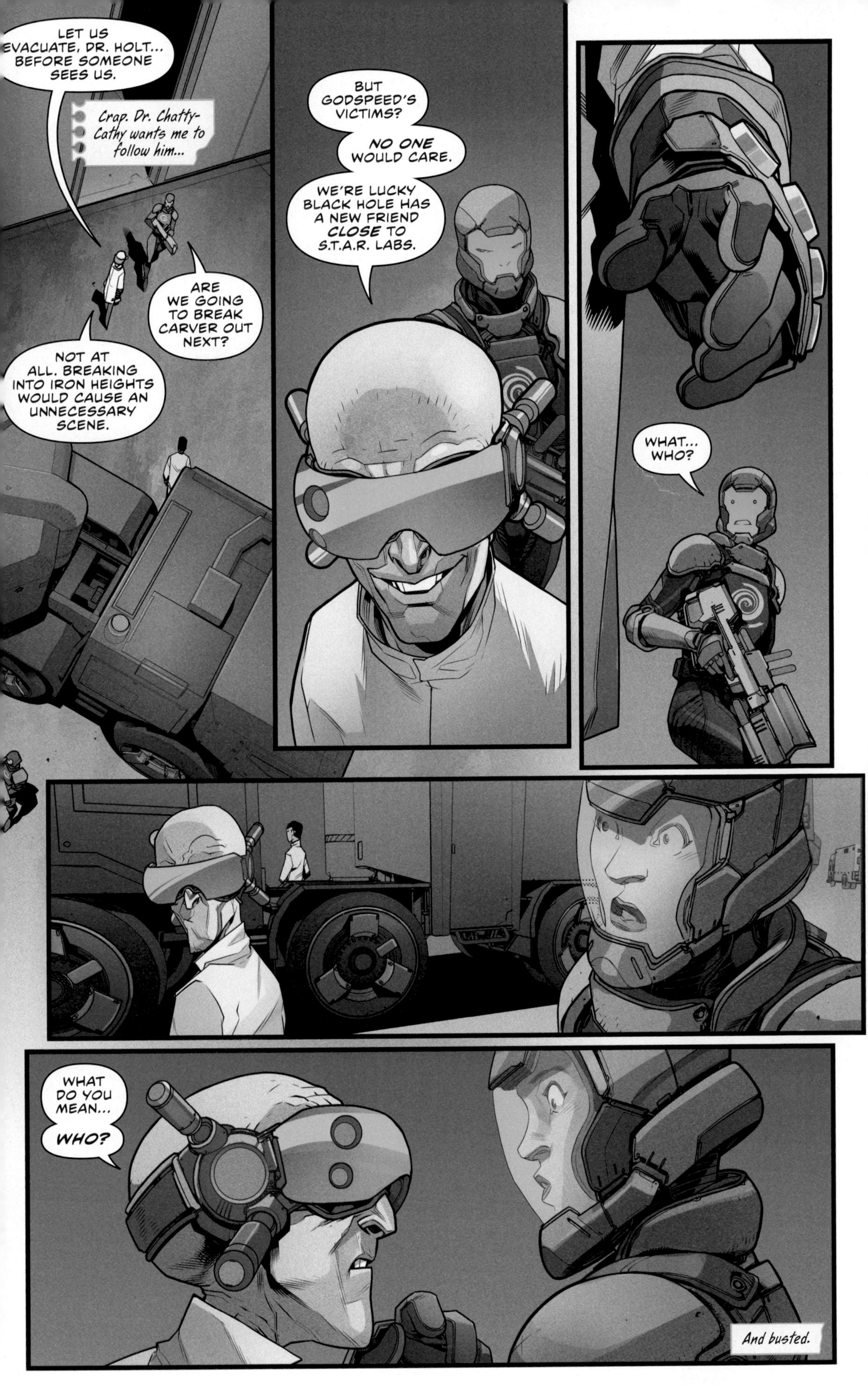
LET US EVACUATE, DR. HOLT... BEFORE SOMEONE SEES US.
Crap. Dr. Chatty-Cathy wants me to follow him...
ARE WE GOING TO BREAK CARVER OUT NEXT?
NOT AT ALL. BREAKING INTO IRON HEIGHTS WOULD CAUSE AN UNNECESSARY SCENE.
BUT GODSPEED'S VICTIMS?
NO ONE WOULD CARE.
WE'RE LUCKY BLACK HOLE HAS A NEW FRIEND CLOSE TO S.T.A.R. LABS.
WHAT... WHO?
WHAT DO YOU MEAN... WHO?
And busted.

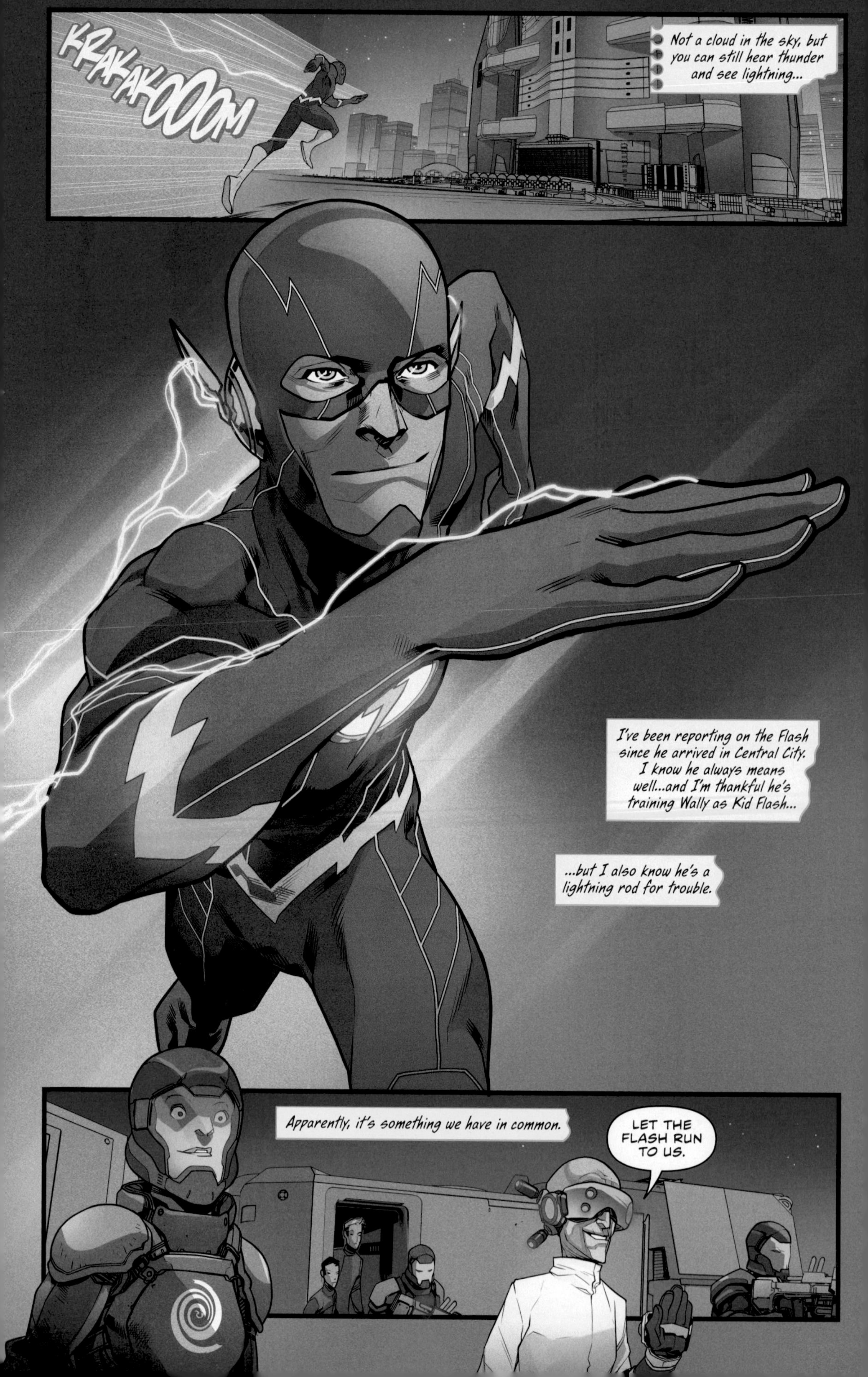
KRAKAKOOOM
Not a cloud in the sky, but you can still hear thunder and see lightning...
I've been reporting on the Flash since he arrived in Central City. I know he always means well...and I'm thankful he's training Wally as Kid Flash...
...but I also know he's a lightning rod for trouble.
Apparently, it's something we have in common.
LET THE FLASH RUN TO US.

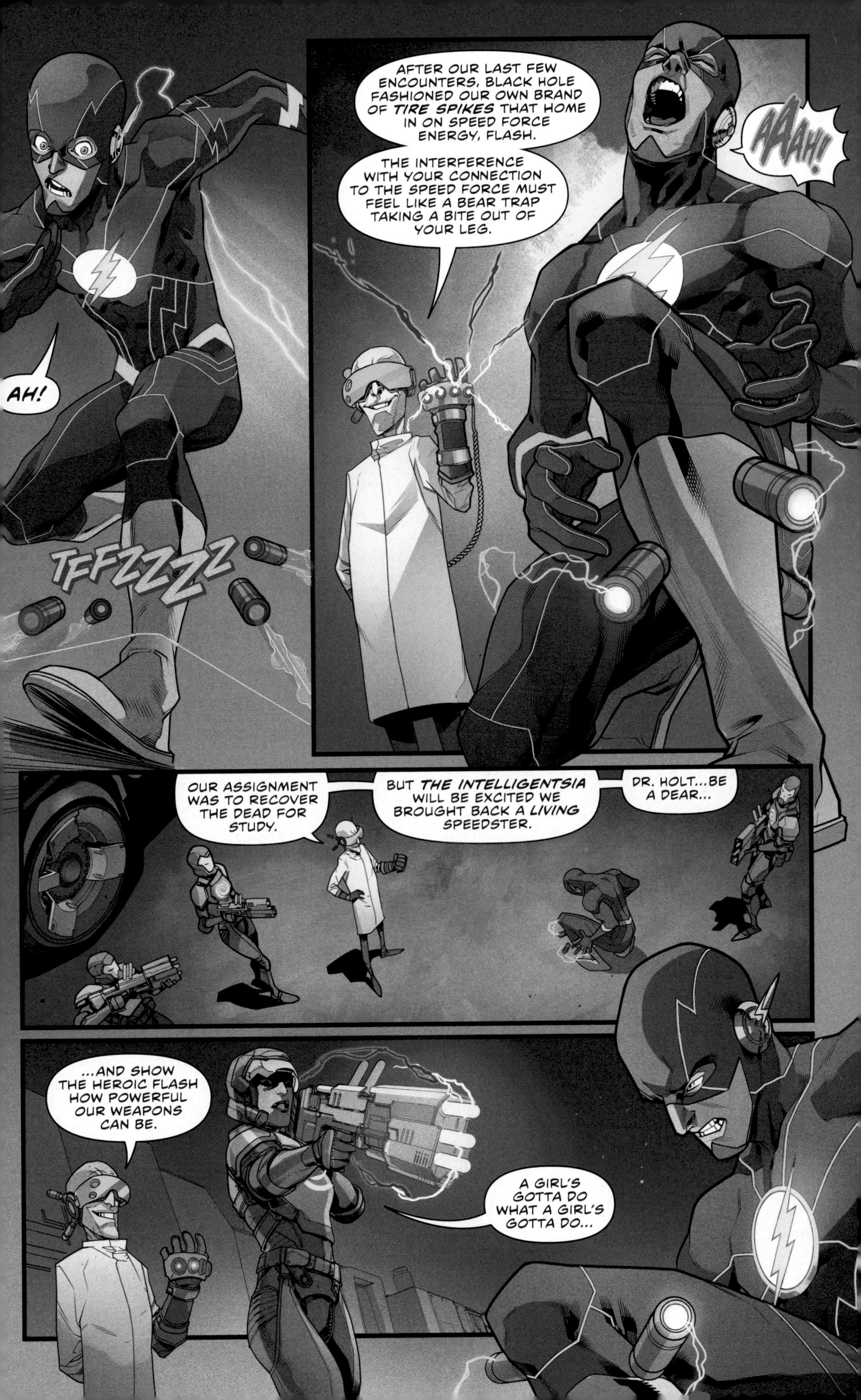
AH!
TFFZZZZZ
AFTER OUR LAST FEW ENCOUNTERS, BLACK HOLE FASHIONED OUR OWN BRAND OF TIRE SPIKES THAT HOME IN ON SPEED FORCE ENERGY, FLASH.
THE INTERFERENCE WITH YOUR CONNECTION TO THE SPEED FORCE MUST FEEL LIKE A BEAR TRAP TAKING A BITE OUT OF YOUR LEG.
AAAAH!
OUR ASSIGNMENT WAS TO RECOVER THE DEAD FOR STUDY.
BUT THE INTELLIGENTSIA WILL BE EXCITED WE BROUGHT BACK A LIVING SPEEDSTER.
DR. HOLT...BE A DEAR...
...AND SHOW THE HEROIC FLASH HOW POWERFUL OUR WEAPONS CAN BE.
A GIRL'S GOTTA DO WHAT A GIRL'S GOTTA DO...

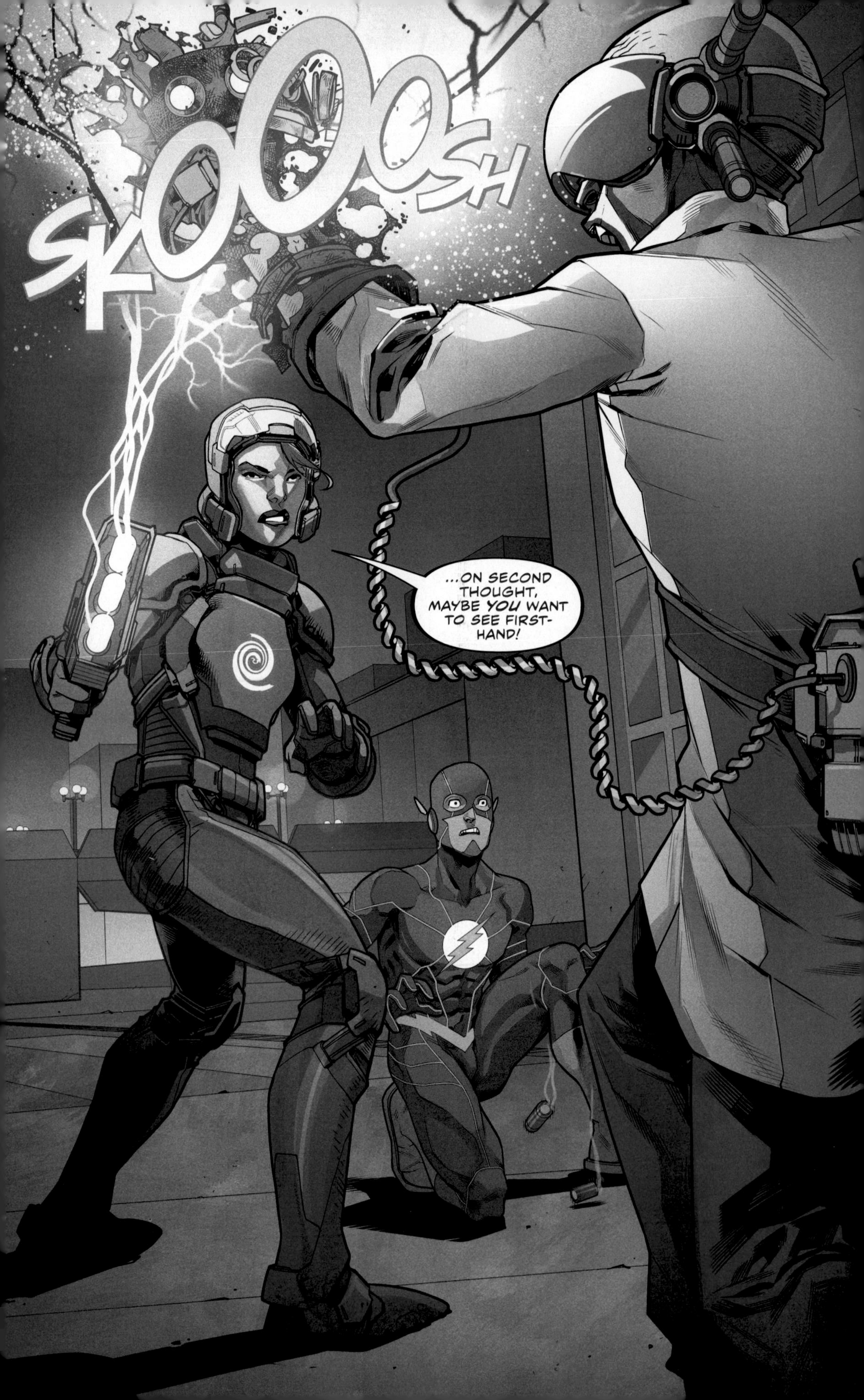
SKOOOOSH
...ON SECOND THOUGHT, MAYBE YOU WANT TO SEE FIRST-HAND!

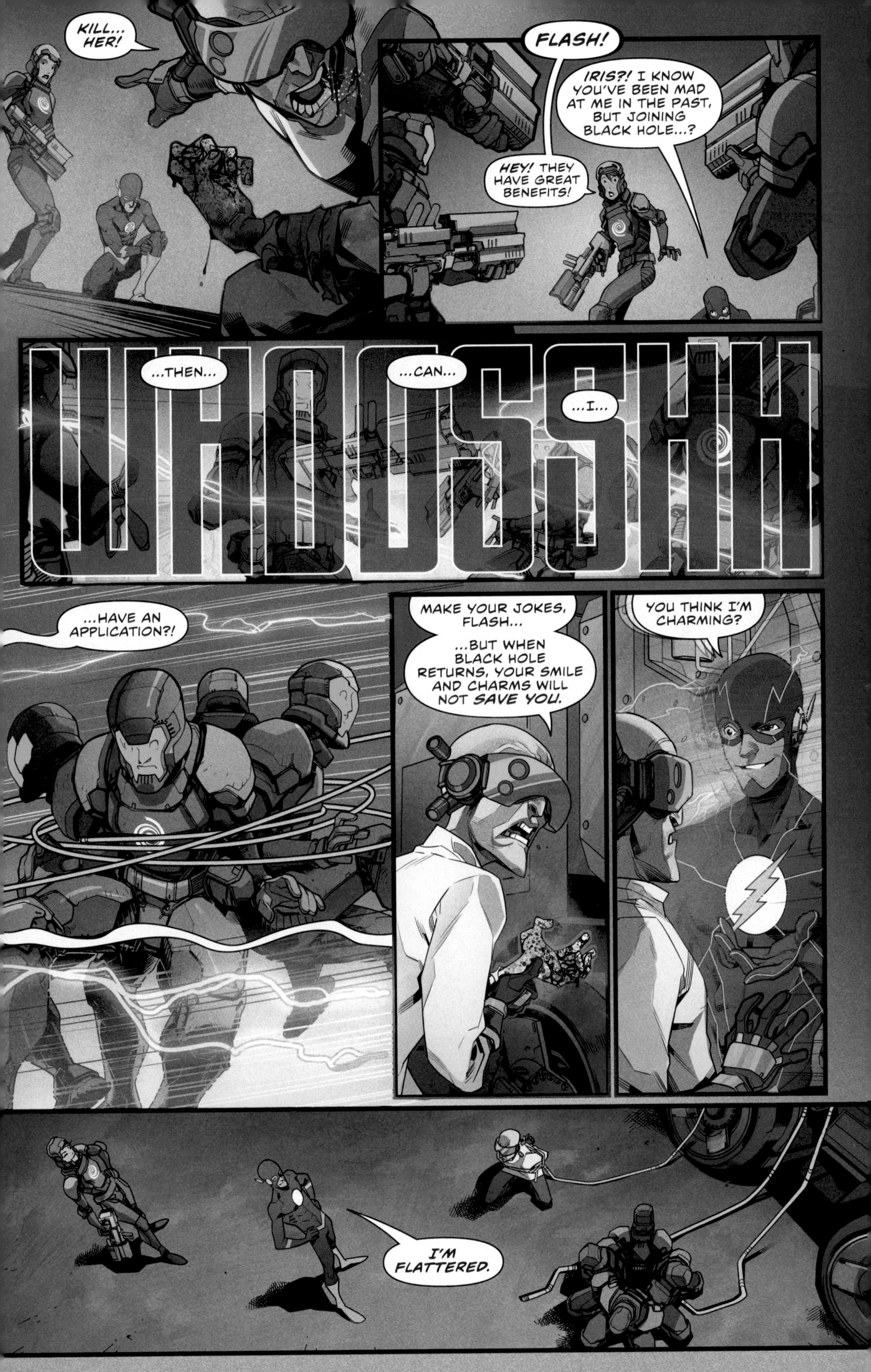
KILL... HER!
FLASH!
IRIS?! I KNOW YOU'VE BEEN MAD AT ME IN THE PAST, BUT JOINING BLACK HOLE...?
HEY! THEY HAVE GREAT BENEFITS!
WHOOSHH
...THEN...
...CAN...
...I...
...HAVE AN APPLICATION?!
MAKE YOUR JOKES, FLASH...
...BUT WHEN BLACK HOLE RETURNS, YOUR SMILE AND CHARMS WILL NOT SAVE YOU.
YOU THINK I'M CHARMING?
I'M FLATTERED.

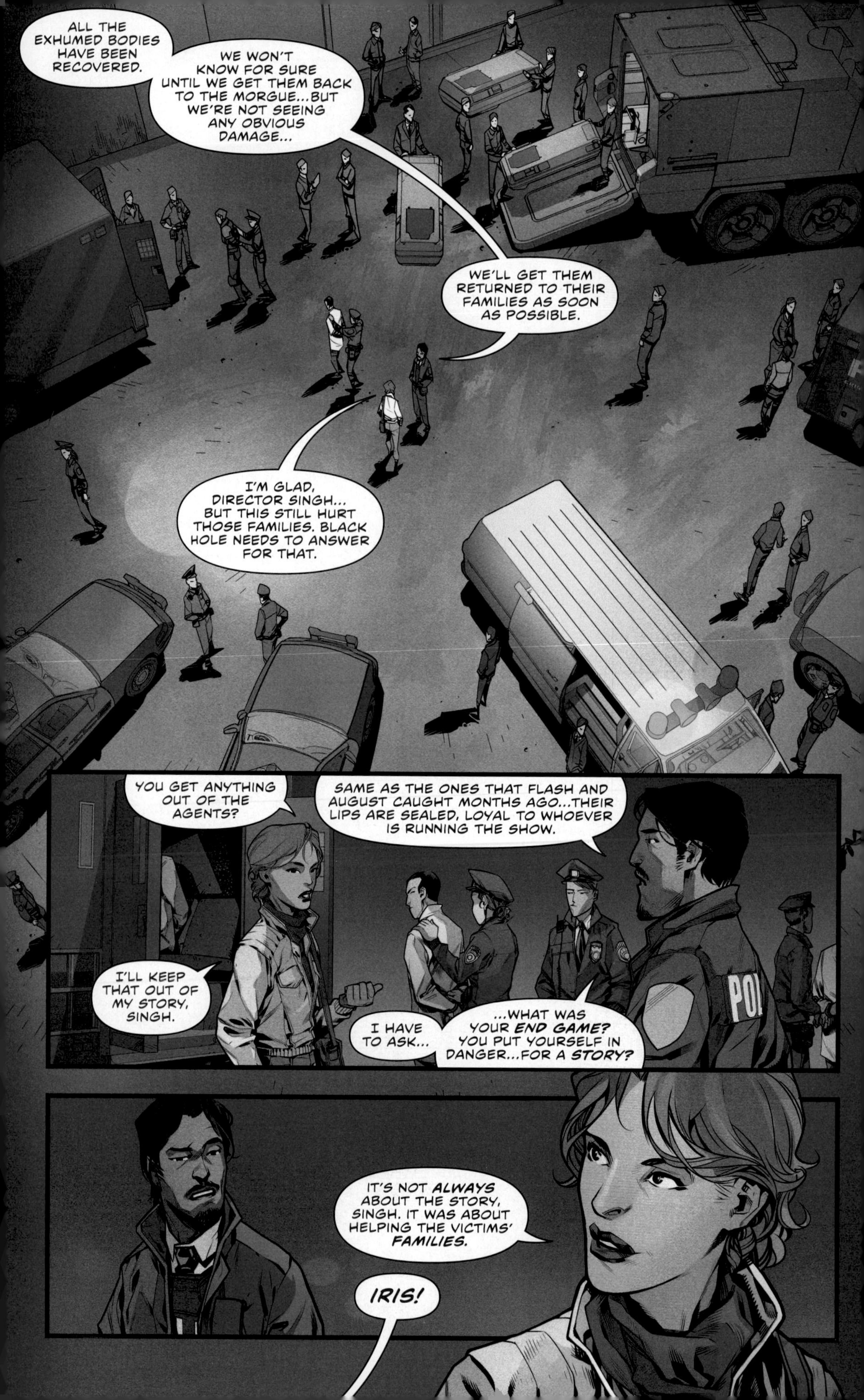
ALL THE EXHUMED BODIES HAVE BEEN RECOVERED.
WE WON'T KNOW FOR SURE UNTIL WE GET THEM BACK TO THE MORGUE...BUT WE'RE NOT SEEING ANY OBVIOUS DAMAGE...
WE'LL GET THEM RETURNED TO THEIR FAMILIES AS SOON AS POSSIBLE.
I'M GLAD, DIRECTOR SINGH... BUT THIS STILL HURT THOSE FAMILIES. BLACK HOLE NEEDS TO ANSWER FOR THAT.
YOU GET ANYTHING OUT OF THE AGENTS?
SAME AS THE ONES THAT FLASH AND AUGUST CAUGHT MONTHS AGO...THEIR LIPS ARE SEALED, LOYAL TO WHOEVER IS RUNNING THE SHOW.
I'LL KEEP THAT OUT OF MY STORY, SINGH.
I HAVE TO ASK...
...WHAT WAS YOUR *END GAME?* YOU PUT YOURSELF IN DANGER...FOR A *STORY?*
IT'S NOT *ALWAYS* ABOUT THE STORY, SINGH. IT WAS ABOUT HELPING THE VICTIMS' *FAMILIES.*
IRIS!

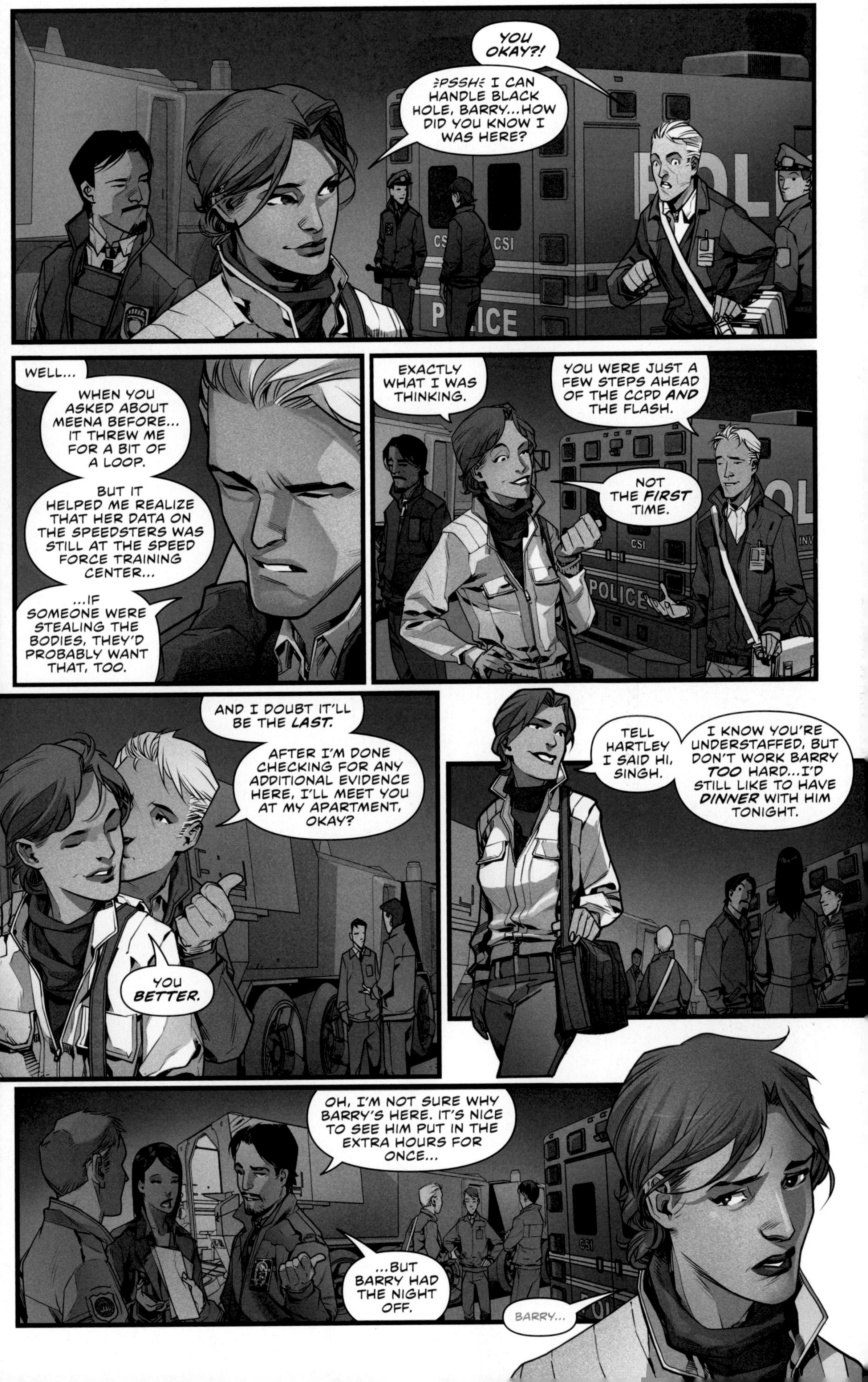
YOU OKAY?!
PSSH I CAN HANDLE BLACK HOLE, BARRY...HOW DID YOU KNOW I WAS HERE?
WELL...
WHEN YOU ASKED ABOUT MEENA BEFORE... IT THREW ME FOR A BIT OF A LOOP.
BUT IT HELPED ME REALIZE THAT HER DATA ON THE SPEEDSTERS WAS STILL AT THE SPEED FORCE TRAINING CENTER...
...IF SOMEONE WERE STEALING THE BODIES, THEY'D PROBABLY WANT THAT, TOO.
EXACTLY WHAT I WAS THINKING.
YOU WERE JUST A FEW STEPS AHEAD OF THE CCPD AND THE FLASH.
NOT THE FIRST TIME.
AND I DOUBT IT'LL BE THE LAST.
AFTER I'M DONE CHECKING FOR ANY ADDITIONAL EVIDENCE HERE, I'LL MEET YOU AT MY APARTMENT, OKAY?
YOU BETTER.
TELL HARTLEY I SAID HI, SINGH.
I KNOW YOU'RE UNDERSTAFFED, BUT DON'T WORK BARRY TOO HARD...I'D STILL LIKE TO HAVE DINNER WITH HIM TONIGHT.
OH, I'M NOT SURE WHY BARRY'S HERE. IT'S NICE TO SEE HIM PUT IN THE EXTRA HOURS FOR ONCE...
...BUT BARRY HAD THE NIGHT OFF.
BARRY...

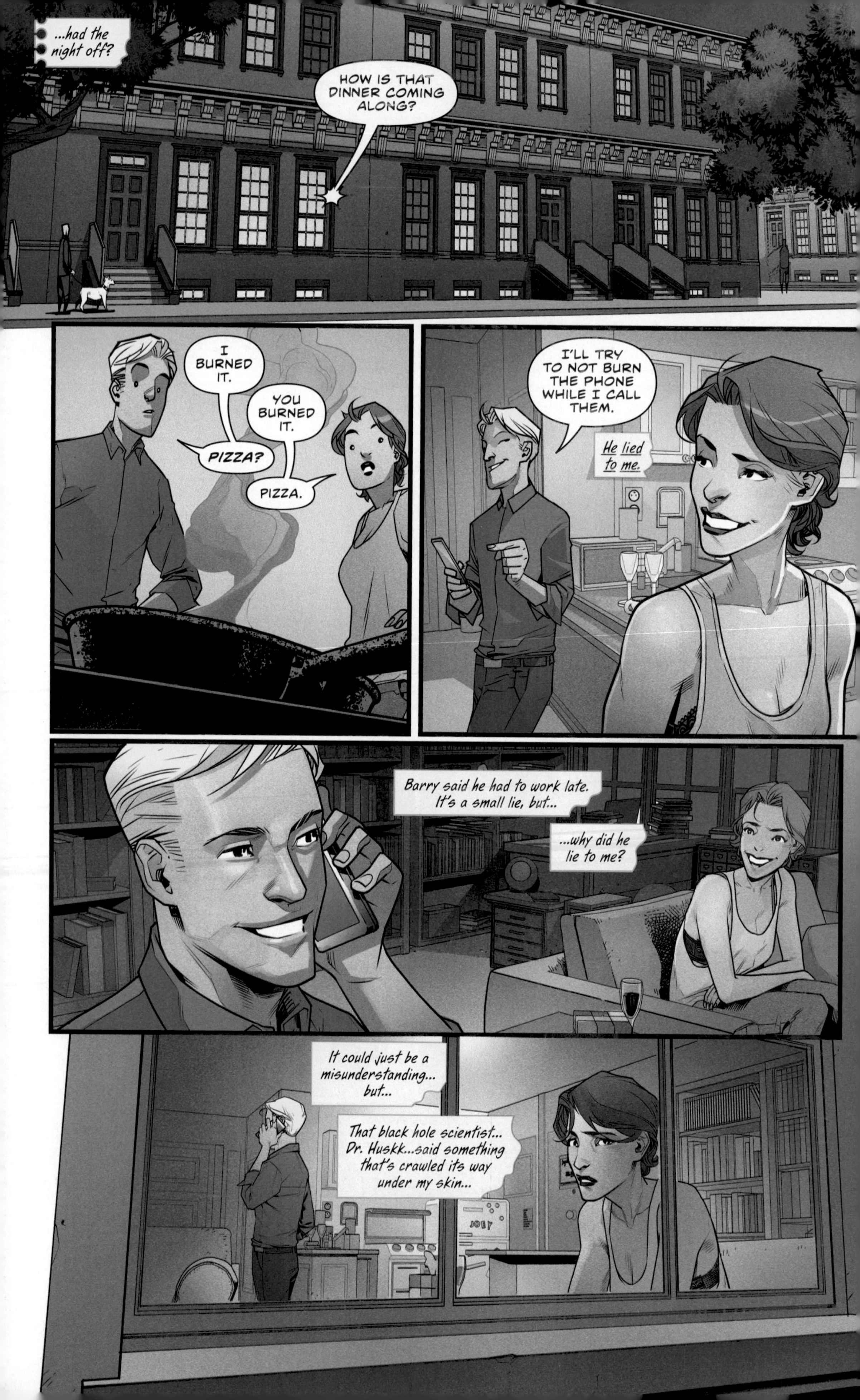
...had the night off?
HOW IS THAT DINNER COMING ALONG?
I BURNED IT.
YOU BURNED IT.
PIZZA?
PIZZA.
I'LL TRY TO NOT BURN THE PHONE WHILE I CALL THEM.
He lied to me.
Barry said he had to work late. It's a small lie, but...
...why did he lie to me?
It could just be a misunderstanding... but...
That black hole scientist... Dr. Huskk...said something that's crawled its way under my skin...
JOEY

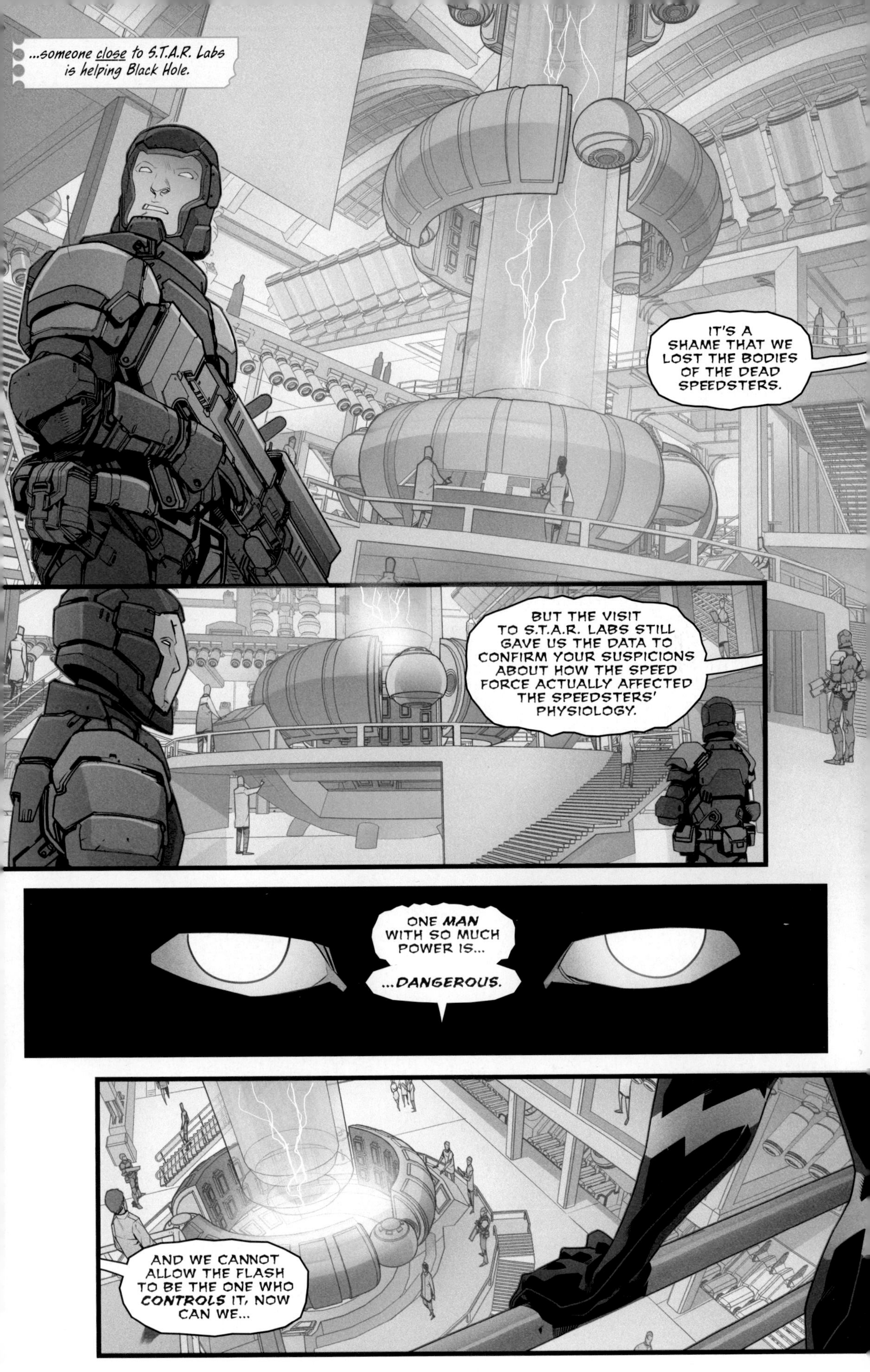
...someone close to S.T.A.R. Labs is helping Black Hole.
IT'S A SHAME THAT WE LOST THE BODIES OF THE DEAD SPEEDSTERS.
BUT THE VISIT TO S.T.A.R. LABS STILL GAVE US THE DATA TO CONFIRM YOUR SUSPICIONS ABOUT HOW THE SPEED FORCE ACTUALLY AFFECTED THE SPEEDSTERS' PHYSIOLOGY.
ONE MAN WITH SO MUCH POWER IS...
...DANGEROUS.
AND WE CANNOT ALLOW THE FLASH TO BE THE ONE WHO CONTROLS IT, NOW CAN WE...

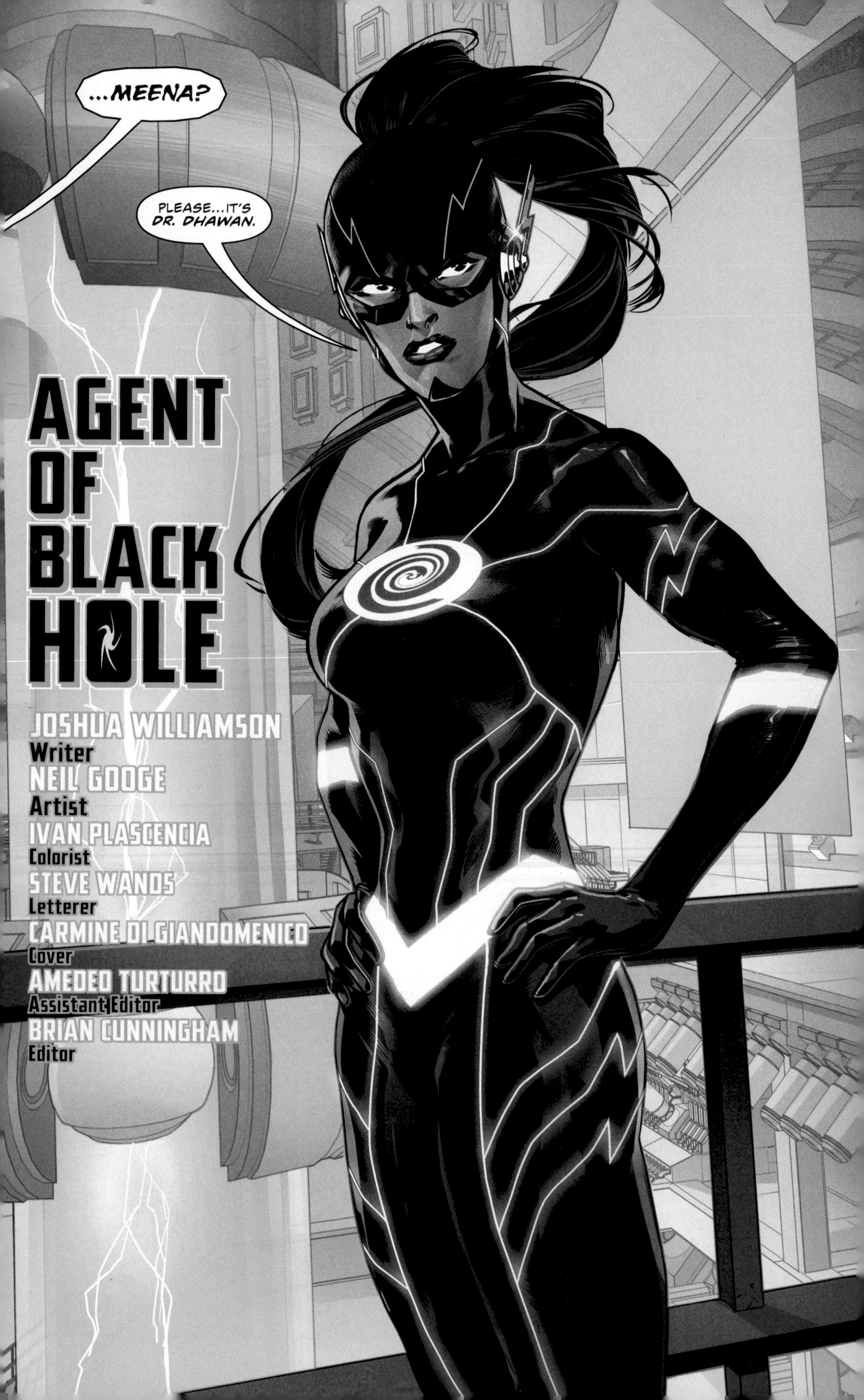
...MEENA?
PLEASE...IT'S DR. DHAWAN.
AGENT OF BLACK HOLE
JOSHUA WILLIAMSON
Writer
NEIL GOOGE
Artist
IVAN PLASCENCIA
Colorist
STEVE WANDS
Letterer
CARMINE DI GIANDOMENICO
Cover
AMEDEO TURTURRO
Assistant Editor
BRIAN CUNNINGHAM
Editor

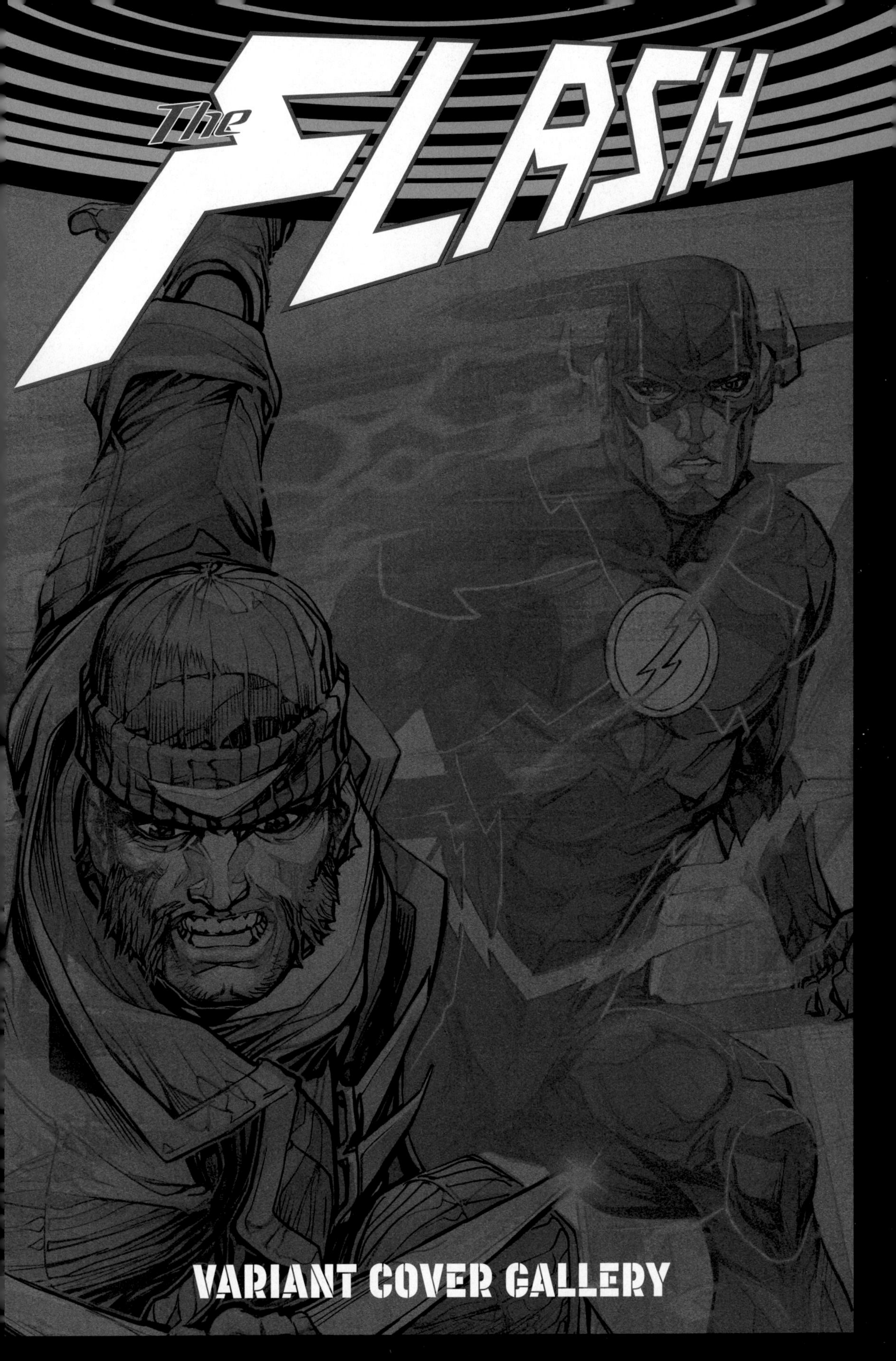
The FLASH
VARIANT COVER GALLERY

THE FLASH #14 variant cover by DAVE JOHNSON

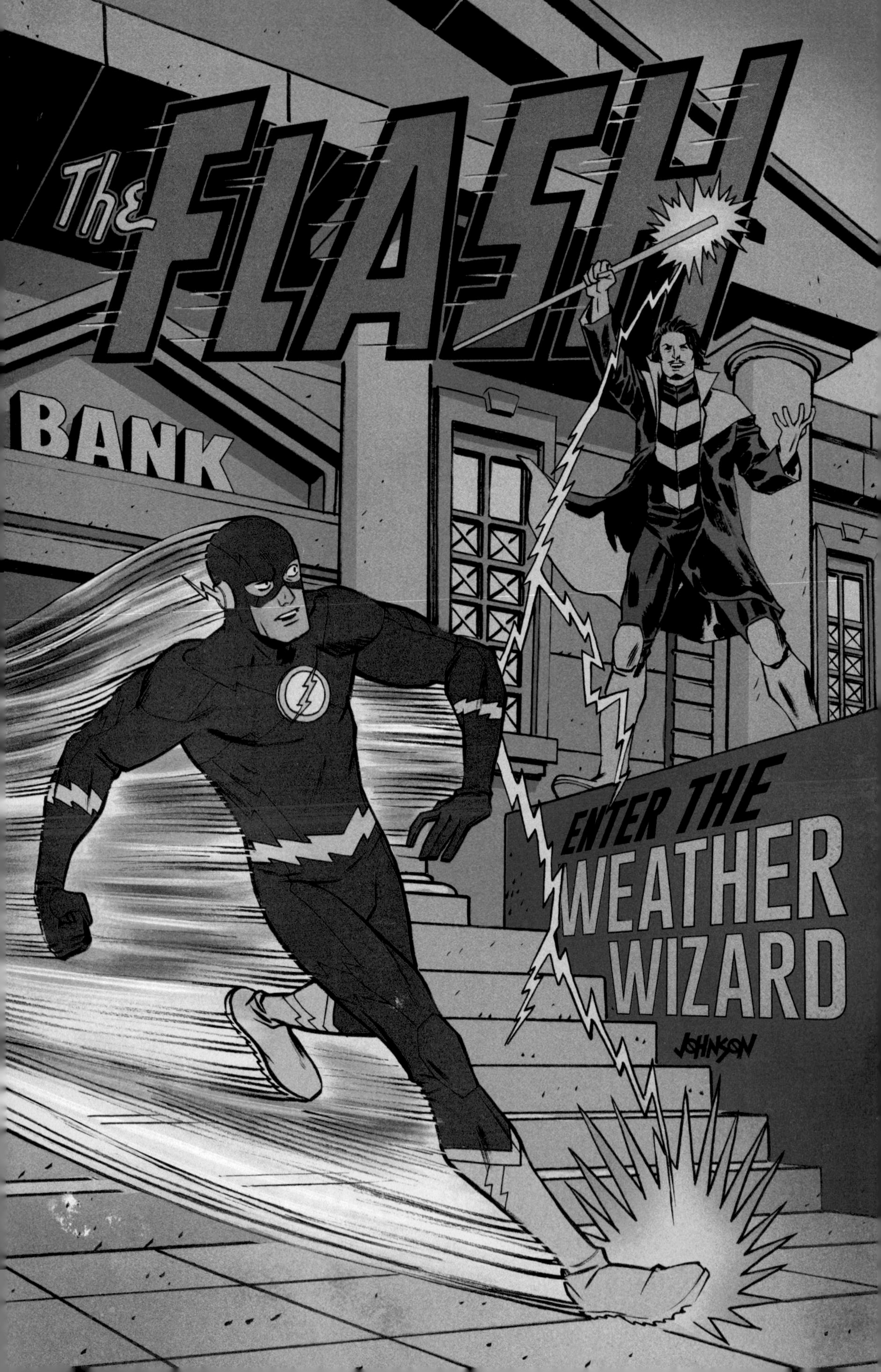

The FLASH
BANK
ENTER THE
WEATHER
WIZARD
JOHNSON

THE FLASH #15 variant cover by DAVE JOHNSON

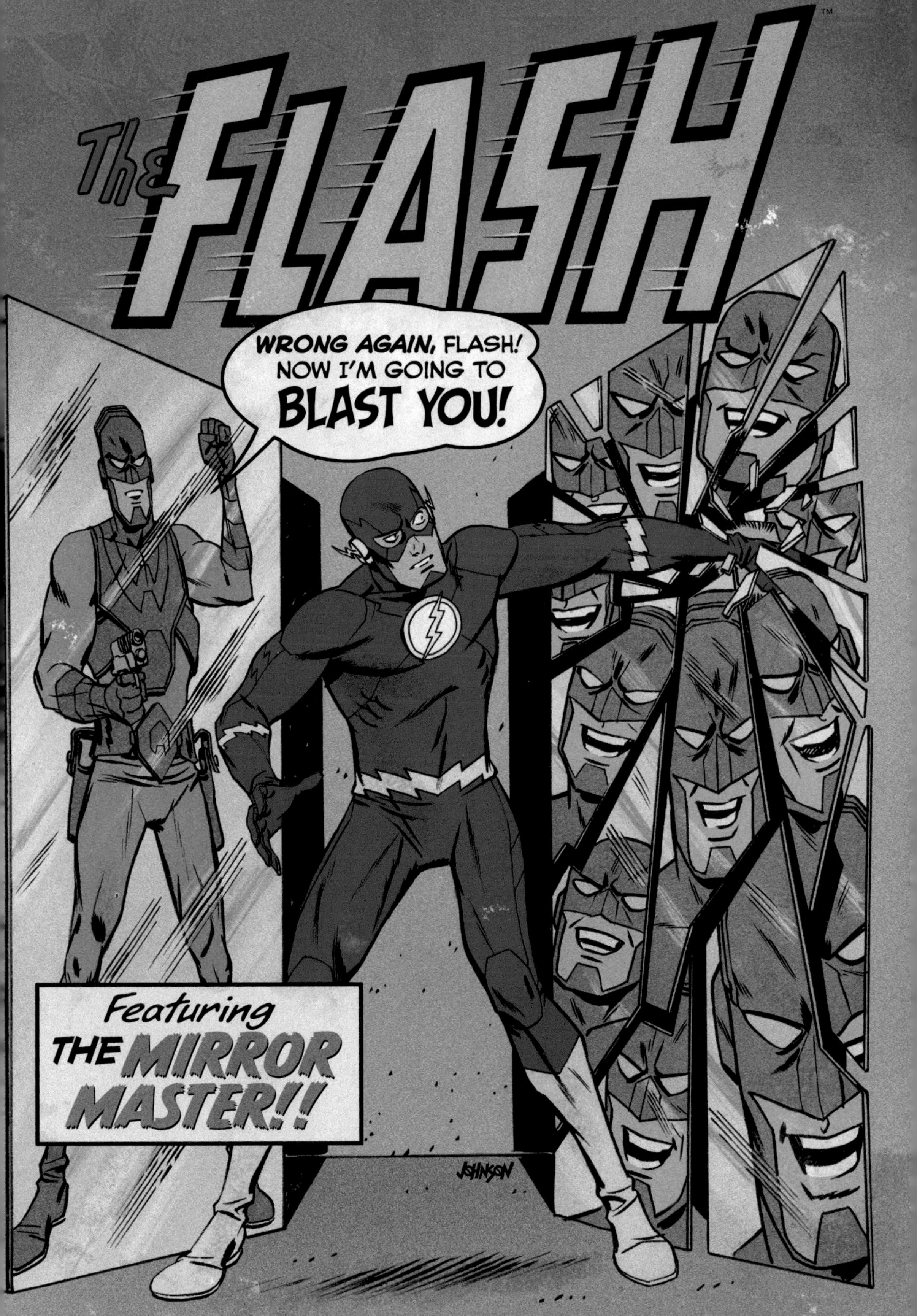
THE FLASH
WRONG AGAIN, FLASH! NOW I'M GOING TO BLAST YOU!
Featuring THE MIRROR MASTER!!
JOHNSON

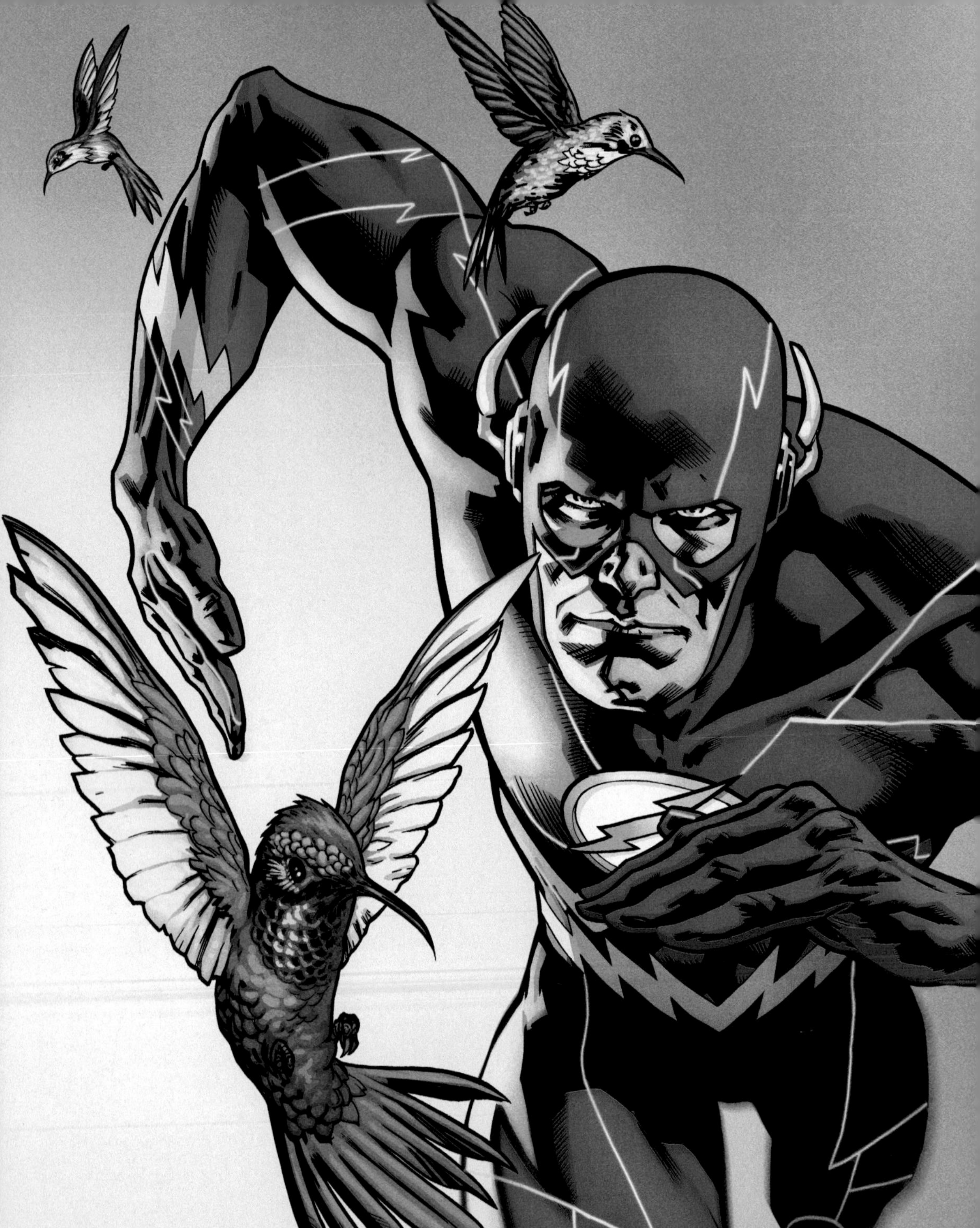
YANICK PAQUETTE 2017
MICHEL LACOMBE

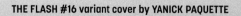

THE FLASH #16 variant cover by YANICK PAQUETTE

THE FLASH #17 variant cover by HOWARD PORTER and HI-FI

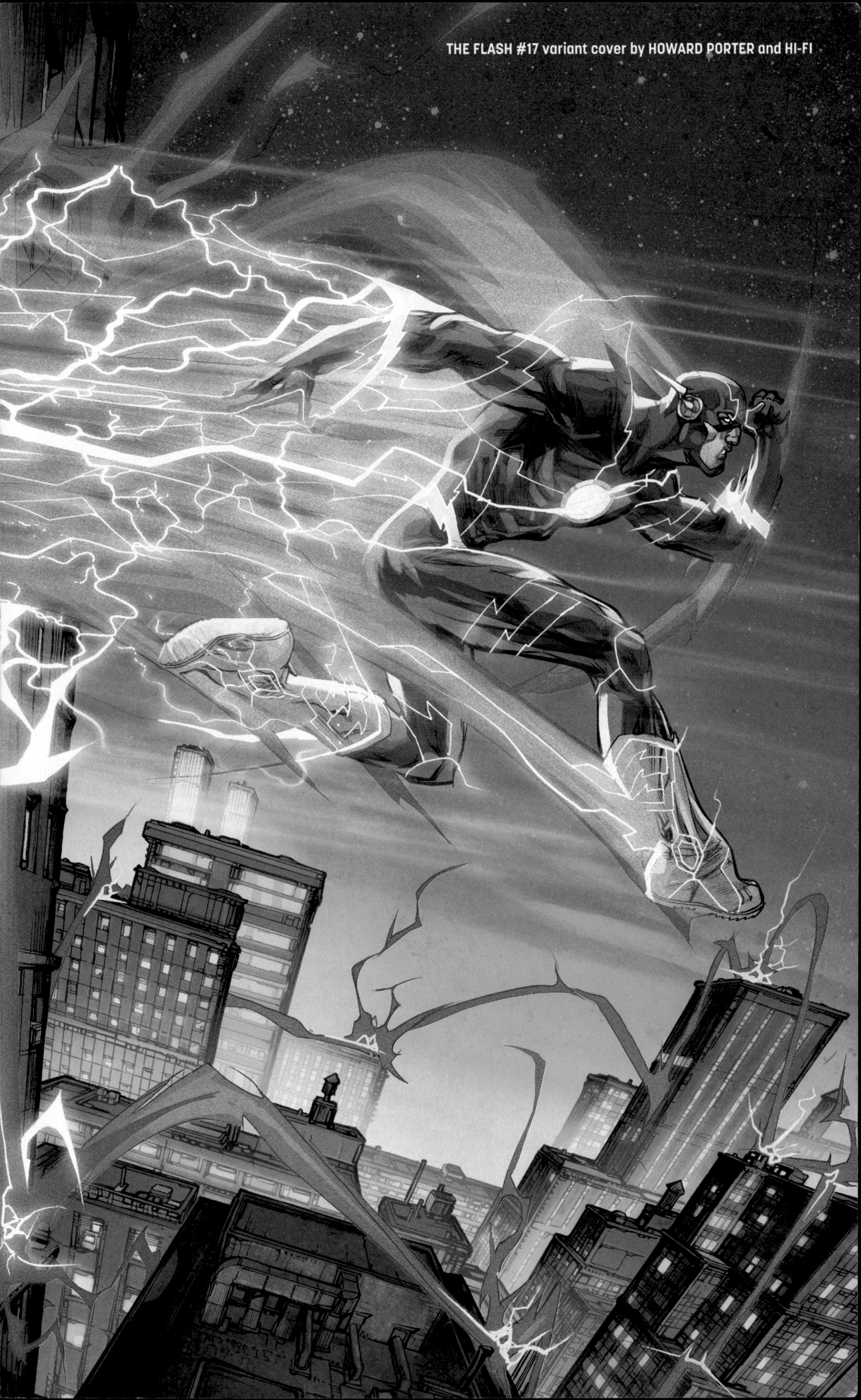

THE FLASH #18 variant cover by HOWARD PORTER and HI-FI

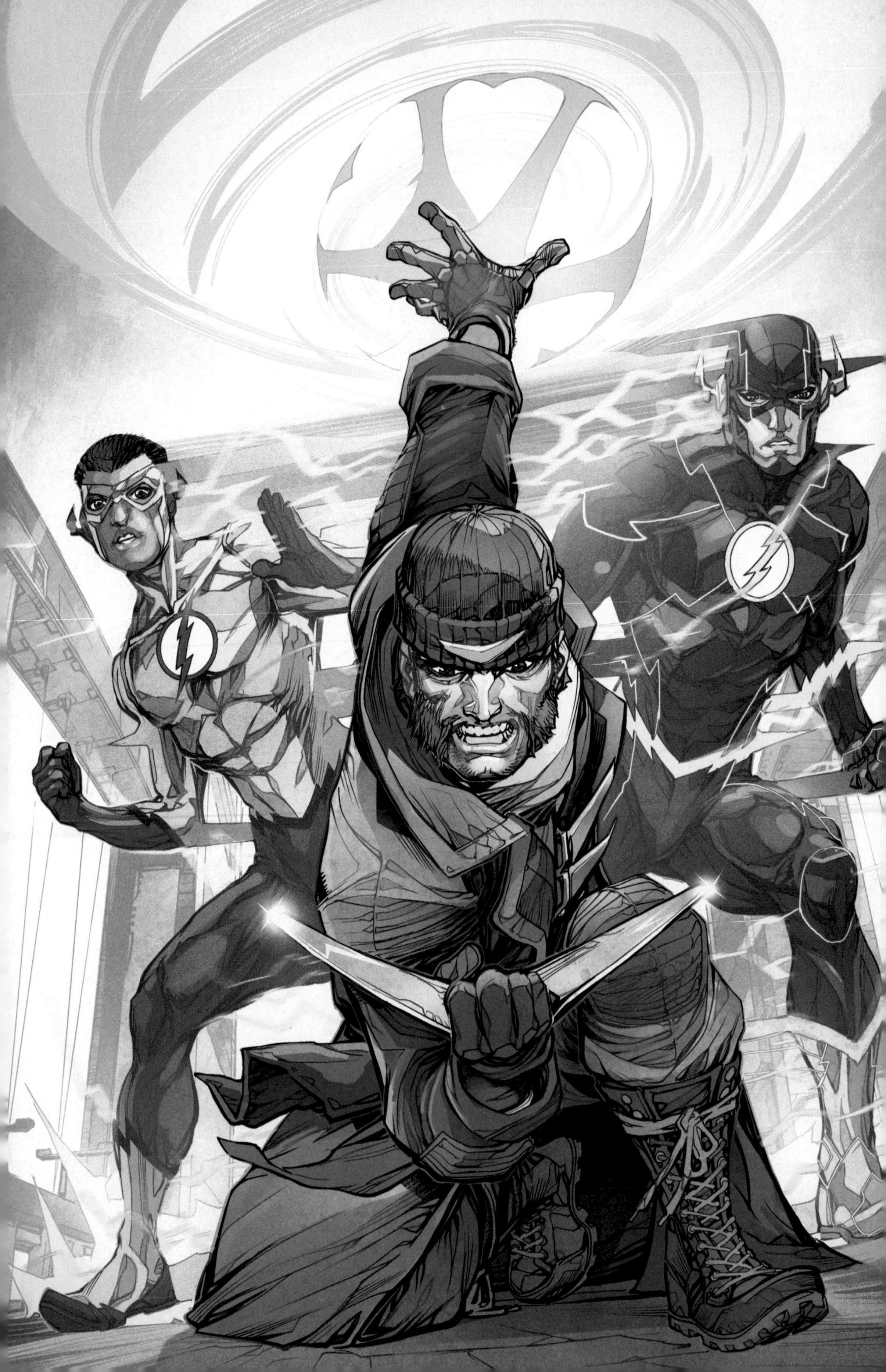

THE FLASH #19 variant cover by HOWARD PORTER and HI-FI

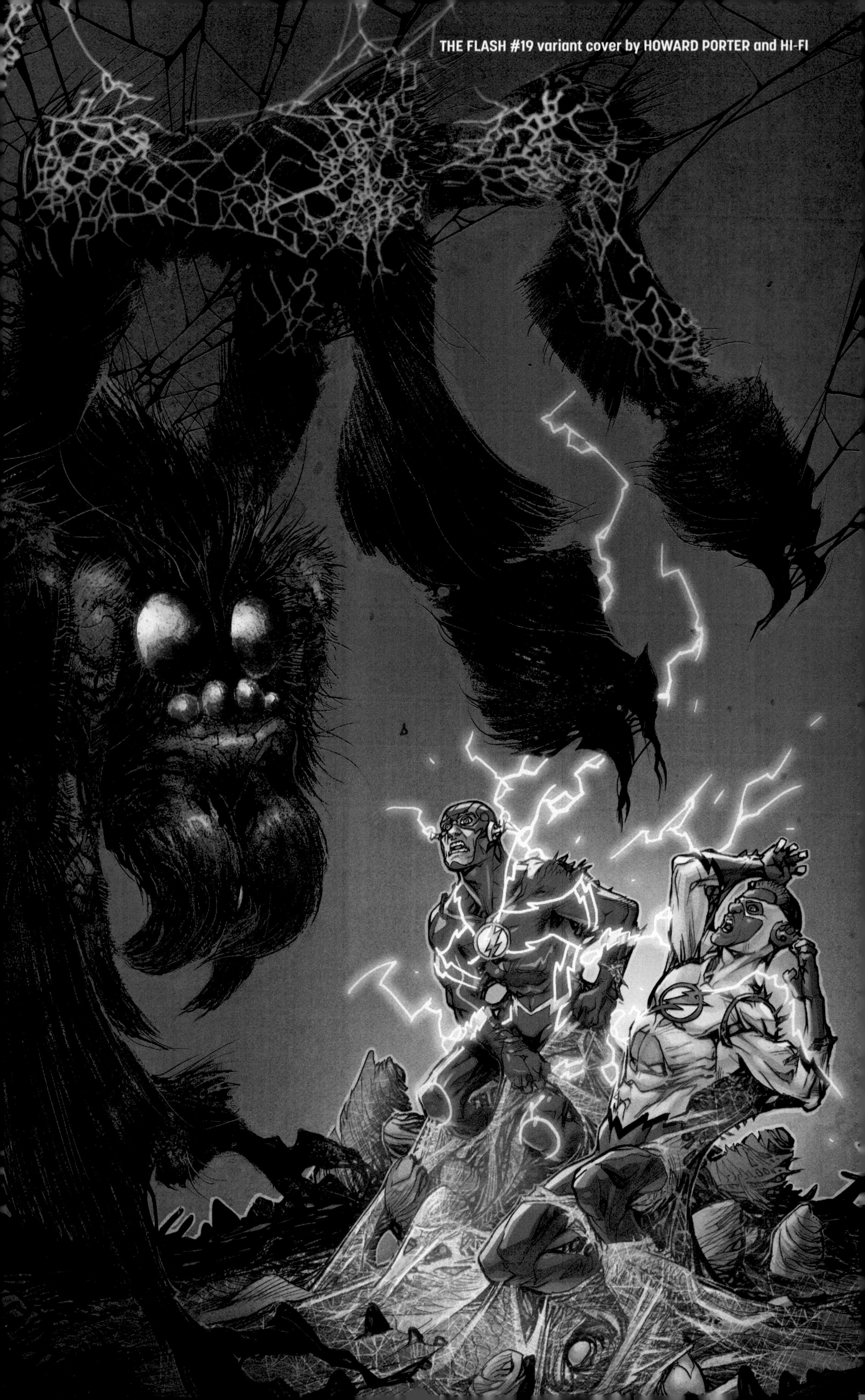

THE FLASH #20 variant cover by HOWARD PORTER and HI-FI

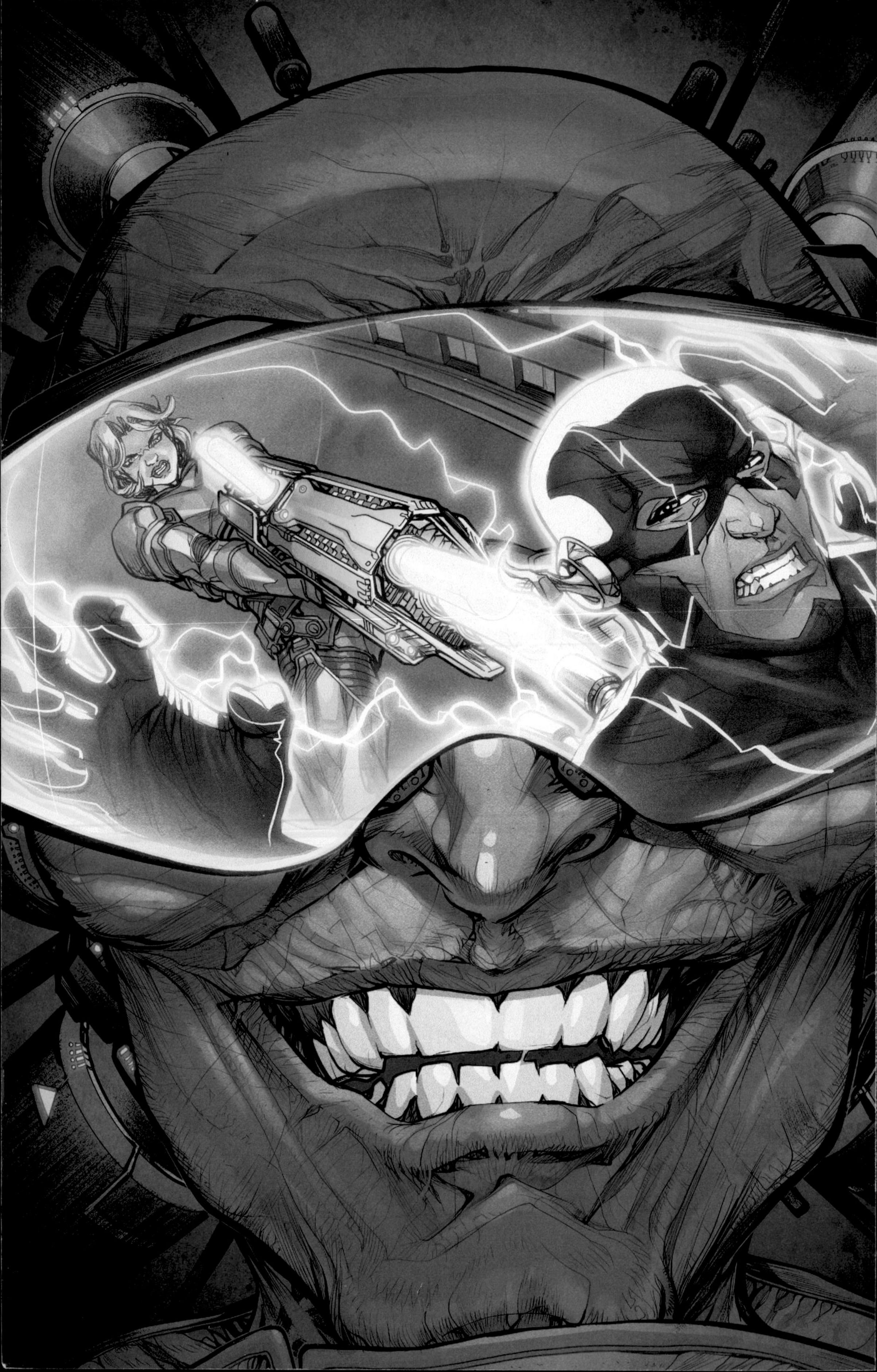

SKETCHES
by CARMINE DI GIANDOMENICO

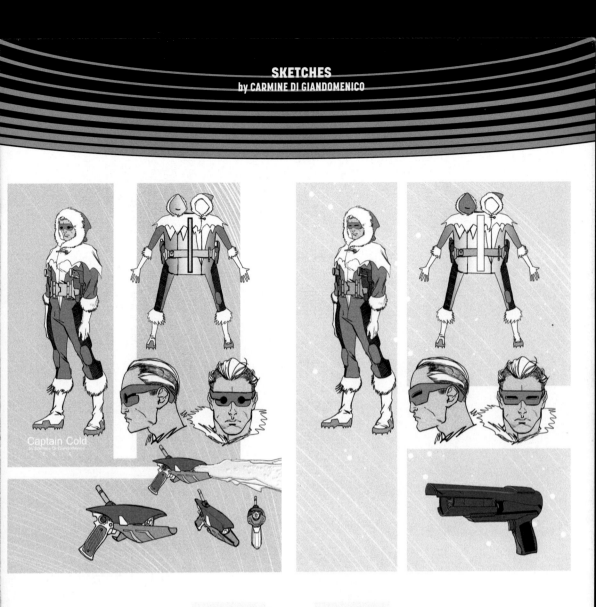

Captain Cold

Bone Dry

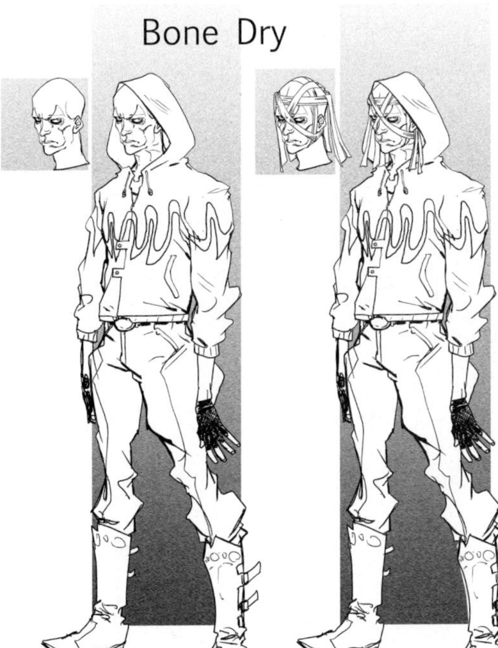

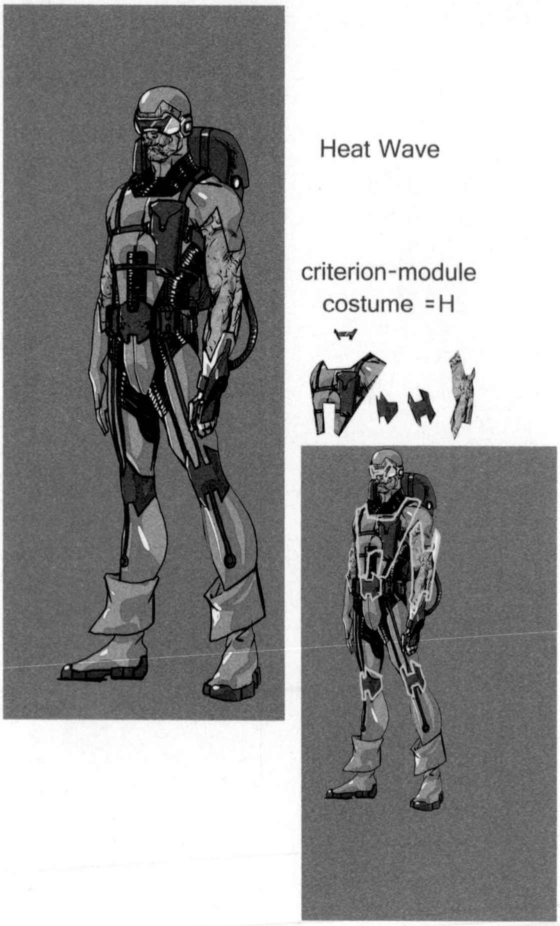
Heat Wave
criterion-module
costume =H

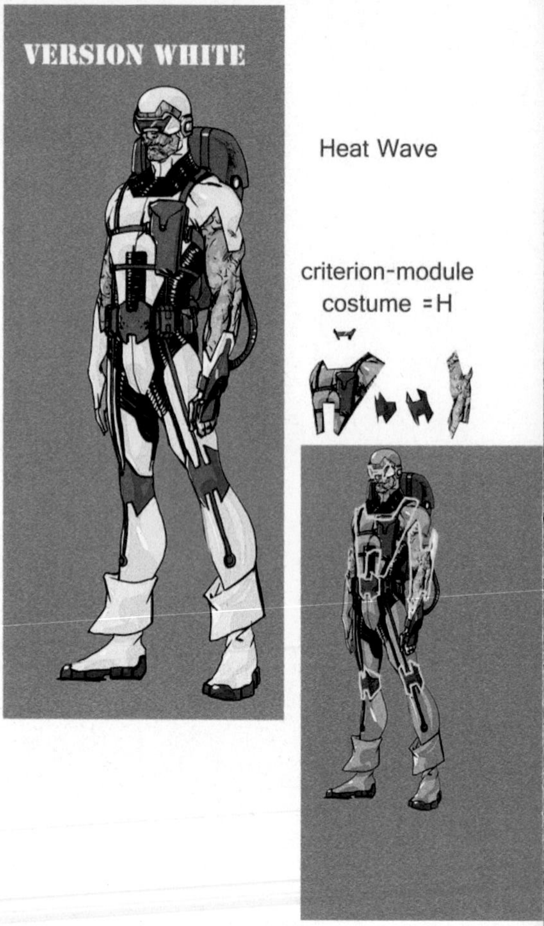
VERSION WHITE
Heat Wave
criterion-module
costume =H

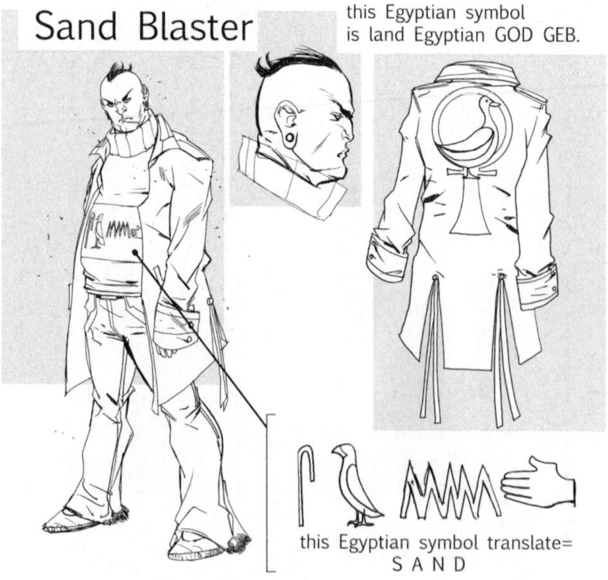
Sand Blaster
this Egyptian symbol
is land Egyptian GOD GEB.
this Egyptian symbol translate=
S A N D